# MORE LIGHT ON
# THE DEAD SEA SCROLLS

*Also by Millar Burrows*

THE DEAD SEA SCROLLS

PALESTINE IS OUR BUSINESS

OUTLINE OF BIBLICAL THEOLOGY

WHAT MEAN THESE STONES?

THE BASIS OF ISRAELITE MARRIAGE

BIBLE RELIGION

FOUNDERS OF GREAT RELIGIONS

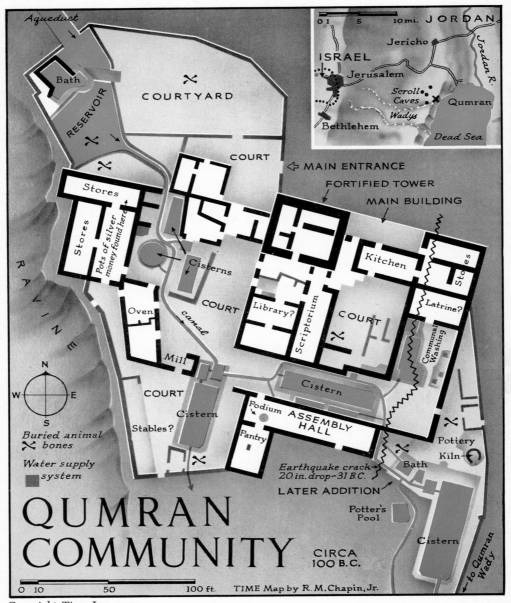

Aqueduct

Bath

RESERVOIR

COURTYARD

Stores

Stores

Pots of silver money found here

Cisterns

Oven

canal

Mill

COURT

Stables?

Cistern

Pantry

Podium

Cistern

COURT

⇐ MAIN ENTRANCE

FORTIFIED TOWER

MAIN BUILDING

Kitchen

Stores

Library?

Scriptorium

COURT

Latrine?

Communal Washing

Cistern

ASSEMBLY HALL

Earthquake crack→ 20 in. drop–31 B.C.

LATER ADDITION

Bath

Pottery Kiln→

Potter's Pool

Cistern

to Qumran Wady

N
W · E
S

✕ Buried animal bones

◼ Water supply system

0 1   5   10 mi.  JORDAN

ISRAEL

Jericho

Jerusalem

Scroll Caves

✕ Qumran

Wadys

Bethlehem

Dead Sea

Jordan R.

# QUMRAN COMMUNITY

CIRCA 100 B.C.

0 10     50          100 ft.    TIME Map by R.M.Chapin, Jr.

# MORE LIGHT ON
# THE DEAD SEA SCROLLS

*New Scrolls and New Interpretations*

WITH TRANSLATIONS OF
IMPORTANT RECENT DISCOVERIES

*by*

## MILLAR BURROWS

WINKLEY PROFESSOR OF BIBLICAL THEOLOGY, YALE UNIVERSITY

*1958*

*THE VIKING PRESS*

*New York*

Library of Congress catalog card number: 58-8133

PRINTED IN U.S.A. BY VAIL-BALLOU PRESS, INC.

# Contents

ⅬⅬⅬⅬⅬⅬⅬⅬⅬⅬⅬⅬⅬⅬⅬⅬⅬⅬⅬⅬⅬⅬⅬⅬⅬⅬⅬⅠ

vii

## PART THREE: RESULTS FOR
## OLD TESTAMENT STUDIES

## PART FOUR: THE ORIGIN OF THE QUMRAN SECT

## PART FIVE: THE IDENTIFICATION OF THE SECT

## PART SIX: THE BELIEFS OF THE SECT

## PART SEVEN: ORGANIZATION AND RITES OF THE SECT

## PART EIGHT: TRANSLATIONS

# *Preface*

More texts have been published, and there has been an enormous amount of discussion of the Qumran texts, since my previous book, *The Dead Sea Scrolls* (*DSS*), was written, two and a half years ago. A review of the new material and recent studies seems to be called for. The interpretation and even the publication of the texts, it is true, have only begun. No complete account will be possible for many years. Enough progress has been made, however, to warrant a survey of the present state of Dead Sea Scroll studies.

Not everything that can be said even now needs to be merely tentative. Some ideas that have been expressed concerning the scrolls and their implications can already be dismissed once and for all, because they depend not on evidence but on mistaken presuppositions. This is true in particular of the widespread claims and fears with regard to the effect of the new discoveries on religious beliefs. Since many people are disturbed on this point, I have felt constrained to deal with it at considerable length. No new material that is still to be published, I am quite sure, will necessitate any change in the fundamental facts and principles I have tried to make clear in this connection. That is by no means true, however, of conclusions and theories concerning the history, life, and faith of the Qumran community. Here we have undoubtedly very much still to learn, and relatively little can be considered finally established. Yet even here certain broad outlines already seem fairly clear and not likely to be changed.

In undertaking this volume I had hoped to be able to give more attention to the texts of the Wady Murabbaat than was possible in *DSS*. It soon became apparent, however, that there was more than enough material for one book in the texts of Qumran. As in *DSS*, therefore, there are only incidental references to the Murabbaat materials in this volume.

The translations in this book will be found full of rows of dots and asterisks, indicating the fragmentary nature of the texts. In order to show just how much is actually preserved, and to prevent drawing inferences from words not actually found in the texts, I have generally refrained from offering conjectural restorations. Occasionally I have restored a word or two where there seems to be no room for doubt as to the reading, but on the whole, even where a gap can be filled with virtual certainty (as in quotations from the Old Testament), I have left blank spaces where they actually occur in the manuscripts. No attempt is made, however, to indicate the extent of the gaps by the number of dots or asterisks. Dots indicate a loss of one or several words; a row of asterisks indicates a loss of one or several lines.

Having regretted my decision not to have an index in *DSS*, I have provided one for this volume and have included in it an index to *DSS* also. Cross-references in the body of the book will help the reader to locate related passages, both in this volume and in *DSS*. Citations of the texts are identified by the columns and lines of the manuscripts and by the pages in *DSS* when the text is translated there. Beyond this no documentation is given.

Acknowledgment is hereby made of the permission graciously granted by *Time* to use the simplified map of Khirbet Qumran by R. M. Chapin, Jr., which appeared in its issue of April 15, 1957. Quotations from the Testaments of the Twelve Patriarchs are taken, with the permission of the Oxford University Press, from R. H. Charles's *Apocrypha and Pseudepigrapha of the Old Testament*. The Oxford University Press has given permission also to quote from Edmund Wilson's *The Scrolls from the Dead Sea*. Permission to quote C. D. Ginsburg's *The Essenes* has been granted by the Macmillan Company.

To the many scholars who have sent me their books and articles

I extend my thanks, with apologies for not naming them individually. To Professors Frank M. Cross, Jr., and G. R. Driver I owe the privilege of being allowed to see advance proofs of their books. I only regret that I did not have time to make more use of them. I am grateful also to Father R. de Vaux for his kindness in answering requests for information.

My wife has once more given me the invaluable assistance of a keen critical reading of my manuscript. The reader cannot know how much harder this book would have been to read without her help in clearing up or eliminating obscure statements. To my secretary, Suzanne F. Taylor, I am indebted for her ready cooperation, industry, and care in copying the manuscript, working extra hours and securing help when needed, and assisting in the compilation of the index and bibliography. Mr. Robert O. Ballou of The Viking Press has again my sincere thanks for proposing the composition of the book and for his considerate helpfulness in the course of its preparation.

MILLAR BURROWS

*Yale University*
*October 30, 1957*

PART ONE

# THE STORY CONTINUED

# I

## Recent Developments

The Dead Sea Scrolls were discovered in America in the spring of 1955. They had been discovered in Palestine, of course, in 1947, or perhaps in 1945, and during the years since then; in Europe they had been the subject of very lively discussion for several years. American scholars had taken part in the publication and study of the texts, and a few articles about them had appeared in newspapers and popular journals; but the general reader was hardly aware of them. Not until *The New Yorker,* in May 1955, published a long article about them by Edmund Wilson were the scrolls really discovered by the American public.

What followed was truly extraordinary. The issue of *The New Yorker* containing Wilson's article sold out in a few days. When the Oxford University Press in the autumn brought out Wilson's article, somewhat expanded, as a book, it immediately leaped into the category of best sellers and remained there for many months. So great was the current created that even my thick, heavy book, *The Dead Sea Scrolls,* published in November, was sucked into the whirlpool of best sellers for a while. The scrolls became a favorite subject for books, articles, and even cartoons. Enormous audiences turned out for lectures about them. Sensational and even silly statements were made, but they only increased the interest.

It is not hard to see why people were so much interested in the Dead Sea Scrolls. Many thought that anything to which *The New Yorker* would devote the greater part of an issue must be interesting, and anything on which Edmund Wilson would write must be important. The story as he told it was fascinating, and a surprising archeological discovery always appeals to the sense of romance. But there was more to it than that. The experience of speaking to many audiences about the scrolls, usually with a time for questions after the lecture, has convinced me that the chief factor in this extraordinary public interest in the scrolls was religious. People wanted to know what these documents would mean for traditional beliefs. Some were anxious lest the foundations of their faith might be weakened; some welcomed what they thought might justify their own rejection of the faith of their fathers; still others were rather amused by what looked like an embarrassment for beliefs and institutions in which they were not interested.

Mr. Wilson had taken up and carried further the suggestions of Professor André Dupont-Sommer which had aroused much controversy in France several years earlier. Dupont-Sommer had said that the Dead Sea Scrolls made Jesus seem like "an astonishing reincarnation" of the earlier teacher of righteousness of whom the scrolls speak. Wilson suggested that the monastery of Qumran, where the scrolls were made, might have been "the real cradle of Christianity." This would mean, he added, that Christianity did not owe its existence to a divine intervention but to the general process of social evolution. The origin of Christianity was a mere incident in human history. That is what really worried thousands of people. We who had been studying the texts were asked over and over again what effect they would have on "the uniqueness of Christ."

The excitement reached fever heat in the spring of 1956, when the press in this country carried reports of BBC radio talks by John Allegro of the University of Manchester, one of the international team of scholars engaged in the study and publication of the scroll fragments at the Palestine Museum in Jerusalem. In these talks the career of the "Essene" teacher of righteousness and the ideas of his followers about him were represented as anticipating Christian history and beliefs even more closely than Dupont-Sommer or Wilson had intimated. The teacher of righteousness, Allegro said, had been crucified; his followers expected him to rise from the dead and return as Messiah and Judge at the end of the world. In part these astonishing assertions were based on texts which Allegro himself published later. For the most part, however, as he promptly acknowledged, they were drawn from inference rather than evidence.

Was Jesus really an Essene? Was his gospel merely derived from the teachings of this pre-Christian Jewish sect? Is the Christian faith just a product of social evolution? Because these questions have caused so much concern and confusion, and because I have been accused of treating them too casually in my previous book, they will have to be given a thorough airing in this volume. In order to have all the facts before us, however, we must first take up the story of the discoveries themselves and bring it up to date. When my book on the scrolls went to press, the 1955 excavation at Khirbet Qumran had been completed, but very little information about it had been released. Four of the caves containing manuscript fragments had just been found while the excavation was going on. The Aramaic scroll found in the first cave in 1947 and the copper scroll found in Cave 3 in 1952 were still unopened. Cave 11 had not yet been discovered.

For the details of what had happened before the spring of 1955 I must refer to my previous book, which from now on I shall for convenience designate simply as *DSS*. A brief review of the story, however, may be helpful at this point. Eleven, if not thirteen, years ago a young Bedouin goatherd in the desolate region south of Jericho, near the northwestern corner of the Dead Sea, happened upon a cave containing ancient Hebrew and Aramaic manuscripts. He now says, in a statement recently published by W. H. Brownlee, that he found the manuscripts in 1945 and kept them for two years. Some of them, at any rate, were sold in 1947 to the Hebrew University, others to the Archbishop of the Syrian Orthodox Church in Jerusalem. The Syrian Archbishop's scrolls were purchased in 1954 for the Hebrew University; all the scrolls found in 1945 or 1947 are therefore now in Israel. They include a complete manuscript of the book of Isaiah about a thousand years older than the earliest Hebrew manuscript of the Old Testament previously known, another manuscript of Isaiah less complete and little later, and several works of ancient Jewish literature which had been quite unknown. In 1949 the cave was rediscovered and excavated, and a great many fragments of manuscripts were uncovered; these and everything found since then are in Jordan, at the Palestine Museum of Jerusalem. (The sites of all these discoveries, of course, are in Jordan.)

Not far south of Cave 1, on the edge of a valley named Wady Qumran, was a ruined building called Khirbet Qumran (i.e., Qumran Ruin). The excavation of this building was begun in 1951 and continued until 1956. It proved to be the headquarters of a Jewish monastic community, commonly identified with the Essenes of whom ancient writers tell us. Established in the last part of the second century before Christ, and occupied, with an interruption of about thirty years, until the First Jewish Revolt against Rome in 66–70 A.D., this building was clearly the place where many of the manuscripts found in the cave had been made.

The year 1951 marks the beginning of other discoveries also. In another valley on the western side of the Dead Sea, the Wady Murabbaat, a few miles farther to the south than the Wady Qumran, Bedouins found in 1951 a quite separate collection of fragmentary manuscripts from the early second century A.D., the time of the Second Jewish Revolt against Rome. Other fragments were brought in by the Bedouins from a place in the same region which has never been definitely located. In 1952 four caves in the Wady Murabbaat were excavated. They yielded pieces of second-century letters, contracts, deeds, and other documents, and also manuscripts of books of the Old Testament later than those from the cave near Khirbet Qumran but still older by several centuries than any other Old Testament manuscripts known hitherto.

While the excavations in the Wady Murabbaat were going on, the Bedouins found another cave containing remnants of manuscripts north of the Wady Qumran, near Cave 1. A rigorous exploration of the surrounding region was undertaken. Many caves were explored, and in one of them was found the copper scroll already mentioned.

During that same busy summer (1952), a third collection of

still later manuscripts was found in the ruins of a Christian monastery, Khirbet Mird, about three miles northwest of Khirbet Qumran. This site was excavated the following year, and manuscripts of the Byzantine period in several languages were found. It was in 1952 also that the Bedouins found a fourth cave in the Wady Qumran very close to Khirbet Qumran, and a little later two other caves were found. By far the richest of all the caves in manuscript fragments was Cave 4. As I have already said, four more caves with scraps of manuscripts were discovered during the 1955 campaign of excavation at Khirbet Qumran. At about the same time a badly damaged scroll of the minor prophets from the second century A.D. was found by Bedouins in a cave of the Wady Murabbaat.

This was the state of affairs when my book, *DSS*, was written. I had not then heard of the four new caves or the scroll of the minor prophets and had very little information concerning the results of the excavation. From now on, therefore, we are entering new territory, though of course we shall not be the first to traverse it. Other books published since mine, including several excellent books in English, have dealt with the new material, sometimes more fully than I am able to deal with it here.

Referring in *DSS* to the purchase of the Syrian Archbishop's scrolls and their transfer to Israel, I expressed the hope that the Aramaic scroll might soon be opened and published. This hope was quickly realized. More of the text of the scroll was recovered than I had thought would be possible. Mr. James Biberkraut, who was entrusted with the opening of the scroll in Israel, subjected it to controlled humidity, cautiously and patiently unrolled it, treated it when opened, and succeeded in recovering three whole columns in the innermost end of the scroll and substantial parts of several other columns. This task was completed before the end of 1955. In the autumn of 1956 a preliminary publication of the text, including columns ii and xix–xxii, was issued by Nahman Avigad and Yigael Yadin under the title *A Genesis Apocryphon.*

Because of the references to Lamech and his wife in small bits of the text which had come loose on the outside of the scroll, it had been supposed that this might be the lost apocryphal book of Lamech. Instead of that, the text was found to consist of stories from the book of Genesis, retold in Aramaic. Naturally this late version of the stories adds no authentic historical information to what is given in Genesis. What it shows is how these stories were understood among the Jews of the last century before Christ. Comparison with other Jewish sources of the same period brings out many details of interest to specialists. The narrative resembles parts of the book of Enoch and even more the book of Jubilees. It may even have been one of the sources for Jubilees. The most significant aspect of the document, however, is its language. Here we have for the first time an extended text of a dialect of Aramaic used by Jews in Palestine in the time of Christ. For the study of the Gospels, and in particular the words of Jesus, this is very important.

The romantic interest in the Dead Sea Scrolls was enhanced by the announcement that the copper scroll—or scrolls, since what had been originally a single scroll was found in two pieces, rolled up separately—had been opened. The story of the protracted effort to open these scrolls is a tale of the triumph of patience and skill over many difficulties. Since the discovery of the scrolls in 1952, scientists in Europe and America had been trying to develop a process by which the brittle, completely oxidized copper might be restored and softened. Success in this endeavor was finally attained, but not in time to use the process on the scroll. When Professor A. H. Corwin of the Johns Hopkins University announced in 1956 that success had at last crowned his efforts, the authorities in charge of the scrolls had already decided to have them cut open, and this had been done in England by Professor Wright Baker of Manchester University. After filling the loose spaces between the convolutions of each scroll with plaster of Paris, running a spindle through the center of the scroll, coating the outside of it with a plastic composition, and baking it, he mounted it so that it could turn on the spindle like a piece of meat being roasted over a fire, and could also move on rails under a very fine circular saw of a kind used for splitting pen-points.

With this saw he then cut narrow strips lengthwise from the outermost layer of the scroll, one after another, turning the scroll after each cut and repeating the coating and baking as often as necessary, until the whole scroll had been cut up into strips. Care was taken to make the cuts where the letters of the text, which had been punched into the copper so that they were visible in reverse on the outside of the scroll, would not be damaged. Each strip was carefully removed, cleaned, placed in a tray made for the purpose, and photographed. As a result of this care, not a letter was lost in the process.

The beginning of April 1956 saw the task completed. Twelve columns of the Hebrew text, of which only about 5 per cent had deteriorated beyond recovery, were thus brought to light. The form of the script points to the middle of the first century A.D. as the time when the scroll was made. The scribe, if he can be so called, made many mistakes in spelling and grammar and sometimes mixed letters of the "cursive" script used for everyday writing with those of the formal script. The text itself has not yet been released; it is therefore impossible to give a full translation now. Only a few paragraphs have been made public, and these only in translation, but they give a general idea of the scroll's contents and confirm the hypothesis of Professor Kuhn of Heidelberg, mentioned in my previous book. About sixty places in Palestine where vast treasures are said to be hidden are listed, though unfortunately they are designated too vaguely to permit exact identification.

Father J. T. Milik, who is in charge of the publication of the scrolls, has given these samples:

In the large cistern which is in the Court of the Peristyle, in a recess at the bottom of it, hidden in a hole opposite the upper opening: 900 talents (Col. i, lines 6–8).

In the cistern which is below the rampart, on the east side, in a place hollowed out of the rock: 600 bars of silver (ii, 10–12).

Close by, below the southern corner of the portico, at Zadok's tomb, underneath the pilaster in the exedra: a vessel of incense in pine wood, and a vessel of incense in cassia wood (xi, 1–4).

In the pit nearby, toward the north in a hole opening toward the north near the graves, there is a copy of this document with explanations, measurements, and all details (xii, 10–13).

The total quantity of treasure listed amounts to something like two hundred tons of gold and silver, as well as other precious materials. That any such treasure was ever actually buried in such places is open to doubt. The archeologists who are working on the scrolls and fragments in Palestine seem to be convinced that the whole thing is purely imaginary. Milik suggests that the document had no official character but was the work of an individual, probably a hermit who lived in one of the caves and was presumably but not necessarily a member of the Qumran community. This theory, however, makes all the more mysterious the use of copper for this scroll, and for this one alone among all that have been found in the region. The preservation of this document must have been considered sufficiently important to justify the use of such valuable material and such a painfully slow method of writing.

But if there really was such an extraordinary treasure, what was it, and what did the community of Qumran, which despised wealth, have to do with it? Had the pooled wealth of the members of the community, who renounced riches and put all they had into the common treasury when they joined the order, become so great that they did not know what to do with it and could only bury it? If so, they were obviously still unwilling to dispose of their treasure altogether and forget it. Were they saving it to support the armies of light in the impending final war with the forces of darkness? Or did this wealth not belong to them at all? Was this the temple treasure, of which Josephus tells us that much was seized by the Romans but some was hidden from them? Were the devout monks of Qumran entrusted with the inventory and list of hiding places just because they were known to be trustworthy and free from covetousness? This has been seriously suggested, but the attitude of the sect to the temple and its priesthood does not favor the suggestion.

A further difficulty is that this theory would put the date of the scroll at the very end of the time when the settlement at Qumran was occupied, if not after its destruction. Jerusalem was not taken and the temple was not destroyed until 70 A.D., two years after the date set by the excavators of Khirbet Qumran as the end of its monastic existence. The war had begun, to be sure, in 66. The siege of Jerusalem lasted five months, and its end could have been foreseen before it began. The temple treasures could have been dispersed, and a list of the places where they were hidden, with an inventory of the amounts deposited at each place, could have been prepared before 68 A.D.

An origin in the Jerusalem priesthood might explain the difference in language between this document and all the other Qumran scrolls. They are written in a "neo-classical" Hebrew, imitating as closely as possible the language of the Old Testament; this is written in a later, more colloquial dialect, more like that of the Mishnah, the oldest part of the Talmud. It is still difficult, however, to imagine how the record could have come into the possession of the Qumran community or a hermit living in a nearby cave. Or are we to imagine a solitary fugitive from Jerusalem taking refuge in this cave with his precious copper scroll after the destruction and abandonment of the Qumran settlement?

Cecil Roth, who believes that the men of Qumran were not Essenes but Zealots, has recently suggested a solution of the problem which he feels is almost too sensational to be mentioned by a "sober don" like himself. From Josephus we learn that in the autumn of 66 A.D. the Zealots captured the treasures of the royal palaces and the "pay-chest" of the Romans. Later some of them established themselves for a while in the temple area, where they had access to the temple vessels and stores of incense. When they hid this treasure they might naturally, Roth supposes, make a crude copy of the inventory on some such imperishable material as copper and fasten it to the wall of a temple chamber. During the siege of the city by the Romans this list would be taken down, rolled up, and smuggled out of the city to the headquarters of the sect. The idea of displaying an inventory of hidden treasure on the wall of even an inner chamber of the temple does not strike one as highly plausible. It is worth recording, however, along with other guesses. In any case this explanation falls to the ground if the Qumran sectarians were not Zealots (see pp. 271–73).

The most formidable objection to any theory which assumes that the list of treasures and hiding places is in any sense authentic is the fabulous amount involved. No treasure ever accumulated in Palestine could have attained such a staggering value. If there is any reference at all to a treasure that ever existed, the figures are unquestionably exaggerated. There would be no point in such an exaggeration of the value of a real hidden treasure. In legend and folklore, however, exaggeration of this sort is to be expected.

It has been suggested that the document preserves a bit of ancient tradition concerning the treasures of the first temple, destroyed by Nebuchadnezzar in 587 B.C. Cherished, perhaps, especially among the priests, and so inherited by the priestly group which established the Qumran community, the tradition may have gained much in the telling through the centuries until its skeleton, the inventory, was inscribed in copper. The probability that the list rests on an old tradition is enhanced by the fact that some of the places named were no longer inhabited in the Roman period. Their abandonment before that time, we are told, has been archeologically demonstrated. Proof of this statement, of course, must await the publication of the text of the scroll.

In any case, the mystery of the use of copper for this document remains. Before the contents of the text had been determined, it was thought that it might be a proclamation or a set of regulations affixed to a wall in the main building of Qumran. But who would publicly exhibit in such a fashion, even in a closed community, a list of hidden treasures? The shape of the document also, a long strip which could be rolled up in a scroll, would be poorly suited to such a purpose. At any rate, the man who made the copper scroll must have considered its contents very important, and this would seem to imply that he believed it to be an authentic record of a real treasure.

An interesting suggestion which meets some of these difficulties has been advanced by Del Medico. The Sadduqites, whom he believes to be the group responsible for some of the scrolls, had initiation ceremonies in the course of which the neophyte was required to take an oath. They would not follow the rabbinic custom of laying the hand on a scroll of the Torah while swearing; instead they might swear by the treasury of the sanctuary. From the Damascus Document, which he considers medieval, Del Medico infers that the Qaraite sect of the Middle Ages used such an oath, but the passage which he cites does not warrant such an inference. Regardless of what the Qaraites may have done, however, the sect of Qumran might conceivably have had such a practice.

To continue with Del Medico's suggestion, the initiation oath included a promise to devote the candidate's possessions to the society. To strengthen his resolution, a scroll of shining copper listing the supposed treasures of the group was perhaps unrolled before him, and he was required to lay his hand on it while taking his oath. No society or sect, of course, possessed any such treasures, but the Sadduqites, who considered themselves the only legitimate priests, may have felt that the temple treasures belonged to them. The tomb of Zadok (Hebrew ṣadoq or ṣadduq), mentioned at the end of the copper scroll, may have been the tomb of Rabbi Sadduq, the founder of this group. Del Medico goes on to say that the copper initiation-scroll of the heretical Sadduqites was confiscated and committed to the "genizah." The advantage of this theory is that it suggests a reason for the use of copper for this document; its weakness is its involvement in the "genizah" theory (see pp. 15–19).

We can only present all these problems as questions to which no sure answer may ever be forthcoming. Perhaps we shall never know whether there really was such a treasure or not. If there was, certainly none of it is likely to be found at this late date. All that we can say with assurance is that the copper scrolls were opened and the study of their text was begun in 1956.

Meanwhile another startling discovery had been made. In February 1956, while the work on the copper scrolls was going on in England, the Bedouins found in the Qumran area, a little to the north of Cave 1, still another cave, the eleventh. In the importance of its contents, Cave 11 rivals Cave 1 and Cave 4. Since the discovery of the first scrolls in 1947, nothing like them in the amount of text preserved in each document had been found. Almost everything from the other caves, important as it was, consisted of small fragments which had to be painfully sorted and pieced together, leaving at best many large gaps in the text. Very little information concerning the manuscripts of Cave 11 has yet been released, but it is known that they include five relatively complete scrolls like those of Cave 1. Part of the book of Leviticus is contained in a beautifully written little scroll, and there are said to be also large parts of an Apocalypse of the New Jerusalem. Whether this is the same composition of which fragments were found in Caves 1, 2, and 4 is not yet known. A scroll of Psalms and an Aramaic Targum of Job are reported also. The world will await with impatience further news about the nature of these latest finds.

The preparation, examination, and publication of the other texts has been going on in the meantime. The first volume in the official publication of texts found or acquired since 1947 appeared while *DSS* was in production, barely in time to be noted at the end of my bibliography. It contained all the fragments found when the first cave was excavated in 1949, together with others that were purchased from dealers in antiquities who had bought them from the Bedouins. A few other texts have been published meanwhile in scholarly journals, including some of those from Cave 4 from which Allegro's startling inferences were drawn. Translations of the most important of these will be found at the end of this volume.

It is an extraordinary fact that this work has continued, though not without difficulties and interruptions, during the trying conditions of the past few years. At the time of the Israeli invasion of Egypt in October 1956, it seemed that Jordan was likely to be the victim of an attack. On November 3, therefore, the manuscripts in the Palestine Museum at Jerusalem were taken to Amman for safety and stored in the vaults of the Ottoman Bank. While there, of course, they could not be studied; they also suffered slightly from dampness. For four months they remained there, but by the end of February 1957 it seemed safe to bring them back. The government appointed the Director of Antiquities, the Assistant

Director, the Mayor of Jerusalem, and the directors of the French
and American schools of archeology as a committee to bring the
manuscripts to Jerusalem and supervise their study and publication. The committee with its precious charge was officially welcomed by municipal officials, and the work on the scrolls was
resumed. It was found necessary, however, before further study
could be undertaken, to take the fragments out from between the
glass plates where they had been carefully placed, and to clean
them again in order to remove any trace of dampness. This trying
chore fell to Father Milik and Dr. Huntzinger, the only members
of the team of scholars present at the time.

Not only have new discoveries been made and more texts published; the discussion of the material has proceeded also at a constantly accelerating pace and in greater and greater volume as
more scholars (and others) took part in it. All this has produced
and will continue to produce much new light on the meaning,
relationships, and implications of these documents. There is now
much more light and less heat than in the early disputes which I
recorded in *DSS*. This is fortunate, of course, but it makes a less
interesting story. It would hardly be practicable, in any case, to
present here a chronicle of the theories and arguments presented
since 1955. Some of them are significant and must be taken into
account as our discussion proceeds, even though this occasionally
entails some repetition of points already treated in *DSS*.

One such point may be considered here. This is the question
whether the Dead Sea Scrolls were the library of the Qumran
community or manuscripts which had been condemned by the
Jewish authorities and committed to the "genizah" (plural "genizot"), a burial place for heretical writings, defective copies of the
sacred books, and other documents which were unlawful but for
any reason could not be destroyed (*DSS*, pp. 75–77). Sukenik,
who purchased some of the scrolls in 1947, maintained from the
beginning that Cave 1 was a genizah, and he was supported in
this view by H. E. Del Medico. Their arguments, however, were
largely forgotten after the excavation of Khirbet Qumran showed
that it had been the center of an active community until the time
of the First Jewish Revolt against Rome. The remains of what

seemed to have been the scriptorium of this monastic settlement, with its long table and inkwells, supported the conclusion that the community had itself produced the manuscripts and had hidden them in the caves for safety in the last perilous days before the destruction of its buildings and the dispersal or massacre of its members. The theory that these were condemned books, which had been buried to prevent them from being used again, was therefore generally abandoned. A vigorous attempt to revive it, however, has now been made by Del Medico, and his arguments deserve attention.

The number of caves in which manuscripts were found and the enormous quantity of this material seem to Del Medico to favor the idea of a genizah, or rather of many genizot. The fact that not all the manuscripts were kept in jars indicates that no great care was taken to preserve them; discarded scrolls, for that matter, were sometimes buried in jars and in caves in early times. The linen wrappings of the scrolls in Cave 1 correspond to the rabbinic requirements for the wrapping of manuscripts relegated to a genizah. Not only the Qumran caves but those of the Wady Murabbaat also were genizot, according to Del Medico. During the Second Revolt (132–135 A.D.) they were used by the Jewish rebels, but before and after that time they served as genizot. The documents found in them do not conform to orthodox usage but are exactly such as would be committed to a genizah by the rabbis.

Del Medico feels, and apparently with good reason, that some Christian scholars have rejected his and Sukenik's view because they have misunderstood the nature of a genizah. The manuscripts found in Cairo near the end of the last century, including the Damascus Document, had been kept in a storeroom connected with a Qaraite Jewish synagogue; this has been commonly called a genizah, and the notion has thus got abroad that a genizah was always near a synagogue, if not attached to it. On the contrary, says Del Medico, a genizah of orthodox Jews is always connected with a cemetery, and in the Orient a cemetery is never near a synagogue. Whether the Cairo genizah is properly so called or not, it belonged to Qaraites, who are not orthodox Jews.

Del Medico's most impressive argument for his contention is drawn from the condition in which the scrolls and fragments were found. Discussing in detail the seven documents found in Cave 1, he concludes that none of them had been preserved with the intention of being recovered later; five of them had been deliberately mutilated before being taken to the cave. Three of them—the Habakkuk Commentary, the War scroll, and the Manual of Discipline—were more or less badly eaten away at one end, so that the bottoms of the columns were destroyed. This was not, Del Medico claims, the work of rats or worms or the result of decay; the ends of these scrolls had been burned in accordance with the rabbinic practice of partially or symbolically burning a manuscript before putting it in the genizah, when it was not clear whether it should be burned or buried. The scroll of the Thanksgiving Psalms had been torn to pieces and crushed together like wastepaper. The second Isaiah scroll had been twisted while wet, having been perhaps dropped by mistake into water. The Aramaic Lamech scroll (Genesis Apocryphon) had apparently been damaged accidentally, perhaps by wine spilled on it, and then deliberately further mutilated before being sent to the genizah. The only one of the seven scrolls of Cave 1 which had not been mistreated in any such way was the great Isaiah scroll, whose relegation to the genizah is sufficiently explained by its unorthodox text, or perhaps simply by the fact that it had been used until it was worn out.

Del Medico ridicules the idea that rats were responsible for all this damage. This would mean, he says, that they had a marked predilection for the bottoms of the pages and did not attack the tops, that they liked some books of Scripture so well as to leave only insignificant bits of them but had a strong aversion for the book of Isaiah; that they even preferred some of the Psalms to others. In the caves of the Wady Murabbaat rats had obviously chewed many manuscripts to pieces and used them to make their nests, but no such nests made of old manuscripts were found in

the Qumran caves. The Wady Murabbaat caves are situated at
about sea level; the Qumran area is a thousand feet lower, where,
says Del Medico, rats could hardly live. This is quite erroneous.
Leading naturalists say that the most characteristic animals of
this region are the rodents. Harding, in the official account of the
excavation of Cave 1, reports that many olive-stones and date-
stones "well gnawed by rats" were found in the cave. These surely
had not been symbolically burned!

Even if rats could be eliminated, worms and decay would still
have to be taken into account. The damage to one end only of a
scroll is easily understood if the scroll had been placed in a jar,
leaving one end more exposed than the other; it must then be
assumed, to be sure, that the bottom end was the one exposed in
each case. That some scrolls suffered more damage than others
may be explained also by the fact that some were better protected
than others. It is still a fact to be taken into account, however,
that some of the scrolls seem to have been left in the caves in the
first place in a damaged condition. How far this is true it is hard to
determine, because, as Del Medico recognizes, those removed
from the caves by Bedouins and illegal excavators seem to have
received rather rough treatment. At the same time it must be
admitted that if any of the manuscripts were already badly damaged when they were left in the caves, their preservation as parts
of a treasured library is hard to explain.

Less impressive are the arguments drawn by Del Medico from
the nature of the scrolls themselves. The book of Isaiah, he says,
was too familiar to require the careful preservation of any particular copy. A librarian would hardly accept this argument, especially if the copy in question was a very old one. The Isaiah
scrolls and the manuscripts of other canonical books which survive only in fragments were not, Del Medico thinks, especially
beautiful or valuable. The fact that many copies of some books
were included in the collection, however, and more of some than
of others, still seems to favor the belief that this was an active,
much used library.

What has seemed to dispose of the genizah theory, since the
first round of discussion, is the excavation of the ruined building,

Khirbet Qumran. This was found to have been the headquarters of a community, the same community that had used the caves in its vicinity. The connection was established by the appearance of the same kind of pottery found in Cave 1, some inscribed potsherds with the same form of Hebrew writing used in the manuscripts, the remains of what might well have been a table on which manuscripts were copied, and even three inkwells. Del Medico, however, sees in all this no evidence against his position. He has a ready explanation for everything. How convincing it is we must consider when we have reviewed the results of the latest excavations. The genizah theory cannot in any case be considered entirely dead. Albright has recently expressed the opinion that Cave 1 was "probably to some extent, at least," a genizah; he apparently means, however, that it was used as such by the Qumran community itself.

Meanwhile other explanations have been offered for the hiding of the scrolls in the caves. In a review of my book and others on the scrolls, which unfortunately I cannot now find or identify, attention was called to a passage in the pseudepigraphical Assumption of Moses as showing that it was a part of the task of a Jewish sect to copy books and store them in caves. In this passage (1:15–18) Moses gives Joshua some books and tells him to anoint them with cedar oil and store them in earthen vessels.

Similarly H. J. Schonfield, in a book graciously dedicated to me and the American Schools of Oriental Research, suggests that the manuscripts were hidden in accordance with the words of the angel in Daniel 12:9, that they might be "shut up and sealed until the time of the end." It is by no means impossible that some such idea was in the minds of the men of Qumran when they hid their manuscripts in the caves. In that case, however, the texts of the Wady Murabbaat would require a different explanation. It must be supposed that they were kept and used in the caves by people lodging there, and were abandoned when their owners moved elsewhere, perhaps at the end of Bar Cocheba's disastrous revolt.

# II

## *New Discoveries*

⎍⎍⎍⎍⎍⎍⎍⎍⎍⎍⎍⎍⎍⎍⎍⎍⎍⎍⎍⎍⎍⎍⎍⎍⎍⎍⎍⎍⎍⎍⎍⎍

The findings of the first three seasons of excavation at Khirbet Qumran (November 24 to December 12, 1951; February 9 to April 24, 1953; and February 13 to April 14, 1954) were summarized with a brief reference to the fourth campaign (February 2 to April 6, 1955) in *DSS* (pp. 54–56, 64–69). A fifth campaign has been carried out since then (February 18 to March 28, 1956). A somewhat clearer and fuller description of the establishment can now be given, though it was so elaborate that the fuller the picture is the less clear it is likely to be. We must try to find a golden mean between a simple but inadequate sketch and a complete but confusing description. The map used as frontispiece for this volume will help to clarify the account.

The main building of the community in the days of its greatest activity was not the earliest one at the site. In *DSS* (p. 68) I remarked that pottery from the eighth and seventh centuries B.C. was found in 1954, but that no remains of buildings of that period had survived. Such remains were found the next year, when the area to the west of the main building was excavated. A wall enclosing a roughly rectilinear area was discovered, and within this enclosure was the only round cistern that has been found at Qumran. Unsuited as the region is and doubtless always has been for human habitation, there evidently was a settlement here in the days of the Hebrew monarchy. Several scholars have argued very plausibly that this was the "City of Salt" mentioned in Joshua 15:62.

The other three cities named in this and the preceding verse, between Engedi and Beth-arabah, have now as a matter of fact been identified with three ruins in a small, level valley called the Buqeah, a few miles northwest of Khirbet Qumran and just below and to the west of Khirbet Mird, the Byzantine ruin excavated in 1953 (*DSS*, p. 64). During the summers of 1954 and 1955 Frank M. Cross, Jr., and J. T. Milik explored this valley and made soundings at the three ruins. They found that all three had been occupied from about the ninth to the early sixth century B.C. and concluded that they were the biblical cities of Middin (or Madon), Secacah, and Nibshan. Cross and Milik suggest further that these were three of the fortresses and store-cities built in Judah by Jehoshaphat (II Chronicles 17:12); a connection with Uzziah's towers and cisterns in the wilderness (II Chronicles 26:10) has been suggested also. All this agrees with the recent demonstration by Martin Noth that the Buqeah is the biblical Valley of Achor, where Achan, with his children and all his possessions, was "stoned with stones" and "burned with fire" (Joshua 7:24, 26; cp. 15:7; Isaiah 65:10; Hosea 2:15). These Israelite settlements, which came to an end about 600 B.C., have nothing to do with the community which occupied the site of Khirbet Qumran some five centuries later, except that what was left of the ancient masonry was incorporated by the new group in their own buildings.

As the first three campaigns of excavation already established (*DSS*, p. 65), the main occupation of the site lasted from about 100 B.C. or possibly a little earlier to the First Jewish Revolt against Rome in 66–70 A.D., with an interruption of from thirty to forty years. The first period was brought to an end by a violent earthquake, probably the one which occurred in 31 B.C. To judge by the coins found in the ruins, the buildings remained deserted through the reign of Herod the Great and were not reoccupied until about the time of his death in 4 B.C. The second period of occupation then lasted until the war with the Romans; its end came in 68 A.D. through a violent military attack, probably by the Romans, followed by a fire which destroyed everything that would burn. There was also a brief period of occupation by

Roman soldiers, and during the Second Revolt in 132–135 A.D. the Jewish rebels held the place for a while.

The first buildings erected when the community was established at about 100 B.C. were relatively modest structures in the area to the west of the main building, which was erected not much later. Not much remains of these earliest buildings. The plan of the main building is now clear; what had been revealed by the first two seasons of excavation was confirmed and elaborated by the subsequent campaigns. The strong tower at the northwest corner is the most conspicuous feature of the building. To the east of this lies the kitchen, with several well-preserved hearths. Along the west side of the square, south of the tower, is a group of rooms, including a long room on the eastern side, next to the central courtyard. Above this room, in the upper story of the building, there had been one like it, the "scriptorium," containing the long table and benches where the scribes copied manuscripts. The remains of these and other indications of scribal activity were found lying above the fallen-in ceiling of the lower room. On the south side of the square was the largest room of all, a long hall with four pillars in the eastern half of it which must have supported a roof or ceiling. It was probably in this hall that the members of the community met for study and prayers and for their meals. Crushed vessels which may have been used for the last of these meals before the building was destroyed were found in a corner of the room. A small room adjoining the hall at the western end contained over a thousand vessels neatly stacked; this was apparently the pantry or storeroom. The east side of the square was occupied by a laundry, a cistern, and a latrine.

To the southeast of the main building, and attached to it, were several pools, a bath, and a large cistern, as well as a potter's workshop. Other cisterns were located at various points, both inside and outside of the main building, with an elaborate system of conduits. The water of the Wady Qumran was brought by a long channel into the complex of buildings at the northwest corner, down through the area west of the main building, and around to the south of it. In the western area were also mills, ovens, what may have been a forge, and silos. There was also in this area a smaller building, in one room of which were found jars containing more than five hundred silver coins of the year 9–8 B.C. These may have been brought in by the members of the sect when they reoccupied the monastery after 4 B.C., or they may have been hidden by a robber while the site was deserted.

A curious discovery of the 1955 season at Khirbet Qumran consisted of nearly forty deposits of animals' bones at rather widely scattered points. They were carefully buried in pots or large pieces of jars. Bones of sheep, goats, lambs, calves, and a few cows were included. It seems also that the bones do not represent whole animals but only the forequarter of each animal. Father de Vaux is convinced that they must be the remains of sacred meals of the community, though there is nothing in any of the texts thus far deciphered to explain them. The number of animals involved, however, is hardly sufficient for a regular rite performed frequently for more than a century. We shall return to this problem when we discuss the community's organization and ritual (pp. 355–78).

To the east of the main building is an esplanade, and beyond it is the cemetery. This contains about eleven hundred tombs neatly arranged in rows. They are not simple graves: a shaft has been sunk, with a *loculus* or niche for the body in its eastern wall. Here the body lies on its back, with the head to the south, about four feet below the surface of the ground. It is protected by tiles or bricks, but no gifts are buried with it.

Six of these tombs were opened in 1953 and twelve others in 1956. In all of these the skeletons were of men. Still farther to the east are more tombs, and there is a smaller cemetery to the south. Six tombs opened in these places were found to contain the skeletons of women or children. Two tombs were opened also in another small cemetery to the north; in one of these a man was buried, in the other a woman. It would seem therefore that the main cemetery was reserved for the burial of men, presumably the regular members of the community. Who the women and children were who were buried in the other places is still a problem. It is connected with the question whether the community included married men and families or only men who had renounced marriage and family life. As we shall see when we come to that subject, the evidence on this point is ambiguous and confusing (pp. 378, 383).

Between Khirbet Qumran and the oasis of Ain Feshkha, on the shore of the Dead Sea and about two miles to the south, there are several springs which may have been used for irrigation. The Roman naturalist Pliny describes the Essenes who lived near the Dead Sea as "companions of palm trees"; the community of Qumran, whether or not it was the group of Essenes to whom Pliny referred, may have cultivated the date palm for food. Milik in this connection recalls the fact that many charred trunks of palm trees were found at Khirbet Qumran. They had no doubt been used as posts and beams in the buildings.

At Ain Feshkha itself de Vaux found in the spring of 1956 the remains of buildings from the same period as those of Khirbet Qumran. Further excavation will be needed to determine their nature more exactly, but it seems entirely probable that here was another center of the same religious group.

Bit by bit these discoveries seem to be filling in our picture of an active community living in caves and huts in the vicinity of the Wady Qumran during the last century before Christ and the first century A.D., having their meals together and meeting for worship and study at the central building, working at the mills and the pottery shop there, and devotedly copying the books of the Bible and other religious literature. Very few who have studied the texts and reports of the excavations have questioned the reality of this picture. There have been, and still are, a few skeptics, however. One of them, H. E. Del Medico, has recently issued a vigorous challenge to the prevailing view and has proposed an alternative explanation of the facts.

I have already presented Del Medico's contention that the caves were used not as hiding places for the treasured library of a religious sect but as "genizot" for manuscripts condemned by the rabbinic authorities. But what does he do with the evidence from the excavation of Khirbet Qumran? He pours out upon it the vials of acid ridicule. Scholars have been guilty, he says, of reasoning in a vicious circle. Starting from the theory that the non-biblical scrolls found in Cave 1 were documents of the Essenes, they proceeded to the excavation of the nearby ruins; now they start from the assumption that these are the ruins of an Essene settlement and proceed to the conclusion that the manuscripts in the caves were an Essene library.

Del Medico denies, in the first place, that there ever was such a sect as the Essenes. This part of his argument we must consider when we take up the identification of the Qumran community (Chapter XXIII). In any case, he says, no ancient writer represents the Essenes as spending their time copying manuscripts. He denies that there was ever any monastic sect in Judaism, that there was ever any settled life in the desolate region of the Wady Qumran, and that there was ever anywhere a Jewish settlement adjoining a cemetery. As for the inkwells found in the ruins of the "scriptorium," were the Essenes, Del Medico asks, the only people in Judea who used inkwells? Their presence is sufficiently accounted for by the presence of a Roman guard or garrison of Jewish insurgents, since in any military organization reports must be sent and received.

In the place of the generally accepted theory of an Essene community and library, Del Medico offers his own hypothesis to explain the evidence. Under the Hasmonean ruler Alexander Janneus (103–76 B.C.) an ancient Israelite border fortress was rebuilt as a military post. During the reign of Herod it was abandoned, because at the time the border no longer followed the western shore of the Dead Sea. During this time, perhaps, the clay which had settled in the cisterns of the fortress may have led a potter to set up a workshop at the ruins for a while, using wood from the ruined buildings as fuel for his kiln.

The cemetery was established by Jews; in fact, says Del Medico, two separate Jewish communities, one perhaps orthodox and the other heretical, seem to have used it. One community established its headquarters at the northeastern corner of the site, the other at the opposite corner near the remains of the potter's shop. The tower of the abandoned fortress was restored for funerary use; the other buildings were erected as adjuncts to the cemetery. The large hall to the northeast and the one on the south side of the courtyard were probably used for the recitation of prayers; the other rooms were used for the ritual washing of the dead, and the cisterns provided water for this and for the purification of those who came with the funeral processions or visited the tombs. Only gravediggers and caretakers lived at the place; Del Medico even finds evidence in a Qumran text that in the first century A.D. there were associations of men who had sacrificed their ritual purity to devote themselves to the care and burial of the dead.

The Romans occupied the place for a while, untroubled by Jewish scruples concerning contact with the dead. During the Second Revolt some of Bar Cocheba's troops were posted there. Still later, it seems, Christians used the cemetery and held their funeral love-feasts there. Del Medico sees a similarity in the arrangement of the Qumran buildings to that of later Christian cemeteries and suggests that Khirbet Qumran may exemplify an early prototype of such cemeteries. The Christian love-feasts, Del Medico claims, offer the only tenable explanation of the deposits of animal bones found in 1955. This, of course, ignores the testimony of de Vaux that most of these deposits were from the second period of the main occupation of the site (about 1 A.D. to 68 A.D.).

The crucial point in Del Medico's whole theory, of course, is its complete separation of the caves and manuscripts from the buildings of Khirbet Qumran, except in so far as the vicinity of a cemetery is an appropriate location for a genizah. Now it is a fact that no manuscripts or fragments of manuscripts were found in the "scriptorium" itself, where they are supposed to have been made. The only connection with them there is the presence of the inkwells and tables. Pottery of the same peculiar type as that first found in Cave 1, however, was found elsewhere in the building. At various points in the ruins, also, potsherds were found bearing Hebrew writing of the same general type as that of the manuscripts. It should be remembered, moreover, that Cave 4, the richest of all in manuscript fragments, was on the edge of the plateau, very close to the ruins. In 1955 a few more fragments were found in rock chambers of the terrace on which the buildings stood.

Aside from the severance of any connection between the settlement and the caves, the chief objection to Del Medico's theory is that it takes too many liberties with chronology. Things which, according to all the evidence, belong together in time are separated. The few Byzantine coins found are taken to justify the idea that Christian funerals and love-feasts were held in the buildings, although these late coins were clearly dropped there long after the buildings had been destroyed. The idea of a lonely potter's shop on the site while it was otherwise deserted ignores the quantities of pottery vessels used in the settlement itself. Del Medico's categorical denial of the possibility of settled human habitation in the Qumran region flies in the face of all the evidence that there was an active community life at the place. The cisterns, baths, channels, silos, ovens, mills, and hearths are more numerous and elaborate than the personnel of a cemetery would require. A military garrison might have used them, but it is difficult to imagine a military function for all the objects found in the rooms or to suppose that the place had any military importance during the particular periods of occupation indicated by the coins. On the whole, the chief interest of Del Medico's ingenious theory, based on much erudition, is that it shows how far one must venture into the improbable to find an alternative for the natural and obvious hypothesis of a monastic settlement.

Turning now to the caves and their manuscripts, we may briefly review what was found in each of them. The scrolls found in Cave 1 in 1947, having been described in *DSS*, need not detain us here, though we shall have to include them later with the other texts in discussing the interpretation and implications of all the material. The fragments excavated in the same cave in 1949, with a few others purchased by the Palestine Museum in 1950, were published in 1955 by Barthélemy and Milik (*Discoveries in the Judaean Desert*, I). This volume appeared just in time to be mentioned at the end of my bibliography in *DSS*, but not in time to be used in the preparation of the book.

The manuscripts found in the other caves, with a few exceptions, have not yet been published. For most of them we are dependent on general descriptions. Cave 2 yielded 187 fragments, many of them quite small. Approximately one-fourth of them belonged to biblical manuscripts. About forty non-biblical manuscripts are represented by one or more fragments. Cave 3 is notable chiefly for its copper scrolls, which we have already discussed. There had been leather scrolls also in this cave, but rats, worms, and dampness had almost entirely destroyed them.

After the first discovery of 1947, the cave whose contents aroused most excitement among scholars was Cave 4, which was not found until September 1952, although it had been almost under the feet of the archeologists when they were excavating Khirbet Qumran. Milik has given an engaging account of the discovery of this cave. Some of the Bedouins one evening were gathered in one of their tents, discussing the scrolls and fragments they had found and the amazing prices they had received for them. An old man who had been dozing woke up and told them that once in his youth he was pursuing a wounded partridge when it suddenly disappeared in a hole in the rock. Following it, he found an ancient clay lamp and some potsherds. When the young men heard this, they at once equipped themselves with a sack of flour, ropes, and lights, and, following the old man's directions, sought the place he had described, near the top of the steep northern slope of the Wady Qumran, near the ruin. With the aid of their ropes they were able to reach the little hole which was soon to be famous as Cave 4.

With their extraordinary new mass of materials the Bedouins went up to Jerusalem in search of purchasers, knowing well that they could command a high price. At the École Biblique, Father de Vaux skillfully bargained with them and finally agreed to pay thirteen hundred pounds for a part of the collection. He also telephoned to the Director of Antiquities at Amman, G. L. Harding, informing him of the new discovery. With two soldiers Harding went at once to Khirbet Qumran and found the Bedouins still busily at work in relays. They had already taken thousands of fragments, which they expected to sell at the rate of one pound per square centimeter.

The government of Jordan promptly appropriated fifteen thousand pounds from funds badly needed for health and agricultural projects. The price expected by the Bedouins was cut in half, but much more money was still needed to buy the outstanding material and preserve it from deterioration or complete destruction. It was wisely agreed that foreign institutions which could find the money should be allowed to purchase some of the fragments, with the understanding that they be left at the museum at Jerusalem until they had been adequately studied and published. In *DSS I* was already able to report (p. 69) that McGill University and the University of Manchester had purchased some of the material on this basis. Other lots were purchased by the Vatican, the University of Heidelberg, and the McCormick Theological Seminary. Thus Canada, England, Italy, Germany, and the United States will eventually have portions of this hoard of ancient religious texts. The fragments could not be bought from the Bedouins all at once, but only in successive lots. Not until the summer of 1956 could the archeologists feel that the whole treasure was at last in hand.

It was the accession of the vast material from Cave 4 which necessitated the appointment of an international team of scholars to study and publish the material. In the publication of the texts from all the caves, they expect to include in one volume everything from Caves 2, 3, 5, and 6, along with their report of the exploration of the Qumran area in 1952, whereas the texts from Cave 4 alone will require at least three volumes, one for the biblical and two for the non-biblical texts.

The biblical manuscripts are a treasure-trove in themselves. There are about a hundred of them. To be sure, they are all fragmentary, consisting sometimes of only one piece or a handful of little scraps. Even when enough of them can be sorted out and fitted together to restore the major part of a column or of several consecutive columns, there are still many gaps and holes which cannot be filled. Bearing this fact in mind, we may speak of "manuscripts," even though very little of some of them can be recovered.

In addition to their scrolls of the sacred books, the men of Qumran had books of selections from the Scriptures. Selections of texts are contained also in phylacteries. Four of these from Cave 4 have been published by K. G. Kuhn. More extensive portions of text were used in the Qumran phylacteries than in those of orthodox Jews. In the wording of the text also, and in the order of the passages quoted, the phylacteries of Qumran are not in accord with later orthodox practice.

Some of the works now known as the apocrypha and the pseudepigrapha were represented in Cave 4, as I have occasion to note later. There were also portions of several non-biblical works known already from other caves and from the Cairo genizah (see p. 16), together with others not represented elsewhere. Brief descriptions of these in alphabetical order will be found in the Appendix at the end of this volume.

Compared with the enormous mass of material from Cave 4, the manuscript fragments of Cave 5 are meager indeed. There are a few pieces of biblical manuscripts, some of them important, and a few of non-biblical works. The fragments from this cave, however, are not numerous; they were all, moreover, very badly decomposed and very hard to clean and handle.

Cave 6 yielded a somewhat larger and more satisfactory lot of fragments, unusual in that more than 90 per cent of them are papyrus. There are some biblical fragments, but those of non-biblical works are the most numerous.

The contents of Caves 7–10 are not yet revealed in any report I have seen, except for the fact that they include inscribed potsherds as well as manuscript fragments, some of the latter being in Greek. As for Cave 11, only a few tantalizing hints have been dropped thus far. It had been a matter of wonder and perplexity that the only cave containing complete or relatively complete scrolls, instead of small fragments, was the one first found by sheer accident in 1947. Now with Cave 11—will it be the last?—we have scrolls again (see p. 13).

The scrolls and fragments of the eleven caves in the area surrounding Khirbet Qumran are by no means all of the same age, and the writings contained in them, even apart from the books of the Old Testament, were not all necessarily composed within the same religious group. At the same time, unless we revert to the genizah theory, they were all obviously preserved, copied, and used by the community which had its headquarters at Khirbet Qumran. In that sense at least they have a certain unity, and, with the possible exception of a few of the oldest manuscripts, all come from the same limited period of time, the period within which the buildings and caves were occupied by the sect now commonly identified with the Essenes.

An entirely separate and quite different body of manuscripts, both in date and in religious associations, is the collection from the Wady Murabbaat (*DSS*, pp. 57f, 87, 320). These come mostly from the time of the Second Jewish Revolt against Rome (132–135 A.D.), whereas the latest of the Qumran manuscripts are from the first two-thirds of the first century A.D. It is not impossible, of course, that manuscripts were deposited in the Qumran caves after the destruction of the community's buildings. It is not inconceivable even that some of the caves may have been used as genizot long after the region was abandoned by the community altogether. Whether this is probable is another question. Here we must fall back on the criterion of paleography (*DSS*, pp. 83ff), and the plain fact of the matter is that the script of the second-century manuscripts of the Wady Murabbaat is definitely and demonstrably later than that of any of the Qumran texts. In the case of the Wady Murabbaat material we are not dependent on coins and other "archeological context"; many of the texts themselves are letters and business or legal documents which bear definite dates. The final proof of the difference in time between the two bodies of material is the fact that all the evidence agrees in presenting a consistent picture.

Not all the Murabbaat fragments are late. As a matter of fact, the oldest fragment in any of the texts from the region of the Dead Sea is a bit of papyrus from the Wady Murabbaat. It is a palimpsest; that is, a new text was written over an older one. The later text, a list of names and numbers in the old Hebrew alphabet, has been dated by the script as far back as the sixth century B.C., the time of the prophet Jeremiah and the Babylonian exile. The older text under it is too faint to be deciphered fully, but it is apparently a letter and can be dated by the script in the eighth century B.C., the time of Amos, Hosea, Micah, and Isaiah. Except for inscriptions cut in stone, clay tablets, and a few inscribed potsherds, this is the oldest known bit of writing in a Semitic language. The only manuscripts in any language that are older are the Egyptian papyri.

From the same time as some of the Qumran manuscripts are two ostraca (inscribed potsherds) of the Wady Murabbaat. Their script indicates a date near the end of the second century B.C. One of them bears only a few letters, but the other lines of text are in a very old form of Aramaic. At the other end of the period covered by the Qumran texts there is a contract in Aramaic from the Wady Murabbaat. It is dated in the second year of the reign of Nero, 66 A.D., just two years before the destruction of Khirbet Qumran.

There are also, of course, much later documents. Even Arabic texts have been found in the Wady Murabbaat, including actually some from the tenth century A.D. written on cotton paper. Evidently the caves of the Wady Murabbaat, which are at a considerably higher altitude than those of the Wady Qumran, were much more used from prehistoric times and throughout all the ages of history.

With the exceptions noted, the manuscript material from the Murabbaat caves and that which was found by Bedouins in unidentified caves of the same region (*DSS*, pp. 61f) is all of the same nature and from the same period. Both biblical and non-biblical manuscripts are represented. The fact of greatest importance about the Hebrew fragments from the Old Testament is that, unlike the Qumran manuscripts, they uniformly exhibit a text coinciding with the Masoretic text (see p. 161).

Of the non-biblical manuscripts, one is a hymn-like composition. Most of the texts, however, are of more historical than literary interest. There is a bill of divorce dated in "the sixth year" (probably 111 A.D.). A marriage contract is dated five years later.

Another fragment comes from the eve of the Second Revolt, 131 A.D. A tiny scrap of papyrus dealing with a sale of real estate bears the date "Year 1 of the Redemption of Israel," that is, 132–133 A.D., the beginning of the Second Revolt. Twelve contracts concerned with the renting of fields and guaranteed by the authority of Simon ben Koseba (Bar Cocheba), the leader of the revolt, are dated in the following year. There are also four fragmentary documents dealing with real-estate transactions, one of which is dated "Year three of the freedom of Jerusalem" (i.e., 134–135 A.D., the third year of the revolt); still another real-estate contract is dated "Year three of the freedom of Israel." All these texts are composed in Mishnaic Hebrew. From the same year comes an unusual document, a bill of divorce given by a woman to her husband. Several contracts are not dated, or the dates are not preserved.

Some of the most interesting texts from the Wady Murabbaat and the unidentified site near it are letters. Two of them from ben Koseba himself to an officer named Yeshua ben Galgola were mentioned in *DSS* (p. 58), with other letters and texts. There is also a letter addressed to ben Koseba, stating that the Romans have moved their camp.

Two phylacteries were found, one in the Wady Murabbaat and the other in the unidentified caves. The order of biblical citations is different in these two examples from the same period, and Milik remarks that the two types are both still in use to this day. In addition to all the Hebrew texts, there are others in Aramaic, Nabatean, and Greek.

A third lot of manuscripts, entirely distinct from both the Qumran and the Murabbaat collections, consists of those found in the ruins of the Byzantine monastery of Marda (Khirbet Mird). The excavation of this site in 1953 was noted in *DSS* (p. 64), and something was said of the manuscripts found there, but a few more details may now be given. There were manuscripts of books of the New Testament, both in Greek and in the Palestinian Christian dialect of Aramaic. In this Christian Aramaic dialect there were also letters, an inscription, and a manuscript of the book of Joshua. There was a fragment of the Wisdom of Solomon in Greek. Many other texts, especially letters, in Greek, Syriac, and Arabic were found. Even a bit of classical Greek literature was found, a fragment of Euripides' *Andromache*. All of these manuscripts came from the fifth to eighth centuries A.D., when the monastic life was especially flourishing in the Holy Land.

Compared to the excitement aroused by the much older Qumran documents and those of the Wady Murabbaat, little attention has been given to the Byzantine texts of Khirbet Mird. Del Medico expresses surprise at this fact. We do not know, he says, what literary and linguistic treasures these carefully written manuscripts may contain. The fragment of Euripides, though four hundred years younger than the Wady Murabbaat documents, still antedates by fully six centuries the Renaissance manuscripts of Euripides, which were the oldest known hitherto.

The work of editing all three collections of manuscript material from the region of the Dead Sea is now well advanced and proceeding as rapidly as can be expected in all the circumstances. The first volume, as we have noted, appeared in 1955. The second, devoted to the discoveries in the Wady Murabbaat, may be published in 1958. The third, which is to contain the archeological report of the exploration of Qumran caves in 1952 and the fragments from the "minor caves" of the Wady Qumran (Caves 2, 3, and 5–10), as well as the copper scroll, is not expected to appear before the end of 1959. It is hoped that the remaining six or more volumes may be brought out at a rate of at least one a year.

Looking back over all the material, as known thus far, we may make a few general remarks by way of summary. Roughly a fourth of all the manuscripts contain books of the Old Testament, according to the Jewish and Protestant canon. Some of the books— notably Deuteronomy, the Psalms, and Isaiah—appear in ten or more copies; this is true also of the twelve minor prophets considered as one book, though not of the individual books in this group.

Most of these books had of course gone through many copies in the course of the centuries before the manuscripts found in the caves near the Dead Sea were made. A few books, however, were not much older than the newly found manuscripts. Ecclesiastes, for example, was probably written not more than a century before the time when a scribe of Qumran made the copy represented by one of the Cave 4 fragments, while Daniel was barely half a century old when it was copied in the Qumran scriptorium.

Only a few of the apocryphal (deutero-canonical) books of the Old Testament have appeared. Tobit in both Hebrew and Aramaic, Ecclesiasticus (Sirach) in Hebrew, and at Khirbet Mird the Wisdom of Solomon in Greek are the only representatives of this group. With a few exceptions, these works were of much more recent composition than the canonical books.

Collections of selected passages from one or more books of the Old Testament are found not only in phylacteries but also in the "Testimonia," the "Florilegium," and some of the other compositions of Qumran Cave 4 (see Appendix). There are also paraphrases of biblical books or portions of them, including the Aramaic Genesis Apocryphon (Lamech scroll) from Cave 1 and paraphrases of Genesis, Exodus, and I–II Samuel from Cave 4. Specimens of Greek and Syriac translations of the Old Testament have been found in the caves of Qumran and Murabbaat and at Khirbet Mird. It is a notable fact, however, that no Jewish Aramaic Targum of any book of the Old Testament is represented among the thousands of scrolls and fragments, with the single exception of the Targum of Job from Cave 11.

The commentaries on a number of books of the Old Testament form perhaps the most surprising class of works among all the manuscripts. The incredulity with which the Habakkuk Commentary was received, and the dogmatic denials that commentaries were written at such an early date (*DSS*, p. 31) seem amusing now that we have parts of commentaries on Genesis, Psalms, Isaiah, Hosea, Micah, Nahum, and Zephaniah. An interesting fact concerning the Qumran commentaries is that, unlike the biblical books, most of them appear in only one copy. Frank M. Cross, Jr., noting this fact, draws from it—rather precariously, I think—the inference that many of the actual manuscripts discovered were the author's original copies. It is at least safe to say that these relatively recent works had not gone through many successive copies.

Two of the books known to us as the Pseudepigrapha, Enoch and Jubilees, are represented in the Qumran manuscripts. Other works which may have been used as sources for some of the Pseudepigrapha are an Aramaic Testament of Levi, a Hebrew Testament of Naphtali, and several compositions related to the Enoch and Noah literature. There were also many other works of the same general nature, but not previously known even in translation. Milik estimates that there were something like six hundred different works among the scrolls and fragments of the Qumran area alone. Only a few of these survived in scrolls even approximately complete; others are represented by a few columns or a mere handful of scraps, and some by only one fragment. As for the general character of the deposits, Milik suggests that most of the caves were the dwellings of hermits, and the manuscript fragments are the remains of their personal libraries. Caves 1 and 4—to which perhaps Cave 11 might now be added—differed from the rest in being hiding places for the central library of the community or of smaller groups of monks or hermits.

How much more material, if any, will still come to light no man can predict. It is known that some has fallen into private hands and is being withheld. Reports of manuscripts from the area that are being offered for sale come now and then to all who are known to be interested in the Dead Sea Scrolls, but a request for photographs usually ends the correspondence, or a photograph of an obviously much later manuscript is sent. Any future find by the Bedouins is almost sure to be reported to the Department of Antiquities or to Father de Vaux of the French École Biblique.

PART TWO

# CHRISTIAN ORIGINS
# IN THE LIGHT OF
# THE DEAD SEA SCROLLS

# III

## Facts and Faith

⎍⎍⎍⎍⎍⎍⎍⎍⎍⎍⎍⎍⎍⎍⎍⎍⎍⎍⎍⎍⎍⎍⎍⎍⎍⎍⎍

In *DSS* I recorded my conviction that the Dead Sea Scrolls would not "require a revision of any basic article of Christian faith" (p. 327). That statement elicited the comment that this depends upon what is considered basic. An astute columnist, Robert Morrill Sand, wrote in the Ridgewood, New Jersey, *Herald News* that what I as a Yale professor would consider "basic articles of Christian faith" might be quite different from "the judgment of, say, a professor of Fordham University, or of the Moody Bible Institute, or of certain Boston oriented Unitarians." This is an eminently fair observation. I had already, in fact, begun to be bothered by the same consideration. Let me therefore try to clarify this point before we go further.

What I meant by basic articles of faith was not those beliefs that mean most to me but the outstanding traditional tenets of the Christian churches through all the centuries. It is quite true that as a liberal Protestant I do not share all the beliefs of my more conservative brethren. It is my considered conclusion, however, that if one will go through any of the historic statements of Christian faith he will find nothing that has been or can be disproved by the Dead Sea Scrolls. This is as true of things that I myself do not believe as it is of my most firm and cherished convictions. If I were so rash as to undertake a theological debate with a professor from either the Moody Bible Institute or Fordham University—which God forbid—I fear I should find no ammunition in the Dead Sea Scrolls to use against them.

Not that everything ever believed by any group or individual that claimed the name of Christian has been confirmed by the scrolls! To claim that would be manifestly absurd. They have not made me any more conservative than I was before. For most of the points on which Christians disagree among themselves, and for most of those on which they all disagree with non-Christians, the Dead Sea Scrolls prove nothing at all; they are simply irrelevant.

There is one point at which the scrolls disprove what some Christians believe, but it is something which no informed Christian believes and no major Christian group officially maintains. There are devout Christians who suppose that the King James Version of the Bible is infallible, and any departure from it is a betrayal of the faith. No person who knows the most elementary facts of the matter believes that. There are those who believe or assume that the Greek and Hebrew texts from which our translations are made are infallible. No person who has studied textual criticism at all could believe that. The most conservative scholars in the most conservative churches recognize that the text has become corrupt at many points in the course of its transmission. If that were not already well known and universally admitted, the Dead Sea Scrolls would demonstrate it conclusively. Such a demonstration, however, was not needed.

More real and lively issues than that have been raised by writers on the Dead Sea Scrolls. The suggestions of Edmund Wilson and others were mentioned at the beginning of this book. Wilson felt that the historical and religious implications of the scrolls must be disturbing to both Jewish and Christian believers. Surprised by what seemed to him a lack of interest in the scrolls on the part of biblical scholars, he could see no explanation except fear or prejudice. The fact that an enormous amount of work was being done on the scrolls, and almost all of it by biblical scholars, seems to have escaped him.

New Testament scholars in particular have been accused of neglecting the scrolls. The fact is that some of the first to deal with this material were specialists in the New Testament. Stendahl remarks that "the pace of publication has obviously been higher in the case of the scrolls than is usual in these areas of research." It is true that at first more Old Testament scholars than New Testament scholars were active in this work. The reason is not far to seek. Those who deal constantly with the Old Testament are more at home in Hebrew and Aramaic studies than those whose major preoccupation is the Greek text of the New Testament, the Greek papyri, and the Greek authors of the New Testament period. Scholars prefer to know something about a subject before they rush into print about it, and it takes time to study ancient texts and analyze their contents, relationships, and implications.

Wilson feels, however, that a "clergyman scholar" is prevented by his religious commitment from facing the implications of the Dead Sea Scrolls. In an otherwise very sympathetic review of *DSS* he declares that this impression has been confirmed by my chapter on the relation of the scrolls to the New Testament. Duncan Howlett rejects as "wholly gratuitous" the assumption that theological commitments will color a scholar's technical studies, but he too complains that theology has made some scholars "very slow in moving toward the conclusions toward which their studies seem to lead." Their caution, he feels, "may be due both to scientific standards and theological reticence."

The indictment was given a new turn by the late A. Powell Davies. Biblical scholars, he said, were not disturbed by what they found in the Dead Sea Scrolls because they had known all along that the origin of Christianity was not what it was commonly supposed to have been. The layman does not know this; he is therefore naturally alarmed when he first learns it.

These are serious charges, and they must be met squarely. Another point, however, must be disposed of first. In suggesting that the Dead Sea Scrolls will disprove the supernatural origin of Christianity, Wilson expresses a laudable hope that this will have the effect of reducing religious prejudice and tension. That would indeed be a consummation devoutly to be wished. If mutual understanding and appreciation between men of different faiths could be brought about by proving that all religions alike were mere by-products of social evolution, and if that could be proved by the Dead Sea Scrolls, something of real value would be gained.

It would not be all gain, to be sure. No doubt countless crimes have been committed in the name of religion; but the comfort, guidance, courage, and inspiration of religious faith are powerful factors for good in human life. They are not to be blindly cherished if founded on falsehood and delusion, but they are far too precious to be discarded without compelling reason. Tolerance that is merely indifference or supercilious disdain is no great mark of intellectual progress.

In any case, for better or for worse, to remove discord between different faiths would require more than a refutation of the divine origin of Christianity. Religious prejudice is not the result merely or mainly of false beliefs. It goes far deeper, and is consequently much more difficult to eradicate. Its roots are not so much intellectual as emotional. They go down into the subsoil of attitudes and feelings formed through personal contacts, beginning in early childhood but not ending there. To imagine that any archeological discovery could affect such a perversion of normal human feelings seems pathetically optimistic. Correct information can do some good. It can remove false ideas of what the adherents of other religions believe and how they feel and act. Personal acquaintance can do still more to remove misunderstanding. Very little, if anything, can be accomplished by finding ancient manuscripts.

In any case, the Dead Sea Scrolls cannot have the effect Wilson desires, because they do not actually prove what he infers from them. If such evidence as they afford could prove that Christianity was a product of social evolution and therefore did not come by divine revelation, that would have been proved long ago. Evidence of connections and influences in early Christianity has never been lacking. Unquestionably Christianity is the fruit of a long historical process. It does not follow, however, that God had nothing to do with it.

If revelation meant a completely new communication from heaven, having no connection whatever with anything that went before it, then the demonstration of any such connection would prove that there had been no revelation. But that is not what revelation means. To say that the gospel was a divine revelation means that it came from God; how it came, and through what human channels, is another question. Both Wilson and Davies have confused these two questions. Wilson speaks of understanding the rise of Christianity as "simply an episode of human history," not as revelation. Davies says that Christianity is now shown to have originated, not in a series of unique events caused by a supernatural intervention, but by a natural process of social evolution.

Are these alternatives mutually exclusive? Davies himself says later, "God can work through natural events in a gradual social evolution just as well as some other way." Exactly! That is precisely my point. But this means that the question *whether* God works in human history and the question *how* he works are two different questions. History may be able to demonstrate a process of social evolution with clear contacts and relationships, but history cannot say whether or not this process is the work of God. That is a question of faith, and cannot be answered on any other basis than that of faith. It is not a matter of establishing facts; it is a matter of interpreting the meaning of the facts.

In *DSS* I said that after studying the scrolls for seven years I did not find my understanding of the New Testament substantially affected (p. 343). This, Wilson objects, is not the issue. From the parallels between the scrolls and the New Testament, he says, scholars have concluded "that both John the Baptist and Jesus must have had some connection with the sect; may perhaps have represented a final stage, when the exponents of the Essene doctrine had detached themselves from the brotherhood proper and were preaching its message in a wandering ministry." Not all scholars who have examined the evidence agree with Wilson's statement. We shall go into this matter later. My point here is that this is not a question that concerns Christian faith at all. The historical connections and antecedents of John the Baptist and Jesus are purely questions of historical fact.

I do not mean that there is no connection between fact and faith. Davies accuses the theologians of supposing that they could "rely upon faith to determine fact." Faith, he insists, must rest on fact. "If the New Testament narrative was not factual, how could one have faith in its principal figure? How could one know, apart from knowledge of fact, that one's faith was not divorced from reality?" Some theologians would protest at this point that religious truth and historical fact are entirely distinct and mutually independent. Some treat even the crucifixion of Christ as an event within the individual's soul, not dependent on what occurred in Palestine under Pontius Pilate. With that position I do not agree. Christianity is grounded in certain historical events, which faith interprets as acts of God. If these events never occurred, they were certainly not acts of God. What is most distinctive in Christian faith could not then be true. Thus far I quite agree with Davies.

The issue becomes confused, however, when he goes on to say that "the truth or falsity of the main events recorded in the New Testament and the implications of those events—also recorded in the New Testament—must be determined *historically*." The truth or falsity of the events must be determined historically, within limits set by the amount and nature of the evidence; but for the implications of the events, all that can be determined as history is what the first Christians believed about them. The truth or falsity of what they believed is not a matter of historical investigation.

Davies makes much of a supposed conflict between history and theology. He predicts a second "battle of the scrolls," not a debate this time about the date and authenticity of the manuscripts but "a rather decisive battle for the entire question of theology against history." What is needed is not a battle but an understanding. Theology and history are not inveterate foes, locked in a struggle from which only one of them can come out alive. They are two mutually supplementary ways of seeking truth, each with its own field and its own methods of inquiry.

Howlett, like Davies, feels that the discovery of the scrolls has raised the fundamental question of the relationship between dogma and fact. "Which," he asks, "is to be given precedence?" Before the scrolls were discovered, he says, this had ceased to be a living issue, "because all the data bearing upon Christian dogma had been squared with it in one way or another." Men are now asking, however, "What is to be the place of the new data in the official doctrines and creeds of the church?"

Now dogma and faith are not the same thing. Put in terms of "official doctrines and creeds," the question seems rather naïve. Official dogmas are not changed overnight. Any change in this sphere, even if desirable, can come only after long study and discussion and the attainment of some substantial agreement within the particular church whose doctrines may be affected. Unless the theologians first decide that a change is necessary, the question of an alteration of official dogmas and creeds will not arise at all.

What is the relation of faith to fact? I have said that history is concerned with facts, and theology with their ultimate meaning. That, no doubt, oversimplifies the matter. History too is concerned with interpretation and meaning as well as facts. It does not raise the ultimate question, however, with which faith is concerned. Its first concern, at any rate, is to establish the facts, and here the theologian must accept the verdict of history. The theologian's task, in other words, follows that of the historian and depends upon it, in exactly the same way and to the same degree that it follows and depends upon the task of the natural scientist. Of course, the theologian is not bound to accept every scientist's or historian's opinions and theories; but when conclusions are sufficiently established to be accepted by a general consensus of competent authorities in these fields, the theologian must abide by the results and adjust his interpretation to them.

The situation here is essentially the same as in the old dispute about evolution versus creation. Unable to distinguish the question *whether* God created the universe from the question *how* he created it, many Christians have felt that to accept the idea of natural evolution would be to abandon their faith in God. Theologians soon recognized that modern scientific views of the universe made it incomparably greater, more majestic, and more awe-inspiring than the world-view which prevailed in biblical times and was accepted without question by the writers of the

Bible. Our new knowledge of the processes of nature demands a correspondingly larger and more profound conception of God and his creative work, but it does not, as once predicted, "usher God to the edge of his universe and bow him out with thanks for past services." With a better understanding of the way God works in nature, we still believe that nature is God's work. Just so we see his work in the processes of history.

The history of our religion is no less a history of God's work if it is shown to be a continuous process involving contacts, relationships, and development. As a matter of fact, Christian theologians have never thought of it as anything other than that. They have always been more or less aware, and increasingly so of late, that Christianity is closely related to other religions at many points and has acquired and assimilated much from other religions. It arose in the first place within Judaism and was first offered to Jews by Jews as the true Judaism, not as replacing but as fulfilling the faith of their fathers. Jesus was the one for whom Moses and the prophets looked.

The Old Testament was accepted as Scripture and is still a part of the Christian Bible. The church was the continuation of the ancient congregation of Israel. Only after it became evident that the Jewish people as a whole would not accept Jesus as the Messiah did Christianity and Judaism become two separate religions. The two branches of the tree grew apart, but they were not separated from the trunk. As Christianity spread in the Roman empire and beyond, it came into contact with other religions too, found that it had something in common with them, and was more or less influenced by them. Judaism itself, in fact, had been influenced by other religions and cultures long before the dawn of Christianity.

# IV

## *Anticipation and Preparation*

⎍⎍⎍⎍⎍⎍⎍⎍⎍⎍⎍⎍⎍⎍⎍⎍⎍⎍⎍⎍⎍⎍⎍⎍⎍

Something like the alarm and confusion caused by the Dead Sea Scrolls was aroused about a century ago when the clay tablets containing the Babylonian stories of the creation and the flood were unearthed and deciphered. They were so much like the account in Genesis that the originality and inspiration of the Bible seemed to be impugned. Babylonian laws also, much older than the laws of Moses, were found to resemble them at many points so closely that some kind of influence, direct or indirect, was indubitable. No longer could it be supposed that Moses had received these laws brand new from heaven. He and his successors had obviously adopted and adapted laws already familiar in the ancient world. The divine inspiration of the Old Testament therefore had to be relinquished or conceived in a new fashion.

Similar contacts between Egyptian wisdom literature and the biblical book of Proverbs were discovered. Clearly the proverbs had not all been newly created by the divine wisdom granted to Solomon. At Ras Shamra in northern Syria ancient Canaanite poems were found, and in them were parallels in metrical forms, language, and ideas with the Old Testament Psalms, so close that a few of the Psalms were seen to be almost certainly Hebrew adaptations of ancient Canaanite hymns. Zoroastrianism, the ancient Persian religion, had beliefs about angels, the resurrection of the dead, and the last judgment that plainly influenced the development of Jewish ideas on these subjects.

Nor were such discoveries limited to the Old Testament. Considerable excitement and serious concern were aroused among New Testament scholars when the mystery cults of the Greco-Roman world were studied and found to be uncomfortably like early Christianity, with salvation by mystical union with a god who had died and risen from the dead, with rites of initiation something like baptism, and with sacramental meals in which the flesh of the cult deity was eaten. The early church fathers recognized these facts and explained them in the same way that much later missionaries in Japan are said to have explained the surprising similarities between northern Buddhism and Roman Catholic Christianity: the devil had planted a counterfeit of Christianity in order to hinder the spread of the true faith. Among modern Christian scholars who rediscovered the mystery cults and their affinities with early Christianity, there were considerable searchings of heart for some time.

Similar misgivings were aroused when Christian scholars began to study the literature of Judaism from the centuries just before and after the birth of Christianity. Here again were found contacts with the New Testament which sometimes disturbed those who had assumed that everything in the Gospels and the Epistles, if inspired, must have been entirely new and different from anything ever said before. In the apocryphal books from the time between the Old and New Testaments and in the rabbinic literature, which recorded the sayings of the rabbis from the last century or two before Christ and from the early centuries of the Christian era, ideas and expressions were found that seemed to be merely echoed in the New Testament. There is that much ground for the statement of Davies that scholars were not shocked by what they found in the Dead Sea Scrolls because they already knew that the origin of Christianity was not what was commonly supposed.

In all the instances mentioned, and in others that might have been mentioned, the same thing has happened. After the first flurry of excitement, an adjustment has been made to the new knowledge, and it has been found that our appreciation of the Hebrew and Christian tradition is not destroyed but enhanced.

We see that, in the framework of ancient Semitic myth and legend, writers of the Old Testament presented a new picture of the meaning of man's life, his place in the world, and his relation to the God who created it and him. In the framework of current legal tradition they presented a new ideal and standard of human conduct under the sovereignty of God. Other ideas and literary forms borrowed from their cultural environment were used in the same way as vehicles of new insights.

Sometimes what seemed at first sight to be real affinities, and must have seemed so to the people of the ancient world, have turned out on closer inspection to be mere surface similarities under which there are profound and crucial differences. This has been conspicuously true with regard to the mystery cults of New Testament times. In the place of their mythical deities, personifi- cations of the vegetation which dies in the hot summer of the Middle East and is raised to new life by the rains of winter and early spring, Christianity offered a crucified and risen Savior who had lived a real human life very recently. There were many people still living who could testify to what they had heard and seen. Their Lord was not a mythical person who was supposed to have been slain by another mythical being in the mysterious ages be- fore history began; he had been crucified under Pontius Pilate.

The fact of historical continuity is therefore nothing new to Christians. Indeed, if anything can be called a basic article of Christian faith it is this. The divine revelation of the gospel, as the church has understood it from the beginning, does not mean that something entirely new and different from anything ever heard before came down all at once from heaven. The Christian revelation was not given apart from history but in history. It was a new stage in a continuous history of revelation, judgment, and redemption, and that history was the history of the people of Israel. The revelation came in and through the nation's concrete historical experiences, interpreted and judged by its prophets and historians in terms of the eternal purpose of God.

In that sense the origin of Christianity was indeed "an episode of human history." What Krister Stendahl calls "the episode dimension" was an integral element in the gospel itself, and Stendahl reminds us that the first Christian theologians were much concerned "to preserve the episode dimension against all tendencies to transform Christianity into a system of timeless truth." The gospel was not a new philosophy. It was the proclamation of an act of God in history, the culminating act in a long series.

In the New Testament itself this understanding of the meaning of the gospel finds expression in the idea of fulfillment. Mark summarizes the proclamation with which Jesus appeared in Galilee in these words: "The time is fulfilled, and the kingdom of God is at hand; repent, and believe the gospel" (1:15). Matthew stresses the continuity between John the Baptist and Jesus by giving identical summaries of the preaching of both: "Repent, for the kingdom of heaven is at hand" (3:2; 4:17). Luke (4:16–21) pictures Jesus in the synagogue at Nazareth reading from the book of Isaiah and saying, "Today this scripture has been fulfilled in your hearing." That is why the Christian church retained the Old Testament as a part of its own Scriptures, though there were some who would have liked to discard it. Marcion, whose views were quickly repudiated by the church, "wanted Christianity to be a new religion," as Stendahl puts it; thus he resembled the modern man who thinks of Jesus as "the founder of a new religion" instead of the fulfiller of ancient prophecy.

Much of the very language of the New Testament is drawn from the Old Testament, which was the Bible of Jesus and his disciples as of other Jews. The word we translate "gospel" is itself derived from the "good tidings" of such verses as Isaiah 40:9; 41:27; 52:7; and 61:1. The word translated "church" in the New Testament is used in the Greek translation of the Old Testament for the "congregation" of Israel. The expression "kingdom of God" goes back ultimately to the frequent references to God's kingdom in the Old Testament, especially in the Psalms and Daniel (e.g., Psalms 103:19; 145:11, 13; Daniel 2:44; 4:3). In the form "kingdom of heaven," to which the Gospel of Matthew is especially partial, it is often used in rabbinical literature. The word "Christ" itself is the Greek translation of the Hebrew word meaning "anointed," which has come over into English in the form "Messiah." The Greek words translated "the Lord's Christ" in Luke 2:26 are exactly the same as those used in the Septuagint for "the Lord's anointed," meaning the king.

Once the basic fact is grasped that Christianity arose as a continuation and fulfillment of the religion of the Old Testament, it ceases to be surprising that many things in the New Testament are found also in Jewish writings. Judaism went on developing and producing literature during what Christians call "the intertestamental period," and its history has continued without a break through the Christian centuries. The destruction of the temple by the Romans and the virtual annihilation of Jewish life in Palestine a little later were far more serious crises for Judaism than the end of the Old Testament period or the rise of Christianity.

What is now called the apocryphal and pseudepigraphic literature was produced during the centuries preceding and following the birth of Christ. The oral traditions of the rabbis, committed to writing later, were developing during the same period. Like the New Testament, all these found their chief inspiration and authority in the Old Testament. Jesus and the apostles were acquainted not only with the Old Testament but also with the subsequent thought and literature of their people.

Those who have been startled by similarities of thought and language between the Dead Sea Scrolls and the New Testament are not aware of the abundance of such parallels in other Jewish sources. Our grandfathers knew their Apocrypha and Josephus, but these are now rarely read by laymen or even by ministers. As Stendahl says, most theological students are "exposed" to many parallels to the New Testament, but they do not "come to grips with the basic problem" of the meaning of such parallels for theology and the work of the parish.

These considerations are very important for a just estimate of the significance of the Dead Sea Scrolls in relation to Christian faith. Fairly close contacts between the scrolls and the New Testament are what we should expect, in view of the fact that the early church and the Qumran sect were both groups of Jews, living at the same time and in the same country. Many parallels with the New Testament in other Jewish sources are at least as close as any that can be found in the Qumran texts.

A few examples will make this clear. The Lord's Prayer may be taken as a case in point. It has often been pointed out that every word of this prayer is typically Jewish. The form of address with which it begins in Matthew, "Our Father who art in Heaven" (6:9; cp. Luke 11:2), appears in sayings of the rabbis. One such saying is this: "On whom can we stay ourselves?—on our Father who is in heaven." Many Jewish prayers address God as "our Father." The petition "hallowed be thy name" is equally typical; the hallowing of the Name is a basic motive of Jewish piety. The petition "thy kingdom come" differs from contemporary Jewish usage in the fact that the verb "come" is not used in connection with God's kingdom in Jewish sources; other verbs which are used with it, however, express substantially the same meaning. The next words in the Lord's Prayer, "on earth as it is in heaven," recall other Jewish prayers. Still other expressions and ideas in the rest of the prayer, such as the conception of sin as debt, are equally Jewish.

Attention has been drawn recently by Paul Winter to several striking parallels with sayings of Jesus in rabbinic literature. In Luke 6:36 (cp. Matthew 5:48) Jesus says, "Be merciful, even as your Father is merciful." The Aramaic Targum Pseudo-Jonathan says at Leviticus 22:28, "As our Father is merciful in heaven, so be ye merciful on earth." In Matthew 7:2 (Mark 4:24; Luke 6:38) Jesus says, "The measure you give will be the measure you get." A passage in the Mishnah expresses the same idea in almost the same words (Sotah I. 7).

The similarities and parallels which have been mentioned show, if nothing else, that in proclaiming their good news the Christian apostles used terms and categories which were familiar to them and their hearers. Sometimes this was done spontaneously and unconsciously, sometimes deliberately. The sermon of Paul on the Areopagus at Athens, as reported in Acts 17:22–31, begins with a reference to an inscription seen on a pagan altar, "To an unknown god," and continues, "What therefore you worship as unknown, this I proclaim to you." In his first letter to the Corinthians, Paul says of his own missionary work that to the Jews he became as a Jew, to those outside the law he became as one outside the law; he became "all things to all men," in order to win some of them (9:20–22).

This was both inevitable and necessary. If the apostles who spread the gospel through the Roman Empire had tried to devise new forms of expression for the new things they had to say, they would not have conveyed any meaning at all. They would have been like those new converts whose joy was so ecstatic that it found utterance in unintelligible "speaking in tongues." It used to be supposed that the Greek in which the New Testament was written, which is quite different from the language of the classical Greek authors, was a special new language created by Providence for the proclamation of the gospel. The discovery of many contemporary documents, written on papyrus, has shown that the Greek of the New Testament was the language used at that time throughout the Greco-Roman world in correspondence, business, and other everyday affairs. The gospel was preached to people in their own language.

Much is being said in these days about communication, the art of getting ideas across to other people. Young people preparing to be teachers, preachers, or writers are told that unless they put what they have to say in a form that their hearers or readers will understand, they will not "communicate." Now revelation, if it is anything at all, is communication. If it is not received, if it does not "register," there is no revelation at all. If the Christian gospel is revealed truth, it is truth not as God himself may be supposed to know it but as man can apprehend it. Not only that; it is truth as it could be received by the minds of men living in a particular part of the world at a particular time in history, the men of Jewish Palestine in the time of the Roman domination, and later the men of the pagan Roman Empire.

All this may seem to have carried us far from the Dead Sea Scrolls, but it is not irrelevant. The surprise so often felt at finding in the scrolls ideas and language like what we have in the New Testament is very largely the result of failure to realize what has just been said. Such contacts were to be expected. If the Dead Sea Scrolls are at all typical of the language and thinking of Palestine at the time when Christianity came into being, the disciples of Jesus and Jesus himself would naturally use these forms of expression and ways of thinking whenever they could, as a means of communication.

All that has been said thus far, however, only leads up to the major issue for Christian faith. The question that has been raised over and over again is what the Dead Sea Scrolls do to "the uniqueness of Christ." It is to be hoped that our little lecture in elementary theology will at least have helped to clarify this issue. The question is not whether anything that Jesus said had been said before, or anything that he did had been done before. It should be clear that he built upon the foundation of the patriarchs and prophets and was received by his disciples as the fulfillment of age-old hopes. He was sent, he said, "to the lost sheep of the house of Israel" (Matthew 15:24). He spoke to Jews in terms of Jewish faith and aspiration. Whatever uniqueness is to be ascribed to him must take account of these facts.

The question remains, however, whether in speaking he said anything at all new, and whether he was himself different from any other teacher or prophet. This basic question leads ultimately to a decision of faith, but that decision must be in accord with historical facts. We must now, therefore, proceed to the strictly historical question of the actual relation between Jesus and the sect of Qumran. Was he acquainted with them? Was he influenced by them? Were his teaching and work anticipated by their history and beliefs?

If Jesus was not what Christians have always believed, if he was not even what liberal, "modernistic" Christians believe, then the sooner we find it out the better. If, on the other hand, a free, unbiased appraisal of the historical and literary evidence leaves Jesus secure in his position as mankind's supreme religious Teacher, that much should be clear to every competent and unprejudiced investigator, even if he is unable to take the final step of faith and accept Jesus as the incarnate Word of God. In short, the facts of history must be allowed to have their say before theological inferences are drawn.

There is a type of Christian faith, already mentioned briefly, which is unwilling to take that position. It is rather strongly represented today and must be recognized. This view regards the affirmations of Christian faith as confessional statements which the individual accepts as a member of the believing community, and which are not dependent on reason or evidence. Those who hold this position will not admit that historical investigation can have anything to say about the uniqueness of Christ. They are often skeptical as to the possibility of knowing anything about the historical Jesus, and seem content to dispense with such knowledge. I cannot share this point of view. I am profoundly convinced that the historic revelation of God in Jesus of Nazareth must be the cornerstone of any faith that is really Christian. Any historical question about the real Jesus who lived in Palestine nineteen centuries ago is therefore fundamentally important.

# V

## John the Baptist

When we compare the New Testament and the Dead Sea Scrolls, one basic fact confronts us at the outset. The New Testament and the Dead Sea Scrolls reflect the same period of Jewish history. Not only do they have the same general background and antecedents; they also deal with the same situation. It has often been remarked by scholars that the Gospels reflect a type of Judaism somewhat different from that of the rabbinic sources, and apparently more influenced by Iranian or Hellenistic ways of thinking. This aspect of Judaism in the New Testament period is especially illuminated by the Dead Sea Scrolls.

Another and very important element in the situation faced by the first Christians and the sect of Qumran was the unrest and bitterness of the Jews under the rule of Rome. The preceding period of the Hasmonean priest-kings had been one of dissension and discontent, but the Romans made matters much worse. The result was a general stirring of Messianic expectations. The evils of the time seemed to be the "Messianic woes," and it was widely felt that the time of deliverance must be near. The Gospels and the Dead Sea Scrolls alike presuppose this situation and address themselves to it. In this important respect the scrolls stand even closer than other Jewish sources to the New Testament.

It was in this situation that John the Baptist appeared. Much interest has naturally centered in his relation to the Qumran covenanters (*DSS*, pp. 328f). There is no reason why one should be reluctant to believe that John was or had been a member of their community. The only question is whether there is good reason to suppose that he was, or that he had anything to do with the sect. There are two ways of approaching this question, and both are exemplified by writers on the subject. One way is to point to such facts as nearness in time and place and infer that John must have had some connection with the sect; the other is to look for specific evidence of such a connection.

The first approach cannot be entirely ruled out. It is true that the place where John baptized penitents in the Jordan River was not much more than ten miles from the Qumran settlement, and his sojourn in the desert before his public appearance may have brought him even closer. "It is impossible," says Cullmann, "to think that John could have been there without coming in contact with the sect." Other writers too, including Daniélou and Howlett, consider "contacts" or "some connection" either "indubitable" or "almost inevitable."

Recognizing the antecedent probability, one must observe that it is not positive evidence. Daniélou feels that in Luke 3:2 "the desert" seems to mean a definite place, and the same word (or, more exactly, its Hebrew equivalent) was used by the Qumran group to designate the region where they lived. True, but the same Hebrew and Greek words are also used often in the Old and New Testaments in a far more general sense. The quotation of Isaiah 40:3 by John the Baptist and also twice in the Manual of Discipline (viii.14; ix.19f; *DSS*, pp. 382, 384) seems to Daniélou "an astonishing proof" of the identity of John's desert and the desert of Qumran. Surely this is pushing the argument too far.

A similar indication of probability is seen in the fact that John came from a devout priestly family. His father had not seceded from the temple priesthood (Luke 1:8f), as the Qumranians had, but it is not improbable that John's retirement to the desert was inspired by a revulsion against the worldliness of the Jerusalem priests. If so, this would give him some sympathy for the Qumran brotherhood.

Here again Daniélou finds what seems to him positive evidence. The "Benedictus" (Luke 1:68–79) of John's father, Zechariah, contains several expressions which are characteristic of the Qumran texts: "to prepare his ways" and "to give knowledge of salvation" (verses 71f); "he has visited us, rising from the deep" (verse 78, as read by the Vulgate—Daniélou sees here an allusion to the star out of Jacob in Numbers 24:17); "the way of peace" (verse 79). But the whole poem is full of Old Testament language; all we can say is that some passages used also by the Qumran sect are echoed here, together with many others.

A somewhat closer point of contact is found in John's ascetic way of life. As Jesus said of him later, he "came neither eating nor drinking" (Matthew 11:18). His fare was in fact even more ascetic than that of the Qumran monks. The Damascus Document mentions locusts as an article of diet, prescribing that they must be roasted or boiled alive (xii.14f; *DSS*, p. 361). Allegro suggests that John's diet may have been restricted by vows of purity taken in the Qumran community, but there is no hint of such vows in the Gospel accounts, and the Qumran texts say nothing of eating locusts and wild honey. Abstinence from wine and strong drink, Daniélou notes, is attributed to the Essenes by Jerome. It was characteristic also, however, of other and earlier groups, such as the Nazirites and Rechabites. As for John's raiment of camel's hair, it has been remarked that this would have caused his expulsion from a community of Essenes, who, according to Josephus, wore white garments.

Daniélou calls attention to John's contacts with Herod Antipas, who "feared John, knowing that he was a righteous and holy man," and "heard him gladly" (Mark 6:20), but had him beheaded to keep a foolish promise. According to Josephus, an Essene had predicted the glorious career of Herod the Great, the father of Herod Antipas, and another interpreted a dream of Archelaus, another son of Herod the Great. How this indicates any connection between John the Baptist and the Essenes is not at all clear.

Brownlee and Fritsch find John's indictment of the Jewish nation characteristic of the sect of Qumran. It is no more so than any prophet's fulminations against apostasy and corruption. According to Matthew 3:17, John denounced the Pharisees and Sad-

ducees in particular; the Essenes are not mentioned, here or elsewhere in the New Testament. This suggests to Daniélou that
John identified himself to some extent with the Essenes. Perhaps
so; but this is at best a weak "argument from silence."

The rite of baptism itself has seemed to many a strong instance
of the influence of Qumran on John the Baptist. The origin of
John's conception and practice of baptism has always been a perplexing problem for historians. The ritual baths of the Qumran
community (see pp. 371–72) offer a tempting explanation.
Murphy points out that, unlike John's baptism, the ablutions of
the sect were self-administered, they were repeated frequently,
and their purpose was to maintain ritual purity. Brownlee suggests, however, that there may have been also a bath to mark
admission to the order, and that the disciples of John may have
practiced other lustrations in addition to their initial "baptism
of repentance for the forgiveness of sins" (Mark 1:4).

As for the purpose of the rite, Josephus says that John baptized
"for the purification of the body when the soul had previously
been cleansed by righteous conduct." The Manual of Discipline
says of one who enters the order "in a spirit of true counsel" that
"in the submission of his soul to all the statutes of God his flesh
will be cleansed, that he may be sprinkled with water for impurity and sanctify himself with water of cleanness" (iii.8f; *DSS*,
p. 373). Brownlee reports a suggestion made to him by Joachim
Jeremias that Josephus, better acquainted with Essene doctrine
than with the preaching of John the Baptist, attributed to him
an Essene conception. Brownlee himself, however, feels that the
statement of Josephus is substantially accurate. In that case, of
course, John may have been closer to the "Essenes" of Qumran
than the Gospels indicate. The decision here must depend on
one's judgment as to the relative accuracy of the evangelists and
Josephus.

Cullman calls attention to the important possibility that John's
baptism may have been derived from a wider movement than
the Qumran sect in particular. Many scholars believe that at the
time when John appeared there were many groups in Syria and
Palestine practicing rites more or less like the baptism of John.

It is difficult to reach a solid judgment on this matter, because the evidence consists largely of questionable inferences from the much later Mandean literature. In the present lack of unanimity among specialists the question must be left open, but the possibility noted by Cullman should not be forgotten. The resemblance between John's rite and the ablutions of Qumran is not, in any case, sufficiently close to establish a direct influence. We may conclude, with N. A. Dahl, that John and the covenanters represent "two movements which are in some respects parallel, but in the main lines independent of each other."

John's announcement of the one who was to come after him affords a point of comparison with the Messianic hopes of the covenanters. According to Mark 1:8, John said that the coming one would baptize with the Holy Spirit; Matthew 3:11 and Luke 3:16 add "and with fire." Murphy thinks that John is speaking here "in terms of the Qumran expectations." Cleansing "with a holy spirit" and sprinkling with "a spirit of truth, like water for impurity," are mentioned in the Manual of Discipline in connection with the future "time of visitation" (iv.21; *DSS*, p. 376).

Those who see a Messianic reference in this section of the Manual associate the spiritual sprinkling with the Messiah, though this would mean that he would receive it instead of administering it. This interpretation of the passage, we shall find, is unacceptable (see p. 316). For the idea of the Messiah as baptizing others with the Spirit, Brownlee refers to a statement in the Damascus Document that God "caused them by his anointed to know his Holy Spirit" (ii.12; *DSS*, p. 350); he understands the verb here as future, though he mentions another possible interpretation of the sentence.

The baptism with fire, which in Matthew and Luke is added to the baptism with the Holy Spirit, recalls the Zoroastrian idea of the destruction of the world by a river of fire, and this idea is reflected by one of the Thanksgiving Psalms (iii.28–36; *DSS*, pp. 404f, cp. p. 329). It seems therefore that John the Baptist was acquainted with a conception of Iranian origin which was known also to the men of Qumran. He may or may not have learned it from them. There is nothing to show how it came to him or to them.

How John thought of the coming one, aside from his being the mighty agent of divine judgment, is not indicated in the Synoptic Gospels. In the fourth Gospel John says that the one who is coming "ranks before me, for he was before me," suggesting the pre-existence of the Messiah in heaven before his coming to earth (1:15, 30). John also, hailing Jesus as the promised one, calls him "the Lamb of God, who takes away the sin of the world," and "the Son of God" (1:29, 34, 36). Brownlee defends the historical accuracy of the fourth Gospel's account of John the Baptist on the basis of comparison with the Qumran documents. We shall consider this question in connection with the relation of the Gospel of John to the Dead Sea Scrolls (pp. 123–30). It may be noted, however, that Brownlee finds the scrolls by themselves inadequate to explain either the judgment by fire or the pre-existence of the Messiah in John's preaching.

In view of the fact that John the Baptist and the Qumran covenanters were living at the same time and not far apart, the points of similarity which we have reviewed make it quite probable that he knew something about their life and beliefs. They may also have heard of him. Whether there was any closer connection is a matter of guesswork; and scholars are divided in their opinions.

Brownlee's suggestion that the Essenes may have adopted John as a boy (*DSS*, p. 328) has been taken up by a number of writers. Speculating as to how this may have come about, Brownlee says that John's parents may have been sympathetic toward the Essenes, though not themselves members of the sect; the prominence of the priests at Qumran may have led John's father to think that there was a greater future for the boy in the community; or the parents may have died, leaving John to be adopted and reared by the Essenes. Henri de Contenson also thinks that John's adoption by the Qumran community is "very likely," and Oesterreicher considers it "not at all improbable." Daniélou remarks that John's parents probably confided their son to the care of the Qumran monks as the parents of Racine entrusted him to the hermits of Port-Royal. It is not certain, however, says Daniélou, that John was an Essene; in any case, he had his own prophetic vocation and founded a new movement. So also Cullmann, while convinced that John must have had some contact with the sect, concludes that "without being a member, he was influenced by them, even if he went on to found an independent Messianic movement."

Allegro points out that John's "mixing with the common man" when he baptized at the Jordan would have made it impossible to remain a member of the community. At the same time Allegro believes that John "belonged to the Essene movement" and considers his adoption by the sect an "interesting suggestion" which "would certainly account for his being in the desert at such an early age." The only basis for the "early age," incidentally, is Luke's statement that "the child grew and became strong in spirit, and he was in the wilderness till the day of his manifestation to Israel" (1:80).

John's separation from the sect, Allegro says, may have come by "expulsion or voluntary resignation, perhaps when he reached this overwhelming conviction of the need to take his message to the common people." Howlett, who takes it for granted that John was an Essene and discusses only what may have made him withdraw, thinks that he may have tried to make Essenism a missionary movement, having reached a conviction that his teaching should not be kept secret. Fritsch too accepts Brownlee's suggestion that John may have become dissatisfied with the sect's failure to call the whole nation to repentance and so fulfill Isaiah 40:3.

Other differences between John and the sect of Qumran have been noted. Murphy points out that he was a prophet of doom, not the legislator of a community. Oesterreicher mentions the "taut organization" of the covenanters, as contrasted with the company of disciples whom John directed to a greater one coming after him. The fact that John addressed publicly all kinds of men, instead of devoting himself to a closed, esoteric group, is stressed by many writers. Rigaux sees in the ease with which John's disciples left him to follow Jesus "a liberty unknown at Qumran."

Fritsch and Oesterreicher especially emphasize the supreme distinction that John pointed the way to Jesus.

Recognizing that John "departed from the ideas of the Dead Sea sect," A. P. Davies insists that "he had to have some ideas from which to make departures." Since "the evidence points so plausibly to the Qumran monastery," he feels it is "scarcely to be doubted" that John and his followers were Essenes "in the broader sense of the term." Rigaux, however, finds "nothing that proves John belonged to the sect"; Cullmann too feels that a connection between the Essenes and the disciples of John "cannot be proved with certainty." The supposed evidence, in fact, tends to evaporate when exposed to the light.

Del Medico explains the similarities between John's preaching and the Dead Sea Scrolls in an original way which at least shows the need of caution in reaching conclusions. The importance ascribed to baptisms and an allusion to a passage in Isaiah suggest to him that one section of the Manual of Discipline(ii.19–iii.12) comes from the sect of John's followers. In another section (viii. 7–16) he sees an extract from a commentary on Isaiah written to explain the coming of John the Baptist. In still another passage (xi.15–22) the mention of "one born of woman" seems to him to indicate that the author belonged to the sect of John the Baptist.

In all this I can find no reason to alter the position taken in *DSS* (p. 329), that John the Baptist probably had some knowledge of the Qumran covenanters and some sympathy with their ideas, though he also differed from them at important points; in some of his ideas and attitudes he may have been influenced by them; he may have visited their settlement, or even possibly have been a member of the sect for a while, though there is no very good reason to think so; in any case, in his public ministry (which is all we really know anything about, aside from his birth) he was entirely independent of them and was sharply opposed to some of their most characteristic tenets.

# VI

## *The Person and Saving Work of Jesus Christ*

⌐⎺⌐⎺⌐⎺⌐⎺⌐⎺⌐⎺⌐⎺⌐⎺⌐⎺⌐⎺⌐⎺⌐⎺⌐⎺⌐⎺⌐⎺⌐⎺

The question most often asked by Christians concerning the Dead Sea Scrolls, we have already observed, is what effect they have on the uniqueness of Christ. Theologians have answered this question by saying that Christ's uniqueness lies not in his teaching but in his redeeming work. To some of us this is considerably less than satisfying, as will appear later, but it is a part of the truth. Some of the most sensational statements that have been made about the scrolls, as a matter of fact, have to do with this aspect of Christian faith. It has been suggested that the story of Christ's coming and saving work merely repeats a pattern which is to be found in the Dead Sea Scrolls. No competent scholar has said quite this, so far as I know, but it has been inferred from statements made by scholars. It is this idea which more than anything else has alarmed believers and delighted unbelievers.

Before considering the connections between Jesus' teaching and the Qumran texts, we must therefore compare the faith of the New Testament concerning his saving work for mankind with the beliefs of the Qumran community. There are two points for comparison here: first, the Messianic hopes of the sect for the future and, second, its beliefs concerning its historic founder or leader, the "teacher of righteousness." The two become one, of course, if it is to be supposed that the teacher of righteousness was expected to return as one of the two Messiahs, or as the prophet who would precede or accompany them. This question is discussed later (pp. 329–41).

Some, if not all, of the writers of the New Testament believed that before his life on earth Christ had been pre-existent with the Father in heaven. So far as I know, there is no hint of a pre-existent Messiah in the Qumran texts. There is not the slightest suggestion that the teacher of righteousness was ever thought of as having been pre-existent. Dupont-Sommer abandoned his original contention that the incarnation of a pre-existent divine being was implied by the expression "his body of flesh" in the Habakkuk Commentary (ix.2; *DSS*, p. 368, cp. p. 152). No such idea is suggested in the Thanksgiving Psalm concerning the birth of the "wonderful counselor" or in the problematic reference to the begetting of the Messiah in the Rule of the Congregation (see pp. 317–18, 300–304). Nowhere is there a suggestion of anything miraculous in the birth of the teacher of righteousness.

The saving efficacy of the death of Christ has no parallel in the beliefs of the covenanters concerning either the teacher of righteousness or the coming Messiah. Much excitement was aroused by Allegro's dramatic statement about the crucifixion of the teacher of righteousness. The question whether the teacher of righteousness was actually crucified will be considered later (pp. 214–17); if he was, he was only one of the many thousands who suffered that cruel but common form of execution. Two thieves were crucified with Jesus.

What gave unique significance to the crucifixion of Jesus was not that he was put to death in that particular way, but that it was he, the altogether righteous Son of God, who suffered death for the sins of others. No such meaning is ever ascribed to the death of the teacher of righteousness. He was persecuted and perhaps put to death for his iconoclastic teaching, as Jesus was; but in this respect, as Cullmann says, the teacher and Jesus both stood in the line of the prophets. Oesterreicher remarks that the teacher's death is left "entirely obscure" in the Qumran texts, whereas "Jesus' death and resurrection are told in the New Testament not once but a hundred times."

A passage in the Damascus Document, unfortunately very

badly preserved (and for that reason omitted from my translation in *DSS*), seems to say of the coming "Messiah of Aaron and Israel" that "he will make atonement for their iniquity." How this is to be done is not indicated in the few words that are preserved. The subject of the verb "make atonement" may have been God, as everywhere else in the Damascus Document. It is equally possible that the form here is passive: "their iniquity will be expiated."

Even Jesus' disciples, Murphy reminds us, found it hard to accept the idea of a suffering Messiah. That it was known at all in Judaism at that time is a debatable question. Brownlee's effort to show that the teacher of righteousness is identified in some texts with the suffering Servant of Isaiah 40–55 is unconvincing (see pp. 316–17). So far as there is any suggestion of atonement by suffering in the Dead Sea Scrolls, the suffering is that of the whole community. Even here more stress is placed on the faithful, obedient life of the covenanters than on their suffering. This is the implication of the Manual of Discipline (viii.1–10; *DSS*, pp. 381f).

Some scholars believe that the followers of the teacher of righteousness expected him to rise from the dead. As first set forth by Allegro, this seemed to imply an individual resurrection comparable to that of Jesus, as related in the Gospels. Further discussion and explanation clarified this point: what Allegro meant was simply that the teacher would be raised in the general resurrection of all the dead for judgment, and that he would then be the Messianic high priest. Many writers, including some who accept this view, have pointed out that it is very different from the Christian belief that "Christ has been raised from the dead, the first fruits of those who have fallen asleep" (I Corinthians 15:20). Since Dupont-Sommer's theory that the martyred teacher of righteousness had already "appeared" in 63 B.C. is untenable (see p. 225), the only remaining possibility is a future reappearance.

No objective historian, whatever may be his personal belief about the resurrection of Jesus, can fail to see the decisive difference here in the beliefs of the two groups. What for the community of Qumran was at most a hope was for the Christians an accomplished fact, the guarantee of all their hopes. God, says Paul on the Areopagus (Acts 17:31), "has fixed a day on which he will judge the world in righteousness by a man whom he has appointed, and of this he has given assurance to all men by raising him from the dead."

The resurrection experience, however it is to be interpreted or explained, confirmed the disciples' faith in Jesus as the Messiah, which had been badly shaken by his crucifixion (Luke 24:21). He who was "descended from David according to the flesh" was now also "designated Son of God in power according to the Spirit of holiness by his resurrection from the dead" (Romans 1:3f). He was now "exalted at the right hand of God," fulfilling Psalm 110:1 (Acts 2:33–35; 7:56; Hebrews 1:13; 12:2).

Being thus exalted, says Peter on the day of Pentecost, Jesus has "poured out" the Holy Spirit on those who believe in him (Acts 2:33). Stendahl points out that here, as in the hope for the resurrection of the dead, "the Christians enjoyed a higher degree of anticipation," that is, they had already experienced what for the sect of Qumran still lay in the future. The covenanters looked for a cleansing "with a holy spirit" and a sprinkling "with a spirit of truth" in "the time of visitation"; Christians had received "the guarantee of the Spirit" (II Corinthians 1:22; 5:5; Ephesians 1:14). For the sect of Qumran, as for Judaism in general, the gift of the Spirit was associated with the Messianic hope; for the church the prophecy of Joel was already fulfilled (Acts 2:16ff).

Not all prophecy, however, was yet fulfilled. Jesus, who had been taken up to heaven, would come again to judge the world (Acts 1:11; 3:20f; 10:42; 17:31); this runs through the whole New Testament. To the question whether the teacher of righteousness was expected to come again as one of the Messianic figures of the last day a decisive answer is impossible (see pp. 331–41). He would in any case be only one of at least three such figures. His coming again, if expected at all, was not for his followers the culminating, ultimate fulfillment of all hopes that the return of Christ was for the early Christians.

The Qumran sect, I have said, expected several Messianic persons. The Christians found in Jesus the fulfillment of all promises and hopes, but they interpreted his person and work in terms of several different categories. First of all, he was the promised king, the son of David. The covenanters also, like all other Jews, looked for the promised "branch of David," whom they called also "the Messiah of Israel" and "the prince of the whole congregation" (see pp. 312–15). The teacher of righteousness, however, was not associated with this hope. He was a priest of the tribe of Levi, not a member of David's tribe, Judah.

Allegro says, "There seems to be nothing which would preclude the acceptance by the Qumran sect of Jesus as the expected Messiah of David's line." This is an astonishing statement. Jesus was so unlike what all Jews expected the son of David to be that his own disciples found it almost impossible to connect the idea of the Messiah with him. It is clear that he did not encourage the use of the title, at least in public (Mark 1:34; 8:30).

To the very end, in spite of all his efforts to instill a very different conception (Mark 8:31–33; 9:31f), the disciples hoped that he would "restore the kingdom to Israel" (Luke 24:21; Acts 1:6). This was what the Qumran sect expected of the Davidic Messiah; he was to be, as Bruce says, "the victorious captain of the sons of light in the final conflict with the sons of darkness"; but, Bruce adds, "Jesus repudiated this kind of Messiahship"; indeed, he "rejected the whole conception of such a warfare."

Except for occasional lapses, the church too has always rejected any such idea of Christ. At the same time, Christians have believed from the beginning that Jesus was the true and only fulfillment of the Messianic hope. It was he who had been "born king of the Jews" (Matthew 2:2). In the city of David had been born "a Savior, who is Christ the Lord" (Luke 2:11). He was indeed a king, but his kingship was "not of this world" (John 18:36).

Oesterreicher remarks that the Qumran community was "almost all expectation." The church too looked to the future, but its ideas of the present and future were anchored in "a clear vision of sacred history." Consequently, while the Dead Sea Scrolls "veil persons and dates," the Gospels are as explicit as possible, even taking pains to "give the long line of the ancestors of the Christ."

If the teacher of righteousness was expected to return as Messiah in any sense, it would obviously be as the priestly Messiah of Aaron. This is what Allegro and others maintain. Schonfield suggests that the very question whether John the Baptist might be the Messiah (Luke 3:15; John 1:19–25) implies a prevalent idea of a priestly Messiah, since he came of a priestly family. This may be so, if we can assume that his descent was generally known. The idea of Jesus as both king and priest appears in the New Testament and other early Christian literature. Milik sees a trace of the idea of two Messiahs in the New Testament, for Mary was related to Elizabeth (Luke 1:36), who was a descendant of Aaron (1:5); Jesus was therefore descended from both the tribe of Judah and the tribe of Levi.

There is no other indication of such an idea in the New Testament, though it was taken up by some of the church fathers. Milik observes quite correctly that the idea of Christ's high priesthood in the Epistle to the Hebrews comes from "an entirely different milieu and mentality." The author of the Epistle notes explicitly (7:14) that "our Lord was descended from Judah, and in connection with that tribe Moses said nothing about priests." Kuhn finds no suggestion at all in the New Testament "that the expectation of the two Messiahs finds its fulfillment in the person of Jesus." Rather, in calling Jesus the Christ, the New Testament "presupposes the Messianic expectation of the average Jew, not the special two-Messiah concept of the Essenes."

The Damascus Document speaks of "the Messiah of Aaron and Israel," as though there would be only one instead of two. Brownlee has inferred from this fact that "in some Essene (or covenanter) circles" there was probably "a tendency toward a unified Messianic expectation" even before the time of John the Baptist. If the Qumran fragments of the Damascus Document (see p. 409) have the word "Messiah" in the singular, as in the medieval manuscripts of the work found at Cairo, this suggestion will be more plausible. Otherwise, it still seems more probable that the change from a plural to a singular form was made in a later copy

(*DSS*, p. 265). The Christian belief that several different forms of the Messianic hope were fulfilled in Jesus does not seem to have any parallel in the Qumran texts.

The covenanters of Qumran expected a prophet as well as the two Messiahs (see pp. 310–11), and Christians considered Christ not only king and priest but also prophet. There is no indication here of any influence from the Qumran sect. The expectation of a prophet goes back to Deuteronomy 18, which both the community of Qumran and the Christian church used as a Messianic proof-text; but other Jews also made a similar use of the same text. The expectation that Elijah would return as forerunner of the Messiah, based on Malachi 4:5f, appears often in Jewish sources, as it does in the New Testament. For some unknown reason, those who searched the prophets at Qumran seem not to have made much use of Malachi's prediction.

Schonfield points out that in rabbinic sources Elijah appears as a priest, a descendant of Aaron, and a Qaraite prayer quoted by Szyszman and Dupont-Sommer asks God to send a teacher of righteousness "to turn the hearts of fathers to their children," which is what Malachi says Elijah will do (4:6). These rather widely separated references suggest that the future teacher of righteousness expected by the Qumran sect may have been associated with Elijah. If we had a Qumran commentary on Malachi, it might be possible to substantiate this conjecture. In the texts recovered there seems to be no support for it. The New Testament, of course, connects John the Baptist, not Jesus, with Elijah; Jesus himself, in fact, made this identification (Mark 9:13; Matthew 17:12f; cp. 11:14).

Stendahl raises in this connection the question whether Jesus thought of himself as the Messiah or as the prophetic forerunner of the Messiah. To readers of the New Testament not acquainted with recent technical studies in the Gospels this may seem a strange question with only one possible answer; among specialists, however, it is a very live issue. The older question whether Jesus believed himself to be the Messiah or merely a teacher or rabbi, Stendahl says, does not present the real alternatives. When it is realized that the real question is whether Jesus conceived his mission as that of the Messiah or as that of the prophet, "the Messianic ideas of the Qumran texts become significant parallels."

Unfortunately, instead of making clear the implications of these significant parallels or the conclusions to which they lead him, Stendahl then goes into an analysis of the New Testament evidence and only comes back to the Qumran texts in another connection. The question of Messiah versus prophet gets lost somewhere by the wayside. How the Qumran material could throw any light on this question is, in fact, rather hard to see. No doubt Jesus thought of himself and his work in terms of current Jewish conceptions, but how he interpreted and applied them can be determined only on the evidence of the New Testament itself. Like his disciples, he may have used more than one traditional category; in fact, it seems to me quite certain that he did.

That even the combination of prophetic, priestly, and kingly offices in one person was anticipated at Qumran has been suggested. Taking up Brownlee's argument that the community conceived its own function as combining all three elements (*DSS*, p. 267), A. P. Davies says that from this to the idea of the teacher of righteousness as prophet, priest, and king "is only a step." It is quite a long step, however, and there is nothing to suggest that the community ever took it. Davies says that the idea may not have been fully developed when the Manual of Discipline was written, but "if it was moving in this direction" the development may have been "complete by the time Jesus could have encountered it." As a remote possibility this can hardly be denied, but those who seek facts or probabilities established by evidence cannot be satisfied with unsupported conjectures.

The term which Jesus most commonly used in referring to himself is one that does not occur at all in the Qumran literature as a Messianic designation. The idea of the "Son of man," who is coming down from heaven to judge the world, is developed especially in the apocalyptic book of Enoch, where some of the very expressions used in the Gospels are found. Either Jesus himself or those who reported his sayings must have been acquainted with this book. It was known also at Qumran, for fragments of it have been found in the caves (see p. 409). The portion containing the

Parables or Similitudes, however, where the figure of the Son of man appears, is not represented by any of the fragments. Milik's inference that this was a Christian work of the second century A.D. (see p. 150) may not win general assent; it may well have been a separate work, however, unknown at Qumran and only later combined with the other parts of the book.

Cullmann remarks that the idea of the heavenly Son of man "is found only on the fringe of Judaism." That would not exclude the Qumran community; the fact is, however, that the idea has not been found in the Qumran texts. Jesus' constant and characteristic use of it is a marked point of contrast between him and the sect of Qumran. It is hard, in fact, to see what basis Fritsch can have for his statement that not only did Jesus know the "profound Messianic teachings of the Essenes" but "his own Messianic consciousness was strongly influenced by their interpretation of the Old Testament prophets."

From the beginning, according to all the Gospels, Jesus was regarded by his disciples as the Son of God. Whatever may have been the original implications of this title, it was not derived from common Jewish usage. Jewish scholars have denied that the expression "the Christ, the Son of God," attributed to the high priest in Matthew 26:63, or "the Christ, the Son of the Blessed," as Mark has it (14:61; cp. Luke 22:67, 70), would ever have been used by a Jewish priest. In orthodox Jewish tradition the Messiah is not a divine being. As Klausner says, "He is a human being, flesh and blood, like all mortals. He is but the finest of the human race and the chosen of his nation."

This seems to be true also of the Qumran "Messiah of Israel," who ranks below the high priest (p. 304). There are a few indications, however, that he may have been considered in some sense the Son of God. The Rule of the Congregation speaks of his being begotten, and while the restoration of the text is uncertain, it is apparently God who is thought of as his Father (see pp. 300–303). If the reading "begets" is correct, there is no doubt an allusion to Psalm 2:7, where God says to the newly crowned king —or to the Messiah, according to the traditional interpretation— "You are my son, today I have begotten you." Both the text and its meaning, however, are too uncertain to warrant any inference.

In the Florilegium the promise to David concerning his son, "I will be his father, and he shall be my son" (II Samuel 7:14), is applied to the expected "branch of David." This implies, says Allegro, the divine sonship of the Messiah. In some sense that is undoubtedly true; the only question is how this sonship was understood, and that is a question we cannot answer. It may be, however, that on this point the Qumran community was closer than orthodox Judaism to later Christian ideas.

There is no indication that the teacher of righteousness was considered divine in any sense. When Fritsch says, for example, that he "must have been regarded as more than human," because salvation came through faith in him, this is surely, as Oesterreicher says, "reading into the text, and not out of it." We shall have more to say later on the meaning of faith in the teacher of righteousness (p. 121). He is never called Messiah, Son of man, or Son of God; neither is he ever called Lord. His followers did not and could not have called him "Redeemer of the world," for as Oesterreicher says, "a world-vision was foreign to them."

Relatively few of the texts actually refer to him at all, and Cullmann and others have pointed out that Josephus and Philo do not mention him in describing the Essenes. "Would it be possible," Cullmann asks, "to describe primitive Christianity without naming Christ?" In short, nothing in the Dead Sea Scrolls concerning the person and work of the teacher of righteousness or any of the expected Messianic figures presents any "threat to the uniqueness of Christ."

# VII

## The Life and Character of Jesus

What do we find when we compare the lives and personalities of Jesus and the teacher of righteousness? It has been suggested, Schonfield remarks, "that Jesus may consciously have modeled himself in certain respects on a pattern created by the earlier teacher of righteousness." It is quite clear that Jesus did deliberately and persistently follow what was "written of the Son of man" (Mark 9:12). In spite of the contrary opinion of many leading New Testament scholars, it seems to me practically certain that he found in Isaiah 53 the pattern for his self-sacrificing life, vicarious death, and ultimate victory. That there was anything in the career of the Qumran teacher of righteousness to add to this pattern is quite another matter. The possibility is worth investigating, of course; the only question is one of evidence.

Dupont-Sommer's initial impression that the Habakkuk Commentary made Jesus seem to be "an astonishing reincarnation of the teacher of righteousness" was supported by a list of points of similarity. As my brief analysis in DSS showed (p. 330 ff.), some of these applied only to the later church rather than to Jesus himself, some were equally true of almost any of the prophets, others depended on very dubious interpretations of the Habakkuk Commentary. The only distinctive point of real similarity was a matter of teaching rather than life or character, the interpretation of the law by a new, direct revelation; and here the radical difference was greater than the apparent resemblance (DSS, p. 331; see also p. 381 of this volume). If Jesus can be called in any sense a reincarnation of the teacher of righteousness—and of course in using the word "reincarnation" Dupont-Sommer did not mean to be taken literally—it would be equally true to say that the teacher of righteousness was a reincarnation of Jeremiah, or of any other prophet who was persecuted for his defiance of established authority and his insistence on fidelity to the revealed will of God.

Howlett complains that the greatest difficulty in comparing Jesus with the teacher of righteousness is that we know so little about either of them. I have indicated already (p. 55) that I do not share the prevalent skepticism as to the possibility of knowing anything about Jesus of Nazareth. It is well to bear in mind, however, Stendahl's reminder that some technical competence is required for the use of the Gospels in this connection. In the various reports of Jesus' acts and words in the different Gospels it is essential to recognize the reflection of "theological, missionary, and catechetical interests" in the early church.

Very important contributions to the understanding of the Gospels have been made in the past forty years. They have made the interpretation of Jesus' life and teaching a much more difficult and delicate task than it seemed before, but they cannot be ignored if dependable conclusions are to be reached. Even so, Allegro is quite right in saying that we have more complete records for Jesus than we have for the teacher of righteousness, and when all is said and done, "Jesus is much more of a flesh-and-blood character than the Qumran teacher could ever be." What we know of the life of the teacher of righteousness actually boils down to very little indeed.

Reading through the Qumran texts, one may find here and there parallels or anticipations of many things in the New Testament, including some of the words of Jesus. We shall consider these presently. If one starts with the New Testament, however, and looks for echoes of the Qumran texts, one can hardly help being most impressed by the enormous differences. I have found this particularly true in going through the Gospels with this question in mind. The carpenter of Nazareth who "went about doing good" through the villages of Galilee and Judea, "the friend of tax collectors and sinners," "eating and drinking," shocking the religious authorities by his indifference to their traditions, but heard gladly by the great crowds of common folk who pressed upon him and brought their sick to him to be healed—this is a very different kind of person from the teacher of the exclusive community in the desert. Their lives have very little in common.

What relation, then, had Jesus with the Essenes or the Qumran community? Was he one of them? Was his band of disciples a chapter of the order? Had he ever been a member of the sect or had anything to do with them? Was his gospel merely a development of their teaching? These, let me say once more, are questions of history, to be investigated as such. There is no reason to be disturbed by them. A man's answer to them will not make him either a better or a worse Christian. Many devout Christians have believed that Jesus was an Essene; I have even encountered a few who seemed offended when this belief was questioned.

In an interesting essay about the Essenes, written almost a century ago and reissued in 1956 by the Macmillan Company, Christian D. Ginsburg complains that both ancient and modern accounts of the Essenes are unreliable. The ancient writers give only "garbled scraps" of information; modern writers "are either too much afraid of, or too much pleased with, the marked resemblance between some of the doctrines and practices of Christianity and Essenism. Hence those who style themselves the true evangelical Christians are very anxious to destroy every appearance of affinity between Essenism and Christianity, lest it should be said that the one gave rise to the other; whilst those who are termed Rationalists multiply and magnify every feature of resemblance, in order to show that Christianity is nothing but a development of Essenism—so that the poor Essenes are crucified between the two."

Ginsburg's essay includes a sketch of the history of studies of the Essenes, from de Rossi in the sixteenth century to his own day. In the course of it he notes that Dean Prideaux, in a book published in 1717, "endeavors to expose the folly of the Deists, who infer, from the agreement between the Christian religion and the documents of the Essenes, that Christ and his followers were no other than a sect branched out from that of the Essenes." Near the end of his account Ginsburg mentions an article by "the able Mr. Westcott" in Smith's *Dictionary of the Bible.* "His fear, however," says Ginsburg, "lest any shining virtues in the Essenes might be thought by some to pale some of the brightness of the Sun of Righteousness, prevented him from appreciating the true character of this order, as well as from seeing that they paved the way to Christianity."

Ginsburg himself had no doubt that "our Savior himself belonged to this holy brotherhood." Judaism was divided into three sects in Jesus' day, and "every Jew had to belong to one of these sects." The fact that Jesus did not appear in public between his twelfth and his thirtieth year implies "that he lived in seclusion with this fraternity." He denounced the scribes, Pharisees, and Sadducees, but never the Essenes. But "he repudiated their extremes" of asceticism and concern for ritual purity.

Before the discovery of the Dead Sea Scrolls it was the general consensus of historians that the theory of an Essene origin of Christianity had been conclusively refuted by Bishop Lightfoot in an appendix to his commentary on Colossians. The new discoveries therefore merely revived an old, long discarded theory. Since they provided a great deal of new material, however, it was only right that the question should be reopened. No longer dependent on the accounts of the ancient writers, scholars could now study the documents of a sect which was either the Essenes or at least very much like them.

As a result the whole question of Essene influence on early Christianity has become again a live issue. A few writers now maintain that Jesus himself was an Essene after all. A. P. Davies has picked up Ginsburg's argument that because Jesus was neither a Pharisee nor a Sadducee he must have been an Essene. One who knew the Scriptures as well as he did, Davies thinks, must have been a member of some sect. That, however, is a gratuitous assumption. The common people, of whom Jesus was one, were not members of any sect.

Much has been made of the "hidden years" of Jesus' youth. They have always afforded a fertile soil for the growth of legends. Stories have been told even of a period of study at a Buddhist

monastery in Tibet. The community of Qumran was at least nearer
home than that. Serious writers have maintained that as a young
man Jesus was initiated into the secrets of the Essenes. Cullmann
rightly pronounces this "pure and groundless speculation." Its
only attraction is its appeal to the craving for mysteries and
esoteric cults. Devotees of such cults in our day are the most
ardent proponents of the idea that Jesus was an Essene.

Another theory finds a point of attachment in the period of
Jesus' temptation in the desert after his baptism. "Jesus need not
have had to spend these several weeks unsheltered," says Davies.
"He could have gone to Qumran." Of course he could have, but
what reason is there to think that he did? Wilson asks, "What are
John and Jesus doing in that 'wilderness' if they had no connection
with the Essenes?" According to our only evidence for his being
there at all, Jesus was undergoing a solitary struggle with temptation. Mark says, ". . . . and he was with the wild beasts" (1:13);
are we to suppose that this means the Essenes?

Daniélou thinks that the "wilderness" must mean the particular
desert where the Essenes had their settlement. The traditional
place of the temptation, he says, is only a little north of Qumran.
It is actually about ten miles, with very rugged and desolate
terrain in between. The desert of Judea includes much more
than the Wady Qumran. The sojourn in the desert, Daniélou continues, appears now as a retreat to a place of prayer. But does
that imply residence in a monastic community? Daniélou remarks
that the monks of Qumran regarded mankind as divided between
the influence of the demons and that of the angels; Jesus was
tempted by the devil and then ministered to by angels. But surely
neither demons nor angels confined their attentions to the sect
of Qumran!

Milik draws a parallel of a different kind between Jesus' temptation and the life of the Qumran covenanters. By its withdrawal to
the wilderness, he says, the community undertook to relive the
experience of the sons of Israel during the forty years of wandering in the wilderness; but by their fidelity to the law the covenanters intended to overcome the temptations to which their
fathers had succumbed. So Jesus, by overcoming temptations like

those of the Exodus period, inaugurated the eschatological period, which meant the return of Paradise. Here is a suggestive analogy, perhaps valid as far as it goes. The major reference of the temptation narrative, however, particularly in Mark, is surely not to the forty years in the wilderness but to the garden of Eden. Adam brought woe on mankind and expulsion from Paradise by yielding to temptation; Christ, the new Adam, overcame temptation and restored Paradise. Whatever analogy one may see here, however, there is no implication of any contact with the Qumran community.

Howlett finds a fatal flaw of the effort to make Jesus an Essene in the very fact that he was baptized by John the Baptist. The influence of John, who had been an Essene, he thinks, would explain the similarities between Jesus' teaching and the beliefs of the Essenes, and the differences between them would not then present any difficulty. If he had himself been an Essene, Jesus would have been baptized in the sect and would not have felt any need of John's baptism.

Allegro, who cannot be accused of minimizing parallels between the Dead Sea Scrolls and the Gospels, recognizes that there is no evidence that Jesus was ever a member of the Qumran community; "indeed," he says, "since his life was mostly spent in Nazareth, such a close connection is highly improbable." At the same time, Allegro holds that Jesus was probably acquainted with other Essene groups; and this is quite likely if, as Josephus and Philo say, there were Essenes living in many towns throughout Palestine.

The theory that Jesus was an Essene has been pushed to its furthest extreme by A. P. Davies, who on the basis of this theory offers a series of highly imaginative reinterpretations of incidents in the life of Jesus. Davies defends his procedure on the ground that he is not "advancing a definite thesis" but only "following a conjecture. But that," he says, "is what historical scholarship is supposed to do—follow a conjecture until it can be seen whether or not it makes a working hypothesis, and if it does, follow the hypothesis until it is proven right or wrong."

That is a fair challenge. Unfortunately there are difficulties in taking it up. One is that the interpretations offered are so far from anything even remotely suggested by the texts themselves that few scholars would consider it worth while to take time to refute them. Another is that definite proof for or against such interpretations is often out of the question, since no specific evidence is available. One test may be, as Davies puts it, whether the events "become more meaningful if we can learn to see them in a clearer context." But fiction often makes events seem "more meaningful" by providing a "clearer context" than sober history warrants. The final test, lacking conclusive evidence one way or the other, must be the degree to which each item in the proposed interpretation and the whole resulting picture agree with our best knowledge of the total historical context.

As an avowedly "controversial hypothesis" Davies suggests what he considers a "more illuminating" interpretation of Jesus' expulsion from Nazareth after announcing the fulfillment of Isaiah 61:1–2. Nazareth, Davies believes, may have been not a town but "all Galilee," or it may have been "a Nazarene encampment or monastery," the Nazarenes being "a Messianic sect, perhaps connected at some time with the Nazarites." (The Hebrew words for "Nazarene" and "Nazirite," *neṣer* and *nazir,* are not related, but that is a small detail.) Davies remarks also that some scholars explain the name Nazareth as meaning "watchtower," and he finds this "quite plausible since there was a tower connected with the monastery at Qumran." (The name Magdala means "tower"; was the home of Mary Magdalene also an Essene encampment or monastery?)

As for the synagogue, Essenes would hardly attend a synagogue of the Pharisees, and Jesus was opposed to the Pharisees; therefore "it is all but certain that he went to a meeting place of an Essenic order," the very one "where he had been brought up." The expulsion of Jesus from Nazareth might then be "the rejection of Jesus by his own sect." Davies states this in the form of a question and says that it is not "set forth as assured exegesis." It is not exegesis at all; it is a new story. At any rate, aside from the tower of Khirbet Qumran, the only suggested connection with the Dead Sea Scrolls is the supposition that it was "the Many" of the sect who invited Jesus to expound the Scriptures and later "cast him forth."

Mark 6:39f, telling of the feeding of the five thousand, says that Jesus told the people "to sit down by companies," and "they sat down in groups, by hundreds and by fifties" (Luke 9:14 says "in companies, about fifty each"). Daniélou sees here an analogy "between the community founded by Jesus and that of Qumran." The latter is directed by the Manual of Discipline to "pass over," at the annual renewing of the covenant, "by thousands and hundreds and fifties and tens" (ii.21: DSS, p. 373). But the crowd of which the evangelists tell was not a "community founded by Jesus." Although Daniélou considers the analogy astonishing, he points out that this was the ancient way of organizing the people (Exodus 18:21–25), so that what we have here is "a traditional rather than a specifically Essene setting."

The question whether Jesus organized a community at all is one on which scholars have found it hard to agree. The word "church" occurs in sayings of Jesus only in the gospel of Matthew (16:18; 18:17). Hyatt and Daniélou feel that the very existence of the Qumran community makes it probable that Jesus formed an organization of his followers. It is true that the sect of Qumran comes closer to the later idea of the church as the true Israel, called out from the apostate nation, than do other Jewish religious associations known to us. The picture of Jesus' life with his disciples, however, as we find it in the Gospels, bears little resemblance to the life of such an exclusive, highly organized, and disciplined group as that of Qumran. Howlett reminds us that Jesus and his disciples were itinerant preachers. The Son of man had no place to lay his head, and he expected those who would follow him to make the same sacrifice (Matthew 8:20).

Hyatt finds also in the Dead Sea Scrolls a suggestion that even the community of goods, as practiced by the early church of Jerusalem, may go back to the lifetime of Jesus himself. Jesus told his followers not to lay up treasures on earth (Matthew 6:19), but to sell their possessions and give alms (Luke 12:33). Judas is reported to have held the purse for the twelve disciples (John 12:6). The more formal arrangement of the Jerusalem church may very well have been a development of this way of living, but it may be doubted that the practice of the Qumran sect makes this any more probable.

In this connection another example of A. P. Davies' interpretations may be mentioned. The Essenes called themselves "the poor"; therefore when Jesus told the rich man who came to him to sell all that he had "and give to the poor" (Mark 10:17–22), he "was in effect telling the wealthy man to join such a sect." But Jesus added, "and come, follow me"; this, says Davies, raises "the interesting question" whether in joining a sect of "the poor" and at the same time following Jesus, "the wealthy man would not have been joining a sect to which Jesus himself already belonged." If so, it is surely implied also that Jesus is the head of the sect, or at least of the branch which he invites the rich man to join. But there is no hint in the passage itself of any Essene connection. Only by starting from the assumption that Jesus was an Essene is it possible to read any such meaning into it. Whether the result makes the story "more meaningful" is perhaps a matter of individual preference.

The account of Jesus' last supper with his disciples naturally suggests comparison with the meals of the Qumran community. The supposed "sacramental quality" of these meals is discussed later (pp. 367–71). Howlett, noting the obvious formal similarities of the Essene and Christian meals, says, "This practice was common in Israel at the time, but a peculiar importance was given to it by both Jesus and the Essenes." The question must still be raised whether the meaning attached to their observances was the same. This comes under the head of Jesus' teaching rather than his life and will be treated in that connection. Here it may be remarked that the procedure of Jesus at the supper conforms to common Jewish practice rather than to anything distinctive of the Essenes or the Qumran community.

The date of the last supper and its place in the Jewish ritual pattern have always been, as Daniélou says, a "great enigma." The difficulty lies in reconciling the accounts in the first three Gospels with that of the Gospel of John. The Passover is celebrated on the night of the fourteenth of Nisan, which is, since the day begins in the evening, the beginning of the fifteenth. According to the Synoptic Gospels, Jesus' last supper was a Passover meal on the night of the fourteenth of Nisan, and he was crucified on the fifteenth; according to the Gospel of John, he was crucified on the fourteenth, and the supper therefore was not a Passover meal. This discrepancy has made it difficult to fix the year of the crucifixion. Was it the fourteenth or the fifteenth of Nisan that fell on Friday that year?

Mlle. A. Jaubert has proposed a resolution of this dilemma on the basis of the Qumran calendar, which, according to her, was the old religious calendar of post-exilic Israel (*DSS*, p. 241). If Jesus and his disciples followed this old calendar, by which the fourteenth of Nisan always came on Tuesday, they would eat the Passover that night. The next three days would then allow time for the crowded events narrated in the Gospels, culminating in the crucifixion, which by all accounts was on Friday. But by the official calendar Friday was the fourteenth of Nisan, Mlle. Jaubert supposes. This, she believes, is what is presupposed by the Gospel of John.

If this explanation is correct, it affords an important link between Jesus and the practices of the Qumran community, though no direct connection is involved if the covenanters were not the only Jews who still followed the old calendar. The two apparently discrepant accounts are reconciled, and it becomes possible to establish the year of the crucifixion. Catholic scholars in particular —including Vogt, Oesterreicher, and Daniélou—seem to be favorably impressed by this hypothesis, though somewhat hesitant in committing themselves to it. The problem is by no means simple. The varying accounts of the last supper have clearly been affected in different ways by later conceptions and practices of the church, so that it is extremely difficult to disentangle the threads of tradition and get back to the historic supper of Jesus with his disciples and to determine its original significance. It is not even certain that Mlle. Jaubert's hypothesis is needed to reconcile the Synoptic and Johannine traditions.

Kuhn's painstaking investigation isolates a primitive Palestinian tradition underlying Mark's account of the last supper. This tradition "does not presuppose the special Jewish Passover, but the Jewish meal in general." It also, Kuhn finds, has "a special affinity to the peculiar practices of the Essene cult meal, as they are now found in the texts from Qumran"; in fact, it is the features which are "unexplainable by Passover customs that find their parallels in the Essene cult meal." At the same time, the strong priestly interest evident in the Qumran meals is entirely lacking in the supper of Jesus; this is no "Essene community."

Kuhn warns the reader that his study "has no direct bearing on what the last meal actually was, historically speaking"; others, however, may feel that it has a very important bearing on this problem, not only showing its complexity but also helping to define it and narrowing down the area of historical probability. As a matter of fact, Kuhn himself goes a little further than the statement just quoted would suggest. The tradition of Jesus' acts and words at the last supper preserved in Mark 14:22–24, he finds, was not connected in the early Palestinian church with the daily meals of the disciples, and therefore "did not develop out of liturgical practice." It is therefore "not a later creation of the Palestinian church." We are thus "forced back to the proximity, rather, of Jesus' last meal as it actually took place."

On the other hand, the conception of the last supper as a Passover meal is found to be, "in all probability, a creation of the Jerusalem church," so that the earlier tradition underlying Mark "comes much closer to what actually happened at the last meal of Jesus." When Jesus' words at the supper, moreover, are freed from the Passover setting, their meaning becomes clearer and they are found to be "not only possible but quite plausible as actually spoken by Jesus." Not the "elements" themselves but their distribution is the point of the comparison to Jesus' body and blood. "Even as all present at the meal partake of the bread and wine, so will they all share in the atonement of his death, of his body to be given and his blood to be shed." Kuhn feels also that with the removal of the Passover setting "the parallelism to the practice of the communal meal of the Essenes becomes far more significant." How this is so is not made clear. It may be observed, however, that if Kuhn is right in dissociating the supper from the Passover meal, the problem which Mlle. Jaubert's hypothesis is intended to solve disappears, and the Johannine dating of the supper finds new support.

Further aspects of Kuhn's study will appear in connection with the rites of the early church; much of it, however, not being concerned with the Dead Sea Scrolls, must be passed over here. It is important for our purpose as an outstanding example of the way in which New Testament scholars are using and must use the Qumran texts. It illustrates the complicated problems involved, the necessity of thorough scholarly competence in dealing with them, and the weakness of hasty, sensational conclusions.

The examples I have given of connections, real or supposed, between the life of Jesus and the Dead Sea Scrolls have not been chosen as straw men to be set up and knocked down. They are taken from writers who adduce them in all earnestness and find them significant. It will be noted that they vary greatly in kind and quality, from sheer fancy to results of solid research. They illustrate very different ways of approaching the questions of anticipation and possible influence. The probability of any direct contact between Jesus and the Qumran community has not been found very great; some acquaintance with Essene groups in Galilee or Judea is not unlikely, but there is little if any specific evidence of it. The supposed parallels between the careers of Jesus and the teacher of righteousness have turned out to be insignificant.

When it comes to a comparison of personalities and characters we have still less material. Aside from the fact that the teacher of righteousness was an independent, prophetic spirit, willing to suffer for his vision of truth and right, we do not know what manner of man he was. If the Thanksgiving Psalms were written by him and can be regarded as autobiographical to any degree, they present a picture of a man overwhelmed by the sense of human sinfulness and helplessness, full of gratitude for his undeserved deliverance from the powers of evil and from the foes who have persecuted him. Much has been made of this idea of him, but the evidence for it is very questionable (pp. 324–29). The teacher of righteousness of whom the commentaries speak may have been, for all we know, a very different kind of man.

If the experience and personality reflected by the Thanksgiving Psalms were his, the contrast between him and Jesus is very marked. His deep consciousness of sin and of the distance between God and man, which, as Daniélou says, is characteristic of saints, is not to be seen at all in Jesus. Daniélou surely goes too far, however, when he says that if Christ is not God, the teacher of righteousness is his superior. Perhaps he has in mind the Johannine Jesus rather than the Jesus of the Synoptic Gospels. But if spiritual conflict and self-abasement are marks of superiority, it must not be forgotten that we do not know what struggles may lie back of the serene assurance of Jesus' affirmations. We are in no position to analyze his self-consciousness. As we have no gospels relating the life of the teacher of righteousness, so we have no psalms revealing the inner spiritual experience of Jesus. The temptation at the beginning of his ministry and the torment of Gethsemane at its end may give some indication. The words spoken to the rich man should be remembered also: "Why do you call me good? No one is good but God alone" (Mark 10:18). Even in the fourth Gospel Jesus can be "deeply moved and troubled" (John 11:33, 38; 12:27; 13:21); he can say, "I can do nothing on my own authority" (5:30).

# VIII

## The Teaching of Jesus: Basic Contrasts

More impressive parallels with the sect of Qumran may perhaps be found in the teaching of Jesus than in his life and character. We have already observed that the significance of such parallels is often discounted on the ground that the uniqueness of Christ lies in his person and saving work, not in the originality of his sayings. To some of us this does not quite seem to meet the issue. What is most essential, of course, as I have said elsewhere, is not that Jesus' words should be new but that they should be true. At the same time, if he was the incarnate Word of God, we can hardly believe that he would have nothing to say except what other religious teachers of his time were saying. The question is first of all one of fact. If the available evidence shows that there is nothing original or new in the teaching of Jesus, as compared with that of the teacher of righteousness or the rabbis, the fact must be recognized, whatever theological adjustment it may necessitate.

What was said earlier about revelation as communication (p. 53) must be kept in mind. "No doubt," says Oesterreicher, "Jesus (and later His apostles) often used the Qumranite idiom to convey His message as He (and later they) used the language of apocryphal writings and of early rabbinical interpreters." Our question now is therefore how far the similarities between the words of Jesus and the Dead Sea Scrolls can be explained as merely instances of using the same religious idiom or starting from the same traditional conceptions. Did Jesus in his use of such accepted terms really bring good news, or did he merely repeat what was already familiar to the Jews in general or the sect of Qumran in particular?

To answer this question we must determine the exact extent and nature of the agreement and disagreement between the Qumran texts and the sayings of Jesus as recorded in the Gospels. In accord with the universal consensus of New Testament scholarship, the first three Gospels and the Gospel of John must be treated separately. As sources for the historic teaching of Jesus of Nazareth we shall therefore use only the sayings recorded in the Synoptic Gospels, leaving the fourth Gospel to be considered later by itself.

If it becomes evident that there is something new and distinctive in Jesus' message, it may be still possible that in some ways and to some extent Jesus was influenced by the Essenes or the Qumran community. Whether or how far this was true will be a question of some historical interest but of relatively little theological significance. It will be merely, as Dupont-Sommer puts it, a question of the point at which "Christianity is grafted on to the tree of Judaism," or perhaps more exactly the branch of the tree out of which Christianity grew.

Our present inquiry can be considerably abbreviated by noting at once that no serious student of the Dead Sea Scrolls has actually denied the originality of Jesus. Dupont-Sommer has affirmed that he "in no way wishes to deny the originality of the Christian religion." To a direct question from the *Saturday Review* he replied, "I never claimed that the Dead Sea Scrolls could strike a blow against the 'uniqueness' of Jesus." Edmund Wilson, while calling in question the supernatural origin of Christianity, says explicitly, "Anyone who goes to the Gospels from the literature of the intertestamental apocrypha and the literature of the Dead Sea sect must feel at once the special genius of Jesus and be struck by the impossibility of falling in with one of the worst tendencies of insensitive modern scholarship and accounting for everything in the Gospels in terms of analogies and precedents."

It is immediately obvious also, to one who compares them, that Jesus could not have been a member of the Qumran sect at the time of his public ministry. His whole point of view was so radically different from theirs that he would have been considered by them one whose "spirit wavered and turned back," so that he went "out from before the masters to walk in the stubbornness of his heart," and could never "come back again to the council of the community" (Manual of Discipline vii.23f; *DSS*, p. 381). Even those who are inclined to believe that Jesus had once been an Essene recognize, with A. P. Davies, that, if so, he "broke rather sharply with the sect." To clarify this matter at the outset, it may be well to point out some of the outstanding differences between Jesus and the community of Qumran.

The life of the Qumran community was distinctly ascetic. They had withdrawn from society to live a life of strict self-denial and discipline in their desert retreat. Jesus said that for the sake of the kingdom of heaven some must relinquish the joys of marriage and family life (Matthew 19:12); he required also that at least his immediate followers free themselves from the entanglement of property (Matthew 6:24). But he "came eating and drinking"; so far was he, indeed, from being an ascetic that those who sought grounds for criticism accused him of being not too austere but too convivial (Matthew 11:19).

The Qumran covenanters were strict legalists—even more strict, says Daniélou, than the Pharisees. Jesus too said, "I tell you, unless your righteousness exceeds that of the scribes and Pharisees, you will never enter the kingdom of heaven" (Matthew 5:20); but his way of exceeding it was not by more strict exegesis and deduction but by going back of all precepts to first principles. Oesterreicher and Cullmann remarked that nowhere in the Dead Sea Scrolls is the teacher of righteousness reported as saying, "You have heard it said . . . but I say to you . . ." Howlett considers the difference in attitudes to the law "the point at which Jesus and the Essenes were in the most fundamental opposition."

The contrast appears in striking fashion in the matter of Sabbath observance. Defending his healing on the Sabbath (Matthew 12:11; Luke 14:5; cp. 13:15), Jesus asks the lawyers and Pharisees, "Which of you, having an ox or an ass that has fallen into a well, will not immediately pull him out on a Sabbath day?" Rescuing even a newborn calf or kid from a cistern or ditch on the Sabbath is forbidden by the Damascus Document (xi.14; *DSS*, p. 360). The teacher of righteousness would probably have frowned on Jesus' statement that the Sabbath was made for man and not man for the Sabbath (Mark 2:27).

The covenanters were ritualists. No doubt they could have joined Jesus in quoting Hosea 6:6, "I desire steadfast love and not sacrifice," though they would not have approved his use of it to defend eating with tax collectors and sinners or plucking grain and rubbing off the chaff with their hands on the Sabbath (Matthew 9:13; 12:7). The Manual of Discipline says that an unrepentant sinner "will not be purified by atonement offerings" and exalts "the offering of the lips" above sacrifices and oblations (iii.4; ix.4, 26; x.6, 14; *DSS*, pp. 373, 383–86). But the covenanters were great sticklers for times and seasons, they exalted the dignity and prerogatives of the priests, and they looked forward to the resumption of the sacrificial cultus. Jesus respected the temple as his Father's house (Luke 2:49) and in blazing indignation drove out the money-changers who made it a den of robbers instead of a house of prayer (Mark 11:15–17). He earnestly desired to eat the Passover with his disciples at Jerusalem (Luke 22:15). There is extraordinarily little indication in his teaching, however, of any interest in ceremonial and priestly concerns. The preoccupation with such matters in the Qumran texts has no echo in the sayings of Jesus.

Especially notable is the contrast between their meticulous concern for ritual purity and his indifference to it. When his disciples shocked the Pharisees and scribes by eating "with hands defiled, that is unwashed," Jesus defended them, saying that what defiles a man is not what goes into his stomach but what comes out of his heart (Mark 7:1–23). "Where," asks Howlett, "could we find a sharper contrast with the Essenes and their system of pools and basins and their requirements for ceremonial washing?" Daniélou remarks that if Simon the Pharisee was scandalized by Jesus' allowing a woman who was a notorious sinner to anoint his feet, it would have scandalized the Essenes even more.

Barthélemy in his notes on the Rule of the Congregation, with its rules excluding from the sessions of the congregation all who were physically imperfect or afflicted, remarks that Jesus healed the blind and the lame who came to him in the temple (Matthew 21:14), and in his parable of the banquet "the poor and maimed and blind and lame" are brought in to take the places of those who have declined the first invitation (Luke 14:21). Cross is so impressed by this difference that he feels Jesus must have spoken "in conscious reaction to sectarian doctrine." The parallel in Matthew's parable of the wedding feast (22:9) does not refer to physical disabilities; the point, in any case, is that all kinds of unfortunate folk whom the respectable religious people considered the scum of the earth would be in the kingdom of heaven when those who despised them were shut out. No specific reference to the Qumran sect in particular is indicated, but the contrast between its attitude and that of Jesus is unmistakable.

The Qumran sect was a closed, very exclusive community. Daniélou observes that the Essenes had to pass through a novitiate of two years before they could partake of the common meals, and each meal had to be preceded by a bath and a change of clothes. It would be impossible therefore for them to eat with tax collectors and sinners. Jesus' eating with those who were ritually unclean, he adds, had a Messianic significance: by it Jesus broke the bonds of Judaism and invited all men into the Messianic community. This is debatable, but it is supported by the saying that "men will come from east and west, and from north and south, and sit at table in the kingdom of God" (Luke 13:29; cp. Matthew 8:11f). Certainly Jesus did not encourage the formation of an esoteric, exclusive society.

Cullmann points out that no tendency to secrecy is to be seen in Jesus' teaching. He did, it seems, forbid his disciples and those he healed to proclaim him as the Messiah (Mark 1:24f; 8:30), but there were fairly obvious reasons for that precaution: popular excitement would provoke suppression by the Roman government, and false conceptions of his mission would hinder his real work. The attention of his disciples was turned not inward but outward; they were organized not for a life of self-centered holiness but for public evangelism (Mark 3:14f). In one passage

Jesus speaks of "the mystery of the kingdom of God" which is given only to the disciples, while "for those outside everything is in parables" (Mark 4:11). Both the authenticity and the meaning of this saying, however, are in considerable doubt among New Testament scholars. Jesus certainly did not intend his parables to conceal truth from the uninitiated; they were obviously used to make his teaching clearer.

Later in the same chapter Jesus says, "Is a lamp brought in to be put under a bushel, or under a bed, and not on a stand? For there is nothing hid, except to be made manifest; nor is anything secret, except to come to light" (4:22). Howlett rather strangely finds this "close to the Essene concept that a secret teaching exists which is to be disclosed." Where he finds any indication that the Essene secrets were ever to be disclosed I do not know. To the saying just quoted from Mark is added another in Matthew 10:26f: "What I tell you in the dark, utter in the light; and what you hear whispered, proclaim upon the housetops." (In Luke 12:2f the command becomes a general statement that everything hidden will become known.) The saying about the lamp occurs several times in the Gospels in different connections. In the Sermon on the Mount, Jesus tells his disciples that they must be the salt of the earth and the light of the world (Matthew 5:13–16).

In four of its most distinctive characteristics—asceticism, legalism, ritualism, and exclusiveness—the Qumran community thus represents the opposite extremes from the religion of Jesus. If he had ever had any connection with it or sympathy for it, he moved far away from it before his public ministry. But what of the chief positive emphases of Jesus' gospel? Are these rooted in the Qumran variety of Judaism? It is instructive to consider a few of them.

Jesus taught his disciples to address God as their heavenly Father and to trust his loving care for them (Matthew 5:43–6:33; 7:7–11; Luke 12:32). God is called Father in the rabbinic literature and the Jewish prayer book, as has been noted, but never in the Dead Sea Scrolls. He is so addressed in the book of Ecclesiasticus (Sirach), fragments of which were found in Cave 2. If the text used at Qumran contained 23:1 and 23:4, which are not in the Cairo genizah fragments, then the prayer beginning, "O Lord,

Father and God of my life," was at least known there; but the only reference to God as Father that I have found in the literature of the sect is in one of the Thanksgiving Psalms: "For thou art a Father to all the sons of thy truth" (ix.35). With Jesus this conception is all-pervasive and decisive. He evidently did not get it from the sect of Qumran.

Equally prominent in the preaching of Jesus is the kingdom of God, or, as it appears in the Gospel of Matthew in more characteristically Jewish form, the kingdom of heaven. In the rabbinic literature this expression signifies the sovereign power and authority of God, to which men must submit. To accept God's rule over one's life is to "take the yoke of the kingdom of heaven." The new world which is still to come is called "the coming age," as it is sometimes in the New Testament also (e.g., Mark 10:30; Hebrews 6:5). At this point the conception of the Qumran community seems closer than the rabbinic conception to that of Jesus, yet, strangely enough, the language is different.

For Jesus the kingdom of God means not only God's eternal, universal sovereignty but also and especially the final, decisive manifestation of his sovereign power in the conquest and destruction of the powers of evil. The kingdom has now come near, Jesus proclaims (Mark 1:15); the disciples are to pray that it may come (Matthew 6:10). Satan still has power in the world, but in his own power to cast out demons Jesus sees conclusive proof that God's kingdom has already broken the power of Satan (Matthew 12:25–28). The men of Qumran also regarded this age as under the power of evil and looked for the divine visitation. But where Jesus spoke of Satan or Beelzebub they spoke of Belial, and they did not use the expression "kingdom of God" for the coming divine triumph. It is as though Jesus and they drew water from the same spring but carried it in different vessels.

The closest resemblance is the degree to which their thinking was dominated by the conception of a cosmic struggle between good and evil, and their sense that a decisive crisis in this conflict was at hand. This was characteristic of the age. Allegro speaks of "the sense of impending doom which pervaded the religious thought of this time." Kuhn's study of the meaning of "temptation" or "trial" in the teaching of Jesus is important here. The temptation from which the disciples must pray to be delivered (Matthew 6:13; Mark 14:38; etc.) means not merely general inclinations or incitements to sin but the assaults of Satan in his desperate effort to defeat the power of God in this crucial phase of the cosmic conflict.

But here again there is an important difference. Both Jesus and the covenanters believed that men must ask and expect God's help in the struggle, but Jesus did not teach that armies and weapons and military tactics could bring victory to the sons of light, or that any victory so won could establish the kingdom of God.

In the sayings of Jesus the coming of God's kingdom is associated with the coming of the Son of man to judge the world (Mark 8:38–9:1 and often). The Qumran sect had its expectations too concerning the agents of the coming redemption, but the Son of man plays no part among them (see pp. 71–72). Here again Jesus seems to be associated with a stream of Jewish tradition quite different from that which flowed through the Wady Qumran. Both had vivid Messianic expectations, but they were not the same.

The contacts between Jesus' teaching and the ideas of the Qumran sect about things to come, we must conclude, are not so close as to indicate any direct connection. This appears to be true also with regard to other subjects. Cullmann remarks that in their understanding of sin and grace the covenanters were closer to the New Testament than to the Pharisees. They were closer, one may add, to Paul than to Jesus, though Jesus by no means minimized the sinfulness of man and his need of divine forgiveness.

# IX

## *The Teaching of Jesus: Parallels*

There are many places in the sayings of Jesus where similarities to the Qumran texts have been noted. They vary greatly in importance, from insignificant verbal parallels to evidence of real spiritual affinity. The word "gospel," used to designate Jesus' message from the time of his first public appearance in Galilee (Mark 1:14f), is undoubtedly derived from the references to good tidings in Isaiah 40:9; 41:27; 52:7; and 61:1. The last of these passages is echoed in one of the Thanksgiving Psalms (xviii.14f), where Gaster remarks that the term for "herald of good tidings" is the "prototype of the term 'gospel.'" The mission of the anointed prophet of Isaiah 61:1 is here assumed by the poet, who designates himself as "thy servant" and "the creature thou hast sustained with thy strength."

Allegro speaks of Essenes "living pious lives of love and humility in the towns and villages of Palestine" and finds it "reasonable to assume that Jesus was acquainted with such people, and that his moral teaching owed much to their influence." Many of the contacts between Jesus' sayings and the Dead Sea Scrolls are in the area of moral teaching. Especially striking are the parallels in the Sermon on the Mount (Matthew 5–7). There is a text from Cave 4 containing a series of beatitudes beginning with the word "blessed," like those of Matthew 5:3ff. The reports published thus far do not indicate whether or not these beatitudes are similar in content to those of the Sermon on the Mount.

The covenanters apparently liked to call themselves "the poor."

Their fondness for the word 'ebyon, one of several Hebrew words meaning "poor," was one of the grounds of Teicher's theory that they were the early Jewish-Christian sect known as Ebionites (*DSS*, p. 51). In Luke 6:20 Jesus says, "Blessed are you poor," while in Matthew 5:3 he says, "Blessed are the poor in spirit." Scholars have not been slow to point out that the War scroll uses the expression "poor of spirit" (with a different Hebrew word for "poor"), along with such expressions as "afflicted" and "perfect in conduct" and in opposition to "hard hearted" (xiv.7).

Cross infers from this passage that the expression in Matthew means something like "meek." Murphy feels that "meek" and "gentle" do not do justice to the idea of perfect conduct in obedience to God's laws. He calls attention to another passage in the War scroll where "stricken in spirit" appears in the same context with "poor" (xi.9f; *DSS*, p. 398); here, however, the "poor" are to be redeemed and the "stricken in spirit" consumed.

On the ground that the Hebrew conception of "spirit" includes the will, K. Schubert maintains that "poor in spirit" means "voluntarily poor," referring to those who had renounced worldly goods. Jesus' audience therefore, Schubert thinks, probably included people "familiar with Essene teaching." The conclusion in this case is more probable than the interpretation on which it is based. If the Hebrew expression meant "poor of will," this would signify weakness of will rather than poverty by choice.

As a matter of fact, the Hebrew word used in the War scroll means "lowly" or "humble" as well as "poor"; it is the word translated "meek" in Psalm 37:11, which Jesus quotes in Matthew 5:5. In short, "poor in spirit" means just what we have always supposed that it meant. The same people are meant in Matthew and Luke; but Luke stresses their actual poverty (adding a "woe" on the rich), while Matthew thinks of their humility under affliction. What word or words Jesus himself used it is impossible to determine.

The assurance given by Jesus to those "persecuted for righteousness' sake" that their reward would be great in heaven, because the prophets had been so persecuted before them (5:11f), "can easily be understood in the framework of Essene ideas," says

Schubert. Some of the Essenes, according to Josephus, had the gift of prophecy, and the Dead Sea Scrolls show that the members of the sect believed that they had supernatural knowledge. Schubert ascribes the idea that the prophets were persecuted to the persecutions under Antiochus Epiphanes and the Hasmonean rulers.

The tradition that Isaiah was persecuted by Manasseh is reported both by Josephus and also in the Talmud, as Schubert explicitly notes. Yet on the ground that Josephus was "relatively well informed about the Essene movement," Schubert finds it "entirely conceivable" that he got his information from the Essenes; he therefore considers it "probable in the light of the Qumran literature" that the tradition "was originally peculiar to the Essenes," though no reference to the persecution of Isaiah in the Qumran literature is cited. Thus "it does not seem improbable," says Schubert, that Jesus, in speaking of the persecution of the prophets, was referring to the Essene tradition. This is an astonishing example of reckless leaping from one conjecture to another. There is really no occasion for dragging in the Essenes.

In the expression "the men of old" (Matthew 5:21, 33) Schubert sees a parallel with "the forefathers" (literally "first ones") of the Damascus Document (iv.8f; vi.2; *DSS*, pp. 352f). Murphy rightly calls this "merely an illustration of a common and contemporary vocabulary." In the reference of Matthew 5:21f to "judgment" and "the council" Murphy finds "no strict parallel" but a suggestion of "the regimentation of Qumran." But surely what Jesus sets before his hearers is not what would happen in the closed community of Qumran; it is a graded series of punishments to which all are liable, culminating in "the Gehenna of fire."

The condemnation of one who is angry with his brother (5:22) is compared by Schubert with the stress on brotherly love in the Manual of Discipline, and the inference is drawn that Jesus refers to "a brother in the religious community," not to mankind in general. The word "brother" actually occurs only twice in the manual of Discipline (vi.10, 22; *DSS*, p. 379). To assume, moreover, that the way a term is used in the Dead Sea Scrolls determines its meaning in a saying of Jesus is, to say the least, precarious.

With what Jesus says of looking at a woman with lust and committing adultery in the heart (5:28) P. Winter compares a verse in the Testaments of the Twelve Patriarchs, "I have never committed fornication by raising my eyes" (Testament of Issachar 7:2). As we shall note repeatedly, the "Essene" character of this document is very doubtful. Winter notes also, however, the expression "eyes of fornication" in the Manual of Discipline (i.6; DSS, p. 371). Here is a real similarity of idea, though not such as to indicate any influence.

A more striking and closer parallel is to be seen in Jesus' appeal to Genesis 1:27 in his condemnation of divorce and remarriage (Mark 10:2–12; cp. Matthew 5:32). The same verse which Jesus quotes as showing God's purpose "from the beginning of creation" is quoted also in the Damascus Document as "the foundation of creation" (iv.21; DSS, p. 352). As Daniélou remarks, this parallel was one of those which led Teicher to regard the Dead Sea Scrolls as Christian documents (DSS, pp. 51, 295–98).

The use made of the quotation is not quite the same. The Damascus Document does not adduce it against divorce but against "taking two wives during their lifetime." What is meant by this expression has been a matter of much debate among scholars. The possessive pronoun "their" is masculine in form, apparently referring to the "builders of the wall" who have committed the offense in question. Winter, however, has recently revived the view that in spite of its masculine form the pronoun refers to the wives, and that what is condemned is remarriage after divorce while the first wife is still living. This makes the meaning agree with one aspect of what Jesus says, though divorce is not condemned by the Damascus Document. It is possible also, if the pronoun is to be given a feminine reference, that what is meant is bigamy, taking a second wife while the first is still alive.

A literal interpretation, giving the grammatical form its proper meaning, takes what is condemned here to be a man's marrying more than once during his life. He could hardly marry at any other time, of course; the phrase "in their lifetime," however, may be used to emphasize the lifelong character of the prohibition. (This understanding of the passage is supported by Hempel in a note to Winter's article.) But in that case the ultimate effect is the same as in Winter's interpretation: if a man can marry only once, remarriage after divorce is thereby excluded.

Winter feels that a connection between the saying of Jesus and the passage in the Damascus Document is "hard to deny." He suggests three possibilities, without indicating a preference for any of them: (1) Jesus was himself the teacher of righteousness of the Dead Sea Scrolls; (2) he quoted from the writings of the sect; (3) a saying derived from the sect's scriptures was wrongly ascribed to him. Of these the first is excluded by many considerations, and there is no strong reason to adopt either of the other two. The parallel is not close enough to require any such explanation. Jesus may have heard of the use made of Genesis 1:27 in the Damascus Document, or he may have applied it as he did quite independently. He combined it in any case with Genesis 2:24, whereas the Damascus Document cites with it Genesis 7:9 and Deuteronomy 17:17.

The prohibition of all oaths in Matthew 5:33–37 (cp. 23:16–22) has been compared with what is said about oaths in the Damascus Document (xv.1ff; xvi.2ff; *DSS*, pp. 363f), but there is no real similarity beyond the fact that the Damascus Document forbids swearing by the names of God (indicated by their first letters). Josephus, as several scholars have noted, says that the Essenes forbade the use of oaths altogether except in the initiation of new members; the Damascus Document, however, presupposes the use of binding oaths in connection with vows and in commitments made before judges.

Many scholars have suggested that the promise made by members of the sect "to love all the sons of light . . . and to hate all the sons of darkness" (Manuel of Discipline i.9f; *DSS*, p. 371) may have been the basis of Jesus' statement, "You have heard that it was said, 'You shall love your neighbor and hate your enemy'" (Matthew 5:43). There is no commandment to hate one's enemy in the Old Testament or in rabbinic literature. There may have been a popular saying to that effect; the Qumran sect was surely not alone in considering it a virtue to hate the wicked. The sentiment was well anchored in ancient Hebrew tradition, as witness

Psalm 26:5, "I hate the company of evildoers," or 139:21, "Do not I hate them that hate thee, O Lord?"

The command to love one's enemies (5:44) is compared by Schubert with the effort of the Essenes to hasten the end by a stricter obedience to the law of Moses. Jesus, he says, "showed that the eschatological event was not dependent upon only the exercise of human will, and that man was not the instrument of revenge." Jesus' command was thus aimed "at a very specific point of his auditors' eschatology." It is only fair to add, however, that the closing psalm of the Manual of Discipline comes much closer to the spirit of Jesus: "I will not render to a man the recompense of evil; with good I will pursue a man" (x.18; *DSS*, p. 386). Many writers have cited this passage as a parallel to Jesus' command to turn the other cheek (Matthew 5:39), as well as the command to love one's enemy.

The command to "be perfect, as your heavenly Father is perfect" (Matthew 5:48) calls to mind the frequent use of such expressions as "blameless conduct" (literally "perfection of way") in the Manual of Discipline (e.g., viii.10, 18, 21, 25f; *DSS*, p. 382). These expressions appear often in the Old Testament, especially in Psalms and Proverbs, where it is clear that no abstract "perfectionism" is implied. Here, no doubt, is the background of both Matthew 5:48 and the Qumran terminology.

It should be noted, however, that "perfect" is one of the words peculiar to Matthew. He uses it again in 19:21, where neither Mark 10:21 nor Luke 18:22 has it. In Luke 6:36, the parallel to Matthew 5:48, the word used by Jesus is not "perfect" but "merciful." An almost exact parallel to Luke's form of the saying in the Mishnah has already been quoted (p. 52). No parallel to any saying of Jesus that has been found in the Dead Sea Scrolls is so close as this.

In the attitude to material possessions Jesus and the men of Qumran were not far apart. They felt as he did that one could not serve God and Mammon (Matthew 6:24). The word "Mammon" occurs in the Manual of Discipline as a word for "property" (vi.2; *DSS*, p. 378); it is used often in the rabbinic literature. The covenanters distrusted "the delight in riches" against which Jesus warned his disciples (Mark 4:19). The Habakkuk Commentary turns the prophet's denunciation of wine into a denunciation of wealth (viii.3; *DSS*, p. 368).

The idea of the Messianic banquet, reflected in such sayings as Matthew 8:11 and Luke 22:28–30, has already been mentioned in our discussion of the last supper; we shall have occasion later to consider the supposed "sacramental quality" of the meals of the Qumran sect and the theory that they were liturgical anticipations of the Messianic banquet (pp. 369–70). Our question here is whether the sect thought of the life of the coming age as a banquet. It would not be surprising to find this idea in the Dead Sea Scrolls, for it is well known in other Jewish sources. I am not aware, however, of any definite evidence of it at Qumran. The lack of such a reference confirms my skepticism regarding the Messianic significance of the community's common meals. One clear reference to anything like drinking the wine new in the kingdom of God (Mark 14:25), fulfilling the meal in the kingdom of God (Luke 22:16), showing forth the Messiah until he comes (I Corinthians 11:26), or to eating and drinking or sitting at table in the kingdom of God or the Messiah (Luke 13:29; 14:15; 22:30), would be sufficient to establish such an idea; but nothing of the sort is said.

The directions for the meal in the Rule of the Congregation suggest to Daniélou a theological significance in Jesus' procedure at the last supper. By putting his hand on the bread, says Daniélou, Jesus signified that he was both the Messiah and the expected priest. This is surely too much to infer. The point in the Qumran regulation is that the priest must be the first to touch the bread; no priest was present when Jesus broke the bread as any rabbi might do for his disciples, or as a father would do for his family.

The strict arrangement of seating by office and rank at the meals and other meetings of the covenanters is taken by Cross and Allegro, in different ways, as providing a background for the dispute among Jesus' disciples as to which of them was to be considered greatest. In Luke 22:24ff this is connected with the last supper. If Jesus and the disciples were "observing this Qumran ritual," Allegro says, the dispute was "occasioned by their order of seating, not as a matter of petty pride, but because their position in the heavenly kingdom was concerned." Cross suggests that Jesus here "is reacting against the Essene protocol." It is "hardly by chance," Cross thinks, that Luke puts the dispute at this place and John 13:12–16 tells of Jesus' washing his disciples' feet after the supper. The fact remains, however, that in Mark 10:42ff and Matthew 20:25ff the same saying of Jesus is given in quite a different setting. The context of a saying in any one of the Gospels reflects the evangelist's thought but proves nothing as to the intention of Jesus.

In the same connection Luke gives also the promise that the disciples will eat and drink at Jesus' table in his kingdom and sit on thrones judging the twelve tribes of Israel (22:30). Matthew does not have the saying about eating and drinking in the kingdom, but he quotes the promise of the twelve thrones with Jesus' words to Peter after the departure of the rich man and connects them with "the new world, when the Son of man shall sit on his glorious throne" (19:28). Cross sees here a parallel with the council of twelve laymen and three priests prescribed by the Manual of Discipline, one of whose functions will be "to render to the wicked their recompense" (viii.1, 6f; *DSS*, p. 381). The words of Jesus, however, refer explicitly to the new age which is to come. The regulation in the Manual of Discipline is accompanied by the clause, "when these things come to pass in Israel," suggesting that the proposed organization had not yet been established when the Manual was written, but the directions given are undoubtedly intended for life in this world. That the council of fifteen was expected also to judge all Israel in the world to come is possible but by no means clear.

The reference to the "new world" (literally, "regeneration") in Matthew 19:28 is mentioned by Gaster in connection with "the making new" of the Manual of Discipline (iv.25; *DSS*, p. 376), which is probably derived from Isaiah 65:17 and 66:22. Here again we have a similar idea but no indication of a closer relationship.

Milik remarks that literary parallels between the Qumran texts and the Synoptic Gospels are not so numerous as the contacts with Paul and John. As an exceptional instance he mentions Matthew 11:25–27, which, as he says, resembles the discourses of Jesus in the fourth Gospel. The relation of this passage to the Dead Sea Scrolls, however, is quite remote; it can hardly be called a literary parallel to anything in the scrolls.

Relatively few parallels have been found for sayings of Jesus outside of the Sermon on the Mount; in fact, there are few, if any, in Matthew 6 and 7 for which any parallels have been found. Schubert finds it "remarkable that the Essene parallels are found almost exclusively in Mt. 5." He adds, however, "It is not only in the Sermon on the Mount that Jesus shows himself versed in Essene rules. As a matter of fact, he also assumes his opponents among the Pharisees to be familiar with them." This, if it could be demonstrated, would be a very interesting and important discovery. Unfortunately, what Schubert gives as the clearest example does not imply any acquaintance with Essene rules on the part of either Jesus or his hearers. It is the saying already quoted (p. 89) about rescuing an animal from a pit on the Sabbath. Comparison with the Damascus Document, as we have observed in connection with the legalism of the Qumran sect (p. 89), indicates only that the general Jewish practice of Jesus' day was not in accord with the harsh regulations of the covenanters.

In Mark 7:9–13 Jesus denounces the practice of evading obligations to one's parents by designating what might have been given to them as an offering to God. A reference to the same practice has been seen in an obscure reference of the Damascus Document to dedicating the food of one's mouth to God (xvi.14f). The text is so broken by gaps in the manuscript that I did not attempt to translate it in *DSS*. The supposed allusion to the practice condemned by Jesus seems to me far-fetched and very doubtful.

The words of Jesus in Matthew 16:18, ". . . on this rock I will build my church, and the gates of Hades shall not prevail against it," come to mind when one reads a passage in the Thanksgiving Psalms (vi.24ff), where the poet says that he "drew near to the gates of death" (an echo of Psalm 107:18), but is now "like one that has come into a fortified city"; then, two lines later, he says,

"For thou dost establish counsel on a rock." The word I have translated "counsel" may also mean "a council" or even "assembly": it is applied, for example, in the Manual of Discipline to "the assembly of the community" (vi.19; *DSS*, p. 379) and in the Thanksgiving Psalms to the "eternal company" of the redeemed (iii.21; *DSS*, p. 404). The passage with which we are here concerned, therefore, may refer to the community of the covenanters. The remainder of the column expresses assurance that the powers of evil cannot break into God's fortress. The parallel with Matthew 16:18 is thus rather impressive. There is no reason, however, to suppose that it is anything but a coincidence.

Another possible connection with this verse has been suggested by Milik in connection with a fragment of the Aramaic Testament of Levi. This text refers to a mountain seen by Levi in a vision, but the end of the line where the word for "mountain" stood is lost. The noun *kepha* (rock), which appears sometimes in the New Testament as "Cephas" and elsewhere is translated into Greek as "Peter" (see John 1:42), is used for Mt. Sinai in a Qumran Aramaic fragment from Enoch 39, and Milik suggests that it may have been used also in the Testament of Levi for the high mountain which "reached to heaven." Calling attention to the possible connection with Matthew 16:18 and perhaps also 17:1–8 (the transfiguration of Jesus), Milik reserves the question for further study. Allegro takes up the suggestion and says that the idea of Peter as the rock on which the church is built "is now clearly seen to stand in this pattern of Jewish apocalypse." The transfiguration also he considers "clearly related to this pattern." That is a good deal to infer, I submit, from a conjectural restoration of a lost word. The apocalyptic pattern will have to be much clearer than it is before these New Testament passages can be fitted into it.

The possibility that the organization of the church, even within Jesus' lifetime, may have been influenced by the sect of Qumran has already been considered (pp. 81–82). The choice of twelve disciples for a place of special responsibility, we found, could have been suggested by the Qumran council of twelve laymen and three priests, but there is no particular reason to think that it was.

A more impressive parallel is the resemblance of Jesus' directions for the treatment of an offending brother in Matthew 18:15–17 to the regulation given for a similar situation in the Manual of Discipline (v.25–vi.1; *DSS*, p. 378). In both cases a rebuke in the presence of witnesses is required before a charge is lodged with the church or council. The procedure is more elaborate in Matthew, involving four steps: first a direct personal approach, then the rebuke before witnesses, the appeal to the church, and finally, if all else fails, the severance of fraternal relations. What is meant by the "church" in this passage, the only place in the Gospels where the word occurs except in Matthew 16:18, has always been a matter of debate among scholars. The question whether Jesus formed an ecclesiastical organization and the possible bearing of the Dead Sea Scrolls on this question have been discussed here (p. 81).

Jesus' selection of Leviticus 19:18, the commandment to love one's neighbor as oneself, as second only to Deuteronomy 6:5, the commandment to love God (Mark 12:31), is compared by Winter with several passages in the Testaments of the Twelve Patriarchs. The pre-Christian date and Jewish origin of this work being at present uncertain, these parallels are less significant than some in the rabbinic literature which have long been known. Winter refers also to the Damascus Document, which quotes Leviticus 19:18 with the substitution of "brother" for "neighbor" (vi.20f; *DSS*, p. 354). The word "brother" is used several times in the context, in fact, and in one instance (vii.1) it is interpreted as the "next of kin." There is nothing in the literature of Qumran like the interpretation of the "neighbor" given by the parable of the Good Samaritan as any person toward whom one can act as a neighbor, regardless of creed or nationality.

Other parallels that have been pointed out between the sayings of Jesus and the Dead Sea Scrolls are less important than those we have considered. Many writers have mentioned the fact that both Jesus and the Qumran sect denounced the religious leaders of the nation. So, of course, did almost all of the prophets in their day. Daniélou suggests that when Jesus called the scribes and Pharisees "sons of those who murdered the prophets" (Matthew

23:31) he may have had the Qumran teacher of righteousness in mind as one of the murdered prophets. This presupposes, of course, the martyrdom of the teacher of righteousness (see pp. 339–340). The possibility cannot be denied, but there is nothing to support the conjecture.

A more plausible connection with the teacher of righteousness may be seen a few verses later. Commentators have been puzzled by the reference in Matthew 23:35 to "all the righteous blood shed on earth, from the blood of innocent Abel to the blood of Zechariah the son of Barachiah." Who was this Zechariah? As Schonfield points out, the reference to him seems to imply that he was the latest in an age-long succession of martyrs. But the prophet Zechariah, son of Barachiah (or Berechiah), lived in the sixth century b.c. The story of an even earlier Zechariah, whose death would fit the statement that he was killed "between the sanctuary and the altar," is told in II Chronicles 24:20f; but he was the son of Jehoiada.

Schonfield mentions several other men by the name of Zechariah who appear in Jewish and Christian history or legend. He concludes that the account in II Chronicles was the basis of a tradition of a martyred prophet who became an antetype of the righteous sufferer; it was "a tradition which had turned into a prophecy." The Qumran sect's teacher of righteousness was such a righteous sufferer, and the inference, suggested rather than stated, is that the example of his life and death may have played a part in the formation of the tradition. The name Zechariah would then indicate the type rather than the individual. It does not follow, of course, that Jesus was referring to the teacher of righteousness under the name of Zechariah, though the naming of Zechariah as the last of the series of martyrs makes this a natural conjecture. That the teacher of righteousness had any connection at all with the Zechariah tradition is itself only an ingenious conjecture.

The closest parallel of all between a Synoptic saying of Jesus and the Dead Sea Scrolls is in Luke 16:8, where Jesus says, "The sons of this world are wiser in their own generation than the sons of light." The designation "sons of light" is so characteristic of the Qumran texts that here if anywhere, it would seem, one may speak of an "Essene" expression. We must remind ourselves, however, that the Qumran community is the only Jewish group of just that time for which we have contemporary specimens of its own literature. What seems to us, in these circumstances, distinctively "Essene" may have been actually much more widespread than we suppose. Obviously Jesus is using a bit of contemporary Jewish vocabulary. That it was peculiar to the covenanters is much less certain.

Another saying reported only by Luke is compared by Daniélou with a Qumran text. In Jesus' lament over Jerusalem he predicts its destruction by enemies, saying, "They will not leave one stone upon another in you; because you did not know the time of your visitation" (19:44). The Manual of Discipline too predicts a "time of visitation" (iii.14, 18; iv.6, 11, 19, 26; DSS, pp. 374–76); there, however, the reference is to judgment and punishment, while in Luke 19:44 it is to an opportunity which has been missed. The words "visit" and "visitation," in both favorable and unfavorable senses, are very common in both the Old and the New Testament.

In Luke 22:53 Jesus says to the priests and officers who have come to arrest him in the Garden of Gethsemane, "But this is your hour, and the power of darkness." This is just one more echo of the conception of a cosmic struggle between the forces of light and darkness which Jesus shared with the covenanters of Qumran and doubtless also with many other Jews of the time.

In all these and other instances of similarity in language and idea, various degrees of relationship may be seen, from merely accidental and superficial resemblances having no significance to real instances of intellectual and spiritual affinity. Most of the contacts are matters of terminology; some point to possible influence by or reaction against the ideas and ideals of the Qumran community. That any of them is the result of direct acquaintance with this particular sect remains uncertain; to me it seems very doubtful.

To one who starts with the teaching of Jesus and looks for parallels in the Dead Sea Scrolls, one outstanding contrast is evident. Where in all the Qumran literature is there anything like

Jesus' parables? Stories more or less resembling his and used in similar ways are to be found in the rabbinic literature. If this method of teaching was used at Qumran, it seems to have left no literary deposit. It is suited, in fact, to such popular teaching as Jesus and some of the rabbis practiced, rather than to intensive study in a tight, exclusive body like that of the covenanters. But what a loss it would have been if Jesus' parables had not been preserved!

There is no question that, as Allegro has put it, "Jesus could have come into contact with Qumran doctrines and even documents." The differences between him and the sect do not exclude the possibility of some contact between him and them. As Cullmann says, "One movement may very well grow out of another and still stand in opposition to it." That was certainly true of the Qumran sect itself in relation to other forms of Judaism.

To my statement in *DSS* that Jesus was more closely related to the apocalyptic literature than to the Dead Sea Scrolls, Wilson protests that some of that literature has turned up at Qumran. If Jesus was acquainted with these writings, Wilson argues, he must have known also the rest of the community's library. This would follow only if such works as Enoch were known only within the sect of Qumran. Definite evidence of an acquaintance with any of the books peculiar to this group is still lacking.

Howlett tries to distinguish what Jesus and the Essenes shared with other Jews from what they alone had in common. Recognizing that the differences "are yet more striking than the similarities," he feels at the same time that the value of the similarities is cumulative. His conclusion is that the disciples of Jesus and the disciples of John the Baptist alike had "similar teachings derived from a common Essenic and anti-Pharisaic background." Oesterreicher finds no connection with any of the sects in the teaching of Jesus: he preserved "all that was true in every segment of the people and of its thought."

A possibility worth considering in this connection has been suggested by Morton Smith in a comparison of the Gospels and the rabbinic literature. When the collections of Jesus' sayings incorporated in the Gospels were made, he says, the church was still a Jewish sect, trying to define its relation to other Jewish groups. New Testament scholars have often seen in the reports of controversies with the Pharisees and other groups a polemic against Judaism; Smith suggests that they reflect the concern of the early Jewish church "to justify itself in Jewish terms." In either case, the points at issue may have been of more concern to the church than they had been to Jesus himself. Instead of inferring, however, as some have, that Jesus was closer to contemporary Judaism than his followers were, Smith sees reason to suspect that the Gospels reflect "a progressive Judaizing of Christianity after Jesus' death." Jesus, he suggests, was one of those disturbing iconoclasts who "take an extreme position from which his followers afterwards try to climb down." He was not less but more original than the Gospels indicate. There is a good deal in the Gospels that supports this hypothesis. If it is true with regard to the parallels between Jesus' teaching and the rabbinic literature, it may be equally true of the parallels with the Dead Sea Scrolls.

Smith notes also the fact that the background of Jesus' ministry seems to be the popular Judaism of the day rather than any official or sectarian form of the religion. The prominence given to casting out demons is a case in point. Smith points out that the early rabbis disliked this element of the popular faith and minimized it. There is likewise little if any reflection of it in the Qumran literature. Much is said of the conflict with Belial and his hosts, but it is all in the realm of faith and conduct rather than physical or mental health. This is especially interesting if the covenanters were Essenes, if the Essenes were closely related to the Egyptian Therapeutae, and if the name Essene itself means "healer," as some believe. The main fact, in any case, is that Jesus ministered to the common people rather than to any sectarian group. "Those who are well," he said, "have no need of a physician, but those who are sick" (Mark 2:17).

Concerning some of the sayings which have been cited, New Testament specialists may raise the question whether they are authentic words of Jesus himself or expressions of later Christian interests and ideas. If evidence of direct dependence upon the Qumran sect had appeared in any of them, that question would have to be carefully considered. No such evidence, however, has been found. Reviewing carefully all the parallels that have been presented and others that might have been cited, one can hardly conclude that the originality of Jesus as a religious teacher has been impaired. Whatever else Christian faith may affirm about him, the impression he made on thousands of his contemporaries, who were better able to judge than we are, still holds good. "What is this? A new teaching!" they cried (Mark 1:27). It is still true, as it was then, that "no man ever spoke like this man" (John 7:46).

# X

## The Apostolic Church

⊔⊓⊔⊓⊔⊓⊔⊓⊔⊓⊔⊓⊔⊓⊔⊓⊔⊓⊔⊓⊔⊓⊔⊓⊔⊓⊔⊓⊔⊓⊔⊓⊔⊓⊔⊓⊔⊓⊔⊓⊔⊓⊔⊓⊔⊓⊔⊓⊔⊓⊔⊓⊔⊓⊔⊓⊔⊓⊔⊓ᴦ

Because of all that has been said about the implications of the Dead Sea Scrolls with regard to the uniqueness of Christ, and because of the crucial importance of this question, I have gone into it at much greater length than will be possible for the rest of the New Testament. The essential issues and presuppositons are, after all, much the same. All that I can do now is to mention some of the principal points involved and to state briefly my own convictions or impressions concerning them.

That the Qumran sect and the early Christian church in Jerusalem had much in common is obvious at once to any reader of the Dead Sea Scrolls who is at all familiar with the book of Acts. First of all is what I have called "the church idea" (*DSS*, p. 332), the idea of a group called out from the nation to be the true Israel. Stendahl points out that, while the Pharisees and Sadducees were parties, the Essenes were distinctly a sect, and in this respect they were closer to the Christian church than they were to the Pharisees or Sadducees. This is certainly true of the Qumran covenanters, whether or not we identify them with the Essenes.

Both the church and the Qumran sect, Stendahl continues, were also Messianic communities, in the sense that their life was conceived in "the framework of promise and fulfillment," as already fulfilling to some degree the life of the impending new age. The great difference here is that the Messiah for whose coming the Christians looked had already lived and died and triumphed over death; the covenanters expected several Messianic figures, none of whom had already lived on earth as Messiah. Stendahl accepts the theory that one of these was expected to be the teacher of righteousness, raised from the dead; in that case the parallel with Christian beliefs would be closer, but we shall find that there is very little reason to adopt this theory (pp. 340–41). In any case, as Stendahl points out, the covenanters did not believe that their teacher was already a Messiah during his lifetime.

Many terms used by the first Christians to designate themselves and their faith were used also in much the same way by the Qumran sect. Both groups called themselves the poor, the elect, and the saints or holy ones. The Christians called their faith "the way," and the men of Qumran used the word "way" both for human conduct and for the activities of the two spirits of truth and error. These expressions are all derived from the Old Testament, but the similarity of their use by the two communities is impressive.

Both groups also believed themselves the heirs of a new covenant, though only the Damascus Document among the Qumran texts makes much use of this idea. There was a difference also in the conceptions of the new covenant. Gaster, Oesterreicher, and others have observed that for the Qumran sect it was a reaffirmation and confirmation of the old Mosaic covenant; for the Christian church the old covenant had been broken by Israel and annulled, and the entirely new covenant promised by Jeremiah 31:31–34 had now been established.

Other items of Old Testament terminology were used in similar ways by the early church and the community of Qumran. More significant is the fact that their ways of interpreting the Old Testament were remarkably alike. As Peter found in Psalm 16:8–11 a prophecy of the resurrection of Jesus (Acts 2:25–32), so the Qumran commentator saw in Psalm 37:32f a prophecy of the persecution and deliverance of the teacher of righteousness. Not only so, but many of the same portions of Scripture were used in this way by both groups.

For the early Christians, however, the fulfillment of prophecy had gone much farther than it had for the Qumran community.

The Messiah had come, the hosts of Satan were already in retreat, the kingdom of God was so near that its power was already manifest in the world. The risen Lord, "exalted at the right hand of God," had "received from the Father the promise of the Holy Spirit" and had "poured out" the gift of the Spirit upon his disciples (Acts 2:33). The Qumran sect expected a "time of visitation" when God would purify a man, "cleansing him with a holy spirit," but this was still in the future. "Instead of the Spirit," says Cullmann, "the Qumran movement had an organization."

The church too, of course, had an organization, though by no means so fixed and definite as that of the covenanters. The twelve apostles exercised a general supervision, but in order not to "give up preaching the word of God to serve tables" they soon found it necessary to have a committee of seven appointed. The parallel between the twelve apostles and the Qumran council of twelve laymen and three priests has already been noted (p. 102). Cullmann suggests a parallel to the three priests in James, Cephas, and John, the three "pillars" of the apostolic church (Galatians 2:9). But two of these were members of the twelve, and none of them was a priest. Many priests joined the church (Acts 6:7), and Allegro suggests that they may have included some leaders of the Essene movement. This is possible; more probably, however, they came from the temple priesthood. Otherwise they would hardly have been called simply priests.

Before its great expansion on the day of Pentecost, the company of brethren numbered "about a hundred and twenty" (Acts 1:15). Milik remarks that this makes ten for each of the twelve apostles, just as the Qumran sect was divided into cells of at least ten laymen with a priest at their head. This is an interesting parallel, though the number ten was also the generally accepted minimum number for the organization of a synagogue.

The resemblance between the "superintendent" of the Qumran community and the Christian bishop has often been noticed. The office of bishop was a gradual development, but Peter already exercised much the same function. Rigaux points out, however, that the Qumran superintendent was not a wonder-worker or a preacher of the new faith to Jews and pagans, as Peter was. Gaster finds in the terminology of the scrolls an explanation of the distinction between bishops and presbyters (elders) in the early church. The bishop corresponds to the superintendent, he suggests, and the counterpart of the elders is to be seen in "the twelve good laymen and true" of the Qumran council. It is very doubtful, however, that there was that much difference between the elders and those called bishops in the New Testament; many scholars believe that they were the same.

Gaster points out that in the later Palestinian Christian dialect of Aramaic the word for "church" was one of those used for the "congregation" at Qumran, and the Qumran term for the "council" of the community was adopted for the council of the church. Both words may go back to the usage of the primitive Palestinian church, and in that case may have been suggested by the terminology of the Qumran sect.

Many writers have compared the "many" of the Qumran sect with the "multitude" of the early church (Acts 4:32; 6:2, 5; 15:12, 30—the Revised Standard Version unfortunately uses five different English words in these five places for the same Greek word). The parallel is not really as close as might be desired. If the early Christians adopted the term used by the Qumran sect, and if they understood it to mean "many," why was it not translated by the common Greek word for "many," which is used, for example, in Mark 10:45 and 14:26? And if the Qumran group wished to say "multitude," they had good Hebrew words for it which they used on occasion. One of them occurs in this sense three times in the Manual of Discipline (v.9, 22; vi.19; in *DSS*, pp. 377–79, I translated it "majority," but "multitude" would have been an equally good or perhaps better translation). If the "multitude" of Acts represents any word used in the Qumran texts, it would be this one rather than the one meaning "many" or "masters" (see pp. 359–62).

Both the church and the sect showed an attitude of considerable independence toward the temple and its priesthood, but the church did not separate itself entirely from the temple. The apostles, like Jesus himself, used the temple at least as a place where they could find people and preach to them. This brought them repeatedly into conflict with the priestly authorities, but they did not withdraw to the wilderness. Some of them persisted to the point of martyrdom. The party of Stephen, however, seems to have had little use for the temple (*DSS*, p. 332).

Concerning the rite of baptism, much of what has already been said of the baptism of John (pp. 59ff) is applicable also to the early Christian practice. Christian baptism was undoubtedly derived from John the Baptist, probably through disciples of his who became followers of Jesus. The new element in the meaning of the rite was that belief in Jesus was added to repentance as a preliminary qualification, and baptism was received and administered in the name of Jesus. There is no reason to suspect that the ritual baths and ablutions of Qumran had any modifying influence on the Christian practice or conception of baptism after its initial adoption by the church.

What has been said about the background and significance of Jesus' last supper with his disciples (pp. 82ff) is still relevant for the Communion meals of the primitive church. There were further developments, of course, in practice and interpretation, but there is nothing to indicate that any of them consisted in a closer approach to the ideas or procedures of the Qumran community. For the many problems still remaining in the early history of the Christian sacrament, the Dead Sea Scrolls offer little if any help.

Like the Qumran covenanters, the disciples in Jerusalem seem to have taken all their meals together, but this was probably, as Kuhn says, a spontaneous continuation of their previous practice while going about through the country with Jesus. It was also a natural expression of their common faith and hopes and fears, their growing sense of separation from the Jewish community about them, and their fervent expectation of their Lord's speedy return. There is as yet no indication of a formal religious rite in the references to "the breaking of bread" in Acts (2:42, 46); in fact, it is only by inference from the "love feasts" at Corinth and their connection with the Lord's Supper (I Corinthians 11:17–34) that one can assume such a connection at Jerusalem.

The varying accounts of the last supper in the Gospels reflect, no doubt, different stages in the history of the rite, but just what belongs to the primitive Palestinian church and what to the Gentile churches of the Hellenistic world is another matter. Such studies as Kuhn's show some of the possibilities but also the limitations of the inquiry. The daily meals of the Jerusalem church, at any rate, were more like those of the Qumran sect than were the more developed liturgical observances of later generations. That they were closer to the meals of this sect than to those of other Jewish groups is very doubtful.

The practice of having all things in common is perhaps the most striking feature in which the Jerusalem church and the Qumran community were alike. The parallel between the story of Ananias and Sapphira (Acts 5:1–11) and the rule in the Manual of Discipline concerning "a man who lies about his wealth" (vi.24f; *DSS*, p. 380) has caught the attention of readers ever since the scroll was discovered, and it has been noted that the punishment at Qumran was relatively lenient (*DSS*, p. 333). Many writers have pointed out also that in the church the sharing of wealth was voluntary, while at Qumran it was required of every member. The unity of spirit and brotherly love seem to have been cultivated with equal intensity in both groups.

The differences between the two communities in life and attitudes have often been pointed out. The separation of the Qumran group from the world, their elaborate system of probation and initiation, the strict observance of ranks and grades, the dominance of the priests, the inferior position of women, and the absence of any mission or message for the world are perhaps the points of greatest contrast with the church. Kuhn remarks that the world-wide mission of Christianity could not have developed if the church had begun as an exclusive group with secret teachings.

In spite of such differences, it is still possible that there were some contacts between the two groups. That the Essenes and early Christians might occasionally visit each other, as Howlett suggests, is rather hard to imagine. Some association with Essenes living in Jerusalem or elsewhere in Palestine is more credible than any direct acquaintance with the settlement in the desert. It is quite possible that dissatisfied members who left the community of Qumran may have been attracted to the disciples of Jesus. A. Metzinger suggests that some who could not complete the two-year novitiate of the sect and some who were expelled may have become followers of John the Baptist or Jesus.

Schonfield finds in James, "the Lord's brother" (Galatians 1:19), who succeeded Peter as the acknowledged head of the Jerusalem church, a person extraordinarily like the Qumran teacher of righteousness and one who suffered in much the same way, though he was not the same person. A. P. Davies suggests that James may have been the leader of the whole Essene movement! Gaster's comparison of the Epistle of James with the Dead Sea Scrolls will be considered later (p. 131); it is pertinent to note here, however, that he accepts the traditional view of the Epistle as written by James, the brother of Jesus, and from the parallels with the scrolls which he finds in it he concludes that the scrolls "open a window upon the little community of Jewish Christians clustered around James in Jerusalem." These first Christians, he continues, "may have been originally the urban brethren of the hardier souls that betook themselves to Qumran and to other camp-settlements in the Desert of Judah." Statements about James by the second-century historian Hegesippus are adduced in support of this conjecture: James was called "the righteous one," says Hegesippus, and like the Essenes he used no oil and wore only linen garments. Hegesippus, however, is not an unimpeachable, contemporary witness. The evidence we have reviewed shows greater differences between the two communities than a higher or lower degree of hardiness.

An important suggestion has been made by Cullmann concerning a possible "bridge between the Essenes and early Christians." The group called "Hellenists" in Acts (6:1; 9:29; and, in some texts, 11:20) did not come from the Dispersion, he says; they were Palestinian Jews. They differed, perhaps, "from the official Judaism, showing tendencies, more or less esoteric, of a syncretistic origin." People of such an eclectic disposition, for whom there was no other name than "Hellenists," would be open to the ideas of an unorthodox sect like the Essenes. Cullmann remarks also that the chapter in which we first meet these Hellenists is the one which tells of the great crowd of priests who joined the disciples. It is hardly likely, however, as we have seen, that these came from the community of Qumran.

Whatever formal elements the church may or may not have derived from the Qumran sect, if any, it is abundantly clear that they were made subservient to a new and quite different faith, in which Christ had a supreme, unique place to which nothing in the Judaism of Qumran is comparable. Milik, at the close of a study which finds more Essene influence in the New Testament than I can see, summarizes the net result admirably: "If thus Essenism carried in itself more than one element which in one way or another fertilized the terrain where Christianity was born, it is no less evident that the latter represents something totally new, which finds no ultimate explanation except in the person of Jesus."

# XI

## *Paul, John,*
## *and the Rest of the New Testament*

ᒐᒐᒐᒐᒐᒐᒐᒐᒐᒐᒐᒐᒐᒐᒐᒐᒐᒐᒐᒐᒐᒐ

From my first acquaintance with the Dead Sea Scrolls in 1947, what has most surprised and impressed me is the agreement of some aspects of Qumran theology with the most distinctive doctrines of the apostle Paul ( *DSS*, pp. 333–36). Cullmann has raised the question whether Paul could have met members of the Qumran sect while he and they were staying at Damascus. The question is unanswerable, because, as Cullmann says, "we do not know when the Essenes came to Damascus." We do not know, as a matter of fact, that they were ever at Damascus (see pp. 219ff).

The affinity, in any case, goes deeper than such an acquaintance as would have been possible at that time. It involves Paul's own religious experience before his conversion. The point at which the very roots of Paul's theology and that of the Dead Sea Scrolls are intertwined is the experience of moral frustration, with the resulting conviction of man's hopeless sinfulness. Paul did not learn this from the Thanksgiving Psalms and the concluding psalm of the Manual of Discipline, nor did the writer or writers of these psalms learn it from him; he and they alike could have found it in the Old Testament, but they also undoubtedly learned it from life.

It has often been said that there were many Pharisees, but Paul was the only one we know of who was overwhelmed and baffled by a sense of inability to keep the law. The authors of the Qumran psalms, though not Pharisees, felt as he did the moral impotence of man without the grace of God. Daniélou reminds us that a strong sense of human sin appears also in IV Ezra, an apocryphal work probably written at about the same time as Paul's letters. In carrying back man's sinfulness to Adam, this book, in fact, presents a parallel with Paul's thought not duplicated in the Dead Sea Scrolls.

Paul finds the seat of the indwelling power of sin in what he calls the flesh. Something like this is occasionally suggested in the Dead Sea Scrolls. Careful comparisons of the passages in Paul's letters and in the scrolls where the flesh is associated with sin have been made by Kuhn and by W. D. Davies. Kuhn finds the statements of the scrolls helpful in understanding what Paul says about the flesh; Davies finds only a rather loose agreement in terminology. Where Paul contrasts flesh and spirit, the scrolls contrast the two spirits of truth and error.

The affinity of Paul's doctrine and that of Qumran goes beyond the conviction of human corruption. The Thanksgiving Psalms and the concluding psalm of the Manual of Discipline express also a profound sense of the righteousness of God, by which a man is given a righteousness he could never attain for himself. There is nothing like this in IV Ezra; I know of nothing quite like it in any other Jewish document. And it is very close to the heart of Paul's faith. Stendahl points out, indeed, that for Paul it "transformed the whole structure of thought and practice to a much greater extent than ever happened at Qumran."

When and how did this assurance of the saving righteousness of God come to the Qumran poets, or perhaps to the teacher of righteousness? We do not know. We know how it came to Paul, and what it meant for him. God's righteousness had been made manifest in Christ, "whom God put forward as an expiation by his blood . . . to show God's righteousness" (Romans 3:25f). The author of the closing psalm of the Manual of Discipline ascribed his deliverance, as Paul did, to election, but he did not take this to mean that he was born more righteous than others. He confessed that he belonged "to wicked mankind, to the company of erring flesh"; but he trusted in his "vindication in the righteousness of God" (xi.9, 12; *DSS*, p. 388).

For Paul salvation meant "the righteousness of God through faith in Jesus Christ" (Romans 3:22). The Habakkuk Commentary speaks of those who will be saved from judgment "because of their labor and their faith in the teacher of righteousness" (viii.2f; *DSS*, p. 368). Not only so; this is said in commenting on Habakkuk 2:4, "But the righteous shall live by his faith," which is one of Paul's favorite proof-texts (Romans 1:17; Galatians 3:11). But the resemblance ends there. For Paul salvation comes by faith instead of works, and without works; for the commentator it is "the doers of the law in the house of Judah" who are saved by "their toil and their faith." Faith in the teacher, moreover, means confidence in his teaching, not in a work of atonement accomplished by his death.

For Paul the Christian is no longer "in the flesh" but "in the Spirit." The conceptions of spirit in the Dead Sea Scrolls and in Paul's writings, like the conceptions of flesh, have been examined by both Kuhn and W. D. Davies. They find a considerable area of agreement between Paul and the scrolls, but also many important differences. Paul speaks chiefly of the Spirit of God or of Christ. He associates the gift of the Spirit with the end of the age. In the scrolls there is no such close connection of the Spirit with any of the expected Messiahs. Kuhn points out also that at Qumran the division of mankind into the lots of the spirit of truth and the spirit of error is by predestination; Paul too is a predestinarian, but at the same time he thinks of the Spirit as received by the believer when he accepts the free salvation given through Christ.

Instead of Paul's conception of the indwelling Spirit as a new power which enables a man to overcome the power of sin, the Qumran sect thought of a struggle of the two spirits within man, with no clear issue until the time of visitation. Paul's idea of the Spirit as a guarantee of future redemption seems to have no parallel at Qumran. Murphy remarks also that the Qumran sect did not have "the spirit of sonship" by which Christians are "sons of God" (Romans 8:14f).

Many parallels in terminology between Paul's letters and the Qumran texts have been pointed out. They include, for example, the only occurrence of the name Belial in the New Testament (II Corinthians 6:15) and the frequent use of the word "mystery" (Romans 16:25; I Corinthians 2:7; Ephesians 3:9; Colossians 1:26f; II Thessalonians 2:7). Parallels have been found also in the ethical sections of the Epistles, but they are no closer than the many contacts with other Jewish and Hellenistic sources. All these may be considered instances of Paul's constant effort to be "all things to all men" (I Corinthians 9:22). Paul has also the conflict of light and darkness and even the expression "sons of light" (Romans 13:12; Ephesians 5:8, 11; 6:12; I Thessalonians 5:4f); but Murphy points out that in sharpest contrast to the covenanters Paul was conscious of being sent to the Gentiles "to open their eyes, that they may turn from darkness to light and from the power of Satan to God" (Acts 26:18).

Contacts of various kinds with the Qumran literature are found in other parts of the New Testament. In his study of the Gospel of Matthew as "a handbook issued by a school," Stendahl compares the way in which the Old Testament is quoted in Matthew with the form and manner of quoting Scripture in the Habakkuk Commentary. In the quotations which the author or editor of the Gospel inserts into the narrative to show how Jesus fulfilled prophecy, Stendahl finds that the Old Testament text is treated according to much the same method as in the Commentary. Stendahl's argument and conclusions are too elaborate to be even summarized here. They have been subjected to searching criticism by B. Gärtner, who finds much more difference than Stendahl does between the conceptions of fulfillment in Matthew and in the Habakkuk Commentary. The discussions of both Stendahl and Gärtner may be commended to all who suppose that New Testament scholars are not giving sufficient attention to the Dead Sea Scrolls.

In Luke's nativity story the song of the angels contains an expression which has been understood in different ways from very early times, as the different readings of the manuscripts show. While the reading followed by the King James Version, "good will toward men," is attested by many of the manuscripts and church fathers, there is even better attestation of the reading, "to men of good will" (2:14). But what does this mean? It has very often been supposed to refer to men whose will is good, men who are well disposed toward others. Many analogies in both Old and New Testament, however, favor the interpretation "men of God's favor." This in turn, however, may mean either men blessed with God's favor, that is, those he has chosen, or those who have won his approval, that is, as the Revised Standard Version has it, "men with whom he is pleased."

One of the Thanksgiving Psalms, Huntzinger points out, contains the expression, "the sons of his good pleasure" (iv.32f; *DSS*, p. 407); another passage reads "the sons of thy good pleasure" (xi.9; *DSS*, p. 414). The Manual of Discipline speaks of "the chosen of good pleasure," that is, "the elect by God's will" (viii.6; *DSS*, p. 381). Here, as Vogt observes, the suffix meaning "his" is omitted, just as the Greek of Luke 2:14 has no possessive pronoun. Vogt maintains that in all these places the word translated "good pleasure" means not "approval" but "will." It is, in fact, the word commonly used for the will of God, both in the Old Testament and in later Hebrew sources. The men of God's will are, then, the elect. Perhaps the best translation would be, "those he has graciously chosen."

The part of the New Testament in which most scholars see the closest and most impressive parallels with the Qumran texts is still, as it was three years ago (*DSS*, pp. 338ff), the Gospel and Epistles of John. The antithesis of light and darkness runs all through these writings, from John 1:4f to I John 2:8–11. In John 12:36 we have the expression "sons of light." In the Manual of Discipline the spirits of light and darkness are called also "the spirit of truth" and "the spirit of error"; these very expressions appear also in the Johannine literature (John 14:17; 15:26; 16:13; I John 4:6).

In the "modified dualism" of John and that of the Qumran texts, R. E. Brown finds a "similar general outlook." The great difference is that for John the Light of the world has appeared, and the victory over darkness is already won. Brown notes also that for John what makes a man a son of light is believing in the light (12:36). Here, as he says, we are "at a distance from Qumran." Along with the characteristic Johannine emphasis on faith as a decision by which men determine their own judgment (3:18f), there is also a hint of predestination (6:37; 15:16). Yet, as Brown says, this is not a "hopeless determinism"; the great stress is on decision.

The Spirit of truth promised by Jesus in John 14–16 is given a title which is very difficult to translate. It means literally "advocate" and is sometimes so translated; in these chapters in the King James Version it is translated "Comforter"; in the Revised Standard Version, "Counselor." Some would prefer to render it "Helper." Cross calls attention to the fact that the Manual of Discipline says, ". . . but the God of Israel and his angel of truth helped all the sons of light" (iii.24f; *DSS*, p. 374); and the War scroll says, "The prince of light thou didst appoint of old as our helper" (xiii.10).

The Johannine conception of the Spirit, who "proceeds from the Father" (15:26) and will be sent to guide the disciples "into all the truth" (16:13), does not correspond closely to the Qumran conception of the spirit who is one of two struggling for the mastery of mankind. The one who in the Gospel of John stands over against Satan, "the ruler of this world" (12:31; 16:11), is not the Spirit but Christ.

One of the key words of the fourth Gospel is "truth," which is also a very prominent word in the vocabulary of Qumran. Albright remarks that its opposite, "falsehood" or "the lie," does not appear so often in John as in the Qumran texts. The description of the devil as "a liar and the father of lies" (8:44) is worth mentioning, however, and in I John the disobedient, unbelieving, and unloving are called liars (2:4, 22; 4:20). Brown considers the parallels between the Dead Sea Scrolls and John with regard to truth and perversity "perhaps the most striking yet advanced." The idea of doing or practicing the truth (John 3:21; I John 1:6) appears also in the Manual of Discipline (i.5; v.3; viii.2; *DSS*, pp. 371, 376, 381).

No idea is more distinctively Johannine than that of eternal life as a present possession of the believer (e.g., John 5:24). Licht remarks that the author of the Thanksgiving Psalms is so convinced that he will be saved from the final judgment that he considers himself already saved. On the negative side, this corresponds to the Johannine doctrine; the Qumran poet's joy and confidence and his assurance of moral victory embody also, no doubt, much of what the fourth evangelist meant by "life." What one familiar with the Gospel misses in the Qumran texts is the conception of a vital energy drawn by the believer from Christ, as the branches draw their life from the vine (John 15:1–8). Even this has at least a partial counterpart in the poet's sense of complete dependence on God.

The love for one another which is demanded of the disciples in the Gospel and Epistles of John is recalled by the requirement of the Manual of Discipline that the members of the sect "love all the sons of light" (i.9; DSS, p. 371). With this is coupled the requirement to "hate all the sons of darkness"; John has nothing like this, yet many writers have pointed out that nothing in the Gospel or Epistles explicitly requires love for those outside the church. Believers are, indeed, warned not to love the world (I John 2:15–17). This does not necessarily refer to persons, yet that is suggested by the statement that the world hates the disciples (John 15:18f; I John 3:13). The Dead Sea Scrolls offer no such motivation for the love of the brethren as is given in the Johannine writings (John 15:9, 12; I John 4:10f, 19). Carried out to its logical implications, such love inevitably leads to the love of all mankind (I John 3:15, 17).

The possible bearing of the Qumran calendar on the date of Jesus' last supper with his disciples, concerning which the Synoptic Gospels and the fourth Gospel seem to disagree, has been discussed (pp. 82f). Kuhn feels that the Johannine account of the supper is "in the style of the communal meals of the Essenes." The only specific point he gives to support this impression is the fact that Peter, instead of asking Jesus directly who is the traitor among them, asks the beloved disciple, whose place at the table is next to the Master, to put the question before him. This, Kuhn thinks, corresponds to the strict order of seating at the meetings and meals of the Qumran community. All that the Johannine narrative suggests, however, is an especially close intimacy between Jesus and the unnamed disciple. Peter simply assumes that his question will be more likely to get an answer if asked by that disciple who enjoys the special confidence and affection of Jesus. There is no indication of a fixed order or rank among the disciples.

Brown calls attention to the frequent and characteristic use of the symbolism of water in the Gospel of John in connection with the ritual ablutions of the community of Qumran. He sees no dependence upon the sect or polemic against it, however, in this symbolism, and it is hard to see what connection there would be. The expression "living water," used in John 4:10f and 7:38, occurs once in the Damascus Document, where it is said that those who turned back from the new covenant "departed from the well of living water" (xix.34; *DSS*, p. 356). This is clearly an allusion to Jeremiah 2:13 and 17:13 and has no connection with the use of the expression in the Gospel. "Living water" is the regular Hebrew term for fresh, running water (Genesis 26:19, Leviticus 14:5, etc.).

The systematic way in which the discourses of Jesus in the fourth Gospel are connected with the Jewish feasts has been associated by some writers with the interest of the Qumran sect in the ritual calendar. Brown sees no connection here, and there is certainly no suggestion of concern for the times when the feasts are to be observed, or of anything that has to do with the sect in particular. It is the celebration of the festivals at the temple that provides the occasions for the discourses.

Many verbal parallels between the Dead Sea Scrolls and the Johannine writings have been pointed out. None is more striking than the statement in the Manual of Discipline that God establishes everything, "and without him it is not done" (xi.11; *DSS*, p. 388), which recalls John 1:3: "All things were made by him, and without him was not anything made that was made." Oesterreicher feels that the language of the Gospel "may well have been an echo" of the Qumran passage, but if so the echo was "greater than the parent sound," because John was speaking of the eternal Word, which was incarnate in Christ. Murphy too thinks that the evangelist "could have found the Qumran formula ready to hand." The similarity caught my eye when I first read the Manual in Jerusalem ten years ago, but I must confess that it did not then and does not now seem to me to indicate any direct connection.

Several more or less characteristic expressions of the fourth Gospel appear also in the Manual of Discipline, though in different connections and sometimes with different meanings: e.g., "eternal life" (3:15, etc.; iv.7, etc.; *DSS*, p. 375), "the works of God" (6:28; iv.4; *DSS*, p. 375), and "the light of life" (8:12; iii.7; *DSS*, p. 373). The words "be one" or "become one" (7:11, 21, 23) are called by Cross "typically Essene diction." So far as they designate the spiritual unity of the brethren, their meaning is the same in the Qumran texts as in the Gospel; here again, however, they are associated with Christ and God in a way that is not at all "Essene."

All these and other contacts between the Johannine literature and the Dead Sea Scrolls have led many scholars to declare that the new material demands a drastic revision of current critical views concerning the Gospel of John (*DSS*, pp. 338ff). The conspicuous differences between John and the first three Gospels have commonly been ascribed to pagan Hellenistic influence. Comparison with the Qumran documents indicates that these elements are derived, as Allegro puts it, "from Jewish sectarianism rooted in Palestinian soil." How far they had come into sectarian Judaism from pagan sources is another question; the point is that they were already domesticated in at least one distinctly Jewish sect. In this connection it is interesting to note that Morton Smith finds the Gospel of John also "a mine of expressions and references which can be paralleled in rabbinic literature."

Some scholars go on from the demonstration of the fourth Gospel's "Jewishness" to argue that it was written at an earlier date than has commonly been supposed. Whether this will ultimately prove to be so remains to be seen; it may be well here too, however, to call attention to Smith's conclusions from the use of the word "Jews" in the fourth Gospel. The Christian group whose point of view is here reflected, he finds, is already in conscious opposition to Judaism. It remembers that Jesus was a Jew and stresses this fact to support its doctrine that the Messiah had come and had been rejected by his own people. This shows, Smith concludes, "the falsity of the common supposition that everything in the Gospels which looks Jewish or which refers to Jesus' being a Jew must belong to the earliest material and be historically reliable."

Albright sees in the new Jewish orientation of the fourth Gospel a refutation of the view that "supposed forms of mild Gnosticism" influenced the thinking of the evangelist. From Gnostic documents found in Egypt only a year before the discovery of the Dead Sea Scrolls, Albright infers that some of the "most pronounced sects" of Gnosticism had developed before 70 A.D., leaving no room for the "relatively harmless early forms" which have been postulated as sources for Johannine ways of thinking. Instead of such hypothetical influences, we have now in the Qumran texts the real background of the Gospel of John in sectarian Judaism. It is safe to say that this position will not go unchallenged. Those of us who claim no special competence in the study of Gnosticism can only await with some interest the outcome of the debate.

Another suggestive but debatable inference is drawn by Albright from the Qumran parallels with the New Testament. These are found not only in the Gospel of John but also in other books of the New Testament, especially the Synoptic Gospels and the letters of Paul; in these other books, however, Albright says, they "are most numerous in the areas where the New Testament books in question parallel the Gospel of John most closely." This indicates, he suggests, that the differences in outlook and doctrine between John and the Synoptic Gospels and between John and Paul are not so great as has often been claimed. Another interpretation, however, may be put on the same facts. If such ideas as the dualism of light and darkness, to take only the most conspicuous example, appear in Paul and the Synoptic Gospels as well as in John, the reason may be that they were widely known in the Jewish world in general and need not have been derived by any of the New Testament writers from the sect of Qumran in particular.

Albright holds also that the difference between John and the Synoptic Gospels "lies in the concentration of tradition along certain aspects of Christ's teachings, particularly those which seem to have resembled the teaching of the Essenes most closely." It is quite true, as Albright says, that any great teacher will be interpreted differently by different reporters. The very different pictures of Socrates given by Xenophon and Plato provide a famous illustration. But the analogy must be carried further: it is quite clear that a creative element is involved, especially in Plato's picture of Socrates. How much in the Gospel of John comes from Jesus and how much from the evangelist himself is a difficult question which cannot be answered by parallels with the Dead Sea Scrolls.

It is somewhat confusing also to be told that the Synoptics and John differ especially at the points of closest resemblance with Essene teaching, and at the same time that the parallels with the scrolls in the Synoptic Gospels are in the areas of closest agreement with John. This seems to imply that where the Synoptics differ from John they also differ from the Qumran sources. That would be hard to substantiate; indeed, the correlation of resemblance to John and resemblance to Qumran in the Synoptics is itself open to question. The parallels that have been pointed out in the Sermon on the Mount, for example, are not in areas of close agreement with John.

Cullmann, in fact, takes a position almost opposite to that of Albright. He associates the fourth Gospel with the Hellenists of the early church, and through them indirectly with the Essenes, and submits that this connection explains the existence of "two such different forms of Christianity as those portrayed by the Synoptic and Johannine Gospels." Both were able to exist within the church from the beginning, he says, "because both found their roots in forms of Judaism present in Palestine." In support of the connection between the fourth evangelist and the Hellenists, Cullmann adduces the statement in John 4:38 that Samaria would be evangelized by others than the apostles, which agrees with the account in Acts 8 of the missionary work of the Hellenist Philip in Samaria. Yet the only "essential and characteristic point common simultaneously to the Qumran sect, the Hellenists, and the Fourth Gospel" that Cullmann can find is opposition to temple worship.

All authorities agree that the Gospel of John is no mere reproduction of Essene thought. Albright speaks of "a wide gulf"; Murphy and Brown both use the expression "a tremendous chasm." Whether there was any direct contact between the fourth evangelist and the Qumran community is still a matter of some difference of opinion, but there seems to be a growing feeling that no such connection can be established. Cullmann's theory of an indirect connection through the Hellenistic wing of the early church has been mentioned. He notes also the possibility, which some consider a strong probability, that the evangelist learned Essene ideas and terminology from the disciples of John the Baptist; but, Cullmann adds, a connection between that group and the Essenes "cannot be proved with certainty." Brown too notes this possibility, but concludes that the resemblances between the Qumran texts and the Gospel and Epistles of John indicate simply a "general acquaintance with the thought and style of expression which we have found at Qumran."

Connections between the Epistle to the Hebrews and the Dead Sea Scrolls have been seen by several scholars. Recent studies of this letter have emphasized its relationship to the preaching of Stephen and the Hellenists, as exemplified by Acts 7. Here would seem to be a fruitful field for further study along the line of Cullmann's thesis connecting the Hellenists with the Essenes. Gärtner considers the use of the Old Testament in this letter much more like that in the Qumran commentaries than what we find in the Gospel of Matthew. Oesterreicher thinks it possible that the Hebrews to whom the letter was addressed were "priests from or sympathetic to Qumran." According to a news dispatch in the summer of 1957, Yadin presented a paper to the Second World Congress of Jewish Studies in Israel maintaining that the Epistle to the Hebrews was written to the sect of Qumran early in the second century A.D. If this report is correct, it is implied that the sect continued to exist for some time after the destruction of the Qumran settlement.

Gaster points out several expressions in the Epistle of James which seem to him to be echoes of the language of the Dead Sea Scrolls. None of them is sufficiently close, it seems to me, to make a direct connection probable. Gaster even suggests that the "scripture" quoted in James 4:5, which is not to be found in the Old Testament, may be a statement in the Manual of Discipline, listing the sins to which the spirit of error incites men (iv.9ff; *DSS*, p. 375). But the sentence in James no more quotes this passage directly than it quotes any verse of the Old Testament. It is probably, I suspect, a faint echo of Genesis 6:3.

Minor parallels in terminology have been seen in other books of the New Testament, but most of them are echoes of Old Testament language or ideas. The explanation given in II Peter 3 for the delay in Christ's return and the final judgment is recalled by the effort of the Habakkuk Commentary to meet much the same difficulty (vii.7ff; *DSS*, p. 368). The idea of the destruction of the world by fire expressed in the same chapter appears also in the Dead Sea Scrolls (see p. 344).

In the Revelation of John there are points of similarity to the Qumran texts, as one might expect in any apocalyptic work of that period. It is not surprising to find some of the same Old Testament passages quoted or echoed in Revelation and in the Damascus Document or the Manual of Discipline. The most remarkable parallel is in the symbol of the woman giving birth to a child in Revelation 12:1–6, which many writers have recalled in connection with the poem in the third column of the Thanksgiving Psalms (see pp. 317f). Licht remarks that while the ideas are similar, the use made of them is not the same. The figure of the dragon and the war in heaven following the birth of the child have no counterpart in the Thanksgiving Psalm. The force of the parallel depends largely, in fact, on the questionable assumption that the psalm has to do with the birth of the Messiah.

There is much about war in Revelation, and it is a war in which Michael and other angels take part. A remote relation with the ideas of the War scroll may be seen; both documents, of course, draw from the Old Testament the idea of the eschatological war. There is no suggestion in Revelation, however, that the saints on earth are to be organized and armed for physical combat with the sons of darkness. The idea in Revelation 20:7ff that Satan will be let loose in the world at the time of the final conflict brings to mind the statement of the Damascus Document that "Belial will be let loose in Israel" (iv.13; *DSS*, p. 352); but this seems to refer to the present age, which the Manual of Discipline calls "the dominion of Belial" (i.18, 23; ii.19; *DSS*, pp. 372f), whereas the loosing of Satan in Revelation will come "when the thousand years are ended" (20:7).

An open-minded review of all the evidence shows, I am convinced, that the similarities between the New Testament and the Dead Sea Scrolls have been considerably exaggerated. There may have been some contact or perhaps contacts, direct or indirect, between the apostolic church and the community of Qumran. Several possibilities have been shown, but, contrary to the opinion of most recent writers on the scrolls, I cannot see anything more than vague possibilities. What the Dead Sea Scrolls actually demonstrate has been well summed up by Albright: they show that the writers of the New Testament "drew from a common reservoir of terminology and ideas which were well known to the Essenes and"—this I would emphasize—"presumably familiar also to other Jewish sects of the period."

# PART THREE

# *RESULTS FOR*
# *OLD TESTAMENT STUDIES*

# XII

## *The Text of the Historical Books, Psalms, and Wisdom Literature*

⊔⊓⊔⊓⊔⊓⊔⊓⊔⊓⊔⊓⊔⊓⊔⊓⊔⊓⊔⊓⊔⊓⊔⊓⊔⊓⊔⊓⊔⊓⊔⊓⊔⊓⊔⊓⊔⊓⊔⊓⊔⊓⊔⊓⊔⊓⊔⊓⊔⊓⊔⊓⊔⊓⊔⊓⊔⊓⊔⊓⊔⊓⊔⊓⊔⊓⊔⊓⊔⊓⊔⊓⊔⊓

In *DSS* (pp. 301–14) the contribution of the Dead Sea Scrolls to the textual criticism of the Old Testament was illustrated by examining the variant readings of the St. Mark's Isaiah scroll that had been adopted in the Revised Standard Version. It was noted, however, that on the whole this manuscript confirmed the accuracy and antiquity of the traditional (Masoretic) text preserved in medieval manuscripts. The fact that this was not the case with the biblical fragments from Cave 4 was mentioned only briefly (pp. 319f). We have now more information about these fragments and those from the other caves; we may therefore conveniently consider the Old Testament books one by one and ask what has been learned thus far concerning the text of each.

It will be seen that many more questions are raised, with regard both to the wording of particular passages and to the history of the Hebrew text in general, than was the case with the scrolls found in Cave 1 in 1947. This is not equally true of all the books of the Old Testament. The six manuscripts of Genesis vary only at a few scattered points from the Masoretic text. For the rest of the Pentateuch we have a mixture of different types of text, indicating connections with various lines of tradition.

One manuscript of Exodus has some affinity with the Hebrew text from which the Septuagint, the standard Greek translation, was made. In Exodus 1:5, where the Masoretic text says that

135

Jacob's descendants numbered seventy when he went to Egypt, the Septuagint says that there were seventy-five of them. The latter number is given in Stephen's speech in Acts 7:14, and it now appears in this Qumran manuscript.

Another manuscript of Exodus, written in the old Hebrew script, exhibits striking agreements with the Samaritan Pentateuch. The Samaritans still use a variety of the old Hebrew script, but the writing of this scroll is not Samaritan. There is nothing in the extant fragments to indicate any connection with the Samaritan sect, yet some of the same variant readings that occur in the Samaritan text are found here too. Many of these consist of additions or expansions of the text. After Exodus 7:18 a statement is inserted telling how Moses obeyed the command given in the preceding verses. The same kind of interpolation occurs in four other places also.

Other instances of an expanded text appear both in the Samaritan Pentateuch and in this Qumran manuscript. In Exodus 32:10 a sentence taken from Deuteronomy 9:20 is inserted. There are also some omissions or transpositions. Exodus 30:1–10 immediately follows 26:35 in the Samaritan text; no fragment has been found to show whether the paragraph occurred at this place in the Qumran manuscript, but in any case it was omitted after chapter 29. There are many other minor points of agreement with the Samaritan text.

What all this shows, of course, is not that the Samaritan readings are better or older than those of the Masoretic text, but that the Samaritan text represents an older textual tradition than had been supposed; and, as F. F. Bruce points out, what we call the Samaritan form of the text was not necessarily peculiar to the Samaritans. Like the traditions preserved by the Masoretic text and the Septuagint, it was widely known among the Jews before the standardization of the text.

Fragments of Leviticus in the old Hebrew script were found in Cave 1 in 1949 (*DSS*, pp. 35, 96–98, 319); another turned up in Cave 6. Representing undoubtedly a very early textual tradition, they agree remarkably with the traditional Hebrew text. The Greek translation also of Leviticus appears in two Cave 4 manuscripts. One of them, on papyrus, is from the last century before Christ. On the whole it reproduces the same text as the later manuscripts of the Septuagint, but it differs from them in not using the word *kyrios* (Lord) for the divine name, transcribing it instead as IAŌ.

Of the other Greek manuscript of Leviticus, written on leather, only 26:2–16 has survived, but in these fifteen verses there are ten variations from the later Septuagint manuscripts and five more readings on which those manuscripts differ among themselves. According to P. W. Skehan, none of these variants has any significance for the revision of the Hebrew text, but some of them represent a very early stage in the history of the Greek translations.

A Qumran manuscript of Numbers in the common square script resembles the Exodus manuscript in the old Hebrew script in containing expansions of the text which appear elsewhere only in Samaritan manuscripts. Thus after Numbers 27:23 a clause based on Deuteronomy 3:21 is inserted: "[And he sai]d to him, your eyes have seen what Yahweh has done to [these] two k[ings]." At other points, however, this manuscript agrees with the Septuagint against both the Samaritan and the Masoretic text. In 35:21, for example, it adds, with the Septuagint, "The murderer shall surely die." In short, this manuscript represents a crossing and fusing of different lines of textual tradition.

The Septuagint itself is represented also at Qumran in Numbers as in Exodus. Fragments of a leather manuscript containing parts of 3:30–4:14 have been identified. In this case, however, there are several instances of the use of Greek words differing from those used in other manuscripts for the same Hebrew text. Possibly, as Skehan suggests, the later manuscripts present a revision of the early translation.

Deuteronomy, as we have observed, is represented at Qumran by scraps of no less than fourteen different manuscripts. Here again we find mixed types of text, agreeing now with one tradition and now with another. Relatively few entirely new readings are found. Only a few of the variants have as yet been published. Sometimes, as in the complete scroll of Isaiah from Cave 1, they will be found to support readings of the ancient versions, especially the Septuagint, which may well be older and better than the readings of the Masoretic text. In Deuteronomy 32:8, where the Masoretic text says, "he fixed the bounds of the peoples according to the number of the sons of Israel," the Septuagint says, "according to the number of the sons of God," and this reading was adopted by both the Revised Standard Version and the Catholic Confraternity translation. It now appears also in the Hebrew text of a Qumran fragment. Other variants in which the Qumran fragments agree with the Septuagint are less impressive.

A rather complicated group of variant readings occurs toward the end of Deuteronomy 32 in the remains of a small scroll which seems to have contained only this chapter, the "Song of Moses." At the beginning of 32:43, where the Masoretic text reads, "Praise, O nations, his people," the Septuagint and the Qumran scroll have "heavens" instead of "nations." The Septuagint adds here a second line, "and let all the angels of God bow down to him," and this is quoted in Hebrews 1:6. The Qumran text reads, "and let all gods bow down to him." (There are also in the Septuagint two more lines, possibly a mere variation of these two; one of these is quoted in Romans 15:10.) The Masoretic text continues, "for he avenges the blood of his servants"; both the Septuagint and the Qumran scroll read, "the blood of his sons," adding, "and those who hate him he will repay." In the last line of the verse, where the Masoretic text reads strangely "his land, his people," the Qumran text agrees with the Septuagint in reading "the land of his people." The Revised Standard Version adopted this reading on the basis of the Septuagint and general probability before the Qumran manuscript was discovered. The insertion of a second line at the beginning of the verse improves the material form. Which of the various forms in which the line appears, if any, preserves the original text is another question. Skehan believes that some Hebrew reading reflected by the Septuagint is more likely to be original than the line as it appears in the Qumran manuscript, which may have been derived from Psalm 97:7.

The historical books which follow the Pentateuch and are

known in the Hebrew canon as "the former prophets" are well
represented at the Qumran caves. Milik says that the manuscripts
of Joshua, Judges, I–II Samuel, and I–II Kings from Caves 1, 4, 5,
and 6 all seem to be derived from the same Hebrew text as that
on which the Septuagint of these books was based. Skehan too
notes the "strong Septuagintal cast" of the fragments of Joshua
and I–II Samuel. Scholars have always had trouble with the text
of Samuel: several of the classics of Old Testament textual criticism deal primarily with the problems of these two books. It
should not be altogether surprising, therefore, that the Qumran
fragments of I–II Samuel are of more value for textual criticism
than those of any other book. The fact that they are unusually
well preserved increases their usefulness.

One leather manuscript had been reinforced with papyrus, and
as a result some portion of every chapter has survived. The complete scroll consisted of fifty-seven columns, thirty-three of I
Samuel and twenty-four of II Samuel. Not only is the text of this
scroll related to that of the Septuagint; it also agrees more closely
than the Masoretic text with the text of I–II Samuel used in the
composition of I Chronicles.

The oldest of all the Hebrew manuscripts of Qumran, as indicated by the form of its script, is another Samuel manuscript,
which Cross dates at the end of the third century B.C. It too is
related to the Hebrew text underlying the Septuagint.

Not every case of agreement with the Septuagint, of course,
signifies necessarily that the Greek translators had before them
the same Hebrew text now attested by the Dead Sea Scrolls. H.
Orlinsky, whose vigorous criticisms of the first Isaiah scroll from
Cave 1 were reported and discussed in *DSS* (pp. 307–11), points
out that where the Masoretic text was obscure or apparently
corrupt the Greek translators and the Qumran scribes may have
made independently the same more or less obvious conjectural
emendations. The Qumran texts do not by any means agree at all
points with the Septuagint; they only occasionally diverge from
the Masoretic text in the same way, and also sometimes diverge
from it in ways not followed by the Septuagint.

This is quite true; on the other hand, Professor Orlinsky would certainly not have us jump to the conclusion that all agreements are purely coincidental. The decision as to a real relationship or common textual ancestry must depend in the long run on the cumulative evidence of a series of agreements, and on a thorough examination of each instance to determine its most probable explanation. In any case, all that can be claimed is that the Qumran fragments have been influenced by the textual tradition that lies back of the Septuagint, not that they reproduce the same Hebrew text that lay before the Greek translators.

Two points may be mentioned at which entirely new readings are presented by the Qumran manuscripts. From Hannah's vow that if God gave her a son she would give him to the Lord, and no razor would touch his head (I Samuel 1:11), it has commonly been inferred that Samuel was a Nazirite (compare Numbers 6:5; Judges 13:5), but this is not explicitly stated in the Masoretic text. Now one of the Qumran texts adds at the end of I Samuel 1:22, "and I will present him as a Nazirite forever, all the days of [his life]." This was not necessarily a part of the original text; it could be a "gloss" inserted by a scribe to bring out the implications of Hannah's vow. If it was in the original text, a copyist's eye, by the common error technically known as *homoioteleuton*, might conceivably have jumped from the "forever" at the end of verse 22 to the "forever" following "Nazirite." In that case, however, it is hard to see why the following words, "all the days of his life," were omitted.

The other unique reading to be noted is from the third-century manuscript. In the Masoretic text of I Samuel 23:11, David asks two questions, and the Lord answers only the second one. David then in verse 12 repeats his first question, and this time it is answered. The Septuagint omits part of the passage, with the result that the reply to the two questions answers only the first. The old Qumran text separates the two questions and gives an answer to each, making a much smoother connection. David asks, "Will Saul come down, as thy servant has heard? O Lord, God of Israel, tell thy servant." God replies, "He will come down." David then asks, "Will the men of Keilah surrender me and my men into the hand of Saul?" God replies, "They will surrender you."

It may be said, of course, that a scribe has here smoothed out a confused passage. It is at least equally probable that the confusion was due to mistakes in copying, and the Qumran fragment preserves the original text.

For I–II Kings we have a few fragments of a Cave 4 manuscript, a part of the first column of one from Cave 5, and a good many pieces of a papyrus manuscript from Cave 6 which shows considerable variation from the Masoretic text. Parts of the last chapter of I Kings and chapters 5–10 of II Kings are included among the extant fragments of this manuscript. Nothing more can be said about it at present beyond the general fact of a relationship with the text of the Septuagint.

One small fragment is all that has been found of I–II Chronicles in the Qumran caves, and nothing notable has been reported concerning it. From the books of Ezra and Nehemiah we have only parts of Ezra 4–5 in fragments of a single Cave 4 manuscript; Esther, as we have observed, is not represented at all in the Dead Sea Scrolls.

Following the order of the books in our English Bibles, we come now to the books of poetry. Parts of two manuscripts of Job, one in the old Hebrew script and one in the square script, were found in Cave 4. The latter survives only in a few scraps, most of which are from chapter 36. The other is represented by three fragments from chapters 13–14. Nothing very important for textual criticism seems to be offered by any of these fragments.

With the Psalms the case is very different, for like Deuteronomy and Isaiah they were copied and recopied many times in the Qumran community. There were fragments of three manuscripts of Psalms in Cave 1, of two in Cave 2, of one in Cave 3, of ten in Cave 4, and of one in Cave 5—seventeen altogether. Fragments containing parts of two consecutive Psalms show that the order of the Psalms was not always the same in the different manuscripts; some of them were probably omitted altogether in some of the manuscripts.

In the medieval manuscripts of the Old Testament and in the ordinary printed Hebrew Bible the Psalms are not presented in poetic form, but the lines are run together like prose. This is true also of one Qumran scroll, which seems to come from the Has-monean period (166 to 63 B.C.). In other Qumran manuscripts, however, the metrical form is recognized, and the lines are separated. Several fragments containing parts of Psalm 119 are arranged in this way, and the acrostic form of the Psalm is made clear. One manuscript, from the Herodian period (37–4 B.C.), arranges the other Psalms also metrically; some of them are so arranged in still another manuscript, but in one Psalm the division into lines is not in accord with the real metrical structure.

The text of the Qumran manuscripts of the Psalms, to judge from the little that has been published concerning it, does not seem to be remarkable in any way. The Herodian manuscript agrees closely with the Masoretic texts; the older Hasmonean manuscript, Skehan reports, has "some good readings and some quite bad ones." He gives examples of both kinds, a few of which may be mentioned here.

In Psalm 38:19 (verse 20 in the Hebrew) the Masoretic text reads literally, "My enemies living are mighty." The King James Version tries to make this clear by expanding it: "But mine enemies *are* lively, *and* they are strong." The Revised Standard Version adopts a conjectural emendation suggested by the paral-lelism with "those who hate me wrongfully" in the second half of the verse. Changing the word meaning "living" to one that means "without cause," it translates, "Those who are my foes without cause are mighty." This conjectural reading now appears in the Hasmonean manuscript. In the following verse, however, where the Masoretic text has "Those who render me evil for good are my adversaries," this manuscript reads, less plausibly, "they plunder me in return for a good word."

In Psalms 69:3 (Hebrew verse 4), where the Masoretic has "My eyes fail while I wait for my God," the Qumran text has the much less impressive reading, "my teeth" or perhaps "my years." Yet in verse 11 of the same Psalm there is an improvement on the reading of the Masoretic text, which is literally, "I wept with fasting my soul." The King James Version here again inserts words to make sense: "I wept *and chastened* my soul with fast-ing." The Revised Standard Version, on the basis of the Greek and

Syriac versions, emends so as to read, "I humbled my soul with fasting." The ancient Qumran manuscript reads, "I chastised my soul with fasting," which may very well be the original reading; in fact, it may have been the basis of the Greek and Syriac renderings.

Psalm 71:6 contains a word which occurs nowhere else and has always puzzled interpreters; it seems to mean literally "my cutter," that is, "he who cut me." This makes the line mean, "Thou art he who cut me from my mother's womb," and most translators interpret it accordingly. Some scholars, however, have suggested that the original word here may have been one which means "my strength," and this is what the Hasmonean manuscript of Qumran actually reads, making the line mean, "From my mother's womb thou hast been my strength."

One variant reading from the Herodian manuscript is reported by Skehan, who, however, does not regard it as correct. Where the Masoretic text of Psalm 102:19 (Hebrew verse 20) reads "his holy height," this manuscript has "his holy dwelling." The difference in meaning is in this case very slight; there is no reason to question the Masoretic reading, though the reasons Skehan gives for preferring it do not seem to me very strong.

From the book of Proverbs parts of 1:27–2:1 and chapters 14–15 are preserved in fragments of a relatively late Qumran manuscript. Only one textual variant of any interest has been noted. For the Masoretic reading in 1:32, "the turning away of the simple," the Qumran text, it seems, has "the cord of the simple," whatever that may mean.

Two manuscripts of Ecclesiastes are represented by fragments found in Cave 4. Four pieces of the older one were published in 1957 by James Muilenburg, as already noted in *DSS* (p. 319); a few more have been acquired since then. This manuscript, from the second century B.C., has a number of readings which do not agree with the traditional text. Most of the differences are very slight, but a few are worth mentioning.

Verse 6 of the sixth chapter begins in the Masoretic text with a word which apparently means "even if" or "although," but its form and derivation have occasioned much discussion. The

Qumran manuscript separates this word into what are supposed to be its component parts, but in so doing produces a difficulty which has always been felt with the same expression in Ezekiel 3:6: the context requires the meaning "if" or "although," but the text seems to mean "if not." Whatever may have been the origin and real significance of this expression, its occurrence here offers some confirmation of its authenticity in Ezekiel. Conversely, the occurrence in Ezekiel strengthens the case for the Qumran reading here in Ecclesiastes. We cannot argue in both directions and claim that each proves the authenticity of the other; we can only say that they mutually support each other, enhancing the probability that the expression may be authentic in both places.

In Ecclesiastes 7:2 this manuscript has "joy" instead of the Masoretic text's "feasting." This is the exact opposite of "mourning," and the same pair of opposites occurs two verses later. At the same time it makes a more prosaic, almost mechanical, contrast than the vivid expression of the traditional text. The very fact that the words "mourning" and "joy" (or "mirth," as the English versions render it here) occur just below in verse 4 may have caused a careless scribe to substitute "joy" for "feasting" in verse 2.

A variant reading in 7:19 is interesting because it is found also in some late Hebrew manuscripts and seems to be supported by the Septuagint. The Masoretic text says, "Wisdom strengthens the wise man"; the Qumran manuscript reads "helps" (*t'zr*), which in the Hebrew consonantal text is the same as the word for "strengthens" (*t'z*) with the addition of one letter. Orlinsky denies that the Septuagint presupposes the Hebrew word for "helps," and he succeeds in showing that in other places the Septuagint uses the Greek word meaning "help" to translate the Hebrew word meaning "strengthen." This almost makes it look as though the Qumran reading was a translation back into Hebrew from the Greek! The fact, however, that fourteen late Hebrew manuscripts also have the same reading as the Qumran fragment makes it more probable that the Septuagint reading here rests on that word, and that the traditional reading arose from the accidental omission of the last letter.

Nothing notable has been reported concerning the two manuscripts of the Song of Solomon represented by fragments from
Cave 4. Like the other books of the "Writings," the last part of
the Hebrew Bible, this one seems to have been preserved in a
form essentially the same as the Masoretic text.

# XIII

## *The Text of the Prophetic Books*

⎍⎍⎍⎍⎍⎍⎍⎍⎍⎍⎍⎍⎍⎍⎍⎍⎍⎍⎍⎍⎍⎍⎍⎍⎍⎍⎍⎍⎍⎍

The first of the prophetic books, Isaiah, was evidently, as we have seen, the most popular in the Qumran community. In addition to the two scrolls from Cave 1, there are more or less extensive fragments of thirteen others from Cave 4. Like the later and incomplete scroll from Cave 1, the Cave 4 fragments agree closely with the Masoretic text. This demonstration of the antiquity of our traditional text in the book of Isaiah is all the more important in view of the quite different indications in other books.

By far the most interesting and useful of all the Isaiah manuscripts for the study of the text is the complete St. Mark's Isaiah scroll—as it may still be called for convenience, although it is now in Israel. It too supports the accuracy, by and large, of the Masoretic text (*DSS*, p. 304). It presents, however, a more popular, less official form of the text than the other manuscripts. It was probably less carefully written and therefore contains a greater proportion of mistakes in copying, but it also preserves a number of ancient readings which were lost in the more orthodox tradition.

It is unnecessary to repeat here what was said in *DSS* concerning the readings in this scroll which were adopted in the Revised Standard Version, with others also which individual scholars considered superior to the Masoretic readings. A few observations growing out of Skehan's special study of this text may be reported, however, as well as a few suggestions brought forward by other scholars since the publication of *DSS*.

Skehan points out that the St. Mark's manuscript illustrates the effect of an "exegetical process" in the transmission of the text; that is, the scribe who copied a manuscript was at the same time an interpreter, who felt free to expand and modify the text in order to bring out what he believed to be its meaning. After the text was officially standardized, in the period between the Qumran and the Murabbaat manuscripts, such exegetical expansions and modifications were no longer permitted; but the fact that they had been common in some quarters before that time is abundantly shown by the Septuagint and the Samaritan Pentateuch. The Qumran sectarians did not feel obligated to preserve any particular form of the sacred text; what seemed to them to convey the meaning, as they understood it, was assumed to be right. Consequently their manuscripts, and above all the great St. Mark's scroll of Isaiah, contained many minor additions and modifications. Usually these were derived from other passages in the same book or in other books. Skehan has listed twenty-seven unique readings of the St. Mark's Isaiah scroll which are clearly drawn from other parts of the book or from the other prophetic books.

Several variant readings in this manuscript which were not adopted in the Revised Standard Version have been defended recently by scholars with more or less success, and in some cases rather far-reaching conclusions have been drawn from them. A few of these may be briefly considered to illustrate the continuing importance of the scroll.

A Danish scholar, Flemming Hvidberg, has proposed a new and startling interpretation of Isaiah 6:13 on the basis of the reading of this scroll. The verse speaks of the threatened desolation of Judah. In the Revised Standard Version, following the Masoretic text, it reads as follows:

> And though a tenth remain in it,
>   it will be burned again,
> like a terebinth or an oak,
>   whose stump remains standing
>   when it is felled.
> The holy seed is its stump.

Translated very literally, the fourth and fifth lines would read, "which in felling a stump is in them." Now in place of the phrase "in felling" the St. Mark's scroll, with a difference of only one Hebrew letter, reads "thrown" or "flung down." The phrase "in them," as often in this scroll, is written in a longer form than in the standard text; this, however, makes it identical in spelling and sound with the word for "high place." Hvidberg supposes that this was the meaning intended here. He points out also that the word translated "stump" does not have this meaning anywhere else but is the common word for the sacred stone pillar of the Canaanites; the word for "felling" also occurs only here, and the root from which it is derived is not used elsewhere of felling trees. The lines would then mean, literally, "which thrown a pillar of a high place." Hvidberg takes this to mean "which lie flung down upon the pillar in the high place."

The last line then means, "the holy seed is its [i.e., the high place's] pillar." The "holy seed," says Hvidberg, means the seed sown in the pagan "gardens of Adonis" referred to in Isaiah 17:10–11; it stands for the god Adonis himself, who was killed and buried. The prophet, according to this interpretation, is saying that the catastrophe which will come upon the land will overwhelm the pagan practices and objects on which God's unfaithful people are relying; the last remnant of Judah will be like sacred trees and pillars of the high places and the "holy seed" of Adonis.

Several things must be said about this interpretation and its basis in the Qumran scroll. Its ingenuity is undeniable. The verse is difficult and obscure at best. Hvidberg's objections to the words "felling" and "stump" are well taken, if better explanations can be found. The references to the sacred pillar and the high place together are striking, if they are really in the text. But the word taken to mean "high place" may still at least equally well mean "in them," as the Masoretic text takes it.

There are grammatical difficulties also. The word "thrown" has the feminine singular form; it agrees with the word "terebinth," but not with the nearer word "oak," which is masculine, and for the two together this form would not be used. Hvidberg's translation, "the terebinth and the oak, that lie flung down," is therefore unacceptable. The only alternative is to translate "a terebinth or an oak that lies flung down." But this is a small point.

A more serious difficulty is that "flung down a pillar of a high place" does not mean "flung down upon the pillar in the high place." The text of the Qumran scroll here, if it means anything, must mean "in which a pillar is thrown down," though that does not make much sense. The net result of all this is that the scroll's reading cannot carry the weight of Hvidberg's far-fetched inferences. I have dealt with his interpretation at some length because it seems to me a good example of the way the Dead Sea Scrolls should not be used for textual criticism and exegesis.

More impressive is the treatment of the same verse by W. F. Albright, agreeing in part with S. Iwry. Like Hvidberg, he takes the phrase corresponding to the Masoretic "in them" to be the word "high place." He also accepts the reading "thrown" of the St. Mark's scroll, but by changing a vowel he gives it the feminine plural form, and he takes it to mean not "cast down" but "cast out." The terebinth is taken to mean a tree goddess; the relative pronoun, by the addition of a syllable, is turned into the name of the goddess Asherah; and the preposition "with" is prefixed to the word "pillar," which is also made plural. Thus Albright gets what he calls a "really classical" description of a high place:

> Like the terebinth goddess and the oak of Asherah,
> cast out with the stelae of the high place.

This at least provides a clear, plausible meaning. The changes in the text are not as violent as they seem at first sight, though the justifications alleged for them are at some points rather forced. The difficulties pointed out by Hvidberg are met.

Iwry's reconstruction of the verse is simpler than Albright's. With very slight and thoroughly credible emendations he secures the meaning,

> like a terebinth, or an oak, or an Asherah,
> when flung down from the sacred column of a high place.

The only difficulty for me in accepting this suggestion is that it is hard to see why and how the trees would be flung down from the sacred column or stone pillar. Albright avoids this difficulty by having the trees (or idols) thrown out *with* the pillars, but this requires a somewhat more drastic emendation of the text.

The net result for both Albright and Iwry is not far from the main point of Hvidberg's interpretation: the pagan objects of the people's religion will be destroyed with them. At best, however, the introduction of these adjuncts of pagan worship is abrupt. If any such reconstruction as Albright's or Iwry's is correct, as it may well be, the failure of scribes to understand the text and transmit it accurately is not hard to understand. The St. Mark's scroll will then have afforded a valuable clue for the recovery of the correct reading.

A quite different kind of defense of a reading consists in showing that it may be explained by reference to a cognate Semitic language. Isaiah 24:6 contains the clause, "therefore the inhabitants of the earth are scorched." In the St. Mark's scroll the verb "are scorched" has a vowel letter (*DSS*, pp. 110–13) which apparently indicates a different pronunciation from that of the Masoretic vowel points. Alfred Guillaume has suggested that the form in the scroll would be correct for a verb corresponding to one known in Arabic which means "be decreased in number." This would make the clause mean, "therefore the inhabitants of the earth are decreased in number," which would be a very close parallel to the following line, "and few men are left." Guillaume does not claim that this explanation is anything more than a possibility, but that much must surely be admitted.

The Revised Standard Version is criticized by F. F. Bruce for not adopting or even mentioning in a note the reading of the St. Mark's scroll in Isaiah 40:12, where, instead of "the waters" (Hebrew *mym*), the scroll has "the waters of the sea" (*my ym*). Many scholars have found this attractive, but there is no ground for adopting it other than a subjective preference, which is hardly adequate. It may be added that the Revised Standard Version never gives a footnote mentioning a variant reading which is not adopted. To do so would necessitate an enormous number of notes.

Isaiah 41:27 begins, literally, "First to Zion, behold them, behold them." The Septuagint reads, "I will give Zion the rulership," or "I will make Zion first." The Vulgate reads, "The first shall say to Zion, Behold, they are here"; the King James Version follows this lead, translating, "The first *shall say* to Zion, Behold, behold them." The English Revised Version reads simply, "*I* first *will say* unto Zion . . ." The American Standard Version is more elaborate: "*I am the* first *that saith* unto Zion." The Revised Standard Version gets about the same meaning by a hazardous conjectural emendation of the Hebrew, reading, "I first have declared it to Zion." The St. Mark's scroll has a unique reading: it differs from the Masoretic text only by the addition of two letters, but uses a verb that appears nowhere else in the Old Testament or in other Hebrew literature. Guillaume points out that in Arabic this verb means "to bring tidings"; thus the scroll has again a close parallel for the next line:

> First to Zion, behold, a bringer of tidings,
>    and to Jerusalem a teller of good tidings I give.

In *DSS* (pp. 313f) a much debated reading of the scroll in Isaiah 52:14 was briefly discussed. Instead of the traditional reading "marred," the St. Mark's scroll has what would ordinarily mean "I have anointed." Here again Guillaume proposes a new explanation. The verb intended, he suggests, is not the familiar one meaning "anoint" but another which would be spelled the same way in Hebrew. It does not occur elsewhere in extant Hebrew literature, but in Arabic it is used of galling a camel's back or fraying a thread, and an adjective derived from it means "ugly." So understood, the reading of the scroll would mean "I have marred," which would differ from the standard text only in being an active verb, with God as the subject, instead of a passive participle. It does not follow, of course, that the reading of the scroll is older or more authentic than the traditional text. Conceivably a scribe of Qumran, acquainted with the verb known to us only in Arabic, understood the word in Isaiah as a form of this verb. The change from the passive participle to the active verb in the first person singular, or vice versa, still requires explanation.

An especially interesting example of important conclusions

deduced from a variant reading of the great Isaiah scroll is afforded by W. F. Albright's study of the ancient Palestinian "high
place," presented first as a lecture at the international congress of
Old Testament scholars at Strasbourg in the summer of 1956.
What gives it unusual interest is its combination of textual criticism and archeology. With the archeological side of Albright's
argument we are not here concerned; suffice it to say that he interprets the high place as a shrine for the cult of the dead. His
treatment of Isaiah 6:13 has already been discussed. Here we
may note his interpretation of a more important passage. In one
of the most familiar chapters of the Old Testament, Isaiah 53,
there is the following rather obscure statement (verse 9):

> And he made his grave with the wicked
> and with a rich man in his death.

The St. Mark's scroll reads:

> And they made his grave with the wicked
> and with rich men his high place.

Albright retains the singular verb of the Masoretic text at the
beginning but changes it to a passive form, so that it means "his
grave was made." He adopts also a conjectural emendation which
other scholars have advocated, making the word for "rich men,"
by a transposition of two consonants, mean "satyrs" (rustic goat-
deities referred to elsewhere in the Old Testament). Others find
this not only unnecessary but also undesirable, because it destroys
the parallelism of "wicked" and "rich" characteristic of some parts
of the Old Testament. This question, however, has nothing to do
with the Dead Sea Scrolls.

The reading "his high place" instead of "in his death" is the
crucial point. The word for "high place" is not spelled as in the
Masoretic text but in accordance with the usual spelling of this
manuscript; there is no reason to question the meaning intended.
The parallelism of "grave" in the first line and "high place" in the
second is impressive and strengthens the case for regarding the
high place as a mortuary shrine. It seems highly probable that
"his high place" instead of "in his death," was the reading of the
original text of this verse.

A variant reading of the St. Mark's scroll in Isaiah 53:11 is cited by Bruce as one that the Revised Standard Version might have been expected to adopt, or at least to mention. Here the King James Version reads, "He shall see of the travail of his soul and shall be satisfied." The Revised Standard Version tries to clarify this by inserting words: "He shall see the fruit of the travail of his soul." The Masoretic text says literally, "From the travail of his soul he shall see, he shall be satisfied." After the verb "see" both of the Isaiah manuscripts of Qumran Cave 1 insert the word "light," making the clause read, "From the travail of his soul he shall see light." This undoubtedly makes sense, but it is a bit too facile to be convincing. The suspicion arises that some scribe, in the tradition back of both the Cave 1 scrolls, felt compelled to insert an object for the verb, though it is not really necessary. And, be it said again, the footnotes of the Revised Standard Version never list variant readings that have been rejected.

The first line of Isaiah 64:2 (verse 1 in the Hebrew) reads in the Revised Standard Version, "as when fire kindles brushwood." The rendering "brushwood," however, is a mere guess, suggested by the context; the word is used nowhere else, and its derivation is unknown. The King James Version, following in part the Greek and Latin versions, translates, "as when the melting fire burneth." The St. Mark's scroll of Isaiah, however, uses here a word differing from that of the traditional text by one letter. Once more Guillaume has pointed out that this corresponds to an Arabic word meaning "brushwood." The meaning "brushwood" is thus supported, and the word in the scroll quite possibly preserves the original reading. It is not impossible, of course, that a scribe somewhere along the line drew the same inference from the context that modern scholars have drawn and substituted for the word preserved by the Masoretes one that gave the desired meaning. The fact that he would have to change only one letter to do this, however, makes it more likely that the change was made in the opposite direction, and that the reading of the Masoretic text is a mistake.

In contrast to such textual reconstruction on the basis of the St. Mark's Isaiah scroll, some scholars have been much more

cautious. A discussion of the subject with very conservative conclusions is given by P. A. H. de Boer in his book, *Second-Isaiah's
Message*.

The book of Jeremiah is not so well represented at Qumran; it
was apparently less popular than Isaiah. Considerable portions of
the last part of Jeremiah were preserved in fragments found in
Cave 2, and there were pieces of three manuscripts of Jeremiah
in Cave 4, as well as a few scraps of a Greek translation. The
text of the Cave 2 manuscript, as compared with the Masoretic
text, exhibits some peculiarities in spelling and grammar, a number of scribal errors, and some variant readings which affect the
meaning; on the whole, however, it represents the same textual
tradition as the Masoretic text. One of the three Hebrew manuscripts of Jeremiah from Cave 4 is very old. The textual relationships of these manuscripts are complicated and have not yet been
thoroughly worked out. The few surviving scraps of a Greek
manuscript of Jeremiah apparently follow the text of the Septuagint. The departures of the Septuagint from the standard Hebrew
text are especially numerous and radical in Jeremiah; it will therefore be all the more interesting to find how far the Qumran manuscripts support the Masoretic text of this book.

Fragments of the book of Lamentations were found in Caves 3,
4, and 5. Again the traditional text preserved in manuscripts several centuries later seems to be supported by the ancient texts
recovered from the caves. Caves 1 and 4 yielded fragments of the
book of Ezekiel, but they offer nothing of particular significance
for the history or the reconstruction of the text. Daniel is represented by scraps of two manuscripts from Cave 1, four from Cave
4, and one from Cave 6. There are some variant readings agreeing
with the Septuagint, but otherwise these manuscripts agree with
the standard text. Even the perplexing shift from Hebrew to
Aramaic at 2:4 and back to Hebrew at 8:1 appears in the fragments exactly as in the late manuscripts.

The minor prophets were well represented in the Cave 4 fragments; elsewhere there were only a few scraps of Jonah in Cave 2
to add to the bits of Hosea and Micah and the full text of Habakkuk 1–2 in the commentaries of Cave 1. Cave 4 also, of course,

had commentaries, including those on Hosea and Nahum among the minor prophets. The Cave 4 manuscripts of the "Book of the Twelve" include at least parts of all the minor prophets, with the possible exception of Obadiah, Habakkuk, and Haggai, which are not explicitly mentioned in the reports I have seen. Skehan says that the text of a Herodian manuscript on which he has been working is "quite ordinary"; Cross, however, finds a complex textual problem in the seven manuscripts with which he has been engaged. No specific variant readings of particular interest in any of these manuscripts have been published as yet.

The biblical text contained in the Qumran commentaries has been mentioned. The phylacteries and the several selections of proof-texts and the like must be considered also, as well as scattered quotations in many other works. These will all have to be combed through eventually in search of significant variant readings, though the freedom in which the men of Qumran sometimes indulged when quoting the Scriptures must be kept in mind. Skehan, who has examined particularly the quotations from Isaiah in non-biblical documents, finds that aside from a few details here and there we cannot learn much from them concerning the history of the Hebrew text of the Old Testament.

A few samples of such variant readings as have been found may be given here to conclude our consideration of the text of the minor prophets. Amos 9:11 is quoted both in the Damascus Document and in the Florilegium. In both places the quotation reads, "And I will raise up the booth of David." Instead of "And I will," both the Masoretic text and the Septuagint say, "In that day I will." What makes this little variation interesting is that the quotation of the same verse in Acts 15:16 agrees with the Damascus Document and the Florilegium against the Masoretic text and the Septuagint.

The Cave 1 Commentary on Micah, quoting Micah 1:3, "For behold, the Lord is coming forth out of his place, and will come down and tread upon the high places of the earth," omits "and tread." Now, as Milik points out, the Septuagint and the Vulgate also exhibit the same omission. Some scholars have long favored the omission of this verb on the ground that it makes the line too long for the metrical structure. This is not in itself a strong argument, but it is a point to be noted along with other considerations.

Orlinsky denies, however, that this affords any evidence of a common Hebrew text behind the Greek and Latin versions and the Qumran commentary; the same verb merely happens to have been omitted in the commentary and in the Septuagint, which was followed by the Vulgate. Orlinsky also calls attention to the fact that some manuscripts of the Septuagint omit not "and tread" but the preceding "and will come down." The two verbs end in the same way in Greek, and a copyist's eye might easily slip from one to the other, causing another instance of *homoioteleuton,* the common error already mentioned (p. 140). Orlinsky's inference is that this is what happened in the Greek manuscripts, sometimes one word and sometimes the other being skipped.

Admitting that this is possible, I would suggest another possibility which seems to me more likely. The two verbs in Hebrew look very much alike and might easily be confused by scribes. If either of them stood alone in the original text of Micah, a scribe might have mistaken it for the other one. Thus two readings would arise: some manuscripts would read "and come down," others "and tread." Then, by the common process called conflation, a scribe, not sure which reading was correct, would include both in his copy, thus producing what we now have in the Masoretic text. The reading of the Qumran commentary may indicate which of the two verbs was original.

An even slighter variation appears at the end of the same verse. In the concluding phrase, "upon the high places of the earth," the Masoretic text omits the definite article before "earth." This is quite in accord with poetic usage in Hebrew, but the missing article is supplied in the Septuagint. It is also supplied in a tiny scrap of the Micah Commentary from Cave 1.

In this instance we must fully agree with Orlinsky that the agreement is accidental. A scribe at Qumran, not too sensitive to the poetic idiom of an earlier age, probably inserted the article quite unconsciously. The Greek translator inserted it because it seemed necessary in Greek. Orlinsky calls attention to the fact that in all our standard English translations the article is inserted, not because it is in the Septuagint and certainly not because the translators were using a Hebrew text which had it. The difference obviously has no significance whatever for the meaning of the text. The only reason for mentioning it here is the warning it provides against using such variations mechanically as evidence.

# XIV

## *General Results for Textual Criticism*

⎍⎍⎍⎍⎍⎍⎍⎍⎍⎍⎍⎍⎍⎍⎍⎍⎍⎍⎍⎍⎍⎍⎍⎍⎍⎍⎍⎍

An enormous amount of work remains to be done on the biblical texts of Qumran. They will afford material for research for many years to come. A few general conclusions, however, have already emerged with a fair degree of clarity and certainty. What is most astonishing, and perhaps most valuable, is the variety of textual types and traditions represented. Skehan remarks that no one manuscript was clearly copied from any other in the collection, nor were any two evidently copied from the same manuscript. They were written at various times over a space of three centuries or more. There is no evidence that for any book of the Bible the community accepted a fixed text as authoritative.

It would be a sad mistake, however, to attribute this diversity to mere indifference and carelessness in quoting and copying. Mistakes were made; deliberate modifications were undoubtedly introduced. There was no sense of a divine origin and authority of words and letters which must be preserved with meticulous accuracy.

Yet on the whole there was a surprising and encouraging degree of fidelity in transmitting the text. Otherwise we should find much more divergence, amounting in time to virtual chaos. We should not find in so many instances such close agreement with later manuscripts, and where differences occur they would not so often coincide with variants found in other traditions or ancient translations.

Clearly, with all the variety, certain fairly definite lines of textual tradition were proceeding side by side in the Qumran community. The prototype of what was later to be recognized as the standard text was there. The types of text represented by the Samaritan Pentateuch and the Septuagint were known also. In some manuscripts one line of tradition may be fairly faithfully reproduced; in others there is a perplexing mixture of traditions. A straight line of development, arranging all the manuscripts in chronological order and showing how one form of the text grew out of another, cannot be reconstructed. If the relationships of the different texts of each book could be determined exactly and presented in genealogical form, we should probably have a collection of pedigrees with a great deal of intermarriage in successive generations.

It is hard to tell whether or not these divergent traditions reflect distinct "recensions" in the proper sense of the word—that is, deliberate revisions made by editors to establish a correct text. The Masoretic text is definitely such a recension, officially established by the rabbis of the early Christian centuries, though not all at one time. The many Qumran manuscripts which substantially agree with the Masoretic text show that it was based on a much earlier tradition, conveniently called proto-Masoretic. The question is whether this tradition itself rested on an earlier recension, and whether the texts which agree more closely with the Samaritan Pentateuch or with the Septuagint are the results of other definite recensions.

W. F. Albright argues that the presence of the proto-Masoretic text at Qumran supports the ancient tradition that the older books of the Old Testament were edited in Babylonia during the exile and brought back to Palestine in the late sixth and fifth centuries B.C. Many modern scholars, as Albright remarks, have believed that there was such an exilic editing of these books; it should be pointed out, however, that most would associate the process with the compilation and composition of the books themselves rather than the establishment of a particular form of the text.

In the St. Mark's scroll of Isaiah, with its correct ancient spelling of Assyrian names (*DSS*, p. 114), Albright sees evidence that this scroll was a copy of one brought to Palestine from

Babylonia, probably between 150 and 100 B.C. In that case, it may be observed, the manuscript was written very soon after its prototype reached Palestine. One wonders whether it was itself made in Babylonia. On the whole it represents the proto-Masoretic Babylonian text; the differences may be attributed to a continuing development of the tradition in Babylonia after the first copies of the Scriptures were taken to Palestine in the fifth century. The Samaritan text of the Pentateuch, with which one Qumran manuscript of Exodus has affinities, was only a slightly divergent form of the proto-Masoretic text.

But what of the Qumran texts that are more closely related to the Septuagint? They prove in the first place, says Albright, that the Septuagint is not a free rendering of the proto-Masoretic text but a very faithful rendering of quite different Hebrew originals. Consequently the marks of Egyptian influence in the Septuagint cannot be supposed to have arisen in the process of translation or in the transmission of the Greek text; they too must be attributed to the Hebrew text used by the translators, which may therefore be regarded as an Egyptian recension. Albright finds reason to believe that in the Pentateuch and the books of Samuel and Kings the revision was made not much earlier or later than the fifth century B.C. The Egyptian recensions of other books might be earlier or later; that of Jeremiah perhaps as early as the sixth century, and that of Isaiah as late as the third.

Such manuscripts as the two of Samuel from Cave 4, Albright believes, belong neither to the proto-Masoretic text of other Qumran scrolls and fragments nor to the recension from which the Septuagint was made, but exhibit a form of the text earlier than either of these. They may even, he thinks, preserve some features which go back to the original Deuteronomic book of Samuel. Whether this conjecture is correct can be determined only by further research and discussion. In the meantime it is conceivable that the text of these Samuel fragments and others is the result of a mixture of different recensions or traditions; in other words, it may be their descendant instead of their common ancestor.

Whatever may be the ultimate result of continuing research

on these complicated problems, it is clear that, as Murphy summarizes the matter, we now have three main lines of evidence to follow in trying to trace the streams of textual tradition back to their source: (1) the Masoretic text itself, which is not a creation of the rabbis but follows an ancient tradition; (2) the Septuagint, whose origin and value are illuminated by the Qumran discoveries; and (3) those Qumran texts which still exhibit a relatively fluid stage in the transmission of the text.

The fact that there was still such a shifting variety of textual traditions at Qumran cannot be taken as characteristic of Judaism in general. Moshe Greenberg reminds us that the sect which left us this treasure of manuscripts had rejected the authority of the Jerusalem priesthood and withdrawn from the main stream of Jewish history. Forms of the text which it was willing to use and copy may have been already rejected by the more orthodox leaders of Judaism. Greenberg believes that the work of the scribes who corrected and edited the text of the Scriptures began as early as the third century B.C. and gained momentum under the Hasmoneans in the second century. The standardized text did not prevail until after the fall of Jerusalem, but as Greenberg puts it, "The prevalence of the standard, not its creation, came after 70 A.D." This agrees with what was said about the Masoretic text in *DSS* (pp. 102–104).

Definite evidence for the time when the process of standardization had reached its goal, and only the officially approved text continued in use, is provided by the manuscripts of the Wady Murabbaat. These come not from a dissident group like that of Qumran, but from the ardent patriots of the Second Revolt, whose leaders, as Greenberg reminds us, included very eminent rabbis. Such unorthodox writings as Qumran affords in abundance were not found in the Murabbaat caves. Here also the text of the Scriptures, still fluid at Qumran, has thoroughly congealed. By the end of the first third of the second century A.D. the text which was to prevail from then on to the present day had practically achieved its final form. As Fritsch says, the work of Rabbi Aqiba in the second century A.D. marks the end of the process of standardization, not its beginning. What remained for the rabbis and

Masoretes of subsequent centuries was only to weed out the few remaining variations in the consonantal text, and later to fix the tradition of the vowels by adding vowel points.

That being so, the diversified texts of the Qumran manuscripts are of great value for the recovery of ancient variant readings which the orthodox scribes rejected and suppressed. Many of these, and many others also, were no doubt preserved by the Septuagint, but their origin and value were problematical. In the Qumran texts we now have such variants in the original Hebrew. No longer do we have to resort to the precarious device of translating the Greek of the Septuagint back into Hebrew. Paul Kahle pointed out this great advantage soon after the discovery of the St. Mark's Isaiah scroll (*DSS*, p. 304). It is now shared by all the fragments from Cave 4 and other caves that preserve readings diverging from the Masoretic text.

It should not be necessary, but perhaps it is, to say again that an old reading is not necessarily a good one. The Qumran texts are full of variant readings which are demonstrably inferior to those of the traditional text. To put the same thing in another way, paradoxical but true, a "pre-Masoretic" reading is not necessarily older than a Masoretic reading. The proto-Masoretic text existed at Qumran and elsewhere along with the divergent texts; on the whole it is fair to say that it was the trunk and they were branches that had sprung out of it. The greatest contribution of the Dead Sea Scrolls to textual criticism is still their demonstration of this fact.

Sometimes, however, the Masoretes and their predecessors must have chosen the wrong reading and discarded the right one. They were conscientious and wise, but they were not infallible. Sometimes the original wording of a verse may have been already lost in all the manuscripts at their disposal. Here and there we may fairly hope to recover from the Qumran manuscripts an older and better text, closer to the original form and meaning.

Every such variant must be carefully examined and judged on its own merits. A reading which seems clearer and more meaningful than the Masoretic text is not necessarily better: an early scribe may have tried to correct what seemed to him an obvious mistake. So often did that happen in ancient manuscripts that it is an established principle of textual criticism, in case of doubt between two alternative readings, to prefer the harsher one as less likely to be the result of a scribal alteration.

Texts were often corrupted by accidental mistakes caused by the carelessness or weariness of the scribe. Both accidental and deliberate changes were all the more likely when there was no dogma of the literal inerrancy of the traditional text. Such exaggerated emphasis upon the exact words and even the forms of the letters as we find among the later rabbis is not in evidence at Qumran. A commentator sometimes quotes a verse in one form and then gives an interpretation which presupposes a different reading. Greenberg reminds us that piety and a critical sense do not always go together. Even in later times pious Jews often ignored questions of textual accuracy. Devout readers of the Bible in our own day, for that matter, often cling to a translation which has meaning and associations for them, even though it has been proved to be wrong.

Every variant reading which is at all likely to represent a better text must therefore be carefully scrutinized before it is accepted. Examples which exhibit some of the problems involved have been given in the foregoing pages. It is essential to determine, if possible, whether the variant represents a tradition or is merely a mistake. Agreement with the ancient versions, especially the Septuagint, is significant at this point.

Even here, however, it may be necessary to consider the question raised by Del Medico, whether the Hebrew text may have been emended under the influence of the versions. In that case, the agreements with the Septuagint noted in many Qumran fragments would not prove that the Qumran scribes preserved a more accurate textual tradition than the Masoretic text, but merely that they used a Greek translation which the orthodox rabbis condemned. The presence of some fragments of the Septuagint in the caves proves that it was known in the community. As Milik points out, however, not more than four manuscripts altogether have been found, two of Leviticus and one of Numbers in Cave 4 and a few fragments of Exodus in Cave 7. This does not indicate that much use was made of the Septuagint in the community.

When all due caution is applied in their use, the biblical manuscripts of the Qumran caves have a unique value for textual criticism. They admit us directly to a stage in the transmission of the text just preceding its final fixation. Their importance is evident in the fact that critical discussion of the Old Testament text, commentaries, Bible dictionaries, and even atlases now find it necessary to give attention to this new evidence.

# XV

## Interpretation, Composition, and Dates

Not only the text and languages of the Old Testament are illuminated by the Qumran texts but also the history of its interpretation. Interesting conceptions and methods of exegesis are exemplified in many of the manuscripts. The men of Qumran had withdrawn to the wilderness of Judea to prepare the way of the Lord by the study of the law, as the Manual of Discipline says (column viii, lines 14–15; *DSS*, p. 382). Some of their literature, therefore, consists of regulations and directions for personal conduct and for the life and worship of the community.

The Manual of Discipline itself is the most extensive and important text of this sort. It is supplemented by the Rule of the Congregation and the Benedictions and by various fragments of similar writings from other caves. Such liturgical works as the Three Tongues of Fire and the Mishmaroth may be included in this category.

The directions and rules recorded in these documents are not presented in the form of systematic deductions from the laws of Moses or other parts of the sacred canon, though an incidental citation of Scripture appears occasionally. It is quite clear, however, from the high veneration for the law frequently expressed, that the sect considered its own rules a legitimate application and expansion of the inspired law.

The most remarkable exhibit of the community's principles and methods of exegesis is afforded by the commentaries on books of the Old Testament. Most of them are expositions of the prophetic books. The Habakkuk Commentary (translated in *DSS*, pp. 365–370) is the best known and complete of them all, but there were also the scant remains of commentaries on Micah and Zephaniah in Cave 1, on Isaiah in Caves 3 and 4, and on Hosea and Nahum in Cave 4. Commentaries on other parts of the canon are represented only by the one on Genesis 49 and the commentaries on Psalms in Caves 1 and 4.

Milik and Cross believe that many if not all of these manuscripts are, so to speak, first editions; they are the authors' own first copies. The compositions they contain, Milik says, are personal in nature rather than in any sense official. One may be permitted to doubt this, at least until further evidence is forthcoming. For the Habakkuk Commentary it seems to me distinctly improbable.

Milik suggests also that these compositions had some connection with the reading and interpretation of the Bible in the regular meetings of the community. It is hardly to be supposed, however, that they were like the assigned papers read by members of a club at its meetings, or that when a member said, "I have a word to speak to the masters" (Manual of Discipline vi.13; *DSS*, p. 379), he meant "I have written a commentary which I should like permission to read at this time." If there was any connection between the commentaries and the formal meetings of the sect, it seems more likely that the commentary would be written after the biblical book with which it deals had been discussed, and its interpretations would then embody the ideas and conclusions of the community. On the whole, however, the individual nature and origin of these documents is easier to believe than any such connection with the group's common sessions.

The interpretations given evince considerable freedom in the handling, not to say manipulation, of the texts. Each sentence or phrase is taken by itself, without inhibitions imposed by the context. Similarity of meaning or of sound may suggest an application; words may be combined or separated without regard to the plain intention of the author. Even the spelling of words may be juggled to produce a new meaning.

Milik distinguishes three types of interpretation in these documents. The commentaries on Habakkuk, Micah, and the Psalms explain the text as referring to the history of the sect itself. The commentary on Nahum applies the text to a different ethnic group in the framework of contemporary history. The commentaries on Isaiah interpret the prophet's words eschatologically. These distinctions, though perhaps useful to some degree, seem to me overdrawn. The Habakkuk Commentary, the only one which is even approximately complete, exhibits all three types of interpretation. The teacher of righteousness belongs to the history of the sect; the wicked priest and the Kittim put it in the framework of contemporary national history; the eschatological application appears in many references to the last days—indeed the whole past and present experience of the sect is conceived as eschatological.

Still another type of exegesis appears in the paraphrases of biblical material. The Aramaic Genesis Apocryphon is the best example of this way of treating Scripture; others are the Cave 4 texts mentioned on page 35. A certain amount of commentary is given with the selected texts included in the Florilegium. An interpretation is implied also to some degree in the selection of texts used in the Messianic Testimonia.

Apart from such interpretations, which we can rarely if ever accept as sound exegesis, the non-biblical texts occasionally offer indirect evidence of the meaning of obscure expressions in the Old Testament. Two examples may be mentioned to show what is possible in this direction.

Several passages in the Old Testament refer to the knowledge of good and evil. Sometimes, as in Deuteronomy 1:39 and Isaiah 7:15–16, this expression is used to indicate the age of a child or youth. Commentators have debated its meaning at great length, but with no final agreement. The Rule of the Congregation says that a boy is to become a member of the community at the age of twenty; he is then ready for marriage and all the responsibilities of manhood. "But he shall not approach a woman to know her by lying with her except when he has fully reached the age of twenty years, when he knows good and evil." On the basis of this passage G. W. Buchanan has raised the question whether the age of knowing good and evil in the Old Testament is twenty years. His conclusion is that this is nowhere an impossible interpretation, and in some places it definitely clarifies the meaning.

R. Gordis accepts this interpretation and declares that it settles the disputed meaning of the knowledge of good and evil in the story of the garden of Eden (Genesis 3). The connection with sexual maturity, he argues, shows that the reference in Genesis is to sexual awareness, with its good and evil consequences. In Genesis and in traditional Judaism, according to Gordis, the age of such maturity and knowledge was not twenty but thirteen. It was raised to twenty in the Qumran community, he suggests, because the sect postponed marriage as long as possible.

The specifically sexual interpretation of the knowledge of good and evil has always seemed and still seems to me unconvincing. No doubt this element was included, but a broader conception of the ability to distinguish good and bad, wise and foolish, and to make right choices—in short, general mental and moral maturity, or, as Buchanan puts it, mature judgment—was, I think, the basic idea. It may be noted that in Isaiah 7:15f the knowledge in question is not simply "knowledge of good and evil" but knowing "how to refuse the evil and choose the good." What is meant corresponds to what we call attaining the years of discretion.

Whether the age at which this knowledge was attained was thought of as thirteen or twenty years old in Isaiah's time is another question, not necessarily answered by the much later view of the Qumran community. Buchanan has shown good reason, however, for believing that the Qumran Rule of the Congregation preserves an ancient tradition representing the meaning of the Old Testament expression. In Deuteronomy 1:39 "your children, who this day have no knowledge of good or evil," are not the same as "your little ones," but are the older children and youths below the age of twenty. In Isaiah 7:15f "when he knows how to refuse the evil and choose the good" means "by the time he is twenty years old." If this is correct, the Qumran document has helped us to understand better a somewhat obscure expression in the Old Testament.

In another instance a text of Qumran seems to explain the origin of a still more obscure biblical expression. In this case it is not the actual meaning of the expression as it is used in the Old Testament that is explained, but rather its meaning in an older story that has been adopted by the biblical writer and modified to suit his purpose. The famous writing on the wall in Daniel 5:25, *"Mene, mene, tekel* and *parsin,"* is interpreted in the following verses with reference to the end of Belshazzar's kingdom. In an earlier form of the story, however, the three mysterious words probably indicated three weights, the mina, the shekel, and the peres or half-mina, each of which had also a monetary value; and these three weights symbolized three rulers of the Neo-Babylonian empire.

H. L. Ginsberg identifies these rulers as Nebuchadnezzar, Evil-Merodach, and Belshazzar; but D. N. Freedman has pointed out that Evil-Merodach does not appear in the book of Daniel and played a very small part in history. On the basis of a Cave 4 text, the Prayer of Nabonidus, Freedman suggests that the second king in the older story was Nabonidus, the father of Belshazzar. Nabonidus too is ignored by the book of Daniel, but he probably had a place in the earlier stories. Chapters 3 and 4 both tell of Nebuchadnezzar, but the Prayer of Nabonidus makes it probable that the story back of chapter 4 was told originally of Nabonidus.

For those who take the book of Daniel literally as history, all this will have no value; for those who understand it as a collection of stories and visions, told to comfort and reassure the author's contemporaries, the new material will be significant. It does not illuminate the meaning of the expression as it is used in Daniel, but it helps us to understand the literary and historical background of the story of Belshazzar's feast. We shall come back to it presently in this connection.

Here we move from exegesis to questions of the composition and date of the Old Testament books. In this area too the Qumran manuscripts have something to offer. For some time it was believed by many scholars that the book of Psalms, for example, contained some quite late material. Many Psalms were attributed to the time of the Maccabean revolt and the Hasmonean kingdom in the second century B.C. More recently there has been a pronounced tendency to push back the dates of the Psalms, though a few critics still believe that there are Maccabean Psalms in the Old Testament.

The Thanksgiving Psalms of Qumran use many expressions from the canonical Psalms, as well as from other parts of the Old Testament. At the same time they exhibit a new type of composition, clearly representing a later literary and religious development. They are themselves, however, not much later in origin than the Hasmonean period and may well have been composed in that period. Thus, indirectly, they indicate that the Old Testament Psalms were of earlier origin. More specific evidence is provided by the Qumran manuscripts of the Psalms. One of these, which is itself apparently from the Hasmonean period, already has the Psalms, on the whole, in the same order and with the same titles as in the Masoretic text. This suggests that not only the individual Psalms but the final compilation of the book were pre-Maccabean.

There are some problems, however. In this manuscript Psalm 32 is missing between Psalm 31 and 33, and this is true also of what Skehan vaguely describes as "another, unpublished, ancient portion of a Psalter, not from Cave 4 at Qumran." Does this indicate that Psalm 32 was written too late to be included in such an old manuscript? It has a few of what have been considered characteristic marks of the Maccabean Psalms, such as the use of the word *ḥasid* (godly, devout). There is no compelling reason to date it so late, however, and there may have been some other reason for its absence from these two old manuscripts; in fact, it may have been included at another place in these manuscripts, in a part of the book that has not survived.

There are a few differences in the arrangement of the Psalms between the Hasmonean Qumran manuscript and the Masoretic text. Psalm 71 is attached without any break to the end of Psalm 38. Skehan suggests that the similarity between the last verses of Psalms 38 and 70 may have caused a copyist or reciter, when he came to the end of Psalm 38, to continue automatically with Psalm 71. Unfortunately the last surviving fragment of the manuscript ends with Psalm 69, so that we do not know whether Psalm 71 was omitted or repeated after Psalm 70. It is entirely possible that for one reason or another both Psalms 32 and 71 were simply moved to places different from those they occupy in the Masoretic text of the Psalms.

In a fragment of another Cave 4 manuscript the end of Psalm 147 is followed by the beginning of Psalm 104. All the other fragments of this manuscript that have been recovered contain parts of one or the other of these two Psalms; it is therefore uncertain whether the scroll was in fact a copy of the whole book of Psalms or of a group of Psalms selected and arranged for a particular purpose.

The scraps of commentaries on some of the Psalms found in Caves 1 and 4 afford further evidence of the antiquity of these Psalms. All that can be said to be proved by them is that the particular Psalms to which the recovered fragments actually refer were composed before the commentaries were written. It is unlikely, however, that such commentaries would be written about books which were not regarded as sacred Scripture; indirectly, therefore, the very existence of these commentaries makes it at least highly probable that the book of Psalms as a whole had already attained what may be called canonical status.

Fragments of a scroll of Ecclesiastes from Cave 4 have been mentioned on page 143. The script indicates a date near the middle of the second century B.C. This is not much later than the time at which many scholars have thought the book was originally written. We cannot tell, of course, how old the book was when this particular copy was made, but the probability of its composition in the third century, if not even earlier, is somewhat enhanced by finding a manuscript probably written not much after 150 B.C.

The prophets of the Old Testament all lived long before the time of the Qumran community. Evidence of the time when their words were written down cannot be expected from the Dead Sea Scrolls and fragments. There is internal evidence in many of the prophetic books themselves, however, that material has been incorporated which comes from a later time than the days of the prophets whose names the books bear. How much later it is may be uncertain, but scholars have found much reason to believe that some of the earliest prophetic books include portions from the Hellenistic period (after 331 B.C.). Fritsch holds that the Qumran commentaries on several of the prophets refute the view that these books contain such late material. That would be strictly true only if we found at Qumran the complete texts of these books, containing the passages in question and clearly dated at least as early as Hasmonean times. Only for the book of Isaiah is this the case, and here it is not a commentary but the St. Mark's scroll of Isaiah that gives us the complete text of the book in a manuscript which cannot be dated much after 100 B.C. at the latest.

The question whether this ancient manuscript supported or refuted the critical hypothesis of a "Second Isaiah" was raised very soon after the first discovery of the scrolls. As I said in *DSS* (p. 321), a copy made at about 100 B.C. could not very well present evidence for or against an editorial process carried out two or three centuries earlier. Milik, however, has recently called attention to a few facts which, he thinks, indicate some memory of the fact that the two main portions of the book were originally separate.

The manuscript consists of 54 columns, and chapter 33 ends exactly in the middle, at the bottom of column 27. But this is not only the end of a column; it is the end of one of the strips of leather of which the scroll consists. And this strip is a short one: it bears only two columns of text, whereas the others usually have four. A new strip then begins with chapter 34. Bearing in mind the differences in spelling and grammar which led Kahle to see two different forms of the Hebrew text in the two halves of the scroll (*DSS*, p. 111), one may be tempted to infer that the scribe of the St. Mark's manuscript copied the two parts of the book from two different manuscripts. This would to some extent support the idea of two originally separate works.

It should be remembered, however, that chapters 36–39, taken almost entirely from 2 Kings 18–20, are already present in the St. Mark's scroll after chapter 35. These chapters have to do with the prophet Isaiah and would surely not have been inserted at this point by a scribe or editor who believed that everything from chapter 34 on came from a different prophet. In other words, if the second half of the St. Mark's scroll was taken from a different manuscript, it was one in which Isaiah's authorship of chapters 34 and 35 at least was already taken for granted. This, of course, does not disprove the reality of the Second Isaiah. The generally accepted conclusion of Old Testament scholars that chapters 40–66 and probably 34–35 also come from a period two centuries or more later than the time of Isaiah rests securely on the internal evidence of the book itself and needs no confirmation from ancient manuscripts.

Fragments of the book of Daniel from Caves 1 and 4 alike already have the puzzling shift from the Hebrew language to the Aramaic at 2:4 and back again to Hebrew at 8:1, as has been mentioned. These manuscripts therefore do not take us back to a time when the whole book was written in either Hebrew or Aramaic. The fact is all the more remarkable because these fragments do take us back to within a century or two of the composition of the book, just before the Maccabean revolt. Henri Michaud feels that the bilingualism shown by the presence of both Hebrew and Aramaic texts at Qumran is enough to explain the curious phenomenon. The author of Daniel was as much at home in one language as in the other, and apparently assumed that his readers were likewise. It is rather hard to believe, however, that he would shift from one to the other without reason. Rather than adopt such an assumption, it would seem wise to agree with Milik that the Qumran fragments afford "nothing new on this irritating problem of the book of Daniel."

The Prayer of Nabonidus from Cave 4 has already been mentioned (p. 169). From Babylonian sources we know that Nabonidus, the last ruler of the Neo-Babylonian empire, spent seven years at Teima in Arabia. The Qumran document is based on this episode. From its similarity to the account of Nebuchadnezzar's seven-year affliction and exile in Daniel 4, Milik infers that the author of Daniel found the model for his story in the Prayer of Nabonidus, but substituted Nebuchadnezzar for the less famous Nabonidus, changed the locale of the episode from Teima to Babylon, and gave the monarch's malady "aspects unknown to medicine."

More probable than such a deliberate literary transformation, it seems to me, is a gradual modification of the story in the course of popular tradition. The stories in Daniel 1–6 have much of the character of folklore. The author of this part of the book seems to have gathered for the encouragement of his persecuted compatriots a collection of popular stories of fidelity and heroism. Nothing is more common in popular story-telling than changes of persons and places, particularly the substitution of well-known names for those less known. The same stories are told about Alexander and Napoleon, about famous but eccentric scholars of Oxford or Cambridge and others equally famous and eccentric at Harvard or Yale. This may well have happened with the story of the affliction and prayer of Nabonidus.

D. N. Freedman rejects the idea of a direct connection between Daniel 4 and the Prayer of Nabonidus but agrees that the story of Nabonidus lay back of the tradition of Daniel 4. The name of Nabonidus, Freedman suggests, was still remembered in Babylonia but not in Palestine; the substitution of Nebuchadnezzar for Nabonidus therefore probably was made after the story reached Palestine.

The great variety of material represented by the Dead Sea Scrolls and fragments raises the question of the canon of sacred Scripture. The Qumran sect was devoted to the divine law and the inspired words of the prophets; it accepted and used all the books in the Hebrew canon, as defined later by the rabbis, except the book of Esther. But it used also many works later condemned by the rabbis as heretical. Did it regard all of these as on the same level of inspiration and authority? Do the ideas and attitudes which appear in the library of this sect throw any light on the history of the Hebrew canon of Scripture?

Here perhaps we should pause and consider again Del Medico's contention that the Qumran texts are not the remains of a religious community's library but a miscellaneous collection of document committed for various reasons to the genizah. Obviously, if he is right, the presence of a book in this collection proves, not that it was accepted by any group of Jews, but that it was rejected. The biblical manuscripts were discarded because they were defective or damaged, the non-biblical works because they were considered heretical.

The fact that no manuscript of Esther was included now finds a striking explanation. In the first century A.D., says Del Medico, it was believed that handling the sacred books outside of the synagogue "soiled the hands"; i.e., it caused the same ritual uncleanness as was contracted by touching a corpse. The one exception was the book of Esther, which was read in the home at the feast of Purim and could therefore be kept in a profane place. Since a scroll of Esther therefore never became unclean, it never had to be committed to the genizah. Neat and tempting as this explanation is, it must yield to the evidence against the whole genizah hypothesis, which has already been presented (pp. 15–19). Some other explanation of the absence of Esther must therefore be found, or it must remain a mystery—unless, indeed, fragments of the book should still turn up, which is not impossible.

Another hypothetical explanation has recently been offered by Cecil Roth. Believing that the men of Qumran belonged to the sect of Zealots, he suggests that they rejected the book of Esther because it recognized and tolerated the Jews' subjection to a foreign government. Here the problem of the sect's identity enters the picture. Neither Roth nor Del Medico accepts the prevalent identification of the Qumran community with the Essenes. A decision concerning Roth's explanation for the absence of Esther from the community's library must therefore be postponed until we have re-examined the question of the sect's identification (pp. 253–74).

New evidence of a distinction between sacred and other literature at Qumran, which affords also a means of determining how each book was regarded, has recently been brought forward. If reliable, this is important, because it indicates that one of the books in the Jewish and Hebrew canon, the book of Daniel, was not regarded as sacred Scripture in the Qumran community. The official publication of the fragments excavated in Cave 1 includes a transcription of the Daniel fragments acquired by Archbishop Samuel in 1948. Commenting on them, Barthélemy remarks that in the other biblical manuscripts of Cave 1 the height of the columns is double their width, whereas the height and width of the columns in these Daniel fragments are approximately equal. Pieces of a copy of Daniel written on papyrus, Barthélemy adds, have been found in Cave 6, whereas the other biblical manuscripts in Hebrew are made of leather.

Cross points out that since Barthélemy wrote this statement a papyrus manuscript of I–II Kings from Cave 6 has been identified. He agrees, however, that the practice of the Qumran scribes in copying biblical manuscripts was fairly uniform. They usually wrote on leather, usually made the columns twice as high as they were wide, and usually used either the old Hebrew script or the formal "bookhand" of the square script, though a very few biblical scrolls in a cursive script were found in Cave 4. Recognizing therefore that there were exceptions to the standard procedure, Cross notes that in at least four Qumran manuscripts the book of Daniel received an "extraordinarily free treatment," which at least "strongly suggests" that it was not considered a part of the sacred Scriptures. Hyatt remarks that the quite recent composition of the book may have been the reason for this attitude.

Although the fragments of Daniel do not completely represent every part of the book, it is of interest to note that they apparently contain nothing of the apocryphal additions to the book found in the Septuagint. Unless evidence to the contrary should appear later, it seems fair to conclude that the stories of Susanna and of Bel and the Dragon and the "Song of the Three Holy Children" were unknown at Qumran. This is significant in view of the internal evidence that much, if not all, of this material was originally composed in Hebrew or Aramaic. If the book of Daniel was circulated in two forms, a longer one containing the additions and a shorter one which did not have them, and the Greek translation was made from the longer edition, it would seem that only the shorter form of the book was used at Qumran.

# XVI

## The Apocrypha and Other Post-biblical
## Works; Languages and Paleography

⎿⎽⎽⎿⎽⎽⎿⎽⎽⎿⎽⎽⎿⎽⎽⎿⎽⎽⎿⎽⎽⎿⎽⎽⎿⎽⎽⎿⎽⎽⎿⎽⎽⎿⎽⎽⎿⎽⎽⎿⎽⎽⎿⎽⎽⎿⎽⎽⎿⎽⎽⎿

The only books of those commonly called the Apocrypha that
have appeared at Qumran are Ecclesiasticus (Sirach) and Tobit.
Both were already known to have been translated from Semitic
originals. Ecclesiasticus has a preface in the Greek version, telling
how the author's grandson translated the book from Hebrew into
Greek in Egypt. But other books also of the Apocrypha were
composed in Hebrew or Aramaic. At least Judith, I Maccabees,
and Baruch were written in Hebrew. Why these were not included in the Qumran library is a question to which only specula-
tive answers can be given.

The Qumran fragments of Sirach and Tobit have not yet been
published, and not much information about them has been released. One of the Aramaic copies of Tobit is on papyrus; the
other one and the Hebrew copy are on leather. The Ecclesiasticus
fragments also are of leather. It may be assumed, in the absence
of information to the contrary, that all these manuscripts are non-
canonical in format and script.

The large number of other works represented by scrolls or
fragments in the caves of the Wady Qumran is clear from the
brief account of them already given (pp. 27–36). Some of them,
we have seen, were already known in Greek or other translations
and were commonly included among the books called Pseudepigrapha. Many others were entirely unknown until they appeared

in the remains of the Qumran library. There is no reason to think that any of these works were venerated as sacred Scripture. Some of them, no doubt, were accorded a high degree of authority as more or less official documents of the sect. The Manual of Discipline is a case in point, yet it is evident that it went through a process of revision during the history of the sect, and was preserved in several forms. Others, though considered spiritually helpful and edifying, were not the peculiar property of this sect and need not have been considered in any way authoritative. Some, whether composed within the community or not, were merely individual compositions which were felt to be worth preserving.

For the works already known in later forms, the Qumran texts help to solve problems of date, composition, and original language. Milik has concluded from a preliminary study of the Tobit fragments that the original language was probably Aramaic. The later versions preserve a longer and shorter form of this book, the longer form being found in the Codex Sinaiticus of the Septuagint and in the Old Latin. The Qumran fragments also represent this longer form; in fact, the Qumran text agrees with the Old Latin in two places where the scribe of the Codex Sinaiticus accidentally omitted fairly extensive passages.

The discovery of Hebrew fragments of Ecclesiasticus revived an old question among scholars. In the Cairo genizah half a century ago were found portions of a medieval manuscript of this book in Hebrew. Most scholars at once assumed that this was a copy of the original text from which the Greek translation was made, but this view encountered difficulties. Several careful investigators came to the conclusion that the genizah text was a late retranslation into Hebrew from the Greek. It is therefore a matter of no little interest to learn that the text of the Qumran fragments, as far as it goes, agrees with that of the medieval Cairo manuscript.

Among the Pseudepigrapha, the book of Jubilees was clearly one of the most popular works in the Qumran community. Not only is it referred to by name in the Damascus Document, but fragments of something like ten manuscripts of the book have been recovered from Caves 1, 2, and 4. The origin of this work has been a subject of much debate among scholars. It has been variously dated all the way from the fifth century B.C. to the first century A.D. The Qumran manuscripts do not make any of these dates impossible; they do, however, show that the book, as preserved in an Ethiopic version and in part also in Latin, is not a Christian edition of an earlier Jewish work but the Jewish work itself. The text of the Hebrew fragments is accurately translated in the Ethiopic and Latin versions. The fact that the Qumran manuscripts are all written in Hebrew, however, weakens the generally accepted hypothesis that the book was composed in Aramaic.

The important work known as the Testaments of the Twelve Patriarchs, which at many points resembles the book of Jubilees, is especially notable for its high moral tone, very close to that of the New Testament. It is also marked by an unusually sympathetic attitude toward Gentiles, which might account for the fact that no texts corresponding to the Greek version of this work have been found in Qumran caves.

Fragments of an Aramaic Testament of Levi appeared in Caves 1 and 4, but Milik argues that this was not a part of the Testaments of the Twelve Patriarchs; it was rather one of the sources used by the author of that work. Portions of this Aramaic work were found in the Cairo genizah more than half a century ago; their text is the same as that of the Qumran fragments. Milik calls attention also to a tenth-century Greek manuscript of the Testaments of the Twelve Patriarchs in the monastery of Mt. Athos. In this manuscript there are two long passages in the Testament of Levi which are lacking in other Greek manuscripts. One of these appears in the Cairo Aramaic fragments, and both of them are found in the fragments from Qumran.

A piece of a Hebrew Testament of Naphtali, recently identified among the fragments, is longer than the corresponding passage in the Greek text of the Testaments.

Combining these facts with many obviously Christian elements in the Testaments of the Twelve Patriarchs, and following in part the arguments of de Jonge, Milik develops a thoroughly credible hypothesis concerning the origin of the book. The passages of

clearly Christian origin, he feels, are not to be explained as interpolations in a Jewish work. The whole book was written by one
author, who was a Jewish Christian. The Aramaic Testament of
Levi, and perhaps the Hebrew Testament of Naphtali, inspired
him to compose a similar work including all twelve of the sons of
Jacob. This accounts for the close parallels with the words of
Jesus and Paul and for the fact that the author, in giving promises
of a Messiah from the tribe of Levi as well as one from Judah,
apparently thinks of both as fulfilled in one person. Daniélou
suggests that the author may have been a former Essene con-
verted to Christianity.

Parts of ten manuscripts of the apocalyptic book of Enoch were
found in Cave 4. Of the five major divisions of the book as it has
survived in the Ethiopic version and partly in Greek, the first and
fourth are represented in four manuscripts, the third in four
others, and the beginning of the fifth in one. There are no fragments from the second part, the Parables of Enoch (chapters
37–71). The third part (chapters 72–92), which consists of elaborate astronomical speculations, is more explicit and clearer in
the Qumran fragments than it is in the versions.

Milik infers from these facts that a Jewish Christian of the
second century composed the Parables of Enoch (part II) and
combined them with the other four parts, originally separate
works, to make a kind of Pentateuch. Not being interested in the
astronomical calculations of part III, he copied them carelessly
and made them relatively unintelligible. The figure of the "Son
of man," who for him was of course Jesus, was what most interested him in the older writings. If we could be sure that the state
of affairs at Qumran accurately presented the whole picture, this
hypothesis would be quite convincing. As it is, it seems for the
present as probable as any that has yet been propounded.

The Damascus Document, though unknown to the modern
world until the discovery of the Cairo genizah, is included by
R. H. Charles in his great edition of the Apocrypha and Pseudepigrapha. Scholars have never reached a unanimous decision concerning the date of its composition. Even the discovery of frag-

ments of it in Caves 4, 5, and 6 at Qumran leaves some of them unconvinced.

Del Medico takes the bull by the horns and examines the five fragments from Cave 6, the only ones yet published. Two of them, he is able to show, can be fitted into the text of the Damascus Document only by assuming a very strange irregularity in the length of the lines. Two others are too tiny to be very significant, containing only a few letters, while the fifth does not fit into any passage of the Cairo manuscripts. As for the fragments from the other caves, which have not been published, Del Medico notes that they are said to contain many regulations which do not appear in the Cairo manuscripts. His conclusion is that at most we can think of texts like those found in the caves as having inspired the medieval Qaraites who, according to him, composed the Damascus Document.

Admitting that these arguments have some force while we have only the Cave 6 fragments before us, we may observe that in at least one of these it would require a surprising degree of coincidence to bring together in the same order as in the Damascus Document so many of what Del Medico calls common clichés. For the unpublished fragments we must accept the statement of Milik that, in spite of noteworthy additions, they present substantially the same text as Manuscript A of the Cairo genizah. Only fragments much more extensive than those of Cave 6 would justify or even suggest such a statement. Milik reports even that the two main divisions of the Damascus Document, believed by some scholars to have been two independent compositions, appear consecutively in a continuous text in the Cave 4 fragments. In view of these facts, it requires either an extraordinary degree of skepticism or an invincible conviction of the late origin of the work to deny that at least some of the Qumran manuscripts actually contained the Damascus Document.

Moving on from writings previously known to compositions with which the Qumran caves have given us our first acquaintance, we may note that the history of some of these also is illuminated by the different forms in which they have appeared in different manuscripts. This is most conspicuously true of the Manual of Discipline. The scroll found in two parts in 1947 (*DSS*, pp. 24f) was clearly incomplete: the last partly filled column was obviously the end of the composition, but the beginning was missing. How much of the scroll had been lost it was then impossible to tell. The additional columns purchased in 1950 filled in the picture in a rather surprising way. Evidently the Manual was followed in the same scroll by the Rule of the Congregation, beginning at the top of a new column, and that in turn was followed by the Benedictions. At the beginning of the Manual, however, very little seems to have been lost.

But that is not all that has been learned about the Manual of Discipline. Cave 4 contained remnants of nine other manuscripts of the same document, presenting what seems in some places to be a better text. Milik assures us that the publication of these fragments will enable us to restore the text of the Manual very nearly as it came from the pen of the author, whom he believes to have been the teacher of righteousness himself.

Two other scrolls found in 1947, the Thanksgiving Psalms and the War of the Sons of Light with the Sons of Darkness, are now matched by fragments of other manuscripts of the same works from Cave 4. As in the case of the Manual of Discipline, these fragments sometimes differ from the Cave 1 scrolls sufficiently to indicate different recensions of the books. Dr. Hunzinger, a member of the "international team" at Jerusalem, says that these fragments give us "a look into the internal history of this literature." They also at many points fill in gaps in the text of the scrolls.

Concerning the contributions of the Dead Sea Scrolls to our understanding of the biblical languages, there is not much to add to what was said in *DSS* (pp. 322–24). Papers dealing with problems in this area are appearing from time to time in the learned journals, but they are concerned with technical details. No general conclusions of major significance seem to have emerged thus far. Fuller publications of the texts will be necessary before that will be possible.

The scrolls help also in the study of post-biblical developments in the Hebrew and Aramaic languages, filling in to some degree the considerable gap between the latest books of the Old Testament and the rabbinic literature. Not a great deal can as yet be added to what was said on this subject in *DSS* (pp. 323f), but the study of the problems involved has been going on quietly among specialists in these languages, and important articles are appearing from time to time in the scholarly journals.

Milik distinguishes eight languages which are represented among the scrolls and fragments from the Dead Sea area: biblical Hebrew, Mishnaic Hebrew, Palestinian Aramaic, Nabatean, Palestinian-Christian Aramaic, Greek, Latin, and Arabic. The last five of these, it will be noted, appear only in the texts of Khirbet Mird, from the Byzantine period (see pp. 33–35). The other three may be reduced to two, Hebrew and Aramaic. It is clear that Hebrew and Aramaic were used together by the Qumran community, and also by the second-century A.D. revolutionaries who left the manuscripts of the Wady Murabbaat. Aramaic had been the popular spoken language of the Jews in Palestine for two or three centuries; Hebrew, however, was not forgotten, and in the nationalistic enthusiasm of the Maccabean revolt in the second century B.C. its more general use had been revived, especially for documents of a formal or official nature.

Aside from the biblical manuscripts and those written in Aramaic, most of the Qumran texts are written in what has been called a neo-classical Hebrew. The writers tried to use a biblical style, imitating especially the Deuteronomic writings, but they did not realize how much their language differed from that of their models. The differences, however, reflect the current use of Hebrew as a living language; they are not merely mistakes in academic composition in a dead language, but echoes of the everyday usage of the time. How far this is true, to be sure, is still a question on which scholars differ. Some find the language of the scrolls inelegant and lacking in spontaneity; others find in it richness, variety, and flexibility. There are differences, of course, among the documents themselves in these respects, corresponding in part to their different purposes and literary types.

The copper scroll, unlike the other Qumran documents, is written in Mishnaic Hebrew, the dialect of the rabbis whose sayings are recorded in the Mishnah. Not much later than the middle of the first century A.D. at the latest, this is the earliest known text in that dialect. After it, the earliest are the second-century texts of the Wady Murabbaat. A few of the Qumran manuscripts exhibit some features of the Mishnaic language, but so also do some of the latest books of the Old Testament itself. An apocalyptic work contained in a papyrus manuscript, two pieces of which are among the Cave 4 fragments purchased by the McCormick Theological Seminary, is composed in what Milik calls "proto-Mishnaic" Hebrew.

After the failure of the Second Revolt against Rome and the virtual depopulation of Judea, the use of Mishnaic Hebrew seems to have been confined to the rabbis and their disciples. Even they soon abandoned it, but at the time represented by the Murabbaat texts it was still used for military communications and (along with Aramaic) for such everyday documents as letters and contracts. In the period of the Qumran texts this late form of Hebrew must have been developing as a medium of general communication, even though official and literary documents were still composed in the self-conscious "neo-classical" language. Noting points of contact between Mishnaic Hebrew and the Punic language of North Africa, a late Phoenician dialect, Milik suggests that the language of the Mishnah represents a widely spoken mixed dialect developed from the Hebrew of Judea and the Phoenician used on the coast of Palestine.

The Aramaic texts of the Qumran and Murabbaat caves fill a great gap in our sources for the knowledge of that language as used in Palestine in the Greek and Roman periods. With the exception of relatively brief inscriptions, especially those of the Palmyrenes and Nabateans, we had previously almost no Aramaic texts from that period. The literary Aramaic of the Persian and Greek periods was known from the Aramaic portions of the books of Ezra and Daniel and from papyrus documents found in Egypt, but the common spoken Aramaic of the Roman period in Palestine had no direct attestation.

This was the language spoken by Jesus and his first disciples, though in a Galilean dialect which doubtless differed somewhat from the dialect of Judea. Much of the New Testament was based at least on an Aramaic oral tradition, and probably also to some extent on Aramaic documents. The new increment of Aramaic texts is therefore of great importance for serious study of the New Testament and Christian origins. The results to be expected cannot be stated in brief generalizations. There will be nothing sensational about them. They will consist of innumerable details of vocabulary and grammar for the use of specialists. Bit by bit, however, they will correct and enlarge our understanding, and every bit will be that much gain.

Later forms and dialects of Aramaic are exemplified by the texts of the Wady Murabbaat and Khirbet Mird. The second-century documents of the Wady Murabbaat and the nearby un-identified site, as compared with those of the Wady Qumran, exhibit relatively slight changes, chiefly in spelling. The Judean, Samaritan, and Galilean dialects already known in later Jewish and Samaritan literature are not represented in any of the Dead Sea collections. The dialect of the Nabatean kingdom across the Jordan appears in papyrus documents from the unidentified site near the Wady Murabbaat.

One of these contains nearly thirty more or less complete lines of a contract dealing with an elaborate transaction in real estate. It is interesting to find here some of the same legal terminology found later in the Talmud. Starcky, who published this contract, sees in it evidence of the existence of a common Aramaic dialect at this time, such as was suggested years ago by Franz Rosenthal. It also illustrates the close relations between Jews and Nabateans. Unfortunately the contract is not dated, but it presumably comes from the same general period as the other texts of the region, the early second century of the Christian era.

A scrap of papyrus with a few letters in the Nabatean script was found in the Wady Murabbaat. A small piece of leather from Qumran Cave 4 is written on both sides in a script resembling Nabatean, but the members of the Jerusalem team are not agreed as to whether it is Nabatean or a Jewish cursive script.

The later Palestinian Christian dialect of Aramaic is found in many of the manuscripts found at Khirbet Mird, both biblical and non-biblical (see p. 33, and *DSS*, p. 64). These were the first texts in this dialect to be found in Palestine itself, those previously known having all come from the monastery of St. Catherine at Mt. Sinai and from the great mosque at Damascus. The texts from Khirbet Mird include the first non-literary, papyrus documents in this dialect that have ever been discovered. One of them, published by Milik, is a letter from a man who calls himself "the sinner Gabriel" to the head of the monastery, asking the latter to pray for him.

In *DSS* the contributions of the Dead Sea documents to the science of paleography were mentioned briefly (pp. 324f). The variety of scripts has of course increased with the discovery of new material. For the common square script the comparison of the Qumran and Murabba'at documents is significant, but considerable development can be traced also within the Qumran material itself. Even the derivation of the alphabet from earlier forms used in the Persian and Greek periods can be seen more clearly than before.

Especially valuable work in this area is being done by F. M. Cross, Jr., following lines laid down previously by his teacher, W. F. Albright. Four fairly definite phases in the history of the square script at Qumran are now distinguished: Archaic, Hasmonean, Herodian, and Cursive. The last is represented only slightly at Qumran but comes into its own in the Murabba'at texts.

The old Hebrew script as used at Qumran has turned out to be an artificial revival in a form so archaic that it is no wonder that the excavators of Cave 1 thought their fragments of Leviticus might be as old as the sixth century B.C. (*DSS*, pp. 35, 97f). Since then the other caves have greatly increased the material in this script.

As if all this was not enough, two cryptic alphabets have been found. Interesting as these are in themselves, however, they are not as important for the history of writing as the other materials. The specimens of Nabatean, Christian Aramaic, and other languages already considered need only be mentioned again in this connection.

The significance of paleography as a criterion for the dating of manuscripts, it will be remembered, was a major bone of contention during the early debates over the antiquity of the Dead Sea Scrolls (*DSS*, pp. 30, 36f, 83ff). The heat of that controversy is now almost forgotten, but one incidental bit of contributory evidence may be mentioned here. In the spring of 1956 Israeli archeologists excavated the ruins of Herod's palace at Masada, above the western shore of the Dead Sea, some distance south of the Qumran and Murabbaat valleys. Here they found a papyrus fragment and a potsherd bearing writing in a script like that of the Dead Sea Scrolls. Since the palace was destroyed in 73 A.D., these bits of writing could not have been later than that date. Thus one more item is added to the abundant evidence for the age of the scrolls.

PART FOUR

# THE ORIGIN
# OF THE QUMRAN SECT

# XVII

## *The 390 Years and the Kittim*

⎴⎴⎴⎴⎴⎴⎴⎴⎴⎴⎴⎴⎴⎴⎴⎴⎴⎴⎴⎴⎴⎴⎴⎴⎴

Many of the questions discussed in *DSS* are still unanswered. Scholars have not yet reached any agreement concerning the origin of the Qumran sect. Much of the argument still revolves about the cryptic indications of the Damascus Document and the Habakkuk Commentary. The 390 years of the Damascus Document (*DSS*, pp. 195–98, 349) still receive a good deal of attention. Schonfield accepts the interpretation which regards the 390 years as indicating a period which began with the destruction of Jerusalem by Nebuchadnezzar in 586 B.C. (As a matter of fact, it now seems clear that the correct date for this disaster is not 586 but 587; this does not affect our problem, however, and the computation of the 390 years has usually assumed 586 as the starting point.) The end of the period in question, called "the period of wrath," is thus placed at 196 B.C. At this time God caused a number of the Jews to repent, but for twenty more years they groped blindly, until God "raised up for them a teacher of righteousness." This calculation therefore places the appearance of the teacher of righteousness at 176 B.C., the year before Antiochus Epiphanes came to the throne in Syria.

Many scholars, however, do not feel that the 390 years can be taken so exactly. Oesterreicher observes that the Qumran documents are deliberately obscure with regard to persons or dates, and this figure is probably symbolic or at best approximate. Fritsch, noting the obvious fact that the number is derived from Ezekiel 4:5, considers it symbolical, yet believes that it was intended to indicate the origin of the community among the Hasidim of the Maccabean period.

All these interpretations assume that the Hebrew text refers to a period *after* Nebuchadnezzar's conquest of Judea. Rowley still defends this understanding of the admittedly ambiguous Hebrew, but he ascribes no evidential value to the number 390. The translation given in *DSS* follows the conclusion of Isaac Rabinowitz that the period in question *ended* at that time and began 390 years earlier (see *DSS*, p. 197). This interpretation was adopted also by Gaster, who reports an interesting Samaritan tradition that "the kingdom of Nebuchadnezzar" lasted 390 years. Thus it was by delivering Judah to Nebuchadnezzar that God "visited" his people, and it was this divine judgment that stirred the faithful to repentance.

The following words, which I translated, "and caused to sprout from Israel and from Aaron a root of planting," are taken by Rabinowitz to mark a new event—"but he caused . . ." To be consistent, I should have followed him in this. The sprouting of the root, then, means the restoration of the community in Palestine after the exile. Gaster takes "visited them" to mean "took care of them" and equates the visitation with the restoration, but the interpretation of Rabinowitz seems to me preferable.

The twenty years of groping are understood by Rabinowitz as an allusion to "the twentieth year" of Nehemiah 1:1. Modern commentators understand this to mean the twentieth year of the reign of Artaxerxes, but the writer of the Damascus Document may have supposed that it meant the twentieth year after the return from the exile. The teacher of righteousness—or "right guide," as Rabinowitz prefers to translate the term—is therefore Nehemiah.

Del Medico reaches a similar conclusion by a different route. Regarding the 390 years as beginning with the destruction of Jerusalem, he says that the figure is purely conventional and drawn from the Bible. The writer of the passage believed the Bible and therefore assumed a return from the exile 390 years after its beginning; the 20 years then brought him to Nehemiah.

Gaster, while accepting the interpretation of the 390 and 20 years given by Rabinowitz, holds that Ezra rather than Nehemiah was the teacher of righteousness. Ezra was a priest, and the term "right-teacher," as Gaster renders it, always designated a priest. Ezra was also, as the "right-teacher" was, an expounder of the law. A different line of reasoning leads N. Walker also to identify the teacher of righteousness of this passage with Ezra. Following the argument of Rabinowitz that the 390 years began with the fourth year of Rehoboam (*DSS*, p. 197), Walker assumes 928 B.C. as the date of that year and, subtracting 390 from it, comes to 538 B.C., the year in which Cyrus gave the Jewish exiles permission to return to Palestine. Like Gaster, Walker takes the visitation to mean the restoration. The 20 years then bring him to 518, when the new temple was dedicated. Ezra, the teacher of righteousness, was raised up later; and still later, in another period of need, a new teacher was given to form the community of the covenanters.

F. F. Bruce adds another suggestion for the interpretation of the 390 years. The Damascus Document says that there will be 40 years from the death of the teacher of righteousness to the annihilation of all the men of war (xx.14; *DSS*, p. 357). Assuming that the ministry of the teacher lasted 40 years, Bruce adds the 390 and the 20 years, the 40 years of the teacher's ministry, and the 40 years from his death to the destruction of the men of war; thus he gets a total of 490, which corresponds to the seven weeks of years predicted in Daniel 9:24ff. This may indicate, Bruce suggests, that the figures given in the Damascus Document reflect an early attempt to establish the beginning and end of Daniel's seven weeks.

Schonfield makes use of the 490 years of Daniel in quite a different way and with a very different result. If we subtract 490 from 536, the date of the foundation of the second temple, we get 46 B.C. If we count the exile as lasting 70 years, from 586 to 516, and subtract 490 from the latter date, we get 26 B.C. Schonfield concludes that the time of the end was expected near the end of the last century B.C., when there was much religious ferment and Messianic expectations were rife. This seems to him to confirm his dating of the Damascus Document and the Habakkuk Commentary in the first century A.D. It does not follow for Schonfield, however, that the teacher of righteousness lived at such a late date. The writer of this part of the Damascus Document, he says, was looking back over a period of time to the teacher of righteousness.

The Habakkuk Commentary, it will be remembered, has much to say of the teacher of righteousness and his adversary, the wicked priest. Here certainly the reference cannot be to Nehemiah or Ezra. Scholars have not yet reached any agreement as to the identity or date of the wicked priest and the teacher of righteousness (*DSS*, pp. 143–86). Some of the discussion still hinges upon the identification of the Kittim, the invading and conquering foreign power which plays a prominent part in the Habakkuk Commentary and the War of the Sons of Light with the Sons of Darkness. A few other documents also mention the Kittim. Readers of *DSS* will recall the long and involved discussions among scholars concerning the Kittim.

After the publication of *DSS* I was surprised by the number of letters I received from people who wanted to explain to me who the Kittim were. All of them assumed that I and other scholars did not know who the Kittim of the Old Testament were, and that the Qumran commentator on Habakkuk must have used the word in the same sense in which it is used in the Old Testament. A more careful reading of what I wrote (*DSS*, pp. 128ff) might have prevented this misunderstanding. The point at issue was what the word meant to the writer of the commentary, who obviously used it to designate a foreign power of his own day. In keeping with a literary convention familiar in Jewish literature, he was applying an ancient term from the Scriptures to indicate an enemy whom it was not prudent to name directly.

There are only two possible alternatives. Either the Kittim were the Macedonian rulers of the Seleucid kingdom of Syria, the chief foes of the Jews from about 200 to 63 B.C., or they were the Romans. When *DSS* was written, the balance of scholarly opinion seemed to be swinging to the Romans, but the question was still open. At present the Romans seem to have such a large majority of the votes that they are practically elected, yet the Seleucids still have a few able advocates.

One of the arguments for taking the Kittim to be the Seleucids, and so for dating the persons and events of the Habakkuk Commentary in the second century B.C., was the fact that the Kittim of Assyria and the Kittim in Egypt are mentioned in the War of the Sons of Light with the Sons of Darkness (*DSS*, pp. 203ff). It was difficult to imagine what these two nations might be in the Roman period, but in the Greek period they seemed entirely appropriate for the Macedonian rulers of Egypt and Syria, the Ptolemies and the Seleucids. This was the interpretation given from the beginning by E. L. Sukenik, and even some scholars who held that the Kittim of the Habakkuk Commentary were the Romans felt constrained to admit that the reference in the War scroll was to the Ptolemies and Seleucids.

In *DSS* I was able to report only a reliable rumor that Sukenik's son, Yigael Yadin, had reached a different dating and interpretation of the War scroll. Before the end of 1955 his commentary on this scroll was published, and it decisively altered the situation. Yadin argues that the scroll was made between 50 B.C. and 50 A.D. The original composition of the book it contains he dates after the Roman conquest (63 B.C.) but before the end of the reign of Herod (4 B.C.).

As compared with the Habakkuk Commentary, Yadin finds not an earlier but a later situation reflected in the War scroll, which is no longer concerned with a struggle between the sect and its opponents within Judaism but with the final struggle of Judaism in general with the Kittim. Indications of dependence in the Manual of Discipline and many contacts with the Thanksgiving Psalms are detected also. The chronological relation of the War of the Sons of Light with the Sons of Darkness and the Damascus Document is found to be not clear.

Yadin's most original and impressive argument, however, is derived from the details of military equipment and procedure in the War scroll. These, he finds, correspond closely with Roman arms and tactics, so closely indeed that the author must have witnessed them himself or consulted contemporary military literature. Latin terms are not used, as in the later rabbinic literature, but the Hebrew words employed by the author are sometimes transparently "translation Hebrew." The word meaning literally "wing," for example, is used in a way unknown in normal Hebrew for a cavalry unit which the Romans called a wing in Latin ( *ala* ).

The Kittim of Assyria and the Kittim in Egypt are explained in terms of the comprehensive plan of war presented in the scroll. Under the head of the sect's eschatological beliefs we shall consider this in some detail (pp. 347–51); here we may note briefly some facts bearing on the question with which we are now concerned. The final war is to consist of three main rounds, lasting altogether forty years. In the first round the whole congregation will fight against three groups of enemies: the hostile neighbors of Israel, the Kittim of Assyria, and the violaters of the covenant within Israel. Of the first group, the Edomites are Israel's neighbors on the south, the Moabites and Ammonites on the east, and the Philistines on the west. The Kittim of Assyria are therefore naturally understood as enemies to the north, the name Assyria being used in a general way for the region of Syria (see *DSS*, pp. 203f).

In the second round the war is directed against the Egyptian Kittim. Yadin stresses the fact that they are not called "the Kittim of Egypt" but "the Kittim in Egypt," and he infers from this that they were people of the same ethnic origin as the Kittim of Assyria, but were living in Egypt. Viewed in that light, of course, they might be either Macedonians or Romans. Egypt, Yadin notes, was not within the biblical boundaries of Israel, but had to be finished off before the more distant "king of the north" could be attacked in the third round. This provides a possible and plausible explanation of the troublesome terms. It shows at least that the Assyrian and Egyptian Kittim do not necessarily mean the Seleucids and Ptolemies of the pre-Roman period.

Dupont-Sommer adduces another argument for dating the War scroll in the Roman period. In the third round of warfare the first year's fighting is to be directed against Aram Naharaim (northern Mesopotamia); the fact that Syria is not mentioned here shows that it has already been conquered in the defeat of the Romans. (This agrees with Yadin's identification of the Kittim of Assyria with the Roman rulers of Syria.) Various peoples in Asia Minor

and southern Mesopotamia are to be subjugated in the next four
years; the sixth and seventh years are then to be devoted to fighting "all the sons of Assyria and Persia and the people of the east
as far as the great desert." The lumping of all these together,
Dupont-Sommer contends, implies the existence of the Parthian
empire.

Unconvinced by these and other arguments for regarding the
Kittim as the Romans, H. H. Rowley still maintains that they are
the Macedonians. He is convinced that the War scroll must be
dated in the second century B.C. The Kittim of Assyria, he thinks,
are "almost certainly" the Seleucids. The Romans had no king before the time of Augustus and in fact never called their emperors
kings. In the book of Daniel the "kings of the north" are clearly
the Seleucids, and Rowley considers this the probable meaning
of the expression in the War scroll. This, however, makes them
the same as the Kittim of Assyria, who have been defeated already in the first round. According to Yadin's analysis, the "kings
of the north" are the rulers of the more distant peoples to be
overcome in the third round of fighting, the nations named in
Genesis 10.

Here we encounter a rather difficult question of interpretation,
which unfortunately depends in part upon the way we fill in a
gap in the text. In the opening sentences of the first column, where
the course of the final war is briefly outlined, the first round of
fighting against Israel's hostile neighbors on all sides is indicated;
then the second and third rounds are summarized as follows:
"And after the battle they shall go up against the king of the
Kittim in Egypt; and in his time he shall go forth with great
wrath to fight against the kings of the north; and his wrath shall
destroy and cut off the horn of their strength." So, at any rate, I
translated these clauses in *DSS* (p. 390); and Rowley's argument
presupposes the same interpretation. Two important words, however, are missing in the scroll and have to be supplied by conjecture; they are "king" and "strength." The word "strength" at
the end of the sentence is purely conjectural. The word "king"
is inserted because a subject in the singular number is presupposed by the following phrase, "in his time," and the verb, "he

shall go forth"; moreover, a "king of the Kittim" is mentioned later in the scroll (xv.2).

This interpretation, however, creates a difficulty. It introduces a struggle between Egypt and the kings of the north which is not mentioned elsewhere in the scroll, and it destroys the threefold division of the war as described in the rest of the scroll. Yadin therefore proposes a different reconstruction, which meets this difficulty but raises others of its own. Instead of "the king of the Kittim in Egypt" he reads "all the troops of the Kittim in Egypt." The phrase "in his time" he interprets as "in its time," that is, the time set for this to happen. The verb "he shall go forth," he thinks, must be a scribal mistake for "they shall go forth," or else the subject is God. A new sentence, then, begins with "and in its time," describing the third round of the war. At the end Yadin supplies "Belial" instead of "their strength." Thus the whole passage reads: "And after the battle they shall go up from there against all the troops of the Kittim in Egypt. And in its time he shall go forth with great wrath to fight against the kings of the north; and his wrath shall destroy and cut off the horn of Belial."

Other translators have presented still other interpretations, a few of which may be noted to show the difficulties and the various possibilities of the passage. To make the matter clearer, I have italicized the words which are inserted in the gaps of the text. Vermès attaches the clause, "and after the battle they shall go up from there," to the preceding sentence, then begins a new paragraph reading: "The *king* of the Kittim *shall go* against Egypt and, in his time, he shall depart in great wrath to fight against the kings of the north, that his wrath may destroy and cut off the horn *of a multitude*."

Delcor and Dupont-Sommer cut the Gordian knot, so far as our present interest is concerned, by separating "the Kittim" from "in Egypt." Delcor reads: "And after the battle *the bands of* the Kittim shall go up from there against Egypt. And in the last extremity, in great wrath He shall go forth to fight the kings of the north, and in his wrath He shall destroy and break the horn of . . ." Dupont-Sommer reads: "And, after this war, *the nations* will go up from there, *and the king* of the Kittim *shall enter* into

Egypt. And, in his time, he shall go forth with great wrath to fight against the kings of the north, and his wrath [shall try] to destroy and cut off the horn *of his enemies*."

Giving, as always, an original twist to the text, Del Medico changes "go up" to "help," inserts "the Macedonian and" instead of "the king (or troops) of," supposes that the word taken by others as the name "Kittim" is a noun meaning "legions," and so reads: "And after the war they shall help from there *the Macedonians and* the legions in Egypt. But finally he shall go forth with great wrath to fight against the kings of the north, and his wrath shall destroy and cut off the horn *of the wicked.*" Those who help the enemy, Del Medico explains, are the apostate Jews in Jerusalem, the legions in Egypt are those of the Ptolemies, and the one who goes forth in wrath is Judas Maccabeus.

This long digression for an exercise in textual emendation and exegesis was occasioned by Rowley's argument that the Kittim in Egypt must be the Ptolemies of the pre-Roman period. It will now be evident that this is by no means an inevitable conclusion. Rowley adds that the mottoes on the banners of the sons of light recall the watchwords of the Maccabean warriors. This is true, and it may have the significance he attributes to it, but the Maccabean slogans might have influenced a writer of the Roman period as well. Thus far the argument for identifying the Kittim with the Seleucids is not convincing.

Rowley suggests also that the forty years of warfare contemplated by the War scroll are the same as the forty years of distress and conflict which the Damascus Document says will intervene between the death of the unique teacher and the Messianic age. At the end of these forty years, according to the Damascus Document, all the men of war will be annihilated (xx.14f; *DSS*, p. 357). The commentary on Psalm 37 also refers to a period of forty years at the end of which all the wicked will perish. Put together, these references suggest a fairly fixed expectation in the Qumran community.

Rowley's inference is that the War scroll must have been written early in the period of forty years and therefore soon after the death of the teacher of righteousness, whom Rowley dates in the pre-Maccabean period. Further discussion of this argument must be deferred until we have reconsidered the identity and time of the teacher of righteousness. It should be observed here, however, that the forty years of the War scroll are not necessarily the same as the forty years of the Damascus Document.

Further evidence of a second-century B.C. date for the War scroll is seen by Rowley in the campaigns of Judas Maccabeus against the Edomites, the peoples east of the Jordan, and the Philistines (I Maccabees 5). These correspond to the first round of fighting in the War scroll, and so indicate that in the second century B.C. "the friends and allies of the sect," as Rowley puts it, "actually embarked on the program of which the author of the Battle Scroll dreamed." In the first century B.C. no such effort to carry out the plans of the War scroll is evident. Now it is true that the campaigns of Alexander Janneus and the other first-century B.C. Hasmonean rulers are irrelevant, because they were not friends or allies of the sect. The scroll, however, does not necessarily refer to campaigns already completed or begun; indeed, it cannot be assumed that the conquests contemplated were ever undertaken.

Dupont-Sommer, as a matter of fact, finds in the first century B.C. a situation which seems to him to be exactly what the War scroll presupposes. Reading, as we have seen, "the king of the Kittim will enter into Egypt," he suggests that we have here a reminiscence of Julius Caesar's expedition to Egypt in 48 B.C. On a subsequent expedition the "king of the Kittim," that is the chief of the Romans, would enter Palestine and encounter there the sons of light, who would annihilate his power, according to the "scenario" of Daniel 11:40–45. Without necessarily accepting quite so precise an interpretation, we may at least conclude that Rowley's arguments for a second-century B.C. date of the War scroll, and for the identification of the Kittim of Assyria with the Seleucids, are not sufficiently compelling to outweigh Yadin's evidence of a date in the Roman period.

A new and important bit of evidence was disclosed by Allegro's publication of a column of the Nahum Commentary. Here, instead of the vague references and cryptic designations of the Habakkuk

Commentary and other documents, we have two pagan rulers mentioned by name, Antiochus and Demetrius. Both are Seleucid rulers, but unfortunately there were three named Demetrius and nine named Antiochus. Actually, only the last four letters of the name Demetrius (. . . *tros*) are preserved, but there seems to be no reason to doubt that this is the name in question. Can we then identify the Antiochus and the Demetrius referred to?

Antiochus is mentioned only as marking the beginning of a period of time. The commentator refers to "the kings of Greece from Antiochus until the rise of the rulers of the Kittim." The words just preceding this are lost, but, to judge from the context, they probably said that there was no one to make the kings of Greece afraid during the period mentioned. Allegro believes that the reference is to Antiochus IV Epiphanes (175–164 B.C.), the Seleucid king whose persecution of the Jews brought on the Maccabean revolt. No scholar seems to have questioned this identification seriously, though Rowley remarks that Antiochus III or Antiochus VII might have been meant.

Disagreement arises concerning the identity of Demetrius. The only direct clue is the statement that he "sought to come to Jerusalem by the counsel of the seekers of smooth things." The "seekers of smooth things" appear again a few lines later and frequently also, Allegro tells us, in other columns of the commentary which have not yet been published. In the Damascus Document (i.18; *DSS*, p. 350) the Jews who were led astray by the "man of scorn" are said to have "sought smooth things." In the Thanksgiving Psalms (ii.32; *DSS*, p. 402) "the congregation of those who seek smooth things" are apparently "the interpreters of lies" (or perhaps more accurately "babblers of lies"), from whom God has rescued the poet. The interpreters or babblers of lies who exchange God's law for "smooth things" are also mentioned later (iv.10; *DSS*, p. 405). Brownlee's acute suggestion that in the word for "smooth things," *ḥalaqot*, the writers of these documents were playing on the word for the legal precepts of the Pharisees, *halakot*, was mentioned in *DSS* (p. 250). Whatever connection there may be, if any, among all these passages, the seekers of smooth things were obviously Jews, perhaps Pharisees, who were regarded as apostates and traitors by the Qumran community.

Who, then, was the Demetrius who sought to come to Jerusalem by the counsel of such renegade Jews? Allegro supposes that he was Demetrius III Eucerus, a contemporary of the Jewish priest-king Alexander Janneus. There is no record to the effect that he ever tried to enter Jerusalem, but Josephus says that, at the request of the Pharisees, Demetrius III came into Palestine, defeated Alexander Janneus in battle near Shechem, and forced him to flee for his life. Very soon, however, the defeated king regained the ascendancy, repelled the invader, and avenged himself on his enemies. According to Josephus, this was possible because many of the Pharisees deserted Demetrius after his victory and went over to Alexander Janneus. Allegro sees in the Nahum Commentary an explanation of this change of heart. Demetrius had attempted to follow up his advantage by taking possession of Jerusalem, but this was more than the Pharisees had bargained for. Gaster supposes that Demetrius even tried to claim the throne of Judah for himself.

If it were clear on other grounds that the Demetrius here mentioned was Demetrius III, this might be accepted as a new fact of history. Rowley reminds us, however, that an attempt to get possession of Jerusalem by another Demetrius is on record. Demetrius I Soter (161–150 B.C.), at the instigation of the false high priest Alcimus, sent to Jerusalem his close friend Nicanor with orders to destroy the Jews (I Maccabees 7). Nicanor attempted to get Judas Maccabeus into his power by deceitful words of peace, but his treacherous designs were foiled, and he was defeated and killed in battle. The "seekers of smooth things," Rowley contends, were the party of Alcimus, who collaborated with Demetrius and Nicanor. The members of the Qumran sect would have regarded them as traitors; in the time of Demetrius III, however, they would not have taken the part of Alexander Janneus, but would more probably have remained aloof from the struggle.

To one who would like to see decisive evidence for one Demetrius or the other, it may seem unfortunate that Demetrius I is not said to have tried to enter Jerusalem himself, but only to have sent Nicanor to get rid of the troublesome Jewish insurgents. If he was the Demetrius referred to by the commentator on Nahum, we must suppose that he "sought to come to Jerusalem" indirectly by sending Nicanor first to put down the opposition and get control of the city. Rowley's view, as he points out, has at least two advantages: the events referred to are all attested elsewhere, and they all took place within less than ten years.

But what has all this to do with the Kittim? Rowley regards his identification of Antiochus and Demetrius as supporting his view that all these sources presuppose a situation in the second century B.C. and therefore favor the identification of the Kittim with the Seleucid kings of Syria rather than the Romans. Here, it seems to me, the Nahum Commentary quite clearly contravenes Rowley's position by making a distinction between the Seleucids and the Kittim. The time during which the kings of Greece, if my inference from the context is correct, had none to make them afraid, is defined as reaching "from Antiochus to the rise of the rulers of the Kittim." The kings of Greece are unquestionably the Seleucids. Antiochus was one of these. Since the rise of the rulers of the Kittim marks the end of the period which begins with Antiochus, the rulers of the Kittim cannot be the same as the kings of Greece. The rise of the rulers of the Kittim seems rather to mean the end of the kings of Greece; in other words, the Seleucid period gives way to the Roman period. To me this seems the most specific and unambiguous evidence we have as yet for the identification of the Kittim with the Romans.

# XVIII

## The Teacher of Righteousness
## and His Contemporaries

⊔⊓⊔⊓⊔⊓⊔⊓⊔⊓⊔⊓⊔⊓⊔⊓⊔⊓⊔⊓⊔⊓⊔⊓⊔⊓⊔⊓⊔⊓⊔⊓⊓

The identification of the Kittim does not necessarily settle the question of the date to which the teacher of righteousness is to be assigned, or the historical persons with whom he and his contemporaries are to be identified. Allegro remarks that even if we agree that the Kittim were the Romans, this does not preclude a pre-Roman date for the teacher of righteousness. The authors of the commentaries tried to find allusions to historical events and persons in the verses of Scripture they were expounding, but they did not assume that the successive references were given in chronological order or that there was necessarily any connection between one and another.

Can we, then, come any closer than formerly to a satisfactory dating and identification of the teacher of righteousness and the persons involved in his career? As I have already said, there is as yet no agreement among scholars on these points. There has been a great deal of interesting speculation, however, and some new evidence has been found. The hypothesis of a plurality of meaning for the terms "teacher of righteousness" and "wicked priest" (*DSS*, p. 162f, 168, 173f, 181f) still has its advocates. Gaster considers it "pretty apparent" that the title "teacher of righteousness" does not indicate any specific historical individual but "denotes a continuing office," "a kind of 'apostolic succession,'" "a series of inspired leaders." The wicked priest may then be any priest hostile to the community or its leader; Gaster does not even include this term in his list of the opponents of the brotherhood.

Duncan Howlett objects that there are too many such designations to be explained in this way. There are not only the teacher of righteousness and the wicked priest, but also the man of the lie, the preacher of the lie, the man of scoffing, and now the lion of wrath. We can hardly regard each of these as designating a series of men. The idea that the commentaries, where these terms appear, had merely, as Gaster puts it, "a stock set of masks" for "a stock set of characters" would be more appealing if there were not so many characters.

Howlett remarks also that no such office as that of the teacher of righteousness is mentioned in the Manual of Discipline. If the "correct expositor" had a regular place in the community's organization, we might expect some reference to him in connection with the study and exposition of the law. If his position was less official and more charismatic, this objection would have less force; it is at best an argument from silence. The lack of any reference to the teacher of righteousness in the Manual of Discipline and similar documents can be explained on the assumption of a succession of leaders, but it can be more easily and plausibly explained if the term refers to an individual leader at a particular time, either in the past or still in the future when these documents were composed. Carmignac holds that the teacher is not mentioned in the Manual, the War scroll, or the Thanksgiving Hymns because he wrote them; this too is possible.

As for the "house of Absalom" in the Habakkuk Commentary (v.9; *DSS*, p. 367, cp. pp. 147–49), we may heartily agree with Gaster that this probably has nothing to do with a man named Absalom. If that had been his name, the commentator would have called him something else. As Gaster says, the name is used as we might use the names of Attila, Machiavelli, Benedict Arnold, or Quisling. The mention of Antiochus and Demetrius by name in the Nahum Commentary is unique in the Qumran documents published thus far.

Most scholars who have dealt with the problem recently still consider the teacher of righteousness an individual leader of the sect, perhaps its founder. Many still believe that he lived in the second century B.C., before the coming of the Romans. Rowley combines several lines of argument, historical and literary, to establish an early second-century date for the career of the teacher of righteousness and the founding of the sect. The Damascus Document expected the Messianic age to come forty years after the death of the teacher of righteousness; therefore this work must have been written before the forty years were over.

The mysterious book of Hagu or Hagi, which seems to have been lost and forgotten later, is referred to in the Damascus Document. Elsewhere it is mentioned only in the Rule of the Congregation. Here the organization of the community has a military character quite lacking in the Manual of Discipline. The situation presupposed by the Rule of the Congregation is like that of the Hasidim, the devout, loyal Jews in the days of the Maccabees. Since only the Damascus Document and the Rule of the Congregation mention the book of Hagu, Rowley infers that these two works were probably written in the same general period. One of them reflects the conditions of Maccabean times; the other was written less than forty years after the teacher of righteousness died. Therefore, Rowley infers, the teacher of righteousness must have lived in the Maccabean period.

This argument would of course be simpler and stronger if the Damascus Document itself more clearly reflected the situation of the Hasidim at the time of the Maccabean uprising. The date of the Damascus Document cannot be established by the mere fact that it mentions a book which is mentioned also in a document that may come from the time of the Maccabees.

The book of Hagu or Hagi is made the object of an interesting line of study by Schonfield. Finding the name quite meaningless, and recalling the frequent use of cryptic and symbolic expressions, he resorts to an old Hebrew form of cipher, which consists of using the first letter of the alphabet for the last, the second for the next to the last, and so on. The first letter is *aleph* and the last *taw*; the second is *beth* and the next to last is *shin*. This type of cipher is therefore called *aleph-taw-beth-shin*, corresponding to A-T-B-Sh, and these are given vowels to make the word *atbash*. An example of such an *atbash* cipher may be seen already in Jeremiah 25:26, where the "king of Sheshach" is mentioned. No such country as Sheshach is known, but by *atbash* the *sh* stands for *b* and the *ch* stands for *l;* thus we get *bbl,* i.e., Babel, the Hebrew form of the name Babylon.

Applying this procedure to the Hebrew consonants of the name Hagu, *hgw,* Schonfield finds that they stand for *ṣrp,* i.e., *ṣaraph,* the Hebrew word for "refine." The followers of the teacher of righteousness, he suggests, called him the "refiner" (Hebrew *ṣoreph* or *meṣareph*), alluding to the prophecy of Malachi 3:1–3, which says of the coming "messenger of the covenant" that "he will sit as a refiner and purifier of silver." That the community led by the teacher of righteousness would use a cryptic form of expression is made probable, Schonfield maintains, by the importance attached to the sacred number 50 and its symbolic value in the Manual of Discipline (*DSS,* pp. 243f). This has no direct bearing, of course, on the date of the teacher of righteousness, but Schonfield argues indirectly that the time just before the Maccabean revolt, when Antiochus Epiphanes was persecuting the Jews, would be likely to promote the use of cryptic forms of expression, and the Hasidim of that period would be "just the kind of people" to use such a cipher as *atbash.*

A further argument is drawn from the use of *atbash* in the book of Jeremiah. It occurs twice in chapter 25 and twice in chapter 51. In the Septuagint, chapters 46–51 immediately follow chapter 25. The section consisting of these chapters, Schonfield says, "has long been held by scholarly opinion" to be a product of the second century B.C. or thereabouts. It contains denunciations of the same hostile nations listed in Psalm 83 and Jubilees 37; the same nations were fought by Judas Maccabeus (I Maccabees 5), and they are to be fought by the sons of light in the first round of fighting of the War scroll. These chapters of Jeremiah, Schonfield suggests, may have been inserted in the book by the Hasidim of Maccabean times. The persecution by Antiochus Epiphanes and his destruction of many copies of the sacred books must have compelled them to do a great deal of restoration, giving them at the same time an opportunity to insert new sections dealing with their own times. As a matter of fact, "scholarly opinion" is by no means so unanimous concerning the late origin of this section of the book as Schonfield implies.

Interesting and suggestive as all this is, one must confess that Schonfield's deductions from the lost book of Hagu are no more convincing than those of Rowley. This is only one strand, however, in Rowley's argument. The forty years between the death of the unique teacher and the Messianic age (if that is what the passage means; see *DSS*, p. 194) are pictured in the Damascus Document as a time of trial and conflict. As we have seen, Rowley identifies this period with the forty years of warfare contemplated by the War scroll. Evidently the warfare had barely begun; hence the document must have been composed near the beginning of the forty years. According to the Damascus Document, the period began with the death of the teacher. The commentary on Psalm 37 also speaks of the destruction of the wicked after forty years, and since the teacher of righteousness is mentioned in this commentary, the forty years are probably those following his death. Thus the War scroll appears to have been written soon after the death of the teacher of righteousness. Having already concluded that it was written in the second century B.C., and that the Kittim of this scroll are the Seleucids, Rowley thus finds another line of evidence for dating the teacher of righteousness in the time of the Seleucids. If he is wrong in his identification of the Kittim in the War scroll, and in dating the War scroll in this early period, the whole elaborate argument collapses.

But Rowley has still another string to his bow. He finds another argument in a study of the literary relations of the Dead Sea Scrolls. In the Testaments of the Twelve Patriarchs and the book of Jubilees there are ideas similar to those of the scrolls. The Messianic expectations of the Testaments, Rowley believes, were influenced by the Qumran sect. In the first-century B.C. Psalms of Solomon, however, no such influence is manifest. In short, the scrolls are more closely related to the literature of the second century than they are to first-century compositions. Here again the argument is more suggestive than conclusive. Much depends on the dating of the works with which the scrolls are compared. That the Testaments of the Twelve Patriarchs come from the second century B.C. is by no means certain (see pp. 179f).

Schonfield, who believes that the Habakkuk Commentary was written in the first century A.D. and reflects events of that time, admits that it can be interpreted as "a dramatization in the historic present, with a topical twist, of events that had happened long before." The wicked priest or the man of the lie may represent the renegade high priests Jason, Menelaus, and Alcimus of pre-Maccabean and Maccabean times (*DSS*, pp. 162f). The exile and murder of the legitimate high priest Onias III (*DSS*, p. 164) may be reflected in what is said of the persecution of the teacher of righteousness by the wicked priest. Or it may be that the wicked priest was Alcimus, as many scholars have maintained, and the teacher of righteousness was his saintly uncle Jose ben Joezer (*DSS*, pp. 168f). All this, however, seems to Schonfield a matter of history repeating itself. Elements from history and tradition, he feels, are repeated in present persons and events.

Schonfield argues at some length that on the basis of certain honored figures of the past an ideal picture of a Suffering Just One had been gradually built up and associated with the hope of a coming Messianic figure. According to this view, we have neither a single historical person represented by the teacher of righteousness nor a succession of individuals so designated, but a traditional, ideal figure made up by the gradual accumulation of elements suggested in part by different historic individuals. Schonfield agrees with Gaster's position, however, to this extent: the traditional and fairly constant description of the ideal figures may have been applied at different times, he says, to different persons who seemed to meet the requirements of the prophecies.

Schonfield has, in fact, suggestions of his own concerning some of these identifications. One to which he devotes much speculation is a man called Asaph whom he supposes to have lived in the time of the Maccabees. In the Assumption of Moses, an apocryphal work of the first century A.D., there is a story about a man called Taxo, who is said to be of the tribe of Levi. Scholars have speculated a great deal about the meaning of the strange name and the identity of the man who bore it. Sigmund Mowinckel, for example, suggested that the name Taxo was from a Greek word meaning "orderer," and that it was a translation of the Hebrew word used in the Damascus Document for the lawgiver of the sect (the "sceptre" of Numbers 21:18; *DSS*, p. 355), whose interpretations of the law are to be followed until the (or a) teacher of righteousness arises at the end of days. He is also identified with the "star," of whom more will be said later. Mowinckel concludes that the Assumption of Moses was written by a member of the sect which produced the Damascus Covenant and the Dead Sea Scrolls. Schonfield's approach is quite different. He assumes that the name is a transliteration instead of a translation of a Hebrew name. Using what would seem to be the Hebrew original, Tacho or Tachu (i.e., *thw*), he finds that by *atbash* this represents Asaph (*'sp*).

The name Asaph has many biblical and legendary associations. In I–II Chronicles, Ezra, and Nehemiah there are many references to a certain Asaph ben Berechiah, the head of one of the three families or guilds of Levitical singers established by David (see especially I Chronicles 6:39; 15:17; 25:1–2, 6; II Chronicles 29:30; Ezra 2:41; 3:10; Nehemiah 12:46). Jewish and Moslem legends make him a trusted counselor of Solomon, who knew the ineffable name of God and performed miracles by its power. A late medical treatise, which traces the origin of medicine to Noah's son Shem, is sometimes ascribed to Asaph. This, Schonfield suggests, explains how the Hasidim and through them the Essenes, as Josephus reports, possessed prophetic and medical writings supposed to have been handed down from the earliest ages. A late Syriac book of Shem refers to Asaph as a Hebrew writer and historian who explained the signs of the zodiac, naming them after the twelve sons of Jacob. Schonfield conjectures further that the reference to Asaph as a seer in II Chronicles 29:30 may have been inserted by the Hasidim as an allusion to a person whom they knew by the name of Asaph.

The Asaph or Taxo of the Assumption of Moses, Schonfield believes, was the teacher of righteousness. Interpreting the name

Asaph as "gatherer" or "collector," Schonfield suggests that it may have been given to the teacher of righteousness because he gathered together the books scattered by the Maccabean war. In II Maccabees 2:14 this achievement is attributed to Judas Maccabeus himself, but, says Schonfield, he must have delegated the actual work to somebody. This might explain the extraordinary literary activity of the teacher's followers.

In the book of Psalms the titles of Psalms 50 and 73–83 ascribe them to Asaph. No doubt these formed a collection used by the "sons of Asaph." Schonfield remarks that Psalms 74 and 83 of this group have been dated by some scholars in the Maccabean period, and he doubts that any of them are much older. This leads to the suggestion that the guild of the sons of Asaph may have been closely associated with the Hasidim, whose spirit these Psalms reflect. The teacher of righteousness himself is thought by many to have been a psalmist and to have composed the Thanksgiving Psalms (see pp. 324–27). It may be recalled, however, that the Qumran manuscripts of the Old Testament book of Psalms do not favor the theory, now generally abandoned in any case, that any of the Psalms were composed as late as the Maccabean period.

To one reader, at least, these elaborate arguments for the existence of "the original teacher of righteousness" in the time of the Maccabees make fascinating reading and elicit admiration for the wide learning and subtle reasoning they exhibit, but they fall considerably short of producing conviction. They impress one as a play of academic imagination, touching reality here and there but then glancing off into free and airy fancy.

The work of the teacher of righteousness and his connection with the history of his time are placed by other scholars at various points in the Maccabean or Hasmonean period. Oesterreicher, like Rowley and others, connects the origins of the Qumran sect with the Hasidim of Maccabean times. When the victorious Maccabees went on from the achievement of religious liberty to the struggle for political independence and power, the Hasidim withdrew their support. The Maccabean leader and high priest was now Jonathan, brother and successor of Judas Maccabeus. Against him was arrayed a little group of devout priests, the "sons of Zadok, keepers of the covenant," with the teacher of righteousness at their head.

Milik holds that Jonathan was the wicked priest. Only in him do we find combined all the characteristics pictured in the Habakkuk Commentary. He was a warrior and a builder. When he "first took office," or, more literally, "begun to rule in Israel," as the Commentary says (viii.9f; *DSS*, p. 368), that is, after he assumed the high priesthood in 152 B.C., he abandoned his previous policy of independence and isolation. The faithful among the Jews, especially a group of priests, resisted him. In 143 he was betrayed and the following year he was put to death. Milik notes that Vermès has suggested Jonathan as the wicked priest but makes his successor Simon share the dubious honor with him. In the Testimonia there is a reference to two "instruments of violence" whom Milik identifies as Jonathan and Simon, but he rejects the idea that both are meant by the wicked priest of the Habakkuk Commentary. Cross holds that the wicked priest was Simon.

H. J. Schoeps also sees the origin of the Qumran sect in a movement of protest against the Hasmonean union of kingdom and priesthood. Not only did Jonathan assume the high priesthood; in 141 B.C. his successor Simon was acclaimed as "leader and high priest forever, until a faithful prophet should arise," and as "captain over them" to be obeyed by all and wear purple and gold (I Maccabees 14:41–47). I–II Maccabees and Josephus fail to inform us, Schoeps says, that there was any strong opposition to these proceedings; we know from apocryphal texts of the period that there was, and the Dead Sea Scrolls have now given us the literature of the opposition party.

Only a descendant of Zadok, to follow further Schoeps' presentation, could legitimately be high priest. The last member of this line to hold the office had been Onias III, who had been exiled and then murdered in 175–174 B.C. (*DSS*, pp. 162–64). Family rivalries and jealousy may have played some part in the opposition to the Hasmonean rulers, but the Hasidim and the devout priests were also sincerely shocked at the assumption of the highest religious office by warriors. They had no objections to war in principle, but the violation of ritual purity and consequent desecration of the temple were for them intolerable.

Their resistance reached the boiling point, Schoeps continues, when a Hasmonean took the the title of king. Whether this was first done by John Hyrcanus (135–104 B.C.), Aristobulus I (104–103), or Alexander Janneus (103–76) is not certain, but the evidence of their coins favors Alexander Janneus. Jewish tradition kept strictly apart the political and priestly offices represented by Moses and Aaron. Since the return from the Babylonian exile, however, the hope of a Messiah who would be both priest and king had arisen. By uniting the offices in himself, therefore, the Hasmonean ruler in effect claimed Messianic status. While the Qumran secretarians did not expect a single Messiah who would be both priest and king (see pp. 298–311), they would undoubtedly see in Alexander Janneus an anti-Christ rather than a Messiah.

The Habakkuk Commentary indicates that the wicked priest drove the teacher of righteousness and his followers into exile. Josephus tells us of the flight of eight thousand Pharisees from the persecution and massacres of Alexander Janneus (*DSS*, p. 200). Like others before him, Schoeps believes that the same series of events is reflected in both cases. The persecution ended at the death of the king, but the fugitive "sons of Zadok," instead of returning to Jerusalem, settled at Ain Feshkha and Khirbet Qumran.

New grist for the mills of all who could use it was provided by Allegro's publication of a column from the Nahum Commentary. Along with its mention of Antiochus and Demetrius, which we have discussed in connection with the Kittim (p. 201), this text speaks of a wicked ruler called "the lion of wrath" or "wrathful lion," who is accused of hanging men alive, an enormity never before perpetrated in Israel. The lion of wrath is mentioned also in a tiny fragment of a commentary on Hosea. The immediate context is lost, but the next line speaks of "the last priest, who put forth his hand to smite Ephraim." Allegro notes the apparent play on the Hebrew words for "wrath" (*haron*) and "last" (*aharon*). Assuming that the smiting of Ephraim is to be connected with the final war against the sons of darkness, Allegro finds significant the association of the last priest and the lion of wrath. This, he thinks, "might tell us something about the identity of the priestly leader of the sons of light." Just what it might tell us we are unfortunately left to guess.

The statement that the lion of wrath hanged men alive is taken by Allegro to refer to crucifixion. He mentions the fact that in Esther 7:9 (English verse 10) the Septuagint renders the same Hebrew verb that is used here by the Greek verb meaning "crucify." It is of some interest to note that in Esther 9:13f the ten sons of Haman are hanged, although they were already killed in verse 10. Here the verb "crucify" is not used in the Septuagint; as a matter of fact 7:10, immediately following the use of "crucify" in verse 9, says in the Septuagint that they "hanged" Haman, though the same Hebrew verb is used in both verses. Allegro points out that a form of the verb which means "crucify" is used by Josephus not only in that sense but also with reference to hanging up the body of a criminal for public exposure after his execution. This explains the specific statement that the lion of wrath hanged men alive.

Josephus reports, as we have noted, that Alexander Janneus, on regaining his throne after being defeated by Demetrius III, crucified eight hundred of the Pharisees who had opposed him. It was then that eight thousand others fled from the country. Allegro sees a reference to this in what is said of the lion of wrath.

Rowley agrees that hanging alive probably means crucifixion, but he maintains that the reference is more probably to Antiochus Epiphanes, who punished parents whose children were circumcised by crucifying them with the bodies of their children hung at their necks. The people crucified at this time would be faithful Jews, including quite possibly members of the sect of the scrolls. The Pharisees who had rebelled against Alexander Janneus would have no connection with the sect. In the time of Antiochus the lion of wrath might be the false priest Alcimus, or Antiochus himself, or the royal agent who conducted the persecutions. Schonfield suggests that the lion might be Demetrius I, in whose reign Alcimus was high priest.

The statement that hanging men alive had not been done before in Israel could refer to Alexander Janneus, Rowley observes,
only if it means that this had not been done before by an Israelite.
By supplying a different form of the verb "to do" Rowley ob-
tains the meaning, "Such a thing had never taken place in Israel
before." One must agree that the form proposed by Rowley is
grammatically preferable to the one given by Allegro, but the
difference is only one of tense. In either case "done in Israel"
means "done among the people of Israel," whether done by them
or to them. If the latter meaning is intended, then Alexander
Janneus is, as Rowley claims, excluded, for Antiochus Epiphanes,
as we have just seen, had previously inflicted the same cruel
death on Jews who were loyal to the traditions of their fathers.

If Alexander Janneus was the lion of wrath, he was also probably the wicked priest who persecuted the teacher of righteousness. The conflict between the teacher of righteousness and the
wicked priest is apparently referred to in a fragment of the commentary on Psalm 37. Unfortunately the text is in bad condition:
only the last letter of the word for "priest" is preserved, and the
reference to the teacher of righteousness has to be conjectured
to fill a gap in the next line. The infinitive "to kill him" follows,
and Allegro supposes that the text originally read, "This means
the wicked priest who sent to the teacher of righteousness to kill
him." There is a tantalizing mention of "the law which he sent
him" (who sent to whom?); then the text continues, with gaps
which can be filled in fairly confidently by the aid of the verse
being expounded: "God will not leave him in his hand, and will
not condemn him when he is brought to trial. He will render to
the wicked his requital, delivering him into the hand of the
tyrants of the nations, to do to him"—and here the fragment ends.
Presumably it is the teacher of righteousness who will not be
abandoned to the wicked priest or condemned, but it is the wicked
priest who is to be delivered to the tyrants of the nations. Such
ambiguity in the use of pronouns is common in Hebrew.

The shift to the future tense—it can hardly be intended in any
other way—is puzzling. Could the conflict have been still going
on when the commentary was written? Allegro considers it pos-

sible that the reference is to the last judgment, and in support of this interpretation cites an earlier part of the same commentary which speaks of a coming time of trial, when the wicked of Ephraim and Manasseh will try to lay hands on the priest (i.e., the teacher of righteousness?) "and the men of his counsel." The text continues, "God will redeem them from their hand, and afterward they shall be delivered into the hand of the tyrants of the nations for judgment."

With these texts Allegro compares also a comment on Psalm 2:1–3 in the Florilegium, where "the last days" are equated with "the coming time of trial." A "season of affliction" mentioned near the beginning of the commentary on Psalm 37 may be, as Allegro suggests, the "time of trial" referred to in the other passages. In the light of all these references, it seems that the conflict is still unfinished. Either the protagonists are still living, or a future resurrection and judgment are contemplated. Allegro considers the latter alternative more probable. We must deal with this question later in connection with the sect's beliefs concerning the future life.

All this seems to Allegro to support his view that the wicked priest was Alexander Janneus. He suggests that the teacher of righteousness had probably instigated the pelting of Alexander with citrons at the Feast of Tabernacles. It was at the time of the frightful massacre which followed this incident, Allegro believes, that the teacher of righteousness gathered a group of faithful priests about him and withdrew to Qumran. Schoeps accepts the identification of the lion of wrath with Alexander Janneus and agrees that he is also the wicked priest of the Habakkuk Commentary and the commentary on Psalm 37. It can hardly be doubted any longer, he feels, that the Dead Sea Scrolls really refer to Alexander Janneus.

Not all scholars are so easily convinced that the teacher of righteousness or his followers were involved with the Pharisees in the rebellion against Alexander Janneus. Still less are they convinced that the teacher was one of the eight hundred who were crucified. This is a major item in Allegro's reconstruction of the history of the sect, and he has dramatized it in a way that at least received a great deal of publicity. In his BBC broadcast of January 23, 1956, he said, according to press reports, that Alexander Janneus had probably given the teacher of righteousness into the hands of Gentile mercenaries to be crucified; the disciples "took down the broken body of their Master" and "reverently buried" him, then settled down "to await his glorious return as Messiah of God." Allegro's colleagues on the international team at Jerusalem immediately published a statement declaring that they found none of these things in the texts. Allegro promptly admitted that his reconstruction of the story was a matter of inference rather than evidence. In his book, which appeared later in the same year, the sensational form of statement was abandoned, but the conjecture that the teacher of righteousness was one of those crucified by Alexander Janneus was repeated.

Whether the followers of the teacher of righteousness believed that he was in any sense the (or a) Messiah we shall have to inquire later. That he was crucified is neither stated nor suggested by any of the texts published hitherto. On the assumption that crucifixion is meant by the hanging alive of the Nahum Commentary, it is strange, as Rowley remarks, that nothing should be said to indicate that the teacher of righteousness was crucified. He may have been, as many thousands were before him and after him. Not the slightest hint of this, however, is given anywhere. The only clear references to his death, as has often been pointed out, are still the two passages in Manuscript B of the Damascus Document which mention "the gathering in of the unique teacher" (xix.35–xx.1 and xx.14; *DSS*, pp. 356f). This expression might very well, though not necessarily, indicate a natural death. Only on the assumption that the teacher of righteousness lived in the time of Alexander Janneus and was one of those who actually opposed him is it possible to infer with any plausibility that he was one of those whom the cruel priest-king crucified. The passage quoted from the commentary on Psalm 37 (p. 215) suggests that the teacher was delivered from his persecutor.

A reference to the time of Alexander Janneus and his successors is found by Schonfield in "the first saints" of the Damascus Document (iv.6; *DSS*, p. 352). (The expression "first saints" is secured by emending an obviously corrupt passage in the Hebrew text, which makes no sense as it stands. With some possible variation, however, the reconstruction is fairly certain.) Schonfield identifies these first saints with the repentant remnant mentioned at the beginning of the document, for whom God "raised up a teacher of righteousness" (see p. 341). They were included, according to Schonfield, among those called in rabbinical literature the first Hasidim. On the basis, presumably, of the 390 years discussed earlier (p. 191), Schonfield says that their rise is dated about 196–176 B.C. All who come after them, the text continues, must live for an unspecified period according to the covenant and the explanation of the laws given to their forefathers. During this time "Belial will be let loose in Israel." At the end of the period "they shall no more join themselves to the house of Judah." Schonfield sees here a prediction that during the time of the Maccabean priesthood's decadence, from Alexander Janneus on, the covenant party will become established as a separate community.

Any effort to correlate the allusions in the Damascus Document with those of the Habakkuk Commentary is pronounced futile by Fritsch. The terms "teacher of righteousness" and "wicked priest" in these two compositions, he thinks, may designate respectively the true and the false priesthood of the temple at any time from the Maccabean uprising to the end of the Hasmonean priesthood. Essentially the same struggle against the corrupt priesthood is reflected in both documents, but different phases of the struggle are contemplated.

Milik is inclined to feel that two different movements, which arose at the same time and had the same background, are represented. That they had close contacts, however, is shown, he points out, by the fragments of the Damascus Document found in the Qumran caves. It is rather hard to believe, in view of this evidence, that there were ever really two distinct groups, though there may well have been a number of different settlements with no absolute uniformity of ideas or practices.

# XIX

## The Land of Damascus

The exact relationship of the "Damascus" and Qumran communities is still uncertain and obscure. Much depends upon the interpretation given to the passages in the Damascus Document which have given it this name. These passages speak of an emigration to "the land of Damascus" under the leadership of one who is called "the star" (vi.5; vii.18; DSS, pp. 353, 355). There are also two references to "those who entered the new covenant in the land of Damascus" (vi.19; viii.21; DSS, pp. 354, 356). The view of Isaac Rabinowitz that these passages have nothing to do with a migration of the sect but refer to the dispersed exiles of Israel in Assyria and Babylonia (DSS, pp. 201f) has had a mixed reception. It has been accepted by some recent writers on the Dead Sea Scrolls, including Gärtner and Howlett.

Others, such as Schonfield, Fritsch, and Milik, still believe that there was a migration to the land of Damascus, though they differ as to the time when it occurred. A very important contribution to the solution of this problem was made by Robert North in an article which appeared after my DSS had gone to press. North showed that the expression "land of Damascus" might very well mean the Nabatean kingdom, to which Damascus belonged during much of the time with which we are concerned. The territory held by the Nabateans sometimes extended to the west of the Jordan River and included the area of the Wady Qumran. It is therefore entirely possible that the migration actually took place, but that it was simply the withdrawal to the Wady Qumran and the establishment of the community there.

In that case, it might also be connected with the flight of eight thousand Pharisees under Alexander Janneus, since the coins found at Khirbet Qumran show that the settlement was established at about that time. As pointed out in *DSS* (pp. 200, 277ff), however, we cannot consider the teacher of righteousness and his followers Pharisees. Perhaps, if North's thesis is to be accepted, we may say that the persecution and flight were not limited to Pharisees but included other opponents of Alexander Janneus. The flight, for that matter, need not be connected with the establishment of the Qumran community. Howlett suggests that many of the Pharisees who fled from Alexander Janneus may have joined the Qumran community.

Gaster regards the community's migration to the land of Damascus and sojourn there as a symbolic way of representing "its sojourn in the forbidding desert," which was considered a dramatic fulfillment of Amos 5:27. In other words, the migration meant simply the sect's "voluntary withdrawal from the normative forms of Jewish life." This, in effect, amounts to the same thing as North's conclusion, the difference being that North regards the expression "land of Damascus" as geographically justified, whereas Gaster takes it as purely figurative. The truth of the matter may very well lie in a combination of North's and Gaster's views. There must surely have been something to suggest the connection between Amos's prophecy of exile beyond Damascus and the community's life in the desert of Judah.

Those who take "the land of Damascus" more literally, or in a narrower geographical sense, differ in their understanding of the relation between the migrating group and the Qumran community. Milik, as we have seen, thinks of two separate though related groups, and this view has been held by others (see, e.g., *DSS*, p. 192). Milik's view of the migration, however, is not quite clear: he speaks of an exodus "in the region of Damascus and to Qumran," meaning apparently that the two groups withdrew at the same time to the land of Damascus and to Qumran respectively. Some scholars, however, connect the withdrawal to the land of Damascus with the abandonment of the Qumran settlement, either in 31 B.C. or in 68 A.D., though the latter alternative is excluded by the presence of portions of the Damascus Document in the Qumran caves (*DSS*, p. 201).

The Manual of Discipline speaks of "going to the wilderness to prepare there the way of the Lord" by "study of the law," and of "clearing the way to the wilderness" (viii.12–16; ix.20; *DSS*, pp. 382, 384). Schonfield takes these to be references to the same withdrawal from Judah mentioned by the Damascus Document. He cites also the instructions given in the Assumption of Moses for preserving sacred writings (2:16f) and the reference at the end of the book of Enoch to books given to the righteous that they may learn the ways of righteousness and be rewarded (104:12f). All these, he feels, have a bearing on the movement to Qumran to copy and preserve sacred writings.

The nature of the migration, if there was one, is of course bound up with the time when it took place. Schonfield believes that the migration can be connected with a situation of which Josephus tells us, and can accordingly be dated almost exactly. After the death of Judas Maccabeus, Josephus says, the transgressors of the law prevailed in Judea, which was afflicted also by a famine. Driven both by want and by their wicked enemies, many at this time forsook their native land and sought refuge with the Macedonians, that is, in the Seleucid kingdom of Syria, the capital of which was Damascus. Judas died in battle in 160 B.C.; the flight therefore occurred in 160 or 159. The same general period is inferred from a passage in the Damascus Document which seems to place the emigration during a period of wickedness and judgment, when faithless Israel is punished by "the head of the kings of Greece, who comes to take vengeance upon them" (viii.11; *DSS*, p. 356). This and a similar passage in the Assumption of Moses (8:1) point clearly, says Schonfield, to the time of Antiochus Epiphanes (175–164 B.C.).

In a special study devoted to "the head of the kings of Greece" Dupont-Sommer argues with considerable cogency that this expression cannot refer to Antiochus Epiphanes. The Damascus Document says that in the time of the visitation in question the devout Jews will be spared, and the chastisement will fall on the rebellious and disobedient (vii.21–viii.3; *DSS*, p. 355). Under Antiochus Epiphanes it was the righteous who suffered and the wicked who escaped. Antiochus, moreover, could not be called "the chief of the kings of Yawan," as Dupont-Sommer translates the expression, because in his time the kings of Yawan would include the kings of Macedonia, Egypt, Pergamon, Bythinia, Pontus, and all the other Hellenistic monarchies, none of whom would acknowledge Antiochus as their chief. A Jewish writer would not so exaggerate the power of the hated persecutor, but would more naturally call him, as the book of Daniel does, "a contemptible person" (11:21). We shall see in a moment how Dupont-Sommer himself interprets "the chief of the kings of Yawan."

Theories which place the migration to the land of Damascus in the time of the Maccabees or Hasmoneans have been discussed in the foregoing pages and in *DSS* (pp. 199f). Rowley puts the emigration to Damascus in the time of Jonathan (160–142 B.C.) or Simon (142–135); Milik dates it in the high priesthood of Jonathan; Vermès at the accession of Simon. If the persecution and exile of the teacher of righteousness are to be connected with the migration of the group, the identification of the wicked priest will determine the date of the migration. So Milik, we have seen, makes Jonathan the wicked priest and dates the migration both to the region of Damascus and to Qumran after Jonathan's assumption of the high priesthood (152 B.C.).

John Hyrcanus (135–104 B.C.), whose assumption of both priestly and royal office was resisted by the Pharisees, has been considered the wicked priest, or one of several wicked priests, especially by those who believe that the devout and revered Pharisee Eleazar was the teacher of righteousness (*DSS*, p. 172f). Aristobulus I (104–103 B.C.) has been seriously considered in connection with some of the statements about the wicked priest in the Habakkuk Commentary (*DSS*, p. 174). The various theories connected with Alexander Janneus (103–76 B.C.) require no further discussion at this point. The last two Hasmonean brothers, Hyrcanus II and Aristobulus II, have both been associated with the figure of the wicked priest by Dupont-Sommer, though he was more inclined later to regard Hyrcanus II alone as the wicked priest (*DSS*, pp. 178–82).

Thus we come down to the beginning of the Roman period, marked by Pompey's annexation of Palestine in 63 B.C. This was the event, it will be remembered, which Dupont-Sommer sees reflected in the most debated passage of the Habakkuk Commentary (xi.4–8; *DSS*, p. 370, cp. pp. 153–57, 179–81; see also this volume, p. 225). Confirmation of the crucial importance of Pompey's conquest is seen by Dupont-Sommer in the Damascus Covenant's reference to "the head of the kings of Greece." Finding that the allusion does not fit Antiochus Epiphanes (see p. 221), Dupont-Sommer proceeds to argue that it fits Pompey admirably. The expression "chief of the kings of Yawan" does not imply that the person so designated was himself a king, but that all the rulers of the Hellenistic kingdoms were subject to him. The eulogy of the Romans in I Maccabees 8:1–16 stresses the fact that the Romans, none of whom "ever put on a diadem" (verse 14), have conquered the kings. The *imperium* conferred upon Pompey by the Senate made him master of the East. The Roman authors glorify his personal dominion over all the conquered kings. None could more fitly be called "the chief of the kings of Yawan."

In further confirmation of his thesis, Dupont-Sommer cites the references to Pompey's occupation of Jerusalem in the Psalms of Solomon, especially the second, eighth, and seventeenth. In the last mentioned the poet complains that the sinners "assailed us and thrust us out" (v.6); the faithful, he says, fled from the wicked and "wandered in deserts to save their lives from harm" (v.19). Thus, in contrast to what happened under Antiochus Epiphanes, the righteous and loyal Jews were now saved by escaping to the desert. This flight, not one under Antiochus Epiphanes or Alexander Janneus, is the migration to the land of Damascus, as Dupont-Sommer sees it. By withdrawing from the country, the devout Jews were delivered from the horrors that befell their unfaithful compatriots, as depicted in other passages of the Psalms of Solomon (13:2f; 15:8–10). The references to Pompey in the

Psalms of Solomon are unmistakable, though he is nowhere named; so also, Dupont-Sommer avers, are the allusions in the Damascus Document. Both the Damascus Document and the Habakkuk Commentary, according to this view, were written during the period of exile in the land of Damascus.

Since the Damascus Document twice mentions the death of the teacher of righteousness, most scholars, including Dupont-Sommer, believe that the teacher was already dead before the emigration to the land of Damascus took place, and the "star" who led the group in this movement was his successor. Not all, however, accept this conclusion. Some believe that the teacher may have been himself the leader of the migration, or even that he may have been himself the "star." These questions will be considered in connection with the Messianic ideas of the Qumran community (pp. 329–41). All that needs to be said here is that the banishment of the teacher by the wicked priest may have no connection at all with the migration to the land of Damascus. If the latter is identified with the withdrawal to the Wady Qumran, this may have been the result of the persecution by the wicked priest. Several scholars, however, interpret the Habakkuk Commentary in the sense that the wicked priest attacked the teacher of righteousness at Qumran some time after the establishment of the community.

According to Dupont-Sommer, "the last priests of Jerusalem," whose wealth the Habakkuk Commentary says will be delivered to the Kittim, were Aristobulus II and Hyrcanus II, the sons of Alexander Janneus and Alexandra. They were the last members of the Hasmonean dynasty to hold office. In the original form of Dupont-Sommer's theory, both brothers were also believed to be represented by the figure of the wicked priest; later, on the understanding that the career of the teacher of righteousness came to an end before 63 B.C., Dupont-Sommer modified his theory to the extent of recognizing Hyrcanus alone as the wicked priest. At the second World Congress of Jewish Studies in Israel in the summer of 1957, Dupont-Sommer announced that a study of texts not yet published had confirmed his identification of the wicked priest as Hyrcanus II. It was Aristobulus II, however, who presumably had the teacher of righteousness put to death not long before the capture of Jerusalem by the Romans. The much debated "appearance" mysteriously mentioned by the Habakkuk Commentary was therefore a post-mortem manifestation of the teacher of righteousness as a divine being at the time when Pompey captured Jerusalem in 63 B.C. (*DSS*, pp. 156, 179–82).

Dupont-Sommer's dating of the events and the documents is rejected by Schonfield on the ground that the literature of that period contains no references to such a person as the teacher of righteousness in the time of Aristobulus II and Hyrcanus II. The theory of Goosens that the teacher of righteousness was the saintly Onias who was stoned to death in 65 B.C. (*DSS*, p. 180) may be recalled; it has not, however, won many adherents. Schonfield submits that if the teacher of righteousness had lived at this time, and if his followers had been a group of the Essenes, he would not have been unmentioned in the literature of his time.

The teacher of righteousness of the Damascus Document, who is dated by Schonfield at about 176 B.C., was not the Messiah, he says, but the traditions about him may have influenced the conception of a coming teacher of righteousness who would be thought of in Messianic terms. For such an expected Messianic teacher of righteousness there would be "many likely candidates" in the first century A.D. It is this coming teacher of righteousness, Schonfield believes, who is the hero of the Habakkuk Commentary (see pp. 331–32). Thus Schonfield has two teachers of righteousness, one earlier than Dupont-Sommer's and one later.

Schonfield finds three periods of the community's history reflected in the Damascus Document. The priests, the Levites, and the sons of Zadok of Ezekiel 44:15 are taken by the Damascus Document as three different groups and identified as follows: "The priests are the captivity of Israel who went forth from the land of Judah, and the Levites are those who joined them; and the sons of Zadok are the elect of Israel, those called by name, who will arise at the end of days" (iv.2–4; *DSS*, p. 352). Each of these, as Schonfield interprets the passage, represents a period in the history of the sect. The first is naturally connected with the migration to the land of Damascus in the time of Antiochus Epiphanes, which was the time of the first teacher of righteousness. The "Levites," described as "those who joined them," stand for a second period in which the accession of new members enlarged the community. This, Schonfield believes, was the time of Hasmonean decadence and the Roman conquest. The third period, that of "the elect of Israel . . . at the end of days," is the one in which the Damascus Document and the Habakkuk Commentary were written. The group was now back in Palestine, with its headquarters at Qumran. This period began near the end of the last century before Christ and lasted until the destruction of the Qumran community.

With this theory is associated an analysis of the Damascus Document and a view of the stages of its composition, but these need not be discussed here. More to the point for our present purpose is the fact that Schonfield takes little account of the occupational history of Khirbet Qumran as revealed by the excavations. He notes the terminal dates set by the excavators, and especially the time of great activity in the first century A.D., but he argues that the destruction of the settlement may have been as late as 72 A.D., and the sect may have reoccupied the site not much later. He ignores entirely the gap of about thirty years in the occupation from 31 B.C. to about the beginning of the Christian era.

These three or four decades when the site lay deserted are used by Fritsch as the basis of a quite different theory. Where others, as we have seen, connect the migration to the land of Damascus with the establishment of the Qumran community, Fritsch suggests that the abandonment of the settlement early in the reign of Herod the Great is to be equated with the migration to Damascus. The reoccupation, apparently not long after the end of Herod's reign, marks, then, the return of the group to Palestine.

Herod, Fritsch says, would not have much sympathy with the moral principles or the Messianic ideas of the Essenes, with whom Fritsch identifies the Qumran community. He probably considered them not only fanatical but politically dangerous. He therefore compelled the group to leave his domain. His death made possible their return and the resumption of their community life.

It will be recalled that the end of the first period seems to have been connected in some way with an earthquake. The fact that a very severe earthquake in 31 B.C. is recorded enables the archeologists to give this exact date for the abandonment of the site. Fritsch dates the abandonment "at or before" the earthquake, and feels that the earthquake would explain the desertion of the site for a generation. Bruce, who agrees that the group may have gone to Damascus during Herod's reign, suggests that the earthquake occurred during their absence. Howlett also regards the hypothesis of Fritsch as probable, though he remarks also that the migration and return may have had nothing to do with political events.

If the migration to Damascus is to be regarded as a movement of the community rather than the Assyrian and Babylonian exile of Old Testament times, and if that movement took them outside of Palestine, the view propounded by Fritsch is quite credible. It involves the composition of the Damascus Document, or parts of it, during the period of absence from Qumran. The presence of fragments of this book in the Qumran caves is then easily understood. The differences between these fragments and the medieval Cairo manuscripts may be attributed to editorial changes in later times. Without rejecting this theory as impossible, I am still more attracted to the view that what is meant by the migration to the land of Damascus is the movement of the group to Qumran itself. The only solid fact we have, however, is that widely divergent views of this matter are still quite possible.

# XX

## The Theories of Schonfield and Del Medico

ⅬⅡⅡⅬⅡⅬⅡⅬⅡⅬⅡⅬⅡⅬⅡⅬⅡⅬⅡⅬⅡⅬⅡⅬⅡⅬⅡⅬⅡⅬⅡⅬⅡⅬⅡⅬⅡⅬⅡⅬⅡⅬⅡⅬⅡⅬⅡⅬⅡⅬⅡⅬⅡⅬⅡⅬⅡⅬⅡⅬⅡⅬⅡⅬⅡⅬⅡⅬⅡⅬⅡⅬⅡⅬⅡⅬⅡⅬⅡⅬⅡⅬⅡⅬⅡⅬⅡⅬⅡⅬⅡⅬⅡⅬⅡⅬⅡⅬⅡⅬⅡⅬⅡⅬⅡⅬⅡⅬⅡⅬⅡⅬⅡⅬⅡ

A tendency to place the persons and events referred to in the Qumran writings in the first century A.D. is manifest in several recent books on the Dead Sea Scrolls. Schonfield's separation of the teacher of righteousness in the Habakkuk Commentary from his prototype in the Damascus Document enables him to find references to events and persons of the Christian era in the historical allusions of the Habakkuk Commentary. The Kittim are the Romans, he maintains, but not the Romans of the time of Pompey. The "guilty house," by whose counsel the rulers of the Kittim "pass on, each before his fellow" (iv.11f; *DSS*, p. 366; cp. pp. 133, 138), is called by Schonfield "the house of idolatry" and identified with the palace of the Roman emperors, and the rulers of the Kittim are the successive procurators sent out by the emperors to rule Judea.

The crucial passage which Dupont-Sommer made the cornerstone of his interpretation of the Habakkuk Commentary receives a new interpretation at the hands of Schonfield. This is the comment on Habakkuk 2:15, which says of the wicked priest or the teacher of righteousness, according to the interpretation put upon it, that "at the time of their festival of rest, the day of atonement, he appeared to them to confound them and to make them stumble on the day of fasting, their Sabbath of rest" (xi.6–8; *DSS*, p. 370; cp. pp. 156f, 179f). Schonfield agrees with Dupont-

Sommer that it was the teacher of righteousness, not the wicked priest, who "appeared." In support of this interpretation he adduces the verse from Habakkuk which is here expounded, and which the commentary alters to read "to gaze on their festivals" instead of "to gaze on their nakedness." Schonfield translates, "in order that God may look at their feasts," but the Hebrew word which he takes to mean "God" is simply a preposition which has been substituted, as happens very often, for the slightly different one in the Masoretic text.

From the supposed introduction of God into the text Schonfield infers that the commentator implies "a reversal of the circumstances, a comeback by the Righteous Teacher." Even if the text were intended to be read as Schonfield takes it, which is entirely improbable, the inference he draws from it would not be justified. The most natural way to interpret the commentator's statement is that the wicked priest is the subject of this clause, as he obviously is of the one that precedes it.

Schonfield does not, in any case, accept Dupont-Sommer's view that the appearing of the teacher of righteousness was his manifestation as a divine being after his martyrdom, and that this occurred in connection with the capture of Jerusalem. More prosaically, he takes the passage to mean that when the wicked priest was persecuting the righteous teacher and seeking to destroy him, the teacher "confounded his persecutors by appearing before them on the Day of Atonement."

Admitting that "to pin the commentary to any known historical event" requires "a stretch of the imagination," Schonfield stretches his imagination and suggests as a possible occasion a persecution of the Jewish Christians in 45–50 A.D. The head of the Christian community in Jerusalem at this time was James, "the Lord's brother" (Galatians 1:19), who was highly respected among the Jews and known as "James the Just (or Righteous)." Schonfield cites later traditions about him, including one to the effect that he was even allowed to officiate as high priest. Tacitly assuming that this obviously apocryphal tale may have been true, Schonfield suggests that James might have "shone forth" or "appeared all resplendent" in the high priest's robe on the Day of Atonement. No doubt this would have confounded any wicked priest who was persecuting James the Just, but to suppose that this was the event referred to by the commentator on Habakkuk exceeds the bounds of historical credibility.

The "house of Absalom," which failed to help the teacher of righteousness when he was persecuted (v.9–12; *DSS*, p. 367, cp. pp. 161f, 166, 169, 179), is supposed by Schonfield to mean members of the Sanhedrin, who should have prevented the illegal conviction of the teacher. This fits the account Josephus gives of the illegal conviction and execution of James by the high-handed procedure of the high priest Ananus. Some members of the Sanhedrin "disliked what was done" and complained afterward, but they apparently did nothing at the time to save the apostle.

Other references in the Habakkuk Commentary seem to Schonfield to indicate Ananus as the wicked priest who persecuted the teacher of righteousness and brought about his death. The commentary speaks of "the last priests of Jerusalem, who assembled wealth and booty from the spoil of the peoples," but all to no avail, for "at the end of days their wealth with their spoil will be delivered into the hand of the army of the Kittim." These last priests, Schonfield contends, must be the last officiating high priests, whose amassed treasure would be taken by the Romans. Josephus, as Schonfield notes, reports the cupidity and rapacity of the last high priests; he tells also how the temple treasures and the wealth assembled by the priests were delivered to the Romans.

What is said of the judgment suffered by the wicked priest, according to Schonfield, corresponds to what happened to the last high priests before the fall of Jerusalem. The Habakkuk Commentary speaks of tortures and vengeance inflicted upon the wicked priest, and connects them with Habakkuk 2:7, which begins, "Will they not suddenly arise, those who torment you?" One high priest was killed by brigands early in the war with the Romans. Later Ananus suffered indignity and death at the hands of the bloodthirsty Zealots.

All this implies that the commentary was written only a little before the fall of Jerusalem in 70 A.D.; and, Schonfield adds, "that is the view we shall accept unless it is shaken by the clear implication of any other passage." What for most of us does more to shake this view than the clear implication of any particular passage is the fact that it involves a date for the composition of the commentary after the community of Qumran was probably dispersed. One need not be superstitious about the date 68 A.D. The destruction of the settlement may have been a few years later than that, though not very many. It is conceivable that a few members of the group may have hidden in the caves for a little while after the community was scattered. But to believe that the Habakkuk Commentary was written during that time and under such circumstances, and that it was left in a jar in the cave almost before the ink was dry, is more difficult.

The reference to the "lion of wrath" in the Nahum Commentary (p. 231) is interpreted also by Schonfield in line with his theory. He believes, as does Rowley (see p. 202), that the Antiochus of the commentary is Antiochus Epiphanes and the Demetrius is Demetrius I. He points out, however, that the commentary refers to an interval from Antiochus to the rise of the Kittim, and follows this with a statement introduced by the word "afterwards." After this comes the reference to the lion of wrath. This implies that the Kittim are the Romans, and the lion of wrath may be supposed to be one of them. Schonfield therefore concludes that the lion of wrath was Titus, who captured Jerusalem and destroyed the temple in 70 A.D.

The fragment of a commentary on Hosea, which contains the only other reference to the lion of wrath that has been published, connects him with "the last priest." Thus the interpretation given by Schonfield for the Habakkuk Commentary is linked up with his interpretation of the lion of wrath. But, alas, this means that now we must imagine the composition of not one but three commentaries after the destruction of the Qumran community, or at best in its last days.

Schonfield does not claim, to be sure, that all these things happened before the commentaries were written. The commentators were predicting what was still to come. They did not always predict exactly what actually happened. It seems to be assumed, for example, that the wicked priest will receive his punishment from foreign enemies. The commentary on Psalm 37 speaks of his being given into the hands of the tyrants of the nations. As it happened, the last high priests during the revolt against Rome were killed in the war of mobs and factions within the besieged city. Like the authors of the apocalyptic literature, the writers of the commentaries had one foot in the present and one in the future. They were so close to the impending events, however, that they saw fairly clearly the shape of things to come.

Other theories have been propounded which connect the allusions of the Dead Sea Scrolls, and the Habakkuk Commentary in particular, with the last years before the destruction of the temple. One of these, advanced as early as 1951, was left out of my discussion in *DSS* because it seemed quite incompatible with the archeological evidence. It has not been abandoned, however, by its author, who has very recently presented it again with some further elaboration. This is the theory of Henri Del Medico. It at least does no more violence to the archeological evidence than does the theory of Schonfield, and Del Medico believes that there is no evidence which, correctly interpreted, cannot be reconciled with it.

Del Medico's theory revolves about the complicated struggles among the Jews during the years just preceding the war of 66–70 A.D. The high priest Ananias aroused a popular revolt by the harsh measures he took to collect the tithes and firstfruits for the support of the temple. In the summer of 66 A.D. Eleazar, a son or grandson of the high priest, put himself at the head of a group of rebels and took possession of the temple. The high priest appealed to the Roman procurator, but Eleazar repulsed the troops sent against him and besieged them in their quarters. A man named Menahem now led a number of followers to Jerusalem and joined forces with Eleazar. Josephus calls him a son of Judas the Galilean, leader of the Zealots, but Del Medico believes that he belonged to a priestly family.

Soon disputes arose between the two groups of rebels. Menahem's followers set fire to the high priest's palace and other buildings, captured the fortress Antonia, and massacred the Roman garrison. The high priest Ananias and his men hid in the sewers.

Menahem now repaired to Masada, a powerful fortress over-looking the Dead Sea, which had been taken from the Romans. Returning soon to Jerusalem, he compelled the Romans to take refuge in the royal towers, and the city was given over to slaughter. The high priest and his followers were dragged out of the sewers and killed.

In the autumn, at the Jewish New Year, Menahem appeared at the temple in royal array. Eleazar and his party attacked him, and the people were ready to stone him. Menahem fled to a place called Ophlas but was found, brought out, tortured, and put to death. His chief followers, one of whom was named Absalom, received the same treatment. The Romans surrendered to Eleazar, now undisputed master of the city. Eleazar promised to spare their lives if they would lay down their arms, but no sooner had they done so than Menahem's followers slaughtered them. This treacherous massacre was followed by violent uprisings and massacres in several other cities. Josephus regarded all these calamities as a divine punishment for the treachery of Menahem's followers; Del Medico suggests that the Zadokites, to whom he believes Menahem had belonged, considered the disasters divine vengeance for the assassination of Menahem, their teacher of righteousness.

The various vague allusions of the Habakkuk Commentary are all interpreted by Del Medico in accordance with this theory. The wicked priest who persecuted the teacher of righteousness is the high priest Ananias. The commentator's statement that he was "named according to the truth" refers to the fact that his name, in its Hebrew form Hananiah, contains the divine name (*hananyah* means "Yah has been gracious"). What is said in the same context about his violent ways of amassing wealth fits what is known of Ananias. Del Medico thinks that "the priest who rebelled," mentioned just before a gap in the text at the bottom of column viii, is not Ananias but Eleazar or some member of his party; the person whose torments are mentioned at the top of column ix, however, is Ananias, who was dragged from the sewers and killed. Schonfield also, the reader will remember, makes this connection.

It was literally one of "the last priests of Jerusalem" who delivered the treasures of the temple to the soldiers of Titus when Jerusalem fell in 70 A.D., corresponding to the commentator's statement that their wealth and spoil would be delivered to the Kittim (i.e., the legions, as Del Medico understands the word). The following clause, "for they are the remainder of the people" (*DSS*, p. 369), is separated by Del Medico from the preceding sentence and taken with the one that follows, so as to yield the meaning, "For these are the remainder of the people: the bleeding men and the oppressed land, the city and all who dwell in it." These, according to Del Medico, are the people of the country, the Zealots whom Ananias oppressed. What follows about the wicked priest is then taken to mean that God delivered him to his enemies, not "for the wrong done to the teacher of righteousness and the men of his party," as I restored and translated the text in *DSS*, but "thanks to [or by the help of] the teacher of righteousness and his party." The priest's wicked treatment of God's elect, the reason for his punishment, is understood to mean Ananias's wicked treatment of Menahem.

The crucial passage about the persecution of the teacher of righteousness by the wicked priest and the appearance of one or the other of them on the Day of Atonement (xi.4–8; *DSS*, p. 370) gives Del Medico a good deal of trouble. His wrestling with it is apparent in the changes he has made in his interpretation since 1951, when his first translation and commentary on this text were published. The expression which I translated "wishing to banish him," and which Del Medico formerly translated "wishing to unclothe him," is interpreted now by almost all interpreters, and probably rightly, "to his house of exile." Del Medico accepts this interpretation in part, but translates "against his house of exile" and makes it modify the immediately preceding words, "the indignation of his wrath," instead of the verb "persecuted" or "pursued."

This disposes of a difficulty I mentioned in *DSS* (pp. 154f), but it involves a curious interpretation of the "house of exile." The word "house" is often used in late Hebrew for the "school" of a particular teacher or party, such as "the house of Hillel." In fact, as we shall see, Del Medico interprets in this sense "the house of Judah," earlier in this commentary, taking it to mean the followers of Judas the Galilean. Here he takes the whole sentence to mean that Ananias pursued Menahem even into his exile, where he had established a school.

The rest of the passage Del Medico finds hard to understand. The Day of Atonement seems especially to pose a problem, for Menahem was killed on the first day of Tishri, nine days before the Day of Atonement. Ananias had been killed on the ninth of the preceding month, Elul, and Del Medico raises the question whether the commentator thought of this as a "day of atonement" for Ananias. The tenth of Tishri, the Day of Atonement, however, was marked by bloody massacres in Jerusalem and other cities. If this is the day to which the commentator refers, how can he say that Menahem, already dead for more than a week, "appeared" at that time? (The possibility that the wicked priest is the subject of the verb is completely ignored.) In rabbinical literature Del Medico finds indications that Menahem was believed to have risen from the dead. Was it believed, he asks, that he had risen first and been seen at Jerusalem on the tenth of Tishri, 66 A.D.? Or was this appearance somewhere else than at Jerusalem? The question is left unanswered. In any case, "the priest whose ignominy was greater than his glory" is identified with Ananias. It is apparently not recorded that he was particularly given to strong drink, but the blood and violence and the desecration of the temple attributed to the wicked priest fit very well the acts of Ananias.

The "man of the lie" is, according to Del Medico, Eleazar. The "preacher of the lie," or as Del Medico translates "orator of the lie," is King Agrippa II, who made many speeches urging peaceful submission to the Romans. The "city of delusion" which he built in blood is Caesarea Philippi, which Agrippa rebuilt. Del Medico applies also to Agrippa II what is said about "the house of judgment" which, according to my translation, is to be judged "in the midst of many peoples" and punished "with fire of brimstone" (x.3–5; DSS, p. 369). Del Medico translates here "the tribunal where God will render his judgment in the midst of many peoples." In the following clause, "and thence he will bring it up for judgment," Del Medico understands "him" instead of "it," making the tribunal the place and Agrippa the object of the judgment. Agrippa had lived in Rome, he says, "in the midst of many peoples," and it is there that God will judge him. In the reference to fire and brimstone which follows, Del Medico sees an allusion to the eruption of Vesuvius in 79 A.D. Surely this makes the date of composition of this document altogether too late to be credible.

The "house of Absalom," which failed to help the teacher of righteousness when he was attacked by the man of the lie (v.9–12; DSS, p. 367), is explained by Del Medico as meaning the ministers of Menahem. His chief minister was actually named Absalom, as Josephus tells us. When Menahem was required by Eleazar to give an account of himself, Del Medico supposes, these ministers tried to save themselves by silence instead of defending their leader. Only the name Absalom affords any foundation for this explanation, and it is a very weak foundation. No such incident, so far as I am aware, is recorded anywhere.

As has been noted in passing, "the house of Judah," in which "all the doers of the law" will be rescued "from the house of judgment because of their labor and their faith in the teacher of righteousness" (viii.1–3; DSS, p. 368), is believed by Del Medico to mean the Zealots, the disciples of Judas the Galilean. Josephus says that the Zealots supported Menahem; he says, in fact, though Del Medico does not accept this statement, that Menahem was the son of Judas. The commentator in this passage is therefore understood to mean that the Zealots had faith in Menahem and endured suffering, and that God would therefore deliver them from human condemnation and punishment. At the time when the Habakkuk Commentary was written, Del Medico says, some of the Zealots were prisoners of the Romans. It is their deliverance that is here promised.

Not only the house of Judah but also the cities of Judah, where the wicked priest "plundered the wealth of the poor" (xii.9f; DSS, p. 370), are identified by Del Medico with the Zealots. The words meaning "the cities of Judah" are exactly the same as those used, for example, in Isaiah 40:9; Del Medico, however, passes over without notice their natural and obvious meaning and pronounces the word for "cities" ambiguous, meaning either "fields" or "disciples." For the meaning "field" he refers to Numbers 21:15, which actually refers neither to fields nor to cities but to the Moabite city Ar. For the meaning "disciple" he cites the name of Er, the son of Judah (Genesis 38:3ff; 46:12). Now since Er was so "wicked in the sight of the Lord" that "the Lord slew him," he hardly seems an appropriate prototype for those who suffered from the rapacity of the wicked priest. Certainly the name Er is no sound basis for taking "cities" to mean "disciples."

I have given this much attention to Del Medico's theory because it is presented with much erudition and ingenuity and should not be merely laughed out of court. The more one examines it, however, the more does one become convinced that it has not sufficient plausibility to outweigh the archeological evidence for the destruction of the Qumran community in 68 A.D. or very soon thereafter. Del Medico complains that the archeologists have assumed the earliest possible or median dates established by the Carbon-14 test of linen from Cave 1 (*DSS*, pp. 81f) and by the Roman lamps found in the same cave (*DSS*, p. 80), instead of recognizing the latest possible dates, which would be 233 A.D. for the linen and about 300 A.D. for the lamps.

Del Medico adds also that there is no way of telling when coins of a given date ceased to be used. This is of course true as a general proposition, but when no coins of later date are found it is safe to assume that the site was not occupied very long after the date in question. The relative numbers of coins of various dates is significant also, and the stratification or archeological context in which they are found must be taken into account. The few coins dated later than 68 A.D. which were found at Khirbet Qumran came from later periods of much less extensive occupation, when the changes in the character of the buildings indicated use by a different group and for a different purpose.

It should be remembered, of course, that for Del Medico the Dead Sea Scrolls are not the library of a monastic community which occupied Qumran; they are heretical scrolls committed to the genizah in the generation following the destruction of the temple. We have already considered and rejected his arguments on that score. The two parts of his theory, however, belong together. If they must stand or fall together, it is hard to avoid the conclusion that neither seems strong enough to hold up the other.

# XXI

## The Theory of Roth and Driver; Other Evidence and Arguments

A theory resembling Del Medico's, yet quite different, has been proposed recently by two Oxford scholars, Cecil Roth and G. H. Driver. An amazing number of details in the Habakkuk Commentary and other texts can be interpreted in line with this theory. On most points an explanation differing from that of Del Medico is given.

The Kittim are of course the Romans, but the War scroll's Kittim of Assyria and Kittim in Egypt find a new interpretation. When Vespasian took his troops to Syria (the Kittim of Assyria), he sent his son Titus to Egypt to get the Fifteenth Legion (the Kittim in Egypt). They met and united their forces on the plain of Acre, which is mentioned in a portion of a commentary on Isaiah published by Allegro. The rulers of the Kittim who "pass on, each before his fellow" (Habakkuk Commentary iv.11f; DSS, p. 366), are the five Roman emperors who came to power during the year 69 A.D. This suggestion was made by Vermès in 1951, but was later withdrawn. The practice of sacrificing to their military standards (vi.4; DSS, p. 367) was first followed by the Romans, so far as is known, after the capture of the temple in 70 A.D.

According to this theory the teacher of righteousness was Menahem, as Del Medico maintains, but the wicked priest was Eleazar, not Ananias. The Habakkuk Commentary says that the wicked priest's "heart was lifted up," and Josephus calls Eleazar "an extremely bold young man." The story of Menahem's assassination, Roth feels, "dovetails amazingly" with the Habakkuk Commentary's "indications" of the "killing" of the teacher of righteousness by the wicked priest on the Day of Atonement, "about this same season of the year." The slight discrepancy in date between the first and the tenth of Tishri is thus easily bypassed, but there are other difficulties which make the dovetailing seem not too neat.

Menahem was killed in Jerusalem, not in a "place of exile." Driver and Roth, however, adopt the other possible interpretation of the word for "exile," taking it to mean "his uncovering" (*DSS*, p. 155); instead of "to his place of exile," therefore, we have "to the place of uncovering him," which is taken to be the equivalent of "into the open." Menahem was dragged out of his hiding place to be tortured and killed by Eleazar's men.

Like Del Medico, Roth and Driver connect the "house of Absalom" with the Absalom who was Menahem's chief follower and died with him. There is no indication that he "kept silence" or failed to come to the aid of Menahem. Driver and Roth, however, take the Hebrew verb of the Habakkuk Commentary (v.10; *DSS*, p. 367) to mean not "kept silence" but "were put to silence." How they interpret the failure of the house of Absalom to help the teacher of righteousness I do not know. In any case, as we have repeatedly observed, the name Absalom in the commentary is probably symbolical. The "man of the lie" is taken by Driver to be John of Gischala, the leader of a Zealot faction in 67–70 A.D., whose falsity is repeatedly denounced by Josephus.

As for what happened on (not "on or about") the Day of Atonement, the outcome of the incident related in the Habakkuk Commentary is anything but clear. Roth apparently assumes—correctly, I believe—that it was the wicked priest, not the teacher of righteousness, who "appeared" at that time. That the result, however, was the death of the teacher of righteousness cannot be taken for granted. Roth, in fact, recognizes the possibility that the incident did not result in the teacher's death. In that case, he says, Menahem's nephew and successor, Eleazar ben Jair, may have been the teacher of righteousness, since he fulfills all the other conditions: he, as well as Menahem, was attacked by a priest on the Day of Atonement, was associated with a man named Absalom, and was chief of a sect which had its center near the Dead Sea. This concession is a credit to Roth's honesty, but it seriously weakens his theory. It would be hard to show that the details of what is said of the teacher of righteousness are met equally well by Menahem and his nephew.

The commentary explains "the righteous" of Habakkuk 2:4, who "shall live by his faith," as meaning "the doers of the law in the house of Judah" (viii.1; *DSS*, p. 368). Eleazar ben Jair was a grandson of Judas (or Judah) the Galilean; he and his followers might therefore well be known as "the house of Judah," as Driver and Roth maintain. The term "sons of Zadok" is much more characteristic of the sect's literature, but this is explained on the ground that Zadok the Pharisee, who with Judas founded the "fourth philosophy," was its leader after the death of Judas, and his name reminded his followers of David's high priest.

Many other points in several of the Qumran texts seem to the authors of this theory to fall into line with it. On the "lion of wrath" of the Nahum Commentary their views diverge. Roth takes this expression as a designation of John of Gischala, whom Driver regards as the "man of the lie"; the "lion of wrath," according to Driver, is another Zealot leader, Simon ben Giora, who is said by Josephus to have "raged like a wounded wild beast." As we have already noted, a little fragment of a commentary on Hosea mentions, along with the lion of wrath, "the last priest, who will put forth his hand to smite Ephraim." Assuming that this "last priest" fought against the lion of wrath, though the text does not say so, Roth sees here a clear reference to Phineas ben Samuel, the last high priest, who unsuccessfully fought John of Gischala and later was allied with him.

John was eventually captured by the Romans and condemned to imprisonment for life, just as the lion of wrath, according to Roth, was to be delivered into the hands of the tyrants of the Gentiles—this is actually said, however, of the wicked priest, not of the lion of wrath. Since Simon ben Giora came from the ancient territory of Ephraim and John of Gischala from the territory of Manasseh, Driver regards the terms Ephraim and Manasseh in these texts as referring to the followers of Simon and John respectively.

The organization of the community by thousands, hundreds, and tens recalls a statement of Josephus that the levies under his own command in 66–77 A.D. were so organized. In contrast to Yadin's conclusions, Roth and Driver maintain that the military tactics reflected in the War scroll were not adopted by the Romans until the late first century A.D., and the weapons described were quite new at that time. Two Hebrew words, referring to a weapon which Yadin identifies with the short, straight Roman sword and Kuhn with a curved sword, are taken by Driver and Roth to refer to the curved dagger (Latin *sica*) from which the most extreme group of Zealots, the "Sicarii," received their name.

One of the most ingenious points in the argument of Roth and Driver is their explanation of a mysterious passage in the Manual of Discipline, which says, speaking of the heavenly bodies, "When they renew themselves, the *M* is large for the holy of holies; and the letter *N* is for the key of his eternal, steadfast love" (x.4; *DSS*, p. 384). This cryptic sentence has evoked a good deal of speculation. Driver and Roth take the *M* and *N* to stand for *mey noah*, "the waters of Noah." The solar calendar which the Qumran sect seems to have followed was dated, according to the book of Jubilees, from the flood. The numerical value of the Hebrew letter *M* is forty, the number of days that the flood continued (Genesis 7:17). The value of *N* is fifty; this signified Pentecost, the Feast of Weeks, which is especially emphasized in Jubilees. *M* and *N* are also the first two consonants of the name Menahem, which in Hebrew would be abbreviated as *MN*.

This explanation ignores the letter *aleph* attached to a verb a few lines earlier, which Brownlee took with the *M* and *N* as forming the word *amen*, used as an acrostic with a Messianic meaning. Barthélemy, supporting Brownlee's interpretation, pointed out that the numerical values of the three Hebrew consonants added up to 91, the number of days in each of the four seasons, according to the calendar of Jubilees (*DSS*, pp. 242ff).

Roth and Driver, however, are not the only scholars who deny the existence of the acrostic and explain the *aleph* in other ways. In support of their own interpretation of the *M* and *N* they cite a rabbinic tradition that the Messiah would be a son of Hezekiah named Menahem, and his period would be 365 days of years "according to the sun," i.e., by the solar calendar. The father of Judas the Galilean and grandfather of Menahem was named Hezekiah.

The occupational history of Khirbet Qumran as shown by the excavations does not disturb Roth and Driver. The Qumran settlement might have been destroyed several years before the almost inaccessible fortress of Masada was finally captured by the Romans. On the other hand, Roth and Driver point out, there is no proof that the settlement was destroyed in exactly 68 A.D. The coins cease at that date, but coins are used for years, and coins of the Jewish insurgents become more and more scarce in the third, fourth, and fifth years of the revolt. As conditions grew worse in Jerusalem, not so many coins were minted. It was also more and more difficult to get supplies to Qumran, to say nothing of newly minted money. Perhaps money was no longer of much use to the community, which had to depend upon pillage to meet its needs.

The dating of the scrolls by paleography also is no obstacle to the theory. Roth and Driver contend that the historical allusions of the Habakkuk Commentary establish its date definitely as "immediately after the year 66." This therefore is a "fixed point" on the basis of which the paleography of the scrolls can be treated "objectively." On this matter I need only refer the reader to *DSS* (pp. 83–101) and to what has been said here (pp. 186f).

The greatest difficulty with any theory that regards Menahem as the teacher of righteousness is not perhaps, after all, the chronological problem. It is the complete lack of resemblance between the two kinds of persons represented by the Qumran sect's teacher and the Zealot leader. No doubt Josephus was prejudiced and used the emotional vocabulary of propaganda in speaking of the Zealots. Menahem may have been a more admirable character than Josephus would have us believe.

The question, however, is not one of character but of the type
of activity for which each man is known. We know little enough
about either of them, but from that little it is clear that, whatever else Menahem may have been, he was a military leader.
There is not the slightest hint anywhere that the teacher of
righteousness ever served in that capacity. Whatever else the
teacher of righteousness may have been, even if we translate his
title "right guide" or the like, he was an expounder of the law
and the prophets. If Menahem in the course of his decidedly
activistic career ever found time for such pursuits, we have no
evidence of it.

Roth draws attention to the fact that Josephus calls both
Menahem and his father Judas "sophists." This word, he says, did
not then have the uncomplimentary connotations it acquired later.
It meant something like "teacher" or "spiritual leader," certainly
something quite different from "military commander" or "brigand
chief." That Josephus represents both Judas and Menahem as
mere terrorists and assassins is merely an expression of his sub-
servience to the Romans and his hatred of all who persisted in
opposing them. By using the term "sophist" Josephus betrays
the fact that the Zealots had "a coherent body of teaching," not
merely a "political principle." Certainly if Menahem was the
teacher of righteousness and the Qumran community consisted
of his followers, they had at least an abundance of ideas and
speculations, if not exactly "a coherent body of teaching." This
hardly meets the difficulty, however. Josephus, who described the
Jewish sects and parties as "philosophies" for his Greek readers,
might have used the word "sophist" in the same loose way for a
leader of one of these groups.

If the identity of Menahem and the teacher of righteousness is
not conceded, Roth feels, we are compelled to assume an incredible series of coincidences. The followers of Menahem withdrew after his death to Masada and held out there against the
Romans until 73 A.D. If an entirely separate community existed
until 68 A.D. at Qumran, "a few miles to the north," then at
least for the years 66–68 there were "two different sects, cut off
from the central revolutionary government in Jerusalem, each of

which venerated the memory of a teacher who had suffered at the hands of a priest, on or about the Day of Atonement, both of them moreover having a close associate named Absalom." With complete conviction Roth adds, "Coincidence cannot have an arm quite as long as this!" He postulates therefore a "Republic of Masadah-Qumran." But the distance between Masada and Qumran is about thirty miles, quite enough to separate two communities even if they were much more alike than those of Qumran and Masada. The leaders of both groups had indeed "suffered at the hands of a priest," but whether they had suffered in the same way is another question. The coincidences are not really so close as they seem to Roth.

A few historical allusions have been found in material not yet published. Milik reports that the Cave 4 fragments of two manuscripts of the "Mishmaroth" type occasionally mention historical events. He gives three examples. In one fragment what seems to be the end of the verb "killed" in the third person feminine singular ($[hr]gh$) is followed by the name Shalomzion. Queen Alexandra, the wife and successor of Alexander Janneus, was named also Salome, or, in the more complete Hebrew form of the name, Shalomzion. Milik suggests that the allusion in this fragment may be to her massacre of her dead husband's adherents. Another fragment bears the third masculine singular form of the same verb, followed by the letter š. Here Milik suggests that the name Simon ($šm'wn$) may have followed the verb as its subject, and that the incident referred to may be the capture of Acre by Simon the Maccabean. The third instance given by Milik is the occurrence of the names Hyrcanus and Aemilius. The Roman governor of Syria in 62 B.C., the year after Pompey captured Jerusalem, was Aemilius Scaurus. The high priest at that time was Hyrcanus II.

In dealing with all these historical allusions, or with what appear to be historical allusions, we must not fail to keep in mind the question whether the references are really to persons who have lived and events which have occurred. Gärtner recalls the way in which past, present, and future are sometimes interwoven in the Damascus Document, as shown by Isaac Rabinowitz, and suggests that this is true also of the Habakkuk Commentary. It is in the commentaries, in fact, that this consideration is particularly important. Schonfield notes that some scholars think the commentators jumped about from one period to another and to the future and back again. Admitting that this may be so, he declares himself "not altogether happy about it." It is quite true, however, I think, that the commentators took each sentence, clause, or phrase by itself, looking for connections with what had happened or what they expected to happen, without being bothered about the chronological order of events. A commentator today, with their presuppositions, might see Stalin referred to in one verse of Scripture, Christopher Columbus in the next, and Napoleon in the next. This does not, however, entirely explain the obscurity of the allusions.

Schonfield suggests two reasons for the fact that the persons referred to are usually not named. One reason is that "they serve as symbols of primeval forces and are not real people at all." The other is that "they cannot be named because they have not yet appeared." They are like the cryptic figures of the apocalyptic literature, except that there is much more "quasi-historical" detail in the Qumran writings. Since the commentators are often referring to future events, it is to be expected that what actually happened at any time will not entirely correspond to what they say. Past events and situations also are sometimes contemplated; the commentators have in mind a story which "only culminates in the future," because they believe that the time of the end has already begun and they are living in it.

One may suppose, though Schonfield does not put it in quite this way, that when anything foretold by the prophets seemed to the commentators to reflect what had already occurred in their day or earlier, they so explained it; when no such application was evident, they referred the prophecy to the future. In a similar way conservative Christian exegetes, assuming that everything foretold by the prophets must sooner or later be literally fulfilled, often connect all "unfulfilled prophecies" with the second coming of Christ. The procedure of the Qumran commentators was probably not so mechanical or deliberate as this may seem to imply;

it was a matter of more or less conscious assumptions. Like some modern scholars who ought to know better, they would accept at face value an appealing "hunch" without subjecting it to critical scrutiny.

The Qumran commentaries were written, as Schonfield says, for the inspiration and guidance of the elect in the time of testing which was imminent or already in process. Schonfield attributes the whole astonishing literary activity of the Qumran community to the desire to be fully prepared for the Messianic age. "Everything would be in the books, nothing neglected, and all the books safely stored for their predestined purpose." The War scroll comes at once to mind as one to which this explanation applies admirably. The Rule of the Congregation, explicitly stated to be "for the whole congregation of Israel at the end of days," is another obvious case in point. Other books were no doubt more directly intended for the present instruction and administration of the community during the interval of waiting, but all were overshadowed by the tense expectation of what was soon to be.

The commentaries in particular would naturally intermingle past, present, and future. Their historical allusions and their predictions might therefore be, and undoubtedly are, sometimes inextricable. Where what is already accomplished and what is still to be can be distinguished, they may be very helpful in dating the documents. Scholars have tried to make use of this criterion in connection with the invading Kittim, for example (*DSS*, p. 141). The only generalization that can be safely made in this respect is that we cannot expect specific and unambiguous historical allusions in the Dead Sea Scrolls. This is amply confirmed by the whole history of the study of the scrolls for the past decade.

Other kinds of evidence concerning the origin and early history of the sect have been detected. D. N. Freedman, comparing the Prayer of Nabonidus with the book of Daniel (see pp. 168–69), finds that the Qumran text preserves a more authentic tradition than that of Daniel. This suggests that the community had access to Babylonian traditions, and so supports the hypothesis that there were members of the group who had come to Palestine from Babylonia at a relatively recent time. Albright had previously drawn the same inference from the text of the St. Mark's Isaiah scroll and the presence of Persian elements in the beliefs of the community, and had interpreted the first part of the Damascus Document to the same effect. Such arguments are suggestive, and where several lines of evidence point in the same direction, they may lead to genuine discoveries. It is necessary, however, to be on guard against the temptation to base large conclusions on too slight evidence. That there was a Babylonian contingent in the Qumran group, or that the group arose among Jews who had recently come from Babylonia, is a reasonable hypothesis which must await further evidence to corroborate it.

Comparisons between the Qumran texts and other Jewish literature have been the basis of conclusions concerning the origin of the sect. Rowley finds that the Dead Sea Scrolls and the book of Jubilees alike lay special stress on the avoidance of idolatry, the observance of the Sabbath, and the celebration of the festivals according to a particular calendar. These were all, he says, live issues at the time of the Maccabean revolt, and were not emphasized in the same way during the later Hasmonean and Roman periods. Alexander Epiphanes imposed idolatry by force in the temple at Jerusalem, outlawed the keeping of the Sabbath, and sought "to change the times and the law" (Daniel 7:25). The prominence of these issues in his reign indicates that both the scrolls and the book of Jubilees had their background in the events of that time.

A somewhat similar but not identical conclusion is reached by Schonfield. In the Qumran texts he sees abundant indications that the sect was influenced by the pseudepigraphic literature written from the second century B.C. onward. Evidence of any such influence in the opposite direction is lacking. At the same time there are notable differences between the Qumran literature and the earlier apocalyptic and pseudepigraphic writings, and equally decisive differences between the Qumran texts and the apocalyptic literature of the period after the destruction of the temple. The books produced by the sect itself, he concludes, come from a limited area and a brief period. The commentaries in particular he would date in "the crucial years of the first century A.D."

It is rather appalling to see how much learning and labor have been expended upon these problems without producing conclusive results or general agreement. The most solid framework for whatever conclusions we may be able to reach is the historical outline provided by archeology. All the arguments on other grounds have proved elastic and inconclusive; they must be tied down to the few solid facts we possess: the establishment of the Qumran community near the end of the second century B.C., the interruption in its occupation in the time of Herod, and its destruction during the First Revolt of 66–70 A.D. This framework makes improbable any theory which compresses too much of the history and literary activity of the Qumran sect into the last few years of its existence. The dates of the events referred to in the texts and the identity of the principal characters have not been established as yet and may never be. In general it seems most probable that the chief persons and most decisive events are to be dated not later than the last century before Christ.

What became of the community after the destruction of the settlement is a question that still arouses curiosity. Perhaps no definite and complete answer to it will ever be possible. The war with the Romans probably seemed to the group as a whole to be the final combat with the hosts of evil for which they had been preparing themselves. Many of them probably threw themselves into the struggle. Milik suggests that the leaders of the revolt may have found the War scroll a useful document for propaganda. That is quite possible, though they can hardly have found it a practical military manual. The disastrous end of the war perhaps caused such profound disillusionment that the sect was never again able to form a cohesive community. At any rate, as Schonfield says, the doctrines of the sect were not all shut up in caves, to be recovered only by chance many centuries later. Much remained in the minds of surviving members and was taken up by Jewish Christian and other groups. In general we may suppose, with Milik, that some members of the sect were reabsorbed by official Judaism, some became Christians, and others joined one or another of the many Gnostic sects of the time.

PART FIVE

# THE IDENTIFICATION
# OF THE SECT

# XXII

## Pharisees? Sadducees? Samaritans?

One thing which is commonly supposed to be finally settled is the identity of the sect. Many recent writers on the Dead Sea Scrolls do not even raise the question. It is widely assumed that the men of Qumran were the Essenes described by Josephus and Philo and a few of the church fathers. Not all scholars, however, are even now convinced that the issue is closed. Some still reject entirely the identification of the sect with the Essenes; others feel that it can be accepted only with qualifications and reservations.

Discussion of this question during the past two years has dealt largely with the same points already presented in *DSS* (pp. 279–94), but it has not merely moved in circles. New considerations and more thorough investigation of matters previously considered have afforded some new matter for thought. Comparisons with other Jewish literature have played some part in the investigation. They at least show what writings may be attributed to the same or closely related sects or schools of thought. The next step is then to identify the sects or schools from which they come.

The argument may move in different directions, according to the point of departure. Fritsch, for example, recalls the theory of certain scholars that Jubilees, Enoch, the Testaments of the Twelve Patriarchs, and the Assumption of Moses were written by Essenes. He then declares that there is reason to believe that these books were produced by the Qumran sect. Considering it a demonstrated fact that the covenanters were Essenes, "or at least

Essenic in character," he concludes that the books in question and others like them are Essene works. This argument, however, rests on the assumption of what we are now trying to find out. The grounds on which Fritsch himself bases his assurance that the people of Qumran were Essenes are of a different sort and must be considered later.

A comparison of the Dead Sea Scrolls with one of the books just mentioned is used in a different way by Benedikt Otzen in a study of the scrolls and the Testaments of the Twelve Patriarchs. The pre-Christian date and substantial unity of the Testaments are assumed. The ethical ideals and attitudes, the dualistic theology, the demonology and angelology, the Messianic ideas, and the historical background of the Testaments and the scrolls, especially the Damascus Document and the Manual of Discipline, are carefully examined. Some details of Otzen's study will be noted when we consider the beliefs of the Qumran sect (pp. 284–88).

His conclusion is that there is no such historical connection between the scrolls and the Testaments as some scholars, particularly Dupont-Sommer, have claimed. The circles from which the Testaments came had no such history behind them as the Damascus Document presents and also had not developed the world-view which finds expression in the Manual of Discipline. The similarities between the new documents and the Testaments are all in the sphere of religion and theology. These writings did not come from the same sect; they do not have the same historical background or reflect the same historical events. They did, however, grow out of the same religious soil within Judaism. This conclusion is important and seems to me well founded.

The mutual relationships and relative age of the Dead Sea Scrolls themselves are involved in this problem. They do not form a completely homogeneous body of literature and were not all written at the same time. Concerning the order in which they were written and the date of each, there is still no general agreement. We have encountered some of the divergent views of different scholars on these points. The relation between the Damascus Document in particular and the rest of the Qumran literature is not yet entirely clear. The combination of close resemblances at some points with marked differences at others indicates that either two distinct though related groups or two different stages in the history of the same movement are represented (*DSS*, pp. 187–94).

Fritsch observes that while the other texts express the views of the community at Qumran, the Damascus Document may present those of groups living in the cities and villages of the country. He prefers, however, the alternative explanation that the Damascus Document reflects a different stage in the sect's development from that which is reflected in the other scrolls. Which stage preceded the other is a question on which judgment must be suspended until all the texts have been published. Fritsch considers it probable, meanwhile, that the Damascus Document is later than the Manual of Discipline.

Carmignac agrees that the Manual is older than the Damascus Document. An elaborate comparison of the scrolls found in 1947 and the Damascus Document leads him to the conclusion that the teacher of righteousness, whom he dates in the latter half of the second century B.C., composed the Manual of Discipline and, somewhat later, the War scroll and the Thanksgiving Psalms. The Habakkuk Commentary and the Damascus Document, Carmignac believes, were written during the first century B.C. by a successor of the teacher of righteousness. The Manual is thus more than half a century older than the Damascus Document.

Otzen comes to the opposite conclusion. The dualistic theory of the Manual of Discipline, he finds, does not appear in the Damascus Document. The historical situation and events depicted in the Damascus Document, including the conflict and break with the Jewish nation as a whole, were, he thinks, the occasion and cause of the emergence of this dualism. The experience of conflict and division was projected on the universe; history became theology. Thus arose the world-view which we find in the Manual of Discipline.

The Habakkuk Commentary, on the other hand, seems to Otzen earlier than the Damascus Document. It was written at Jerusalem, he believes, in the midst of the struggle with the wicked priest, who was probably Alexander Janneus. When the Damascus Document was written, this struggle was over and the group had withdrawn to Damascus, but the memory of the conflict was still fresh. The Manual of Discipline was not written until much later, perhaps not before the first century A.D. Dupont-Sommer, it will be remembered, dates both the Habakkuk Commentary and the Damascus Document during the sojourn in the land of Damascus.

It should not be forgotten that the Damascus Document itself has now appeared at Qumran in more than one redaction, indicating that it had a literary history of its own. This suggests a relatively early origin. Del Medico, who still considers the Damascus Document a medieval Qaraite work, says that it consistently represents a particular group, but that the Manual of Discipline is a mosaic of fragments from many different groups. His painstaking effort to separate the sources and assign each to the sect in which it originated is not convincing, but his contention that the Manual is a composite work is undoubtedly sound. In short, we cannot regard either the Damascus Document or the Manual of Discipline as a unified work which can be dated at a particular time. This does not invalidate such studies as those of Otzen and Carmignac, but it necessitates some qualification of their conclusions. The relations of these and other Qumran documents among themselves and with other Jewish literature are more complicated than any simple theory recognizes.

For our present purpose the result of these comparative studies is largely negative. Any attempt to assign the Qumran literature on such grounds to a particular sect or party in Judaism is, for the present at least, doomed to failure. If we had definite bodies of literature which could be attributed with certainty to the Pharisees, the Sadducees, the Essenes, or any other division of Judaism, the situation would be different; but that is not the case. To establish the identity of the covenanters of Qumran we are restricted to the same kind of evidence that scholars have used to determine the associations of the apocryphal and pseudepigraphical writings. This consists largely of what we are told about the various sects in the apocrypha, the histories of Josephus, the rabbinical literature, and the New Testament.

It is generally agreed and may be assumed without further discussion that the roots of the Qumran sect go down into the movement of the Hasidim of Maccabean times (*DSS*, p. 274). The most important outgrowth of that movement, judged by its historical consequences, was the sect or party of the Pharisees, the fathers of the "normative Judaism" of the rabbis and the orthodox Judaism of subsequent centuries. The views of scholars who regarded the Qumran covenanters as Pharisees were briefly considered in *DSS* (pp. 278, 293f).

Otzen recalls the fact that, before the discovery of the Dead Sea Scrolls, L. Ginzberg and Hvidberg regarded the Damascus Document as a Pharisaic work, and he agrees that the community which, according to him, migrated to Damascus and created both the Damascus Document and the Habakkuk Commentary issued from Pharisaic circles. The Manual of Discipline, however, together with the Testaments of the Twelve Patriarchs, he finds far removed from the legalism of the Pharisees. From this difference he infers that a new, non-Pharisaic influence was felt by the group during its sojourn in the land of Damascus. This influence came from Jews of the type best represented by the Testaments of the Twelve Patriarchs, Jews who revered the law but did not insist on minutiae as the Pharisees did.

The possibility of a connection between the Qumran sect and the Sadducees was discussed briefly in *DSS* (pp. 275–77). The prominence of the priesthood in the community and the characteristic use of the term "sons of Zadok" ("Sadducee" and "Zadokite" being the same word in Hebrew) are the chief reasons for suspecting such a connection. Long before the discovery of the Dead Sea Scrolls there was much debate over the question whether the Damascus Document, which many prefer to call the Zadokite Document, came from a Sadducean community. The problem is complicated by the fact that the name Zadok has varied associations in Jewish history and literature, and several groups at different times have been called Zadokite.

This question has been thoroughly studied by Robert North. The term "sons of Zadok," he finds, refers to some historic or supposedly historic individual, but it is uncertain whether he was the high priest of David and Solomon, the Zadok of Socoh named by a rabbinic source as the founder of the Sadducees, the Pharisee named Zadok who according to Josephus founded the "fourth philosophy," or some unknown or legendary person. Whoever he may have been, both the Sadducees and the Qumran Zadokites probably looked back to the same Zadok as their founder or ideal prototype. In any case, the term Zadokite or Sadducee became practically another word for "priest."

The Sadducees of the New Testament period were the priestly party which had achieved both religious and civil authority. The name Zadokite may have been used also, however, for other priestly groups or for the priesthood in general, not all of whom belonged to the party of the Sadducees. Both the Sadducees and the Qumran sect claimed that they or their priestly leaders were the true "sons of Zadok." Since this is the basis of the name Sadducee, North submits that the Qumran covenanters should be called Sadducees, even though they were a separate group and hated the priestly party which was in power at Jerusalem. Advocates of the Essene theory, says North, insist that there were different groups of Essenes; in the same way we may speak of different groups of Sadducees.

Since the covenanters of Qumran did not acknowledge the legitimacy of the priests then in control of the temple and its worship, they considered any sacrifice performed by these priests unlawful, but they probably still regarded the sacrificial laws as binding. That they offered sacrifices of their own, apart from the temple, is most improbable. Their position may very well have been like that of orthodox Jews to this day, for whom sacrifice has been impossible since the temple was destroyed, but who look for the restoration of the sacrificial cultus when the temple is restored in the days of the Messiah. In that case, the Qumran covenanters might well consider themselves as the real Sadducees, and the party in power as those who said they were Sadducees but were not.

The theology of the Sadducees is known to us only from the reports of outsiders, which are neither comprehensive nor impartial. They are said to have accepted only the written law, rejecting the oral law developed by the Pharisees, though they had their own traditional interpretations, which were in many ways more strict than those of the Pharisees. They rejected the belief in the resurrection of the dead, and also the Pharisaic beliefs about angels. In these matters the sect of Qumran seems to have been, as North says, "quite different and immensely richer and more spiritual in doctrinal content," but he reminds us that we have no writings of the Jerusalem Sadducees to compare with the Dead Sea Scrolls.

North considers also as "middle links" the later sects of the Qaraites and the Dositheans, whose affinities with both the Sadducees and the Qumran sect have been the subject of much discussion among scholars. He comes to no definite conclusion except that all these possible connections, "frail and hazy" as many of them are, must be considered in reaching a decision as to the "ultimate affiliation" of the Qumran covenanters.

The possibility of some kind of historical connection between the Qumran group and the Sadducees cannot, at the present stage of the investigation, be dismissed as impossible or unworthy of serious consideration. It has been argued recently by W. S. LaSor that the Sadducees and the covenanters of Qumran had the same background and origin but came later to a parting of the ways. LaSor even suggests that the house of Absalom of the Habakkuk Commentary means the Sadducees.

In the hands of Del Medico, as we have observed, the Dead Sea Scrolls become compilations of selections from many Jewish and even Christian sources. Among the groups whom he finds represented in the scrolls are the followers of Zadok the Pharisee, the associate of Judas the Galilean in the revolt against the Romans in 6 A.D. and in the inauguration of the Zealot movement. As a distinct movement, Del Medico holds, the Zadokite sect arose at about 60 A.D.; until 66 they were allied with the Zealots, but after the outbreak of the war against Rome they became enemies.

With the ascendance of the rabbis after 70 A.D, all dissident groups had to struggle to survive. The Zadokites then became a secret society, with initiation rites and grades of membership. The sections of the Manual of Discipline that Del Medico regards as the statutes of Zadokite lodges are therefore dated at about

90 A.D., and the compilation of the work is accordingly assigned to the late first or early second century A.D. Filled as it was with heresy, Del Medico says, this composite work must have been seized by Rabbi Gamaliel II and committed to the genizah at about 115 A.D.

This ingenious theory at least calls attention to a fact that should be recognized. There is no ironclad proof that the manuscripts came from the community which had its headquarters at Qumran. If they did not, then the destruction of the settlement does not establish the last possible date when they could have been left in the cave. Here, as often, we must be content with probability, but the probability is actually overwhelming. There is so much evidence, indirect but significant, that very strong evidence to the contrary would be needed to outweigh it.

Such a mass of manuscripts in caves so closely grouped about the Qumran settlement could hardly be placed there by persons unconnected with the community except in some period when the site was completely deserted. Against that supposition the evidence of paleography is decisive: the manuscripts were written at different times during a period of three or four centuries, the greater part of them coming from the latter half or third of that period. This was just the time when the community at Qumran was most active. Such a theory as Del Medico's has to deny the force of the paleographical evidence.

The possibility of a connection between the Qumran sect and the Zadokites of the first century A.D. is considered by Schonfield also. He considers it possible that the Damascus Document, or at least the first part of it, which he calls the Testamentary Work, may have been called the "Book of Zadok." The Zadok whose tomb is mentioned in the copper scroll, he believes, was probably the high priest of David's time, whom the sect venerated; but in the Jewish and Christian accounts of the origin of the Sadducees he finds evidence of a new development at about 25 B.C., when there was great Messianic excitement and the time of the end was believed to be at hand. A man named Zadok may have had something to do with this development, Schonfield suggests, but he considers it more probable that the sect's use of biblical references to the sons of Zadok gave rise to a belief that it had been founded by a man of that name. Citing Jewish and Christian evidence of the multiplicity of Jewish sects at this time, Schonfield concludes that it was widely felt to be a time "to take to the wilderness, to separate from the ungodly, to write and store away appropriate books, . . . perhaps also to hide away treasure for the Wars of Messiah." In this "multiplication of groups" the followers of John the Baptist formed one and the Qumran sect another. The obscure statements of Jewish and Christian sources which connect the origin of the Sadducees with this period are therefore derived from traditions about the Zadokites, but these Zadokites were not the followers of Zadok the Pharisee, the associate of Judas the Galilean.

All this may seem to have taken us rather far from the Sadducees, but the points mentioned are all related. It is quite clear that the Qumran sect and the party commonly known as Sadducees were not the same; they were bitter opponents. It may be, as North says, that the sect had split off from the Sadducees. The covenanters of Qumran certainly considered themselves the true sons of Zadok, and the movement had probably arisen within the priesthood (*DSS*, p. 276). The covenanters may therefore have been the Zadokites who were confused with the Sadducees in later Jewish and Christian writings. They were not, however, a group founded in the first century A.D. by Zadok the Pharisee, for they had been in existence for more than a century before his time. Whether they had any later connection with his followers in the last days before the destruction of the temple we shall have to consider later.

Provocative suggestions of contact with the Samaritans have appeared here and there ever since the first discovery of the scrolls. The manuscript fragments in the archaic Hebrew script naturally recalled the continued use of a form of that script by the Samaritans to the present time (*DSS*, pp. 84, 95, 97); affinities with the Samaritan dialect were noted in the language of the scrolls (*DSS*, p. 115); similarities in religious practices and beliefs were detected also (*DSS*, p. 287); even a polemic against the Samaritans was suggested as the basis of a peculiar textual variant (*DSS*, p. 313). The Jewish Christian "Pseudo-Clementine" literature connects the Sadducees with a Samaritan named Dositheus, said to have been a disciple of John the Baptist and the predecessor of Simon Magus. What is told of the Dosithean Samaritans reveals contacts not only with the Sadducees but also with the Essenes. North gives some attention to these contacts in his study of the Sadducees and the Qumran sect, but reaches no definite conclusion.

A comparison of the Samaritans and the Qumran covenanters has been made by John Bowman. He finds no indication of a connection between them, but points out that there are many similarities between the beliefs held by Samaritans to this day and those of the Qumran sect. The Samaritans consider themselves the sons of light, and they call the chief of the forces of evil Belial. They look for a redeemer called the Taheb, who corresponds to the Messiah of Israel of the Qumran documents. Their high priest is the anointed one (Messiah) of Aaron.

These beliefs, Bowman says, are survivals of the teachings of the ancient Samaritan sects. The similarities between them and the Qumran sect, he concludes, do not indicate any direct contacts but are to be explained by the fact that their backgrounds were similar. In other words, both arose out of the same situation of ferment and tense expectation. The ideas they had in common were probably shared by others of the many sects which arose during the same period among Jews and Samaritans alike, for while the Jews had no dealings with the Samaritans, they were exposed to the same winds of doctrine that were blowing through the whole region. There is even said to have been a Samaritan branch of the Essenes.

# XXIII

## Essenes? Christians? Zealots?

⎏⎏⎏⎏⎏⎏⎏⎏⎏⎏⎏⎏⎏⎏⎏⎏⎏⎏⎏⎏⎏⎏⎏⎏⎏⎏⎏⎏⎏⎏⎏⎏⎏⎏⎏⎏⎏⎏⎏⎏⎏⎏

Were the Qumranians, then, Essenes? As has been said, a majority
of the writers about them now assume that they were; few even
acknowledge that the question is open for discussion. Milik says
that the basic identity of the sect and the Essenes is now accepted; the discussions now going on deal with the origins of the
sect, the foreign influences manifest in it, and its influence on the
New Testament. Fritsch feels that it has been "shown quite conclusively" that the covenanters of Qumran were Essenes, though
he guards himself by adding "or at least Essenic in character."
Howlett mentions the "steadily dwindling group of scholars" who
still insist that this identification "has not been proved with in-
controvertible finality," and he admits that this is true; the only
difficulty of which he seems to be aware, however, is the insignificant fact that the Dead Sea Scrolls do not use the name
"Essene." Discussions of the origin of Essenism and its relation
to other sects or parties now commonly use the Dead Sea Scrolls
as Essene documents.

So far as there is any discussion of the main question of identity,
the considerations adduced are still largely those presented in
DSS (pp. 279–94). The geographical argument, based on the fact
that Pliny and Dio Chrysostom locate the principal Essene settlement close to the Dead Sea, is naturally an important factor in
the situation. Pliny says that Engedi lay "below the Essenes."
Fritsch accepts Dupont-Sommer's dubious suggestion that this
may mean "south of the Essenes." The Essene settlement, Engedi,

and Masada would thus be mentioned in order from north to south. It is quite possible that Pliny followed that order in describing the major points of interest on the western side of the Dead Sea, but the phrase in question is not impressive evidence. Other writers have not failed to point out that the ancient world did not think of north as up and south as down. Dupont-Sommer himself, in proposing this interpretation, mentioned also the possibility that the Qumran monastery was only one of many Essene settlements scattered throughout the Dead Sea region.

Milik, apparently assuming that "below" means "south of," argues that Khirbet Qumran must be the place of which Pliny speaks because no other important ruin has been found between Engedi and Jericho. He recalls also what Philo and Josephus say of the work of the Essenes as farmers and artisans. Many indications of both industrial and argricultural activity have been provided by the excavations at Khirbet Qumran. The nearby oasis of Ain Feshkha provided a place for their work as farmers.

The differences between the sect of the Dead Sea Scrolls and the Essenes described by Philo and Josephus have not been entirely forgotten, but most writers find it easy to dispose of them. Fritsch suggests that some of them may disappear when all the Qumran material is published, or at least prove to be less serious than they now seem. There were many communities of Essenes, and what was true of some may not have been true of others. Some of the differences between the Essenes as described by ancient writers and the Qumran community as reflected in its own literature may thus be explained as differences between branches of the same general movement. The fact that Philo and Josephus say nothing of the teacher of righteousness or the new covenant, for example, is explained by Fritsch on the supposition that the teacher of righteousness founded a schismatic group among the Essenes.

Other differences may reflect different stages in the history of the movement. The contrast between the militant spirit of the War scroll and the extreme pacifism attributed by Philo to the Essenes is mentioned by Fritsch, who suggests that the War scroll may have come from an earlier period, such as the time of the

Maccabean revolt. This is not in accord with the most probable date of the War scroll (see p. 195), and there are indications that neither the Essenes nor the Qumran group were pacifists at the time of the rebellion against Rome; the general proposition, however, that there may have been changes in attitude and belief with changing times, is undoubtedly true. Schonfield observes that the elaborate organization of the community must have taken time to develop; this is confirmed by the fragments from Cave 4 representing various recensions of the Manual of Discipline, the Damascus Document, and the War scroll. Schonfield recalls also the references in the Damascus Document to many generations, afflictions, and years of sojourning.

·If the word "Essene," or "Essenic," as some prefer, is taken to include all the more or less similar marginal sects which arose in Judaism from the persecution of Antiochus Epiphanes to the destruction of the temple, it is quite safe to say with A. Powell Davies that the movement "almost certainly contained divisions or sects" and that these "were constantly changing and developing." Even if Essenism is thought of as a specific sect we must of course make some allowance both for change and for some variety at any one time. The only question is how much divergence is compatible with belonging to one and the same sect.

We may accept Albright's judgment that there will probably be disagreement for some time between those who regard the Qumran covenanters as "the Essenes proper, described by Josephus," and those who consider them "a splinter sect which emerged from" the Essenes. Albright goes on to say that "opinion increasingly favors the former alternative"; this, however, is much less certain. Fritsch may be right in saying that the similarities between the Essenes and the covenanters "far outweigh the differences." He is on less solid ground when he affirms that "any difference can be attributed either to prejudice and faulty reporting by Philo and Josephus or to our own inadequate knowledge of the history and teachings of the Qumran sect."

To say, as Fritsch does, that the term "Essene" is to be applied to the Qumran community "in its widest sense as used by Josephus" is a contradiction in terms. Josephus may have included under this name a few related but distinct sectarian groups; he did not, so far as we can judge by his description, use it in a wide enough sense to include the Qumran sect. If we include it, we are using the term in a wider sense than he did. H. J. Kandler, after a fresh, detailed comparison, comes to the conclusion that the sect of Qumran cannot be identified with the Essenes of Philo and Josephus but belongs to the realm of Essenic sects.

Not all scholars are yet ready to consider the Qumran covenanters Essenes in any sense. Del Medico goes so far as to deny that the Essenes ever existed. According to him, Philo, who was never in Palestine, simply invented "these virtuous Essenes, inhabiting villages in an idealized Palestine." His purpose was probably to show that the monastic way of life, "a typically and uniquely Egyptian phenomenon of the first century of our era," was compatible with Judaism. That there were Jewish monks like Philo's Therapeutae even in Egypt seems to Del Medico uncertain; he is quite sure there were none in Palestine.

Pliny is commonly believed to have visited Palestine in the train of Vespasian, but Del Medico denies that he ever saw the country. The calm retreat of disillusioned old men which he describes is no more credible than the luxuriant vegetation which he makes rise from the arid desert. Pliny merely elaborates what Philo has said; Dio Chrysostom, who cannot be trusted anyway, simply follows Pliny.

As for Josephus, his works are translations and full of interpolations. The Hebrew Yosippon has all the episodes in which Essenes figure but never mentions them. The Latin Hegesippus has nothing about them except in one doubtful passage, probably corrupt, of some manuscripts. The Slavic version contains the account of the three sects but omits all other references to Essenes.

The basic passage in the *Jewish Wars* (II. viii.2–14) was interpolated, Del Medico maintains, by a Greek who probably lived in Italy at the beginning of the third century A.D. It was based on what had been said about a century earlier by Hippolytus, who confused the Essenes with a sect that lived on the east side of the Jordan, but said little about them that was not true of Jews in general. The interpolator of Josephus turned what Hippolytus said into a satire against the Jews; another interpolator toned down this aspect by inserting sentences which do not appear in the Slavic version. This second interpolator is responsible also for the references to Essenes in the *Antiquities,* which simply describe the customs of the Palestinian peasants. None of the ancient writers and interpolators, says Del Medico, pictured the Essenes as monks who copied manuscripts, so that one could label as Essene any place where one found a Roman inkwell.

Here, as on other points where Del Medico has blazed a trail of his own, his arguments should be carefully checked and either substantiated or refuted. No other scholar, so far as I know, has attempted to sever the connection between the Essenes and the Qumran sect in such a radical fashion. There are others, however, who remain unconvinced that the Qumranians were Essenes. The position of Allegro, for example, is notably noncommittal. He usually speaks of the "Qumran sect" or the "covenanters." The location of the monastic settlement described by Pliny, he says, "corresponds exactly with that of the Qumran monastery," and he notes the similarities of practice and doctrine, but, without drawing any conclusion, he moves at once to the Essene communities throughout Palestine, in which he sees "a very possible means of access to Qumran ideas for Jesus, if we are to see both groups as part of the same religious movement."

Otzen feels that the similarities between the Essenes and the Qumran community have been overemphasized. The motives and ideas back of the similar practices, he says, reveal a broad chasm between the two sects. As the Essenes are represented in both of our chief sources, they are thoroughly Hellenized. Jewish in origin, they stand on the threshold between Judaism and syncretism. Citing a list of non-Jewish elements in their beliefs, rites, and ethical ideals, he concludes that even if we postulate a common origin, the two movements developed in diametrically opposite directions. Both departed from the prevailing Pharisaism, but while the Essenes moved eagerly toward syncretism, the group which produced the Manual of Discipline sought to return to the religion of the prophets.

Schonfield finds the affinities of the covenanters with the Essenes on the one side and the primitive Jewish Christians on the other equally impressive, but he sees peculiarities in the covenanters' party which prevent identification with either Essenes or Jewish Christians. The stress on entering the covenant and the separation from Judah exhibit a sectarianism narrower than that of the Essenes. The fact that at the sacred meal of the Rule of the Congregation the chief priest and the priestly elders take precedence over the Messiah of Israel seems to Schonfield fatal to the identification of Essenes and covenanters. The party of the new covenant may, he says, be considered Essene in a broad, generic sense, but if so its autonomy and special emphasis must be recognized.

A new point in Schonfield's view is his suggestion that the Essenes and the New Covenant Party, as he calls the Qumran sect, were two different groups which in turn occupied the site of Khirbet Qumran. Accepting de Vaux's conclusion that there was an Essene settlement there from about 100 B.C., but maintaining at the same time that the literary activity of the covenanters began late in the last century before Christ, Schonfield suggests that with the consent of the Essenes, or after they abandoned the site, the covenanters "repaired the buildings and set up their own establishment—perhaps somewhere about 25–20 B.C.—following Essene practice closely in their organization, and acquiring and being assisted by the literature in the possession of the Essenes."

Schonfield strangely ignores the interruption in the occupation of the site for more than thirty years, beginning in 31 B.C., though his theory could easily be adjusted to that outstanding fact in the history of Qumran. If the relationship between the Essenes and the covenanters was as close as he supposes, however, there would seem to be no real necessity for maintaining the distinction between them. Schonfield himself, as a matter of fact, is inclined to accept the identification of the Qumran community with what Josephus calls "another order of Essenes," who were not celibates as the Essenes in general were. His conclusion is that the covenanters were "probably a distinct and rather specialized sect associated in the last phase of its existence with the Essenes and to an extent not yet fully clarified with the Judaeo-Christians, but identical with neither."

That the Qumranians were actually Christians has been argued since 1951 by J. L. Teicher (*DSS*, pp. 51, 99, 184, 295–98). In this theory he has few if any followers, but he has continued to defend it. In a recent article on the Essenes he notes Del Medico's effort to make the Essenes a fictitious group, and says that the Dead Sea Scrolls will not prevent the Essenes from evaporating "into thin air," for these documents "are Christian, not Essene." Since Teicher holds at the same time that the Essenes themselves were Christians (see the following paragraphs), the contrast here is more rhetorical than logical.

The accounts of the Essenes and Therapeutae attributed to Philo, Teicher says, represent an attitude toward Greek culture so different from what appears in his genuine writings that if he wrote them he must have done so "under the effect of a touch of schizophrenia." Teicher does not, however, consider these accounts Christian forgeries, as some earlier scholars did; they are bits of Christian literature, he says, which became associated with the name of Philo, perhaps merely through being included in a manuscript of his works.

Citations from some of the church fathers are given to show that they considered the Essenes "a species of Christians." That they were right is "a daring thought," but Teicher is willing to "risk it." It would give the Essenes "a proper habitat in the annals of history" and would dispose of "the endless and tiresome debate about the influence of Essenes upon Christianity." There are scholars and others than scholars, one may remark, who do not seem to find this debate tiresome even now. It must be said also that if the Essenes were indeed a species of Christians, they were a very strange species, as different from the church of their time as they were from other Jewish groups. This should be evident from our discussion of the relation between them (pp. 111–18).

Teicher claims, however, to have "direct and positive proof" that the Essenes were "non-Pauline Christians." According to

Josephus, the Romans tortured the Essenes to death during the First Jewish Revolt, when they would not "blaspheme the legislator" or "eat what was forbidden to them." The Romans did not compel Jews on pain of death to violate their religious scruples, Teicher says; therefore the Essenes were not Jews. But if the statement of Josephus is to be accepted, the argument can be reversed: the Romans tortured the Essenes to make them do violence to their convictions; the Essenes were Jews; therefore some Jews at least were so tortured by the Romans. Teicher adds that what Josephus says of the Essenes applies in detail to "the early non-Pauline Christians, as we know them from the Dead Sea Scrolls." Here is a new variation on the theme of Essenes and Qumranians: the covenanters of Qumran are Christians, but they are also Essenes; therefore the Essenes are Christians!

Two difficulties are recognized by Teicher but easily met. The ascetic type of communal life seems incongruous with Christianity; but, says Teicher, the life of the Jerusalem church was communal and austere, and other Christian communities probably imitated it. More difficult to reconcile with his theory is the fact that the Essenes existed, according to Josephus, before the Christian era. But the name "Essene" appears in such a variety of forms in the sources that we cannot tell what its original form or meaning was. In any case, both the early Christians and certain groups of Jews were called "the poor." If Christians could share one name with Jewish groups, they might also be known by another name which had been used by Jews.

The discoveries at Qumran, Teicher boldly asserts, "proves conclusively that the site was occupied in the first two Christian centuries, and occupied by Christians." Any real proof to this effect would profoundly alter the whole trend of studies in the Dead Sea Scrolls. In the end, however, Teicher modestly states that his identification of Essenes and Christians is only "a promising working hypothesis."

It is rather curious to note how the theories of Teicher, Schonfield, and Del Medico coincide at some points yet diverge sharply at others. Teicher's idea that the early non-Pauline Christians inherited the name "Essene" from a pre-Christian Jewish sect recalls Schonfield's theory of an Essene occupation of Qumran preceding the occupation by the covenanters. Both Teicher and Del Medico postulate a Christian occupation of the Qumran settlement. Del Medico and Schonfield, however, agree in rejecting Teicher's opinion that the Essenes and Qumranians were Christians, though Del Medico says that the Qumran genizah may have included Ebionite writings seized by the rabbis. The Ebionites, says Del Medico, at least existed. Sections of several of the scrolls are in fact attributed by him to Christian sources.

The insuperable difficulty for any theory that would make the Qumran covenanters Christians is that the two communities, with all their affinities and possible contacts, were much too different to be identified. If the time when Qumran was occupied and the scrolls were written could be extended to the second or third century A.D., comparisons with the Ebionite sect of Jewish Christians might have more force. For the period before 70 A.D., however, we are dependent upon the New Testament for our knowledge of Christian practices and beliefs. If the picture given there is not reliable, we have no evidence at all for judging what primitive Christianity really was. To claim that the Dead Sea Scrolls are Christian and reflect early Christianity more accurately than the New Testament does would obviously beg the question, even if it could be proved that the scrolls were late enough to be Christian documents.

The theory that the covenanters of Qumran were Zealots has been encountered already in our discussion of the origin of the sect and the identification of the teacher of righteousness (pp. 232–45). Several points not mentioned in that connection may be mentioned here. One interesting detail is Roth's suggestion, previously noted, that this theory explains why no fragments of the book of Esther were found in the Qumran caves: its recognition of a foreign dominion over the Jews would make this book unacceptable to the Zealots.

The prevalent conception of the Zealots as a political party of super-patriots is the result, Roth suggests, of the misleading account given by Josephus, though Josephus himself speaks of them as a "fourth sect of Jewish philosophy" and calls their leaders "sophists." Josephus, says Roth, does not really describe the Jewish sects, but merely gives a brief inventory to serve as a foil for his long, exaggerated, idealized account of the Essenes.

Even if his identification of the teacher of righteousness should prove to be mistaken, Roth claims, a comparison of the Qumran literature with the history of the Zealots shows that they fit together with marvelous precision. When Judas the Galilean rebelled against the Romans after the death of Herod the Great, he seized the city of Safed in Galilee, but soon lost it again to the Romans. After that he disappeared for ten years. It would be quite natural if he took refuge with his followers at Damascus, which was nearer and probably safer than Jerusalem. This was the migration to the land of Damascus of which the Damascus Document speaks. Here Judas and his followers had leisure to revise their covenant. The Thanksgiving Psalms reflect the experiences of Judas in his exile and divine deliverance; he may even have compiled them himself.

When he appeared again in Judah, Josephus tells us, Judas propagated his doctrines. This was exactly the time when the Qumran settlement was reoccupied. Like Schonfield, Roth holds that the group which came to Qumran at about 6 A.D. was not the same as that which had abandoned the place in 31 B.C. Judas and his followers, he suggests, now used this site as a base while appearing in the eyes of the world to be peaceful Essenes.

Judas died fighting against the Romans. The brief reference in Acts 5:37 seems to imply that he was killed at the time of his rebellion in 6 A.D. In that case he did not have much time to make use of a base at Qumran. Two of his sons were crucified by the apostate Jew Tiberius Alexander, who was procurator in 46–48 A.D. Another son, Menahem, then became the leader of the sect. In 66 A.D. he made Masada the military center of his group; but, Roth says, the community at Qumran continued its literary activity.

After Menahem's death at Jerusalem in the same year, his nephew Eleazar ben Jair took his place at the head of the group at Masada, where they kept aloof from the rest of the Jewish insurgents and held out against the Romans until 73 A.D. The community at Qumran continued a few years longer, following current events with interest and writing its commentaries and other texts, including the War scroll.

With every wish to do full justice to this theory, which is propounded with extraordinary enthusiasm and conviction, I am bound to say that my conclusion as stated in *DSS* (p. 295) is unchanged: "Possibly some members of the community joined the Zealots in the last decades before the destruction of the temple. Any closer connection than that, however, can hardly be postulated. The community of the Dead Sea Scrolls was quite certainly much older than the movement inaugurated by Zadok and Judas."

To this I must now add that the distinction drawn by Schonfield as well as Driver and Roth between the sect which occupied the Qumran settlement in the last century B.C. and the group which reoccupied it in the first century A.D. is more ingenious than convincing. The retention of the same general plan and apparently the same use of the buildings in the second period distinctly favors either the identity of the groups or at least a direct continuity. If it was not the same individuals who returned nearly forty years after they had abandoned the site, it was the same community, and it may well have included some of those who had lived there before. The composition, copying, and editing of the community's literature cannot all be assigned to the second period of occupation.

All these continuing attempts since 1955 to establish the identity of the Qumran sect have been no more conclusive than those which preceded them. The insistence of Del Medico that very different groups are represented among the texts has at least this validity: no rigid standard of uniformity in belief, ritual, or organization was imposed on the writings used and preserved by the covenanters. Like the Bible, many other books which they copied and read may have been inherited from other groups.

The current tendency to use the term "Essene" in a broad way to include the Qumran sect along with others of the same general character is not seriously objectionable. With Schonfield, Bruce, and Oesterreicher, we may consider it possible, though by no means certain, that Josephus was thinking of the Qumran community when he wrote of the "other order" of Essenes, which practiced marriage (*DSS*, p. 291). It is thoroughly possible, even probable, that Pliny's Essenes were the men of Qumran. One must still, however, protest against the current tendency to use together what Josephus and Philo say of the Essenes and what the Dead Sea Scrolls reveal concerning the sect of Qumran, on the assumption that both bodies of data apply to one and the same group. To some it may seem pedantic to maintain this distinction, but for the purpose of accurate historical knowledge it is essential.

PART SIX

# THE BELIEFS OF THE SECT

# XXIV

## *God, Spirits, Angels, and Demons*

⎣╶╴⎢╻╶╴⎢╻╶╴⎢╻╶╴⎢╻╶╴⎢╻╶╴⎢╻╶╴⎢╻╶╴⎢╻╶╴⎢╻╶╴⎢╻╶╴⎢╻╶╴⎢╻╶╴⎢╻╶╴⎢╻╶╴⎢╻╶╴⎢╻╶╴⎢╻╶╴⎢╻╶╴⎯

It has already been said that the literature of the Qumran community was not subject to any strict theological censorship. A book that was sufficiently valued to be copied and preserved must have been considered helpful and sound, but it was characteristic of the sect, as of Judaism in general, to be more interested in ideas that seemed stimulating and inspiring than in conformity to a strict standard of orthodoxy. There were no creeds, no decisions of councils, no *ex cathedra* pronouncements of a supreme authority.

At the same time it is to be expected that certain characteristic ideas and attitudes will appear in writings produced within the community, and this is what we actually find. J. Licht, in a study of the Thanksgiving Psalms, finds that when the phrases and motifs which recur frequently are put together and their meaning is determined, a comprehensive system of theological thought emerges. This, as he observes, is surprising in the Judaism of that period. Using the theological passage in the third and fourth columns of the Manual of Discipline (*DSS*, pp. 374–76) as a standard, Licht checks by it his inferences from the Thanksgiving Psalms, noting also some differences "both in details and in stress."

Variations in doctrine among the Dead Sea Scrolls, Licht points out, can be explained largely by the different purposes and interests of the texts. The Thanksgiving Psalms deal especially with matters of inner, individual experience. The Manual of Discipline is concerned with the organization of the community and the administration of its affairs. The conflict with external foes dominates the Habakkuk Commentary. The War scroll contemplates the impending crisis. Differences in time of composition explain other points of divergence, and some may be attributed to differences between individuals or divisions within the sect. In the main, however, the scrolls represent the same basic theology. No difference among them is fundamental.

In recent discussions of the Dead Sea Scrolls the conviction of the absolute sovereignty of God is seen more and more to be basic for the sect. According to its belief, the operations of nature follow unchanging laws which God has ordained from the beginning. It is interesting to observe here already something of the ambivalence of Greek and modern ideas of "natural law." What is for science simply an observed uniformity in nature is for religious faith an expression of God's will.

The incomprehensible mystery of God's eternal decrees profoundly impressed the men of Qumran. Typical examples of the characteristic use of the word "mystery" are noted in *DSS* (pp. 255f), including the statement of the Habakkuk Commentary that "the mysteries of God are marvelous" (vii.8; *DSS*, p. 368). Licht defines the meaning of the word "mystery" in the scrolls as a "divine unfathomable unalterable decision." One more adjective is needed to make the definition complete: "wonderful" or "awe-inspiring." Among the divine mysteries, as Licht notes, are "the mysteries of sin," which are a part of the universe ordained by God.

In what would seem to us Calvinistic fashion, though it is in direct line with the faith of the Old Testament, the Qumran theologians attributed God's mysterious acts to his will to manifest his own glory. To glorify God was, as they saw it, the chief end not only of man but of God himself. Quite in the manner of Paul, they were able to believe that the wicked were created to serve as objects for the demonstration of God's mighty wrath. The blessings of the righteous also redounded to his glory.

Man cannot understand God's ways, but he can trust in his justice; yet even the conception of divine justice is colored by the stress on God's sovereignty. In the Old Testament the same Hebrew word is used for justice, vindication, and even victory. In the Thanksgiving Psalms the justice of God usually means, as Licht defines it, "his unquestionable right to do as he pleases." This is very close to the central conception of the book of Job, and the Qumran writers often seem to echo Job's despairing cry, "How can a man be just before God?"

But God is also merciful; if he were not, man's case would be hopeless. Expressions of humble gratitude for deliverance from helpless involvement in sin abound in the Thanksgiving Psalms. As Licht observes, the dominant emotion is not simply joy but gratitude for God's gifts, among which the ability to live a righteous life is paramount.

The sect's conception of the universe was in accord with its conviction of the sovereignty of God, though this was combined with strange ideas of non-Jewish origin. No taint of polytheistic mythology is to be found in their thinking. All the exotic elements which they adopted, directly or indirectly, from Persian or Babylonian thought were adjusted and subordinated to their faith in God as the sole Creator of heaven and earth.

Near the end of the scroll of Thanksgiving Psalms the expression "to create new things" occurs. This probably is an echo of the reference in Isaiah to God's creating new heavens and a new earth (65:17; 66:22); it may possibly, however, as Gaster supposes, imply a continued process of creation. Gaster recalls a famous Jewish prayer which says that God "renews every day the work of creation." He mentions also "the rabbinic doctrine of periodic renewal," which, however, is not the same thing. The text of the passage in the Thanksgiving Psalms is too much broken by holes in the manuscript to permit a clear understanding of what is meant. All that can be inferred from it with certainty is God's power to create, change, and destroy, while remaining eternally the same.

The community's interest in the universe and its operations is shown by their possession of manuscripts of Enoch and other related writings (see pp. 177–80). These matters were no doubt included in the secret teachings of the sect, which they vowed not to divulge to those outside of their circle (Manual of Discipline ix.17; x.24; *DSS*, pp. 383, 387). Cryptic scripts are used in some of the texts, and there is an esoteric astrological work in a mixture of scripts among the documents from Cave 4.

Ideas concerning the Spirit of God and good and evil spirits play a large part in the conception of the universe in the Dead Sea Scrolls. In the Old Testament, E. Schweitzer reminds us, the Spirit of God is associated first of all with extraordinary manifestations of divine power. The result of this emphasis in later Judaism was to relegate the operation of the Spirit either to the remote past or to the Messianic age. In the later parts of the Old Testament, however, there was also a tendency to think of God's Spirit as the power for righteous living, primarily in the community of the future but also to some extent in the present. In post-biblical Judaism the growing stress on the individual's decision for good or evil opened the door to the Persian conception of a cosmic struggle between light and darkness, in which every man had to choose one side or the other. Thus the way was prepared for the idea of the two spirits which is expressed in the Manual of Discipline (iii.13–iv.26; *DSS*, pp. 374–76, cp. pp. 257f).

The struggle between the spirits has a future aspect: it is for an appointed period, at the end of which will come "the time of visitation" when evil will be judged and destroyed. This idea, Schweitzer points out, is incorporated into the Jewish conception of obedience to the law, so that the struggle is centered not so much on the final consummation as on the present moral conflict; but this conflict itself is made a part of the cosmic process which God initiated at the creation of the world. It is not man's spirit that struggles with evil but the power of God. The mythological form of expression is only a new means of representing this basic Hebrew conviction.

The spirits of light and darkness which struggle in man's soul and in the universe are sometimes called angels. Thus it is made clear that they are both God's creatures and subject to him, even though for the appointed period he allows the one whose way he abhors to be active. It is equally clear, however, that the two spirits or angels are powers outside of man, which not only help or hinder him but control his life in accordance with each individual's divinely assigned "lot."

The dualism of the Qumran theology is thus primarily ethical but with a cosmic dimension. It may be, as both Fritsch and Schonfield suggest, that conflicts with human enemies had something to do with the development of this conception. It undoubtedly takes a distinctly military form in the War of the Sons of Light with the Sons of Darkness. Schonfield remarks that the disappointment during the period of Jewish independence following the Maccabean revolt, when the end failed to come and evil prevailed, fostered a doctrine of two powers which the later rabbis of the Talmudic period had to condemn as a dangerous heresy.

Otzen compares the dualism of the Manual of Discipline with the Greek and late Jewish idea of the macrocosm and microcosm. According to this conception, what occurs in the universe at large, the macrocosm, is mirrored on a small scale in the individual man, the microcosm. The double aspect of the Qumran dualism, both cosmic and ethical, corresponds to this idea. Otzen finds also that the two spirits are thought of in different ways under these two aspects. In man we have a psychological dualism, with the spirits of good and evil struggling in his heart. This conception is not mythical but spiritual. In the universe, on the other hand, we have a cosmological, mythical dualism, in which the two spirits are thought of in mythological, not spiritual, terms.

The connection between these two types of dualism is seen by Otzen in the idea that the division of mankind to which each individual will belong is determined by the outcome of the struggle in his own soul. This, it seems to me, does not accurately represent the thought of the Manual of Discipline. No doubt the element of personal decision and effort was recognized in practice, but little room is left for it in the passage in question. Schweitzer's judgment, that the outcome both in the universe and in the individual soul is determined not by the spirit of man but by the power of God, is more in accord with the implications of the text.

It is true and important that the dualism of the Qumran texts is not a contrast of matter and spirit. It is not an absolute dualism, grounded in the nature of things. Both of the two spirits are creatures of the one God and subject to him. Otzen, however, finds a trace of absolute dualism in the statement of the Manual of Discipline (iii.19; *DSS*, p. 374), "In the abode of light are the origins of truth, and from the source of darkness are the origins of error." (Otzen takes the word which I render "abode" as another Hebrew word which means "spring," and this reading is possible.) Mandean sayings which speak of the powers of evil as derived from black water or a great spring are cited, and Otzen suggests that the language of the Manual of Discipline at this point may have been influenced by such non-Jewish ideas, even though the implied absolute dualism was not accepted. Certainly if such a conception was recognized at all, it was rejected.

The major purpose of Otzen's study is a comparison of the Dead Sea Scrolls with the Testaments of the Twelve Patriarchs. In the Testaments he finds a dualistic doctrine, but it differs from that of the Manual of Discipline in being only a "microcosmic" dualism, without the "macrocosmic" aspect. Chapter 20 of the Testament of Judah speaks not only of the two spirits but also of a spirit of understanding that can turn whichever way it wishes. Here, it seems, each man's spirit is free to choose between the two spirits. Elsewhere, especially in the Testament of Asher, there are many references to the two ways of good and evil and the two inclinations which reside in every man's breast. The idea of the two inclinations or impulses is characteristic of the rabbinic literature, and the idea of the two ways played a large part in early Christian literature. Outside of the passage cited from the Testament of Judah, the conception of the two spirits is not clearly present in the Testaments of the Twelve Patriarchs. There are passing references to "Beliar" (a corrupt form of the name Belial), to "the angels of the Lord and of Satan," to "the evil spirit," and to "the angel of peace." The idea of a struggle between good and evil in the universe is notably lacking.

In the Testaments of the Twelve Patriarchs, as in the dualism of the Manual of Discipline in its "microcosmic" aspect, the two spirits are conceived, Otzen says, in quite unmythological, psychological fashion. This may be true if the two spirits of the Testament of Judah and the two inclinations of the Testament of

Asher are considered identical, but the scattered references to God, Beliar, angels, and spirits in several of the Testaments make this doubtful. The Testament of Benjamin says, "The inclination of the good man is not in the deceitful power of the spirit of Beliar" (6:1).

It is not entirely clear, in fact, how far the distinction between "mythological" and "psychological" holds good for the Manual of Discipline. The struggle between the two spirits in a man's heart seems to be conceived quite realistically as a conflict between two personal beings. Molin believes that the evil spirit is Belial. Otzen himself remarks that in late Judaism there was a tendency to mythologize the idea of the good and evil impulses, so that the evil impulse was confused with Belial and the demons. In both the Manual of Discipline and the Testaments of the Twelve Patriarchs he recognizes traces of the same tendency, and a mixture of the two ways of thinking. His contention that in general the spirits of the "microcosmic" struggle are not conceived mythologically thereby loses much of its force. It does not seem to me, indeed, very significant.

The spirit of light is called also the spirit of truth in the Manual of Discipline; he is no doubt the same as the angel of God's truth who is said in the same passage to help the sons of light. It is therefore natural to ask whether he can be identified with one of the archangels named in other Jewish literature. Two of these, Michael and Gabriel, are already mentioned by name in the book of Daniel; the apocryphal and rabbinic writings have a number of others, classified according to their functions. The term "prince" is sometimes applied to them, and the spirit of light is called the "prince of lights" in the Manual of Discipline (iii.20; *DSS*, p. 374). The Damascus Document says, "For of old arose Moses and Aaron through the prince of lights" (v.17f; *DSS*, p. 353). One of the archangels is named Uriel, which means "God is my light," and he is said in some sources to be the ruler of light. Otzen argues therefore that the spirit of light is the archangel Uriel.

Molin hesitates between Uriel and Michael as the angel with whom the spirit of light is to be identified. Yadin argues strongly that he is Michael. The War scroll says, "The prince of light thou didst appoint of old as our helper; in his lot are all the sons of righteousness, and all the spirits of truth are in his dominion" (xiii.10). The function of the prince of light is thus to help the sons of light, as the angel of God's truth is said to do in the Manual of Discipline. Later the War scroll says that God "will send eternal help to the lot he has redeemed by the power of the angel he has made glorious for rule, Michael, in eternal light, to give light in joy to all Israel, peace and blessing to the lot of God, to exalt among the gods the rule of Michael and the dominion of Israel over all flesh" (xvii.6–8; *DSS*, p. 399). It is therefore Michael, Yadin concludes, who is the prince of light appointed to help the sons of light. As for Uriel, Yadin points out that he is not named among the four angels of the presence in the War scroll; in his place we find Sariel (see below).

Otzen identifies the angel of God's truth with Michael, but distinguishes him from the spirit of light. The help given by the angel of God's truth, says Otzen, is probably intercession, and the angel who appears as intercessor in late Judaism is Michael. In the Testaments of the Twelve Patriarchs "the angel that intercedeth for you" is mentioned, and it is said that "he is a mediator between God and man, and for the peace of Israel he shall stand up against the kingdom of the enemy" (Testament of Dan 6:2). A few verses later it is said that the angel of peace will strengthen Israel (6:5). These expressions, Otzen says, fit only Michael. Why Otzen considers the angel of God's truth different from the spirit of light and truth is not apparent. Yadin's view that they are the same and to be identified with Michael seems much more probable.

The War scroll (ix.14–16) gives the names of four archangels which are to be inscribed on the shields of the four "towers" of the army. (The Hebrew word for "tower" is here used like the Latin *turris*, for a solid military formation.) The names given are Michael, Gabriel, Sariel, and Raphael. Yadin compares this list with others which appear in the pseudepigrapha and in rabbinic literature. The names of Michael, Gabriel, and Raphael appear in all of them. In Enoch 40–71 the fourth angel is Penuel; in the rabbinic Midrashim he is always Uriel. Sariel never occurs in these lists, but Enoch 20 gives seven names, and in the Greek text one of these is Sariel.

From these facts Yadin infers that in the period when the Parables of Enoch (chapters 37–71) were composed, the name of the fourth archangel was not yet fixed, and it would be in this period that Sariel might be named instead of Penuel or Uriel. If we knew when this part of the book of Enoch was written, says Yadin, this would be a useful indication of the date of the War scroll. It is of some interest to recall here that no manuscript of this part of Enoch has been found at Qumran, and that Milik therefore regards the Parables as the work of a Jewish Christian of the second century A.D. (see p. 180). Yadin adds that the sources vary in the functions they ascribe to Uriel: in some he is the ruler of light, in others the ruler of darkness and Sheol. The idea of the four archangels as connected with four military units, corresponding to the "towers" of the War scroll, is found also, Yadin points out, in rabbinic literature.

In his commentary Yadin speaks of the four archangels as "angels of the presence," but they are not so designated in the War scroll. The "angels of the presence" are mentioned, however, in other scrolls. One of the Thanksgiving Psalms, in a badly damaged passage not translated in DSS, has the expression "in the lot together with angels of the presence" (vi.13). The scroll of Benedictions (iv.25f) says that the priest will be "like an angel of the presence in the holy dwelling," and will "cast the lot with the angels of the presence." Fragments of three manuscripts concerning the angels of the presence were found in Cave 4. The term occurs frequently in the pseudepigrapha and the rabbinic literature.

Other designations of angels, familiar either in the Bible or in the apocalyptic literature, appear in the Dead Sea Scrolls, especially the Thanksgiving Psalms and the War scroll. The term "holy ones," used in Daniel and Enoch, is especially common in the War scroll but appears also in the Thanksgiving Psalms and the Manual of Discipline. The expression "glorious ones" occurs also. The word "gods" is often used in the War scroll and the Thanksgiving Psalms, clearly with reference to angels, who are also sometimes called "sons of heaven," "the host of heaven," or "the eternal host." Sometimes a familiar Old Testament word for "mighty ones" or "heroes" is applied to the angels. Very often, as in other Jewish literature, they are called simply "spirits." The word "angel" itself, literally "messenger," is used frequently, especially in such combinations as "the holy angels." Several Qumran manuscripts have to do with "the angel of peace."

Other terms are used for particular angels, or for angels with particular functions. One of the Thanksgiving Psalms uses a term which, as Mansoor points out in a note on the passage (vi.13), occurs along with the word "angel" in Job 33:23; elsewhere in the Old Testament it means interpreter, spokesman, or mediator. In the Thanksgiving Psalm, Mansoor translates it "intercessor." The passage in Job speaks of "an angel, a mediator, to declare to man what is right for him."

The next line in the Thankgiving Psalm contains an incomplete word which Mansoor restores as a noun meaning "herald" or "announcer." Wallenstein postulates a different form from the same root, meaning "proclamation" or "announcement." The preceding word means "one who brings back"; Wallenstein therefore renders the two words together as "reporter." This is more convincing than Mansoor's understanding of the noun by itself as meaning "announcer," for it is hard then to see how the preceding word can be taken. In either case the meaning "reporter" or "announcer" is involved. But this makes it probable that the word in the preceding line means not "intercessor," as Mansoor takes it, but "one who declares," or the like, as the context in Job implies. Wallenstein translates it "interpreter," Gaster "intermediary."

Dupont-Sommer has an entirely different understanding of the whole line. Instead of "There is no intermediary" (or "intercessor" or "interpreter"), he reads, "None deals insolently with sons," and instead of "announcer" or "proclamation" in the next line, he reads "his fruit." This seems to me much less probable; all admit, however, that there are too many gaps and doubtful letters in the text to permit any certain reconstruction. The mediating and announcing angels must therefore be left up in the air, where perhaps all good angels belong.

The use of the word "prince" or "commander" for some of the angels has already been noted in connection with "the prince of lights." It is used frequently for the chief angels, and the term used for their dominion is one derived from the same root, as Yadin has pointed out. In the book of Daniel, Michael is called "one of the chief princes" (10:13), "your prince" (10:21), and "the great prince who has charge of your people" (12:1); "the prince of Persia" and "the prince of Greece" are mentioned also (10:13, 20), evidently as patron angels of the nations. Mansoor remarks that in the rabbinic literature the word "prince" is used regularly for a guardian angel.

The word "angel" is used also in the Dead Sea Scrolls for an evil spirit. The spirit of darkness, as we have seen, is called also the angel of darkness in the Manual of Discipline (iii.20f; DSS, p. 374). Later in the same passage there is a reference to "destroying angels" (iv.12; DSS, p. 375), who are mentioned also in the War scroll (xiii.12) and in the Damascus Document (ii.6; DSS, p. 350). Otzen observes that they seem to stand on the borderline between angels and demons. As the agents of divine punishment they might be considered good angels; the fact, however, that Belial or Beliar is the agent of punishment in the Damascus Document and the pseudepigraphic writings makes it seem probable that the destroying angels here are thought of as subjects of Belial.

The use of the name Belial for the chief of the hosts of evil is characteristic of the Dead Sea Scrolls. Yadin counts thirty-three instances: twelve in the War scroll, five in the Manual of Discipline, ten in the Thanksgiving Psalms, and six in the Damascus Document. To these may be added one occurrence of the name in a fragment from Cave 1; the texts from the other caves may be expected to add to the number.

Belial is clearly the same as the spirit or angel of darkness. All the evil spirits and the sons of darkness are said to be in "the lot of Belial." The present age of the world is called "the dominion of Belial" in the War scroll (xiv.9) and the Manual of Discipline (i.18, 23f; ii.18; DSS, pp. 372f). But just as the Manual says that there is an appointed period, at the end of which error will be destroyed forever (iv.19; DSS, pp. 375f), so the War scroll says that God "made Belial for destruction" (xiii.10f), and in the end he will be destroyed, "when the great hand of God is raised against Belial and against the whole army of his dominion with an eternal smiting" (xviii.1).

The use of the name Belial, corrupted to Beliar, is one of the close points of contact between the Dead Sea Scrolls and the Testaments of the Twelve Patriarchs, where Otzen cites thirty-one instances. If this work is a Christian composition, this is all the more remarkable in view of the fact that the name Belial occurs only once in the New Testament (see p. 122). It is not very common in Jewish literature.

In the book of Jubilees the evil one is called Mastema. As a proper name this word does not occur in the Dead Sea Scrolls, but as a common noun meaning "enmity" it appears several times. The Manual of Discipline, speaking of the angel of darkness, refers to "the dominion of his enmity" (iii.23; DSS, p. 374). The War scroll speaks of Belial's "hostile purpose" or "purpose of enmity," using the same word (xiii.4; DSS, p. 399), and a little later calls Belial "the angel of enmity" (xiii.11). The Damascus Document also mentions "the angel of enmity" (xvi.5; DSS, p. 363). Another passage in the War scroll, using another noun from the same root, refers to Belial and "all the mysteries of his enmity" (xiv.9). Yadin suggests that the translator of the book of Jubilees may have mistaken this rather unusual noun for a proper name.

As has been said, the dominion of Belial is only for a limited period. Meanwhile he not only rules the sons of darkness but also grievously afflicts the sons of light. But they are not left to their own resources in fighting him. They are mightily aided by "the God of Israel and the angel of his truth." In the final struggle, in which Belial and all his hosts will be destroyed, the War scroll prescribes the strictest ritual purity for the sons of light, "for holy angels are together with their armies" (vii.6; DSS, p. 395). In the moment of triumph the elect will acknowledge the divine help by which they have prevailed: "Thou, O God, terrible in thy royal glory, and the congregation of the holy ones are in the midst of us. . . . For holy is the Lord, and the King of glory is with us together with the holy ones; mighty ones and the host of angels are in our musters, and the One Mighty in battle is in our congregation; the host of his spirits accompanies our steps" (xii.6–8).

# XXV

## Man, Sin, and Salvation

In the whole Qumran theology nothing is more distinctive than the doctrines of man and sin. They are, in fact, one doctrine, for man is thought of chiefly as a sinner, utterly hopeless but for the grace of God. As J. P. Hyatt says, this is a more pessimistic view of man than is usually found in Jewish sources. The inherent sinfulness of man is of a piece with his weakness and insignificance before the sovereign majesty and power of God. This conception is especially characteristic of the Thanksgiving Psalms, which express over and over again what Licht calls "an almost pathological abhorrence of human nature." The poet includes himself in what he says of man in general; often he speaks in the first person singular, as though he were speaking only of himself. Yet it is clear, as Hyatt says, that while this overwhelming sense of man's weakness and sinfulness may have come to some degree from the poet's own temperament and experience, he draws conclusions for all mankind. Licht points out that there is no suggestion of a particular act by which man first became a sinner, such as the fall of Adam; rather it is the contrast with the utter holiness and majesty of God that produces the crushing realization of man's weakness and sinfulness.

Not all men, however, are hopelessly lost in sin. We have seen, in connection with the sect's dualistic conception of the universe, that all mankind is divided into two "lots." Every man belongs either to the sons of light or to the sons of darkness. The sons of darkness are wholly governed by the power of Belial, but the warfare between good and evil extends also into the souls of the righteous. God has allowed the two spirits to be mingled and to struggle for mastery even in the hearts of the sons of light. Dominion over them belongs to the "prince of lights," yet "by the angel of darkness is the straying of all the sons of righteousness" (Manual of Discipline iii.20–22; *DSS*, p. 374).

In speaking of the dualism of the sect, we have already observed that it was not a metaphysical dualism of matter and spirit or of body and soul. The whole man is on one or the other side in the cosmic struggle. There are many passages, however, which use the terms "flesh" and "spirit" to denote the contrast of the human and the divine, though only in a very general way. Human nature as such is characterized as "flesh," with special reference to its inherent sinfulness and weakness. The implications of the term "spirit" are much less clear, because the word is used in many different senses. According to the Manual of Discipline, a candidate for admission to the sect must be examined "as to his spirit and his deeds" (vi.17; *DSS*, p. 379); the sons of Zadok are "weighed" and the members are assigned their rank in the group "according to their spirits" (ii.20; v.21; ix.14f; *DSS*, pp. 373, 378, 383); when a member falls away from true devotion and obedience it is said that his spirit "wavers" or "turns back" (vii.18, 23; *DSS*, p. 381). All this corresponds to common biblical usage, by which "spirit" often indicates a person's disposition, character, or self.

The Damascus Document condemns men who defile or make abominable their "holy spirit" (vi.11; vii.3f; *DSS*, pp. 353f). Here the meaning seems to be essentially the same, with the added implication that the righteous man must regard his own God-given spirit as holy. The Manual of Discipline, however, reflects also a somewhat different conception. Concerning the members of the community it says that "in a spirit of true counsel for the ways of a man all his iniquities will be atoned . . . and in a holy spirit he will be united in his truth" (iii.6f; *DSS*, p. 373). So in the "time of visitation," God will consume every "spirit of error" in man's flesh, "cleansing him with a holy spirit," and "will

sprinkle upon him a spirit of truth, like water for impurity"
(iv.20f; *DSS*, p. 376).

From these and the many other passages that might be cited,
it seems impossible to derive a clear, consistent meaning for the
word "spirit." As in the Old and New Testaments and in common
usage to this day, it is used with many meanings, including those
of the angelic or demonic beings that serve or oppose God, the
good and evil influences that these exert on men, and the character, disposition, or self of the individual. Still other uses of the
word will be seen when we examine the sect's doctrine of salvation.

The realm to which each man belongs has been determined by
an eternal divine decree. The division of all mankind into two lots
no doubt seemed to the members of the sect a simple matter of
observed fact, and the assumption that they were themselves the
sons of light and all others were sons of darkness obviated any
difficulty in drawing the line between the two divisions. They
were painfully aware that the spirit of darkness was contending
with the spirit of light even in their own hearts, but they recognized with humble gratitude that they belonged to the lot of God.
As Licht remarks, the Manual of Discipline and the War scroll
present an objective generalization of the twofold division of
mankind, while the Thanksgiving Psalms present the individual's
subjective consciousness of having been allotted to the position
of the righteous.

The whole conception is a corollary of God's absolute sovereignty and man's complete dependence upon him. According to
the Iranian conception of life and the universe, which unquestionably influenced the Qumran community directly or indirectly,
each individual chose for himself which side he would take in the
cosmic conflict. The men of Qumran, however, subsumed everything under their strict monotheistic belief in God as the sole
Creator and Lord of the universe.

How this hard predestinarianism could be adjusted to human
freedom and moral responsibility was a problem no more solved
by the Qumran sect, as Kuhn observed several years ago, than it
was by later Christian theologians. Apparently it was not even

felt as a problem. Schweitzer raises the question, however, whether the whole idea of the two spirits may not have been simply a mythological way of conceiving the necessity of decision in human life, not only once and for all but repeatedly day by day. It would then amount to the same thing as the rabbinic doctrine of the good and evil impulses or inclinations, according to which one must constantly choose which impulse he will follow. Schweitzer points out that in the Testaments of the Twelve Patriarchs, where we have noted both the two spirits and the two inclinations, the necessity of a free moral decision is also strongly emphasized. This is not, however, the doctrine of the Manual of Discipline. There, as also in the Thanksgiving Psalms, the point of view appears to be rigidly predestinarian. A man is judged according to his spirit, but his spirit is as it has been given him.

The deterministic point of view is carried even to the point of astrological speculation. Milik informs us that a fragmentary document from Cave 4 gives the signs of the zodiac and connects them with the months and the days of each month; it also states the meaning of thunder under a particular sign. Another Cave 4 manuscript reported by Allegro describes the physical proportions of persons born under each sign of the zodiac. Especially significant for the subject before us is the fact that this document states also the proportion of people born under each sign that are assigned to the spirits of light and darkness respectively. This text is written in a mixture of different alphabets, and while the words run from right to left, the letters of most of them are written from left to right.

The impending day of visitation, when the wicked will be punished, bulks large in the thought of the Qumran community. Licht observes that the author of the Thanksgiving Psalms faces with terror the catastrophe which threatens the greater part of mankind, even though his confidence that he will be delivered makes him also "agreeably thrilled" by the prospect. In the assurance that he will be spared, he considers himself already saved and gratefully praises God's saving mercy.

A study of the literary form of the Thanksgiving Psalms by H. Bardtke throws light also on their conception of salvation. Examining them according to the categories which have been distinguished in the Old Testament book of Psalms, Bardtke finds that the Thanksgiving Psalms of Qumran exhibit a mixture of two literary types, the "individual complaint" and the "individual thanksgiving." In both connections, however, there are differences between the Old Testament Psalms and those of Qumran. Persecution and other calamities are referred to, but the chief ground of complaint in the Qumran Psalms is man's constant propensity to sin. The poet's distress is described in terms of an attack by a multitude of foes before whom he stands firm in his devotion to God's law, but his ability to do this manifests the marvelous grace of God in his election, not any merit of his own. The deliverance for which he thanks and praises God is therefore grounded in the divine election.

Frequently the complaint and thanksgiving lead to a third element, reflection on the smallness of man and the greatness of God. To the expression of a personal experience there is added a more general, didactic note. Sometimes the tone and language recall the Wisdom Literature of the Old Testament. Like other post-biblical Jewish psalms, the Thanksgiving Psalms of Qumran thus prove to have a purpose not only of self-expression and personal devotion but also of teaching and edification. In one of them (xi.3–14; see *DSS*, pp. 413f) Bardtke finds a description of the way of salvation, summarizing the ideas of the Manual of Discipline "as in a catechism." Even the description of the enemy, to which much space is given in the longer Thanksgiving Psalms, agrees with the description of the evil spirit in the Manual of Discipline. The comparison may perhaps be pushed too far, but Bardtke has succeeded in demonstrating a didactic purpose in the scroll of Thanksgiving Psalms. Molin also recognizes such a purpose. He finds in the scroll a guide for the meditation and devotion of the members of the sect.

Salvation consists not only in deliverance from calamity and judgment; it includes deliverance from sin itself. The sons of light are saved by the faithful study and observance of the law, but they are able to keep the law only because they have been placed under the dominion of the spirit of light. The first effect of their election is therefore, as Licht points out, a righteous character. Both a good character in general and also specific moral traits are expressed by the word "spirit." As the sons of darkness have a "spirit of error," a "spirit of wickedness," a "spirit of fornication," or an "apostate spirit," so the sons of light have a "spirit of the counsel and truth of God," a "spirit of truth," a "spirit of knowledge," or an "upright spirit."

Having the divine gift of righteousness, the sons of light rejoice also in the forgiveness of sin. One of the Thanksgiving Psalms, in true biblical fashion, says that God "pardons those who repent of transgression and punishes the iniquity of the wicked" (xiv.24). The expression "those who repent of [literally, turn from] transgression" was probably used also in an incomplete line of another Thanksgiving Psalm (xvii.15); it appears once in the Manual of Discipline (x.20; *DSS*, p. 386) and twice in the Damascus Document (ii.5; xx.17; *DSS*, pp. 350, 357). But the grace of repentance is given only to the elect. Thus, as Licht says, the expression "those who repent of transgression" is used practically as a name of the sect. Forgiveness and the gift of a righteous character or "holy spirit" are in fact two aspects of the same divine work.

The writer of the Thanksgiving Psalms, overwhelmed by the consciousness of human depravity, is all the more grateful for his cleansing from this contamination. He speaks of it in terms of the atonement provided, in the religion of the Old Testament and in later Judaism, by ritual acts; but it is quite clear, as Licht points out, that he is thinking of inner moral purification. Rites of purification were undoubtedly practiced by the Qumran community, and great care was taken to guard the ritual purity of the members, but the Manual of Discipline warns in no uncertain terms that for him who "refuses to enter God's covenant" and gives "free rein to the stubbornness of his heart" there is no possibility of atonement by ritual means. "He will not be purified by atonement offerings, and he will not be made clean with water for impurity; he will not sanctify himself with seas and rivers or be made clean with any water for washing" (ii.25–iii.5; *DSS*, p. 373).

Since the sons of light are the members of the sect, salvation is an affair of the community as well as the individual. The personal aspect of salvation is almost exclusively stressed in the Thanksgiving Psalms, yet even here it is evident that the author is concerned with the life and thought of his group. Molin suggests that the Psalms may have been used in the community's corporate worship. Licht sees a conflict between the poet's intensively personal attitude and his thought and life as a member of the group. He finds the conflict resolved by the claim to leadership which the Thanksgiving Psalms express or imply. It is true that the poet sometimes speaks as a leader and teacher of others; I must confess, however, that I see no indication of a conflict between his individual experience and his relation to the group. Religious leaders are usually men of intense personal experience of religion.

Salvation involves also the victory of the hosts of light in the final conflict with the forces of evil. This appears most strikingly in the War of the Sons of Light with the Sons of Darkness, but it is implied also, in a different way, in the sect's withdrawal to the wilderness "to prepare the way of the Lord" by the study of the law, as presented in the Manual of Discipline (viii.12–15; *DSS*, p. 382). There is very little of the idea of a "history of salvation" in the Dead Sea Scrolls, aside from the Damascus Document. Bardtke remarks that the Thanksgiving Psalms make no allusion to God's saving acts in history. Moses and the law are mentioned, but it is the law itself that interests the poet rather than any historical event. Yet the sect is aware of a divine plan for the future and believes itself called to be the new Israel in which God's purpose will be realized.

Milik may therefore be right in supposing that the members of the sect considered it necessary to relive for themselves the experience of Israel in the desert before the conquest of the promised land. The purpose of their community life, from this point of view, was to meet the conditions for overcoming evil, and in so doing to have a foretaste of the heavenly life which they would ultimately enjoy. This life of preparation included planning and training for the war with the Kittim. The War scroll exhibits a curious combination of preoccupation with military equipment and procedure and utterly unrealistic directions for the conduct of the war.

# XXVI

## The Two Messiahs

⎍⎍⎍⎍⎍⎍⎍⎍⎍⎍⎍⎍⎍⎍⎍⎍⎍⎍⎍⎍⎍⎍⎍⎍⎍⎍⎍⎍⎍⎍⎍⎍⎍⎍⎍⎍⎍

No aspect of the Qumran theology has evoked more discussion than its Messianic beliefs. Publication of a few new texts from Cave 4 has contributed important data on this subject. The term "Messiah" itself (literally "anointed") occurs in many of the texts; other Messianic titles also are used, and in some passages where there is no explicit mention of a Messiah scholars have seen reflections of Messianic ideas. The question whether the teacher of righteousness was in any sense a Messianic figure has been much discussed also. It is necessary therefore not merely to supplement with a few details what was said in *DSS* (pp. 264–67) but to review the whole subject.

The word "Messiah" has for Christians, of course, very definite associations. Some Jewish writers on the Dead Sea Scrolls have complained that Christian interpreters have read Christian ideas into the use of this title in the scrolls. L. H. Silbermann, for example, complains of "the tendentious practice of capitalizing certain key words in our translation and our thinking." He is distressed because "no one seems to have any compunction about translating *mšwḥ* or *mšyḥ* as Messiah with a capital M, ignoring the palpable fact that Messiah is a word loaded with two millennia of connotations beyond its use in our Ms" (the Manual of Discipline). It is surprising that the use of a capital letter makes all that difference. Silbermann himself translates the passage in the Manual of Discipline which he is discussing (ix.10f), "until the coming of a prophet and the anointed High Priest and the

Davidic king." He might at least have written "high priest," if not "davidic." Gaster translates, "Until the coming of the Prophet and of both the priestly and the lay Messiah," though in a note he spells the word "messiahs."

It is true, of course, and one would have thought it was obvious, that the Hebrew word meaning "anointed" was used in many different ways from the time when it was first applied to the kings and high priests of ancient Israel. If we decline to see so much significance in the conventional use of a capital letter (just as we continue to write "Bedouin" out of deference to the dictionary), let it not be thought that we are injecting any special meaning into the word "anointed." After all, the distinction between capital and small letters was unknown to the Qumran community. Our task is to find in what sense or senses they used the word "anointed." W. S. LaSor would use the word "Messiah" only where an "eschatological reference is certain." This, however, would only beg the question and obscure the problem.

The passage in the Manual of Discipline to which Silbermann's article is devoted speaks of "the Messiahs of Aaron and Israel." The Damascus Document speaks three times of a single Messiah of or from Aaron and Israel (xii.23; xix.11; xx.1; *DSS*, pp. 355f, 361). As was noted in *DSS* (p. 265), the plural form may have been changed to the singular in the Damascus Document by a later scribe to whom the idea of two Messiahs was not familiar. It has been suggested by Norman Walker that the change was made as a consequence of the combination of royal and priestly offices by John Hyrcanus (135–104 B.C.), which led the covenanters to expect a Messiah who would be both high priest and king. This seems entirely improbable, because John Hyrcanus can hardly have been admired by the covenanters, if the sect existed in his time. His assumption of royal dignity shocked and alienated many devout Jews.

Yadin, citing Segal and Gaster, holds that the belief in two Messiahs was one of the reasons for the sect's opposition to the Hasmonean priest-kings. According to Schoeps, it was the sect's opposition to the Hasmonean dynasty that gave rise to the idea of two Messiahs, and this "Messianic schizophrenia" ended with the collapse of the dynasty. The earlier expectation of one redeemer who would be both priest and king was then resumed. It will be interesting to learn, when the Qumran fragments of the Damascus Document are published, whether they include the passages in question, and if so whether they speak of one or two Messiahs of Aaron and Israel.

On the basis of Hebrew syntax and usage, LaSor argues that when two words are used together, as Aaron and Israel are used here, they designate a unit. "Aaron and Israel" together thus designate the community. What the Manual of Discipline means, therefore, is not that there will be a Messiah of Aaron and a Messiah of Israel, but that the sect as a whole will have two or more "anointed ones," whatever that term may then mean. This contention, however, is based on the grammatical usage of the Old Testament rather than on that of the Dead Sea Scrolls. In the Manual of Discipline itself we read of "the spirits of truth and of error" (iii.18f; *DSS*, p. 374). Surely this does not imply that truth and error together form a unit, to which both spirits belong! Most scholars agree that two "anointed ones" are meant, and that the terms Aaron and Israel refer respectively to the priesthood and the laity. In other words, there will be a priestly Messiah and a lay Messiah, an anointed high priest and an anointed king. K. Schubert has suggested that the sharp division of the community into priesthood and laity was what led to the doubling of the Messiah.

Whether the two Messiahs are eschatological figures or belong to the present world order is another question. Silbermann insists that they are to be connected with what the rabbinic literature calls "the days of the Messiah" which are "in time," not to "the coming age" which is "out of time." According to a rabbinic tradition which he cites, the anointing oil was hidden by King Josiah, and since then the high priest has been called "the priest of manifold garments" instead of "the anointed priest." The prophet who is to come will restore the anointed priesthood as well as the Davidic monarchy, and thus re-establish "the proper pattern or structure of Israel." Whether the line was actually drawn so sharply at Qumran between the days of the Messiah and the coming age is not entirely clear, but I am inclined to agree with Silbermann on this point.

That two Messiahs are expected, one of Aaron and one of Israel, is confirmed by the Rule of the Congregation, where the Messiah of Israel appears separately. This document is explicitly connected by its opening words with "the last days." The Messiah of Aaron is not mentioned by that name, but he may be the priest who presides over the meals of the sect and takes precedence over the Messiah of Israel himself (ii.17–22; pp. 304–305). This important text has evoked a variety of interpretations among scholars. Some regard it as a picture of the Messianic banquet; others see in it a set of directions for present procedure, supplementing the similar passage in the Manual of Discipline (vi.4–6; *DSS*, p. 378).

Milik believes that the reference is to "the present community, but in an apocalyptic perspective." Cross calls attention to the statement that these directions are to be followed whenever as many as ten men are present; this, he thinks, shows that the passage is not concerned with the Messianic banquet of the future. In the meal here pictured, he holds, the community anticipated the future banquet liturgically, as the early Christian church did in its sacramental meals. How the presence of the Messiah of Israel is to be explained on that basis it is difficult to see. It is hardly to be supposed that he was impersonated by a member of the sect, yet the idea of an imagined or spiritual presence is excluded by the fact that when his turn comes the Messiah puts forth his hand and takes bread with the others.

Much depends, unfortunately, on the meaning of a word which is completely illegible in the photographic reproduction of the text. The editor, Barthélemy, says that a careful examination of the manuscript shows this word to be a verb meaning "begets," and both Cross and Allegro have testified that an infra-red photograph confirms this reading. The next two or three words, including the subject of the verb, are missing; then come three words meaning respectively "the Messiah," "with them," and "shall come." Barthélemy and most other interpreters insert the word "God" as subject of the verb, and after it a particle which indicates that the next word, "the Messiah," is the object of the verb.

This makes the clause mean, "If God begets the Messiah," which is, to say the least, startling.

The question then arises whether the next word, "with them," goes with this clause or with the following verb, "shall come." To read "If God begets the Messiah with them" does not make sense, but Barthélemy feels that a connection between "with them" and "shall come" is unlikely. He therefore adopts a simple emendation suggested by Milik: by lengthening the last letter of the verb he changes it to one meaning "brings." This yields the reading, "if God brings the Messiah with them," which Barthélemy attaches to what precedes as part of the title of the section. The verb "shall come" then begins a new sentence.

Much depends also on the way the gap in the text is to be filled. Dupont-Sommer supplies "the Lord" instead of "God," omitting the sign of the direct object. He keeps the verb "begets," however, and takes with it the phrase "with them," reading "when the Lord shall have begotten the Messiah among them." The meaning "among" for the preposition used here is unfortunately questionable.

Gaster too rejects Milik's emendation, but, on the supposition that the verb is completely illegible, he proposes a different restoration, supplying a verb which occurs a few lines later in the text and which means "meets" or "is present." He therefore translates, "In the event that the anointed (king) should be present with them." This implies that in the time for which these directions are intended the monarchy will have been restored and there will be a king, who may or may not be present at any of the common meals. The reference would then be to any one in a succession of kings, not to a single eschatological Messiah. The testimony of those who have studied the manuscript and the infra-red photograph, however, leaves no doubt as to the verb actually written in the manuscript.

Cross accepts Milik's emendation. If the reading "begets" is to be retained, however, and "God" is to be supplied as the subject, there may be, Cross observes, an allusion to Psalm 2:7, "You are my son, today I have begotten you." A reference is possible also, he suggests, to Isaiah 66:9, "Shall I bring to the birth and not cause to bring forth? says the Lord; shall I, who cause to bring forth, shut the womb? says your God." The verb here translated "cause to bring forth" is the one which means elsewhere "beget." Cross mentions also Psalm 110:3, where, by reading different vowels with the same consonants, some Hebrew manuscripts and the Greek and Syriac versions have the verb used in Psalm 2:7, meaning "I have begotten you," instead of the word meaning "your youth."

Robert Gordis declares Milik's emendation incompatible with Hebrew syntax and usage. He adopts an alternative suggestion of Barthélemy that there may be in the verb "begets" an allusion to Ezekiel 36:12, with a variant reading found in the Septuagint, "I will beget" instead of "I will bring" or "cause to walk." The troublesome phrase "with them" is taken by Gordis with the following clause, making the sentence read, "When God begets the Messiah, with them shall come the priest." This interpretation at least takes seriously the words in the manuscript that can be read with certainty. I must confess, however, that to me the Hebrew syntax of the sentence, as Gordis takes it, still seems peculiar. After an "if" or "when" clause it is not normal, to say the least, to begin the final clause with a prepositional phrase. One wonders also why the high priest's coming with them should be made dependent upon the begetting of the Messiah. At the same time, to take the verb "shall come" as the beginning of the final clause makes a strange Hebrew sentence. The only way to justify it would seem to be to emphasize the "jussive" force of the verb: "let the priest come."

Kuhn, writing before the confirmation of the manuscript's reading by Cross and Allegro, questions not only the verb at the end of the line but also the conjunction which precedes it. He supposes that the line ended with two words referring to the leaders of the community, with whom the earlier part of the line is concerned, and that the title of the section was completed with these words. In this we are no longer free to follow him. His reconstruction of the beginning of the next line, however, is still suggestive. On the ground that the following clause calls the person here referred to "the head of the whole congregation of

Israel," while the remainder of the section puts the priest above the Messiah of Israel, Kuhn maintains that "the Messiah" here mentioned is not the lay Messiah of Israel but the priestly Messiah of Aaron. He therefore fills the gap at the beginning of the line with the words "And the priest," so that the subject of the following verb, "shall come with them," becomes "the priest the anointed one," that is, "the anointed priest." This would be eminently satisfactory if only we could dispose of the verb "begets" at the end of the preceding line, but that is possible only if we assume a scribal error and emend the text.

H. N. Richardson tries to get around these difficulties in still another way. Accepting the text of the manuscript, he reads the verb with different vowels, making it mean "is born" instead of "begets." He then supplies at the beginning of the next line, as subject of the verb, "the prophet," so that the clause, taken with what precedes, means "when the prophet is born." A new sentence then begins, "The Messiah shall go in with them," and this is followed by the clause, "because he is the head of the whole congregation of Israel," which all other interpreters take as referring to the priest. This is suggestive, but it is not free from difficulty. Richardson's reading of the verb presupposes a spelling (the use of $y$ as a vowel-letter for $\bar{e}$) which is at best rare in the Qumran texts, though it occurs a number of times in the St. Mark's Isaiah scroll. To read "the prophet" is not impossible, but it is surely uncalled for. Richardson takes the term, in any case, as a designation of the Messiah, so that the passage still refers to the Messiah's birth, though it does not imply a divine origin or status. One wonders why he did not supply "the prince" instead of "the prophet."

If the verb "begets" is retained, the subject must surely be God, and the object must be the Messiah. The word "beget" must then be used in the same way as in Psalm 2:7, where it refers to the adoption and establishment of the king as God's son (see II Samuel 7:14). No other kind of reference to begetting is credible in the context of a series of directions for the community's meetings "in the last days."

How what follows is to be restored is still a problem. Even the priest is not actually named in what is preserved of the text; he has to be supplied to fill a gap following the verb "shall come." The next line, however, clearly mentions "the sons of Aaron, the priests," and Kuhn's point that the priest takes precedence over the Messiah of Israel in the rest of the text holds good. It is true also, as Kuhn points out, that the mention of "the Messiah," instead of "the Messiah of Israel" or "the Messiah of Aaron," is surprising. It would be a relief to read with Kuhn "the anointed priest," if it could be fitted into the rest of the text. That being impossible, it is almost certain that "the priest" followed "shall come" as its subject.

The next words, "head of the whole congregation" are then best read not as a title of the priest, but with a preposition (restored at the end of the gap in the text), making the clause read, "the priest shall come [or enter] at the head of the whole congregation." Cross, who proposes this reading, points out that the same phrase, "at the head of," is used in the Manual of Discipline, the Benedictions, and the Damascus Document, as well as the Old Testament. Three lines later, where Barthélemy reads, "and afterward the Messiah of Israel shall be seated," both Kuhn and Cross read "shall enter."

It would be a pleasure to close this discussion with a new and convincing solution of the problem, but nothing that I have been able to think of is any better than the suggestions made by others, and none of these is more convincing than the original proposal of Milik and Barthélemy, unsatisfactory though it is. To have a text of such outstanding theological importance so incomplete and uncertain is tantalizing. Its implication as to the divine origin or adoption of the Messiah must remain uncertain. The passage as a whole, however, clearly presupposes at least the idea of the royal and priestly Messiahs, with the latter in the place of highest honor.

The subordination of the Messiah of Israel to the priest recalls the way in which the "prince" is subordinated to the priests in Ezekiel 40–48. The word "prince" actually appears in some of the Qumran texts, and it is natural to ask whether it refers to the Messiah of Israel. Milik finds in the Benedictions a blessing for the Messiah of Aaron and another for the Messiah of Israel. He admits that his arrangement of the fragments "remains very hypothetical," but, having worked out what seems to him the most probable order of succession, he finds first a blessing for the members of the congregation in general, next a blessing for the high priest, then a blessing for the rest of the priests, and finally a blessing for "the prince of the congregation." The last named is probably the same as the "prince of the whole congregation" of the Damascus Document (vii.20; *DSS*, p. 355) and the Messiah of Israel of other texts. The high priest must be the Messiah of Aaron if these blessings are intended for the congregation of the last days.

North notes that the high priest is not actually mentioned in the text except in Milik's restoration of a damaged line, which, North says, is "conjectural and based on hints which seem to us somewhat fragile." Milik's assignment of blessings to the two Messiahs is regarded by North as only complicating the problem. Other scholars, however, have not been so skeptical. Dupont-Sommer follows Milik's division of the text throughout. With reference to the "prince of the whole congregation," he points out that the same title is used in the War scroll (v.1). It occurs also in a commentary on Isaiah, as convincingly restored by Allegro. In the following lines of the blessing, Dupont-Sommer observes, this "prince" is said to be the one who will "restore the kingdom of his people forever" and "renew the holy covenant"; there is also, as Milik notes, a clear allusion to Isaiah 11:1–5. It is thus abundantly clear that this blessing is intended for the royal, Davidic Messiah, the Messiah of Israel.

Gaster accepts Milik's arrangement on the whole, but takes the last part of Milik's blessing for the priests as a blessing for the king, and for the last blessing renders "prince of the congregation" as "president of the community," interpreting the title according to rabbinic rather than biblical usage. This, however, introduces another important leader not in evidence elsewhere in the Qumran literature. In the Damascus Document, Gaster translates this title "the leader of the community" and, in the War scroll, "the leader of the entire community."

In the War scroll what seem to be Messianic titles are applied to the leaders in the final war, but, as Milik remarks, it is hard to tell whether these leaders are to be identified with the two Messiahs or whether they are merely precursors of the Messiah. If the Messiahs of Aaron and Israel were to be regarded as simply the anointed priests and kings in a succession, this question would have no meaning. The phrase "until the coming of a prophet and the Messiahs of Aaron and Israel," however, quite clearly excludes such an interpretation. An exultant invocation in the War scroll (xii.9–12; *DSS*, p. 398) has been taken by Milik as a eulogy of the Messiah of Israel, but Yadin is surely right in rejecting this interpretation: the "mighty one," "man of glory," "thou who doest valiantly," is certainly God himself.

The "prince of the whole congregation," as has been seen, is probably the Davidic Messiah. Certainly, as Yadin notes, the War scroll does not imply any opposition to the tribe of Judah or the family of David; on the contrary, David's victories over the Philistines are proudly recalled as an example of divine deliverance (xi.1–3; *DSS*, p. 397). In this connection Yadin points out that in the Damascus Document (v.1f; *DSS*, p. 352) the prescription of Deuteronomy 17:17 concerning the king is applied to the "prince," and the writer proceeds to speak of David. Yadin therefore concludes with good reason that "the prince of the whole congregation" is the military head of the community in the final war, as the chief priest is its religious head. The community, he continues, did not accept the Hasmonean union of priesthood and kingship in one person, but held as its ideal the biblical picture of priest and prince standing side by side with clearly differentiated functions.

Another passage of the War scroll (xi.7f; *DSS*, p. 398) uses the expression "thy anointed ones" (or "Messiahs"), and describes these as "seers of testimonies" through whom God has made known the ordering of his battles. The preceding line quotes Numbers 24:17, the same verse that in the Damascus Document is applied to "the prince of the whole congregation" (vii.20; *DSS*, p. 355). This was evidently a favorite proof-text of the Qumran sect: it is quoted also in the Benedictions, the Testimonia, and the commentary on Genesis 49. The designation of the "anointed ones" as "seers of testimonies" recalls Psalm 105:15 (I Chronicles 16:22), "Touch not my anointed ones, do my prophets no harm." The idea of an anointed prophet occurs elsewhere in the Old Testament only in I Kings 19:16 and Isaiah 61:1.

The latter passage speaks of an anointing by the Lord with his Spirit. Yadin connects this with a sentence in the Damascus Document, "And he caused them by his anointed to know his Holy Spirit and a revelation of truth" (ii.12; *DSS*, p. 350). Yadin reports that an examination of the manuscript at Cambridge has convinced him that the word translated "a revelation" (*ḥwh*) is actually the one used in the War scroll, meaning "seers of" (*ḥwzy*). He suggests therefore that "his anointed" (*mšyḥw*) is a copyist's mistaken reading of "anointed ones of" (*mšyḥy*), so that the sentence should read, "And he caused them to know by the anointed ones of his Holy Spirit and the seers of truth." In my photostat of the manuscript, Yadin's reading seems possible but by no means certain.

Another passage in the Damascus Document refers to the prophets as "the holy anointed ones" (vi.1; *DSS*, p. 353); here too the manuscript reads "his anointed one," but in the context this form is impossible and the emendation "anointed ones" is generally accepted by scholars. The reference to prophets as "anointed ones" is clear in both passages.

Whether the chief priest of the War scroll is the Messiah of Aaron is uncertain. He is not so called, nor is the word "anointed" applied to him. Two priests are mentioned as having special parts in the preparations for battle. Before the warriors go out to their assigned positions for the battle, the chief priest offers a prayer, standing before the whole army. After the various units have taken their places in the battle array, seven priests go out; one of them walks up and down before the ranks, exhorting and encouraging them, then the other six sound their trumpets (vii.8ff; *DSS*, p. 395; also xv.5ff). The one who encourages the troops is called "the priest appointed for the time of vengeance by all his brethren." Gaster confidently identifies him with "the priest anointed for battle" of whom the Talmud speaks. Yadin notes that the two titles are somewhat similar, but that the function of the "priest appointed for the time of vengeance" is that of a second priest in the Talmud, who walks about repeating the words of the "priest anointed for battle" so that all the soldiers can hear them.

The conception of the two Messiahs in the Qumran scrolls has revived discussion of the Messianic ideas in the Testaments of the Twelve Patriarchs. The idea of a Messiah from the tribe of Levi appears in this book, but also the traditional hope of a Messiah from the tribe of Judah. In other words, we have here both a priestly and a kingly Messiah. The relation between them, however, is obscure. Some interpreters have held that the two offices are to be understood as combined in one person, a descendant of both the tribes of Levi and Judah. If the book is a Christian work, as some scholars maintain (see p. 179), this is what we should expect. Early Christian writers referred to Jesus' descent from Judah through Joseph and from Levi through Mary, who was related to Elizabeth, the wife of the priest Zechariah.

Some passages in the Testaments can be taken in this sense; in others, however, it is hard to maintain. The Testament of Simeon, for example, says, "For the Lord shall raise up from Levi as it were a high priest, and from Judah as it were a king" (7:2). Otzen notes that Aptowitzer, in order to uphold the theory of a single Messiah from both tribes, has to assume that this text read originally, "the Lord shall raise up from Levi and Judah a high priest and king."

The problem is complicated by the fact that if the Testaments of the Twelve Patriarchs is a Jewish work, it undoubtedly contains Christian interpolations. The verse just quoted continues, "God and man; he shall save all the Gentiles and the race of Israel." It is sometimes a delicate task to distinguish what is Christian from what is Jewish.

There are other passages which indicate two distinct persons. Kuhn points to a verse in the Testament of Judah as decisive. Here, after exhorting his sons to "love Levi," Judah continues, "For to me the Lord gave the kingdom, and to him the priesthood, and he set the kingdom beneath the priesthood" (21:2). This certainly is no Christian interpolation. If it has any Messianic reference at all, it implies two Messiahs. It may, however, refer simply to the historic kingship and priesthood of the Old Testament. That meaning would be natural in either a Jewish or a Christian composition. This may also be the meaning of a verse in the Testament of Issachar which says, "And to Levi he gave the priesthood, and to Judah the kingdom" (5:7). Another passage in the Testament of Judah, however, clearly refers to the future: "And among men of another race shall my kingdom be brought to an end, until the salvation of Israel shall come. . . . For the Lord swore to me by an oath that he would not destroy my kingdom from my seed forever" (22:2f).

Kuhn cites also a somewhat puzzling statement in the Testament of Reuben: "For to Levi God gave the sovereignty and to Judah with him and to me also, and to Dan and to Joseph, that we should be for rulers" (6:7–12). Reuben goes on to say that Levi will know the law, give ordinances, and "sacrifice for all Israel until the consummation of the times as the anointed high priest of whom the Lord spake." He will "bless Israel and Judah, because him hath the Lord chosen to be king over all the nation." His seed (i.e., presumably, Judah's) "will be among you an eternal king."

Other passages say simply that deliverance will come to Israel from Levi or from Judah or from Israel and Judah. On the basis of the verses which have been cited, in particular Testament of Simeon 7:2, Otzen concludes that all these passages imply a belief in the two Messiahs. Kuhn claims that this belief appears throughout the Testaments "with complete unanimity." That seems to me somewhat more than the evidence justifies; it is fairly clear, however, that the expectation of two Messiahs, a priest and a king, lies at least in the background of this work, be it Jewish or Christian.

The book of Jubilees tells us of Jacob's taking his sons Levi and Judah to see Isaac and be blessed by him (31:4–20). Levi is blessed first and promised that he and his sons shall be the Lord's priests through all generations; Judah is then blessed and told that he will be a prince, and all the Gentiles will quake before him and his sons. Here too Kuhn sees the doctrine of the two

Messiahs, but again his conclusion seems a little too confident. Rowley infers from this passage that the kingdom is subordinated to the priesthood, presumably because Levi is blessed first; this may be so, but Levi was born before Judah and would naturally receive the blessing before his younger brother.

The expectation of two Messiahs has a background in the Old Testament. Not only did the kingship and priesthood exist side by side in Israel and Judah before the Babylonian exile, with many vicissitudes in the relations between them, but after the end of the exile we find the priest Joshua (or Jeshua) and the prince Zerubbabel working together to rebuild the temple (Ezra 3:2). After an enforced interruption, they resumed the task with the help of the prophets Haggai and Zechariah (Ezra 5:1f; Haggai 2:20–23; Zechariah 3–4; 6:9–14).

In Zechariah 4:14 Joshua and Zerubbabel are called "the two anointed ones" (literally "sons of oil," not "Messiahs"). Walker suggests that they were the first Messiahs of Aaron and Israel, prototypes of the future priestly and royal Messiahs. Yadin quotes a Talmudic saying, previously cited by Louis Ginzberg with reference to the Damascus Document: "The two sons of oil— these are the two anointed ones, one anointed for battle and one anointed to be king over Israel."

Zerubbabel soon disappeared, and there was no Jewish king until the Hasmoneans assumed the title, but the high priests retained much power under the Persian and Greek rulers, as they did later under the Romans. Kuhn remarks that even in the Second Revolt (132–135 A.D.) the high priest Eleazar and the Messianic leader Simon ben Koseba (bar Cocheba) stood side by side, though the priest was now subordinate to the military leader.

The statement in the Manual of Discipline from which our discussion of the two Messiahs started refers also to a prophet, who will either appear with them or precede them. The expectation of a prophetic forerunner of the Messiah was strong in Judaism, as the New Testament and the rabbinic literature testify. On the basis of Malachi 4:5, he was commonly identified with Elijah. No other Qumran text, apparently, mentions so explicitly this expected prophet. The promise of a prophet like Moses in Deuteronomy 18:18f is quoted in the Testimonia and may, as Milik supposes, refer to the prophetic forerunner rather than the royal or priestly Messiah. Numbers 24:15–17, the prophecy of the "star" and "scepter," and Deuteronomy 33:8–11, Moses' blessing on Levi, are cited also in the Testimonia. It may very well be, therefore, as Milik observes, that scriptural justification for the hope of three Messianic persons—prophet, priest, and king—was found by the sect in the Pentateuch. One wonders, indeed, whether the threefold hope may have been derived in the first place from the study of these and other verses in the law as well as the prophets.

# XXVII

## Other Messianic Titles and References

⎍⎍⎍⎍⎍⎍⎍⎍⎍⎍⎍⎍⎍⎍⎍⎍⎍⎍⎍⎍⎍⎍⎍⎍⎍

Other titles than those we have noted are used in some of the texts for one or the other of the expected Messiahs or for persons associated with them. A "righteous branch" for David is prophesied by Jeremiah (23:5; 33:15), and the term is picked up by Zechariah (3:8; 6:12). The commentary on Genesis 49, expounding verse 10 of that chapter, uses the expression "until the Messiah of righteousness [or true Messiah] comes, the branch of David." The Florilegium quotes II Samuel 7:11ff, the promise spoken to David by Nathan, and comments, "This is the branch of David, who will arise with the interpreter of the law." On the basis of these passages Allegro is probably right in restoring the words "the branch of David" in a fragmentary line of a commentary on Isaiah. A different word for "branch" is used in Isaiah 11:1 and quoted in another fragment of the same commentary. There can be no question that in all these places the reference is to the royal Messiah of David's line, who is elsewhere called "the Messiah of Israel."

The verse in Genesis 49 mentioned in the last paragraph contains a word meaning "staff" which is used also in Numbers 21:18. The same word can also mean "lawgiver"; in fact, it is so translated in the King James Version in both Genesis 49:10 and Numbers 21:18, though in both places the context shows that the meaning "staff" was intended. The commentary on Genesis 49, interpreting the words "nor the staff from between his feet," says,

"For the staff is the covenant of kingship, and the families of Israel are the feet."

The Damascus Document, after quoting the verse from Numbers and giving a fanciful interpretation of the well and the princes, proceeds, "And the staff [or legislator] is he who studies the law" (vi.7; *DSS*, p. 353). Another passage explains the star of Numbers 24:17 as "the interpreter of the law who came to Damascus" (vii.18f; *DSS*, p. 355). The Hebrew words here translated "he who studies the law" and "the interpreter of the law" are the same; they can also be translated "the searcher of the law." The same expression occurs also in the Florilegium's comment on II Samuel 7:11ff, quoted on page 401.

If the interpreter of the law is one of the three coming persons mentioned in the Manual of Discipline, he may be either the priestly Messiah or the prophet. Milik identifies him with the former, and this seems reasonable, since he is to appear with the branch of David, who is undoubtedly the Messiah of Israel, the prince of the whole congregation. In one of the passages of the Damascus Document cited above (vii.18–20) the prince of the whole congregation is said to be the "scepter" of Numbers 24:17. The same passage, however, says that the interpreter of the law, who is identified with the star out of Jacob, "came to Damascus." This seems to make him a figure of the past, whatever the migration to Damascus may mean. Gaster, to be sure, interprets the statement in a general way: the star, as he translates the passage, "refers to every such interpreter of the Law as indeed repairs to 'Damascus,'" the term "Damascus" being taken in a "purely figurative" sense. If, as seems more probable, the reference is to the past, it is natural to ask whether the interpreter may have been the teacher of righteousness himself. Schonfield considers this possible but suggests also that the interpreter of the law may have been the teacher's successor in the leadership of the community. Cross suggests that the historic interpreter of the law may have been David's high priest, Zadok.

Elsewhere Schonfield identifies the teacher of righteousness with the lawgiver, who is explicitly said in another place to be the interpreter of the law (vi.7). The same passage says that the community is to obey the rules given by the interpreter of the law until "the arising of him ·who will teach righteousness at the end of days" (vi.9–11; *DSS*, pp. 353f). Here we have a future teacher of righteousness, to come at the end of a period which began with the lawgiver or interpreter of the law. Yet, as we have just seen, the interpreter of the law is also a future figure who will arise together with the branch of David!

Is this simply a difference in the use of traditional terms in different documents? If so, it must have been as confusing to the men of Qumran as it is to us. Or was there a double conception of the interpreter of the law, as there was of the teacher of righteousness? This seems more probable. As there had been a teacher of righteousness in the early days of the sect's history and there would also be a teacher of righteousness in the last days, so there had been an interpreter of the law in the past and there would also be an interpreter of the law in the future. But then we must still ask again whether the past teacher and interpreter were the same historic person, and whether the future teacher and interpreter would be one person or two.

Isaac Rabinowitz, who interprets the historical allusions of the Damascus Document as references to Old Testament history (*DSS*, pp. 197–99, 201f), and holds that the teacher of righteousness in the past was Nehemiah (see p. 332), believes that the interpreter of the law was Ezra. He points out that the only place in the Old Testament where the verb meaning "search," "study," or "interpret" is used with the law as its object is Ezra 7:10, where it is said that Ezra "had set his heart to study the law of the Lord, and to do it, and to teach his statutes and ordinances in Israel." The statement that the interpreter of the law "came to Damascus" is understood by Rabinowitz simply as an allusion to the Babylonian exile. In that case, however, it would seem more natural to say that the interpreter came from Damascus, not to Damascus, for Ezra did not go into exile but came out of exile.

If it may be assumed that all these terms had a fairly uniform meaning for the members of the sect, we may draw a few inferences with some assurance, even though a few points remain uncertain. The group looked for the promised branch of David, the Messiah of Israel, the prince of the whole congregation, the king. With him would come the Messiah of Aaron, the religious head of the community, who would rank above the military and political Messiah. Whether the interpreter of the law who would arise with the branch of David would be the priestly Messiah or another person is not clear. There would also be a prophet, who would come either with or before the two Messiahs; perhaps it was he who was called also the interpreter of the law. The relation of the teacher of righteousness who would appear in the last days to these other figures is a question that must be deferred until we have considered a few other texts which have, or are thought to have, Messianic significance.

The theory of Barthélemy that there are Messianic variant readings in the St. Mark's Isaiah scroll was noted in *DSS* (pp. 265, 313f). The scroll's reading in Isaiah 52:14, "so I have anointed his appearance," was singled out as the most impressive of these variants. Another explanation of this reading, offered in 1952 by A. Guillaume, was not mentioned in *DSS;* it has recently been presented again and a little more fully. The third consonant in the Hebrew verb meaning "anoint" represents both of what were originally two distinct sounds. They are still distinct in Arabic. If instead of the one that is used in the word "anoint" we use the other of these two sounds, we get a different verb. It does not occur anywhere else in Hebrew, but it exists in Arabic and may once have been known in Hebrew. It is used of galling a camel's back, fraying a thread, and changing men into animals. An adjective from this root means "ugly." The reading of the St. Mark's scroll thus means, according to Guillaume, "so I have disfigured his appearance from (being) that of a man."

It is precarious to assume the use of a word unknown elsewhere in Hebrew, yet we may be quite sure that the Old Testament has not preserved the whole vocabulary of the ancient tongue. In this text, which scholars have always found difficult, Guillaume's suggestion is plausible and very attractive. Not the least of its advantages is that it yields substantially the same meaning indicated by the context and traditionally found, with some difficulty, in the Masoretic text. The difference is that instead of a passive we have an active verb, whose subject is God. The supposed Messianic variant disappears.

In *DSS* (pp. 266f) I refer briefly to the contention of Brownlee that the suffering Servant of the Lord of Isaiah 40–55 was believed by the Qumran sect to be fulfilled in a Messianic sense by the teacher of righteousness, and also by the community itself. One phase of Brownlee's argument calls for special attention here, because it has been adopted by other scholars. The passage in the Manual of Discipline concerning the two spirits (see pp. 280–293) contains a few sentences in which Brownlee and others see a reference to the Messiah (iv.20–22). The most relevant portions read, as translated in *DSS* (p. 376), "And then God will refine in his truth all the deeds of a man, and will purify for himself the frame of man, . . . cleansing him with a holy spirit. . . . And he will sprinkle upon him a spirit of truth. . . ."

The word rendered "a man" is a common term for an adult male human being. As Brownlee himself notes, it is used a few lines lower in a general sense ("the heart of a man"), and similarly in the closing psalm of the Manual ("with good I will pursue a man"). Why it should be supposed to indicate the Messiah here is not apparent, but we shall encounter this word again in another connection. Some scholars accept the Messianic interpretation. Gaster and Dupont-Sommer reject it and interpret the passage as referring to the individual son of light who is to be purified in the coming time of visitation. This seems to me clearly correct.

Both Gaster and Dupont-Sommer also accept, as I did in *DSS*, a correction of Brownlee's translation first proposed by Yadin. Where Brownlee reads, "He will refine him more than the sons of men," implying a distinction between the Messiah and other men, Yadin shows that what Brownlee takes as a phrase meaning "more than the sons of" is really a noun meaning "frame," "structure," or the like. Wernberg-Møller, reviewing Kapelrud's book in the *Journal of Semitic Studies* for July 1957 (p. 295), still takes the expression as a phrase, "from the sons of man," but understands it to mean "some of the sons of man," i.e., "a part of mankind."

This removes the distinction between the Messiah and mankind in general, but Yadin's explanation seems to me better.

Following what has been quoted, the text continues, "to make the upright perceive the knowledge of the Most High and the wisdom of the sons of heaven, to instruct those whose conduct is blameless." These expressions may be taken to indicate that the "man" is an individual with a mission like that of the teacher of righteousness. In the context, however, they more probably express the purpose of the purification of all the elect. Certainly the abrupt introduction of the Messiah simply as "a man" in a passage dealing with men in general would seem very strange. It would be somewhat surprising also that the Messiah should need such a radical cleansing from sin. In short, the passage has nothing to do with the Messiah.

A very different text, and one much harder to interpret, is the poem in column iii of the Thanksgiving Psalms (lines 3–18). My translation in *DSS* (pp. 403f) is open to improvement; at several points I would now translate somewhat differently, but no English version can reproduce the ambiguities and word-plays of the original. Scholars differ widely in their understanding of even the subject of the poem. Following the pioneer study of Chamberlain, many see in it a picture of the birth of the Messiah from the Qumran sect; some find references also to the birth of the Antichrist from Judaism and the destruction of him and his followers.

Dupont-Sommer, Carmignac, and Licht may be mentioned among those who have espoused some form of the Messianic interpretation. Gaster understands the poem as referring to the "Messianic Travail," known in rabbinic literature as "the pangs of the Messiah." Allegro sees a connection with the idea of atonement by suffering: the sufferings of the sect are "borne for the atonement of the earth," and out of them will come "the Saviour of the world." Baumgarten and Mansoor do not reject the Messianic interpretation but do not explain how far they agree with it; they indicate, however, that at least part of the poem refers to the poet's own suffering. Kuhn and Silbermann reject the Messianic interpretation altogether, understanding the references to a storm-tossed ship, a besieged city, and a woman in travail as all figures of the peril and anguish which the poet has undergone. Molin is impressed by Silbermann's arguments but considers a Messianic reference still possible.

The outstanding point in favor of the Messianic interpretation is the application of the term "wonderful counselor" from Isaiah 9:6 to the child who is born, though Chamberlain himself at first held that it referred here to God. Many Old Testament references to suffering Zion as a woman in travail are cited as parallels, but these have nothing to do with the Messiah. The strange symbol in Revelation 12 of the woman in heaven giving birth to a male child who is threatened by a dragon is naturally adduced also. The degree of emphasis on the birth of the child, not merely on the mother's suffering, may be taken to indicate a Messianic reference, but it may also signify simply the poet's deliverance from his peril. Licht holds that the poet introduced the figure of the woman in childbirth with reference only to his own affliction, but soon passed on to the thought of the Messiah's birth, and the mother then became less important than the child. From the woes attending his birth the author moved on to other woes affecting the whole world.

Another indication of Messianic significance is found in the use of the same word for "a man" which occurs in the "two spirits" section of the Manual of Discipline. There we have found no reason to see in it an allusion to the Messiah (see p. 316). If it is clearly used here in that sense, however, it may reasonably be considered a quasi-technical Messianic term in other texts, though it certainly cannot be given such a meaning everywhere. Brownlee, with reference to the use of the word in this Psalm as well as the Manual of Discipline, suggests as the basis of its Messianic application II Samuel 23:1 and Zechariah 13:7. In the former place David is called "the man who was raised on high, the anointed of the God of Jacob." In Zechariah the mysterious "shepherd" is called by the Lord "the man who stands next to me."

In Numbers 24:17 the "scepter" of the Hebrew text is translated in the Septuagint by a Greek word meaning "man." It is not the word usually used for the Hebrew noun with which we are here concerned, but it is so used twice in this chapter of Numbers, referring both times to Balaam. It is also used for the same Hebrew word in Jeremiah 17:5, referring to "a man who trusts in man," and in Daniel 8:15 with reference to "one having the appearance of a man." How it came to be used in Numbers 24:17 is a mystery; possibly the Greek translator used a Hebrew text which read "man" instead of "scepter," but that would only push the mystery back one step. Brownlee cites also a passage in the Testaments of the Twelve Patriarchs where Numbers 24:17 is quoted according to the Septuagint (Testament of Judah 24:1), and another which speaks of a coming "man working righteousness" (Testament of Naphtali 4:5). Vermès points out, however, that in these passages the "man" is the royal, Davidic Messiah, not the suffering Servant.

For the idea of the "man" as a suffering Messiah, Vermès refers not only to Zechariah 13:7 but also and especially to Lamentations 3:1, "I am the man who has seen affliction." Neither the Thanksgiving Psalm nor the Manual of Discipline, however, says anything of the suffering of the "man." In the Manual he is to be cleansed from his sin, but this is to be done by "a holy spirit" and by sprinkling upon him "a spirit of truth," not by suffering. In the Psalm it is the mother, not the child, that suffers.

While a Messianic meaning in the word "man" seems to me only barely possible, the echo of Isaiah 9:6 in the term "wonderful counselor" is most easily explained as a Messianic reference. The mother may then be the community. The child is called his mother's "first born," and Dupont-Sommer remarks that this makes the Messiah the first born of the community. Immediately after the reference to the "wonderful counselor," where I translate "a man comes forth from the waves," Dupont-Sommer translates, "and he will deliver each one from the waves." This he takes to be an indication of the Messiah's work, redeeming men from death and perdition. I cannot say that I find this convincing. It has the strange effect, for one thing, of making the supposedly Messianic term "a man" refer here to the redeemed instead of the redeemer. Chamberlain and Vermès at first understood the clause in this way, but both later changed their interpretation. Baumgarten and Mansoor and also Gaster understand the line as I do.

The reference to the birth of the Messiah's adversary, as seen in the poem by Dupont-Sommer, Licht, and others, begins in the twelfth line of the column, with the sentence beginning in my translation, "She who conceived nought" (*DSS*, p. 403). From here on, according to Licht, the subject is the birth of evil, the bursting forth of Sheol into the world. The word which I translate "nought" is ambiguous. Chamberlain and Dupont-Sommer take it to mean "a viper," representing the Messiah's adversary, the Antichrist or Belial himself. Two women are therefore distinguished, one representing the community of the righteous and the other the congregation of the godless.

The word meaning "viper" or "nothing," as the case may be, occurs also in the second column of the scroll (line 28), where it is combined with one meaning "worthlessness" (*DSS*, p. 402). In Isaiah 42:14, "I will cry out like a woman in travail," the verb meaning "I will cry out" is spelled with the same consonants as the noun in question here. Gaster suggests that the poet, recalling the verse in Isaiah, took the verb for the noun which it resembles, and so secured the expression, "She who conceived nought," or, as Gaster paraphrases it, "They that carry in their wombs the seeds of worthlessness." This explanation would apply equally well if the poet had the meaning "viper" in mind.

Silbermann retains the meaning "groaning" or "crying," as in Isaiah 42:14, and translates "a groaning or crying mother." The contrast, however, between the woman who is pregnant with a man and her who is pregnant with "a viper" or "nought" should not be ignored. The former has given birth to her child before the latter is mentioned. What the woman who has conceived nothing or worthlessness might mean, if not the symbolic mother of Belial, I am unable to say. The name Belial itself, for that matter, means "worthlessness"; the expression may therefore refer to the prince of darkness, whether it means "nought" or "viper."

It is difficult to reach a decision in this case. For myself, I am skeptical as regards the whole Messianic interpretation, but I am not prepared to pronounce it impossible. The poem remains obscure at many points, however we take it. In any case, as Licht points out, it tells us nothing about the person or work of the Messiah, unless of course we accept Dupont-Sommer's improbable interpretation of line 10.

Another debatable reference to the Messiah has been found by Allegro in a fragment of a commentary on Isaiah which he has published. Expounding verses 28–32 of Isaiah 10, the commentary has several sentences, unfortunately incomplete, in which Allegro sees evidence of a "triumphal march to Jerusalem" by the Messiah. One line contains the clause, "when he goes up from the plain of Acco to fight against"—here the text breaks off, but two lines lower we read, "and as far as the boundary of Jerusalem." The passage in Isaiah on which this is based outlines a rapid march on Jerusalem from the north by the Assyrians.

Allegro at first supposed that the name Acco was incomplete, and that what was meant was the valley of Achor, just above Khirbet Qumran (see p. 21). He inferred therefore that the Messiah was expected to march against Jerusalem "from the vicinity of Qumran." Becoming convinced that the place named was actually Acco (i.e., Acre, on the Mediterranean coast north of Haifa), he envisaged the Messiah's landing at Acco, "the nearest port of entry to the New Testament battlefield of Armageddon."

It seems strange that the Messiah should be expected to come, like the Kittim, from the west. Even stranger is it, in spite of the free exegesis of the Qumran commentators, that a prophecy concerning a dreaded foe of Israel should be applied to the coming of the Messiah. In a small fragment which apparently refers to Isaiah 10:27 and perhaps the beginning of verse 28, "the prince of the congregation" seems to be mentioned. (The word "prince" is incomplete, but the restoration is practically certain.) The next fragment continues with a quotation of verses 28–32, followed by a reference to a "word for the end of days" and the clause about going up from the plain of Acco. Then comes a fragment commenting on verses 33 and 34, which refers to the nations and three times to the Kittim, all in the plural. Allegro supposes therefore that the singular form, "when he goes up," must refer to the "prince of the congregation," that is, the Messiah. But the quotation of Isaiah 10:32 which immediately precedes this comment, and to which it must refer, ends with the statement that the invader "will shake his fist at the mount of the daughter of Zion, the hill of Jerusalem." It is this statement, not the reference to the prince of the congregation in the earlier comment on verse 27, that affords the antecedent for the reference to an individual's going up from the plain of Acco.

Roth and Driver, it may be remembered, interpret this text as referring to the meeting of Vespasian and Titus near Acre before the attack on Jerusalem in 70 A.D. This is too late to be easily accepted as the event referred to by the commentary on Isaiah. It is altogether probable, however, if not certain, that the Romans took the place of the Assyrians in the mind of the commentator, and that what he expected "for the end of days" was an attack on Jerusalem by the Romans proceeding from the plain of Acco. What the Messiah would do then is not stated until later, when the commentator comes to chapter 11. This he naturally applies to "the branch of David who will arise at the end of days." He will receive "a glorious throne, a holy crown, and many-colored garments." Then, the commentator says, "over all the nations he shall rule, and Magog"—but, alas, the text is broken again at this exciting point!

The comment on Isaiah 11:3 which now follows is interesting in connection with the subordination of the coming king to the priesthood. Quoting the prophet's statement, "He shall not judge by what his eyes see, or decide by what his ears hear," the commentator says (after another unfortunate gap in the text), "as they instruct him, so he will judge, and according to their directions"—again there is a break, but presumably the sentence was completed, "he will decide." The next line, also incomplete at beginning and end, says, "one of the priests of renown shall go forth, and in his hands garments"—presumably the many-colored garments already mentioned.

Allegro sees here a reference to a coronation ceremony based on Psalm 45, where many-colored garments are mentioned, though actually it is the king's bride who wears them there. Further details, as Allegro says, may yet be found in other frag-

ments. That the king should be crowned by a priest is not surprising, but that he should be required to follow priestly instructions in pronouncing judgment is more notable. Deuteronomy
17:18–20 directs that the king shall copy and study the book of
the law. The Qumran sons of Zadok did not feel that the Messiah
could be trusted to interpret the law for himself.

# XXVIII

## The Teacher of Righteousness

A question that has been much discussed by interpreters of the
scrolls is the relation, if any, between the Messiah and the teacher
of righteousness. From the reference in the Damascus Document
to a teacher of righteousness who will arise at the end of days
(vi.11; *DSS*, p. 354), it has been inferred that the sect expected
its teacher of righteousness to return as Messiah at the end of the
world (*DSS*, pp. 265f). Being a priest, he would not, of course,
be the Davidic king, the Messiah of Israel. He might, however, be
the priestly Messiah of Aaron. On the other hand, he might
equally well be the coming prophet, if indeed he was expected to
return at all. In order to clarify this problem we must consider
more fully the ideas of the sect concerning the teacher of righteousness. His identity and the time in which he lived have already been discussed (pp. 204–18). Here we are concerned with
the beliefs of his followers concerning him and the part he was
expected to play, if any, in the Messianic consummation of the
age.

Involved in this problem is the question of the teacher's relation to the literature of the sect, apart from the few texts which
mention him. The Thanksgiving Psalms in particular have been
thought by many scholars to be the work of the teacher of righteousness himself. This possibility was first suggested by Sukenik.
Michaud claims that a thorough study of the whole scroll trans-
forms the possibility into a practical certainty. The poems, he
says, are the outpouring of a strong personality, and the only

individual mentioned with admiration in the Qumran texts is the teacher of righteousness. Bruce agrees that the man whose personal experience and devotion find expression in the Thanksgiving Psalms "could hardly have been anybody other than the teacher of righteousness." Milik finds in the hymns a system of thought and a program of life which only an exceptionally strong personality could have produced. Dupont-Sommer remarks that the author may not have been the teacher himself but perhaps one of his disciples; in any case, however, he feels that the poems are profoundly marked by the teacher's personality and doctrine. Howlett also thinks that the poems, while not necessarily written by the teacher, afford reliable information concerning him. He complains, in fact, that they have been "so far almost entirely neglected" as a source of such information.

Others are less sure of a direct connection between the teacher and the Psalms. Eissfeldt holds that the possibility of his authorship is undeniable, but that the "I" of the Psalms may be in many cases a collective expression of the community. The Psalms may be, he suggests, exercises for confessional meditation. Vermès thinks it is possible to distinguish in the scroll prayers which could be used by any member of the community and others which can only refer to the teacher of righteousness. Molin too notes the occasional impression of a collective subject, but he feels that more often an individual is speaking. Any member of the sect could be the author; there may even have been several authors, though this is improbable.

Like Eissfeldt, Molin regards the Psalms as exercises in meditation. He suggests that this scroll may be the Book of HGW— i.e., "Book of Meditation"—mentioned in the Damascus Document and the Rule of the Congregation (*DSS*, pp. 188, 247, 359, 362). Other hymnlike compositions represented by manuscript fragments may have a better claim to be that mysterious book; but it was probably a manual for the instruction of novitiates and for devotional study in the order, and this was also, as Molin sees it, the purpose of the Thanksgiving Psalms. This meditation, however, was intended to enable those who practiced it to enter into the experience of a profound, original spirit. Who this was we do not know. He may have been the teacher of righteousness. We do not know enough about the community and its history to identify him.

Bardtke admits that many of the Psalms may reflect personal experiences of the teacher of righteousness, but he warns that to draw conclusions as to their authorship would be premature, because we do not know the other persons of the sect, the trusted fellow workers of the teacher of righteousness or those who preceded or followed him. The author of the Psalms was a great spirit, an energetic and skilled pastor of souls. The hymns are not the work of several different authors. Bardtke concludes, however, that everything which may be attributed to the personal experience of the teacher of righteousness may equally well be understood as expressing the experience and duties of every member of the sect.

While condemning Bardtke's conclusion as too reserved, Michaud recognizes that there are difficulties in identifying the author of the Thanksgiving Psalms with the teacher of righteousness. He feels, however, that these difficulties can be met. He recognizes the possibility of a collective "I," as in the Old Testament Psalms, but the literary unity of the Qumran hymns seems to him to indicate the expression of a single personality. The abundant echoes of Old Testament language make it more difficult to get specific information about the teacher of righteousness, yet Michaud finds that only the language is reminiscent; the inspiration is original.

Michaud's confident affirmation of the teacher's authorship is balanced by Licht's equally decided denial. The writer of the Thanksgiving Psalms, he contends, may have been a leader of the community and an important one, but he was not as prominent as the teacher of righteousness. The fact that he considered himself a great leader does not make him the head of the whole sect. He applied to himself a traditional pattern. Like the "superintendent" of the Damascus Document, he was a teacher of the law and felt for the community the compassion of a father for his sons. The pattern which fits him best, however, is that of the "instructor" or "wise man" of the Manual of Discipline, who was not the leader of the whole congregation but any man in an important position. In a very human way, Licht holds, the poet was inclined to exaggerate his own importance.

The scroll of Thanksgiving Psalms is not the only one for which the teacher of righteousness has been given credit. Milik thinks it probable that he composed also the Manual of Discipline and perhaps also the Damascus Document. An elaborate series of "conjectures" has been propounded by Carmignac. Comparing the scrolls with one another, he classifies them in two groups, distinguished by vocabulary, style, method of using the Scriptures, form of presentation, and interests. In one group, which comprises the Damascus Document and the commentaries, there are many references to the teacher of righteousness. In the other, consisting of the Manual of Discipline, the War of the Sons of Light with the Sons of Darkness, the Thanksgiving Psalms, and perhaps other texts, the teacher of righteousness is not mentioned at all. The reason, Carmignac suggests, is that the books in the latter group were written by the teacher of righteousness himself, and therefore naturally do not refer to him in the third person. The other books, which do so refer to him, sometimes quote from the books which he wrote.

Developing the hypothesis further, Carmignac believes that the order in which the teacher composed these works can be ascertained and even fitted into the history of the movement. Assuming the identity of the Qumran sect and the Essenes, he argues from Josephus that the origin of the Essenes is to be dated at about 160 or 150 B.C. The Damascus Document indicates that the teacher of righteousness, who was not the founder of the sect, came twenty years later, that is, about 140–120 B.C. Allowing about ten years for him to achieve experience and authority, we may then date the Manual of Discipline, together with the Rule of the Congregation and the Benedictions, at about 130–115 B.C. The War scroll would follow after an indeterminable interval; the Thanksgiving Psalms were not written all at once, but many of them seem to come from the latter part of the teacher's life, probably between 110 and 100 B.C.

So far as the dating of the compositions is concerned, many

objections to this theory might be raised. Most, if not all, of the dates are almost certainly too early. It is very doubtful also that all these compositions were written by the same man; some of them, indeed, are clearly composite and have had a history of their own. The reasons for attributing them to the teacher of righteousness, however, are as impressive, or almost as impressive, for the Manual of Discipline and the War scroll as they are for the Thanksgiving Psalms. One may very seriously doubt that he wrote any of them, though of course it is not impossible.

Those who see the personality and individual experience of the teacher of righteousness reflected in the Thanksgiving Psalms draw far-reaching conclusions. The teacher is portrayed as a man opposed, persecuted, betrayed, and abandoned. He was, Dupont-Sommer says, the perfect image of the man of sorrows, the suffering Servant of the Lord of Isaiah 40ff. Circumstances and events of his life are deduced by Michaud: he was an orphan, brought up in a devout religious group and under strict discipline; in his youth he received a revelation of God, probably while studying the Scriptures; his enemies or perhaps his own colleagues or disciples forced him into exile in Egypt; there he formed a group of followers under great difficulties and taught them the law; the new covenant was apparently revealed to him also in Egypt. Not every question is answered, however: we cannot tell whether the teacher's exile in Egypt was before or after the establishment of the community at Qumran.

With all due respect for the industry and ingenuity with which all this has been extracted from the text, I must say that I do not find it convincing. Michaud's inferences concerning the poet's spiritual experience and theological position are more acceptable, and they agree with the findings of other scholars. To reach such specific conclusions concerning the teacher's life, however, is possible only by taking literally expressions which are almost certainly figurative. The references to Egypt are a case in point. In at least one instance, in fact, the reference is secured by a questionable restoration of the text.

Still less convincing is Howlett's attempt to connect passages in the Thanksgiving Psalms with historical situations and events.

Without claiming certainty, he finds in the Psalms an "exciting intimation" that the teacher of righteousness may have been Eleazar the Pharisee, who denounced John Hyrcanus to his face (*DSS*, pp. 172f), and a possible corroboration for the surmise that Eleazar was not put to death but "continued and probably increased his denunciations." After the break between the Pharisees and John Hyrcanus, Howlett concludes, there was a division among the Pharisees themselves, and the strictest group withdrew to Qumran, where "one of their members" (not Eleazar after all?) came to be revered as the teacher of righteousness. Apart from the very dubious assumption that the Qumran covenanters were in any sense Pharisees (see pp. 253–57), such fanciful inferences remind one forcibly of the traditional titles attached to the Psalms of the Old Testament, which attempt to connect each Psalm with an event in the life of David.

On the assumption that the author of the Thanksgiving Psalms was the teacher of righteousness, something like Messianic claims on his part have been seen in some passages. In the seventh column of the scroll (line 12; *DSS*, p. 410) the poet refers to God's "separating by me the righteous from the wicked." Michaud compares this with the statement of the Habakkuk Commentary (v.4; *DSS*, p. 367) that "into the hand of his elect God will deliver the judgment of all the nations." These two passages, says Michaud, must refer to the same person, and "his elect" means the teacher of righteousness. It is fairly certain, however, that the word "elect" here is plural. It remains true, of course, that the poet thinks of himself as having something to do with the separation of the righteous from the wicked, perhaps by his teaching and leadership.

In the last relatively complete column of the Thanksgiving Psalms (xviii) there are two lines (14f) which, broken as they are, clearly echo Isaiah 61:1f. One who "brings glad tidings of thy goodness" is mentioned; then the very phrase "to bring good tidings to the afflicted" is used, and in the next line "those who mourn" appear. Michaud finds here a suggestion that the teacher of righteousness identified himself with the anointed prophet who speaks in Isaiah 61. If so, and if there is any connection with the

Messianic expectations which we have examined, it is the promised prophet who is contemplated rather than either of the two Messiahs. The allusion, however, may not be quite so precise. Any teacher of the sect might consider himself divinely commissioned "to bring good tidings to the afflicted."

Oesterreicher remarks that if the Thanksgiving Psalms were written by the teacher of righteousness or in his name, he thought of himself not only as a father and nurse of the community, one by whose teaching the "eternal planting" of God was abundantly watered, but also as a sailor who could not steer his course, a man beset by panic and confusion. The poet's sense of human frailty and sinfulness and of utter dependence upon God need not, of course, be thought inconsistent with a conviction of a divine mission. A humble feeling of unworthiness and inadequacy has often been characteristic of prophets and apostles.

It must be said, indeed, that nothing in the Thanksgiving Psalms establishes a connection between their author and any of the eschatological figures mentioned in other texts. If the obscure Psalm in the third column is concerned with the birth of the Messiah, it remains the only Messianic passage in the scroll. But are the "man" of column iii and the teacher of righteousness one and the same? So Vermès argues. Accepting the Messianic interpretation of the "man" both in the Manual of Discipline and in the Thanksgiving Psalms, and the understanding of many of the Thanksgiving Psalms as referring to the teacher of righteousness, he asserts that the "man" and the teacher are the same person.

In the commentary on Psalm 37 Vermès finds striking support for this conclusion. Using the same Hebrew word for "a man" as the debated passages in the scrolls, verse 23 of this Psalm says, "The steps of a man are from the Lord, and he establishes him in whose way he delights." The commentary, with a slight reconstruction of its text, says of this verse, "This means the priest, the teacher of righteousness." It does not follow, however, that the "man" of the Thanksgiving Psalms is the teacher of righteousness, even if the teacher wrote them. It is hard to believe that the poet who so often speaks in the first person would refer to himself in such an obscure and involved way as this interpretation implies.

Is there sufficient reason to suppose that any Messianic or eschatological function was attributed to the teacher of righteousness? The Damascus Document speaks once of "the arising of him who will teach righteousness at the end of days" (vi.10f; *DSS*, p. 354). It also speaks of a teacher of righteousness who had been raised up in the past (i.11; *DSS*, p. 349) and a "unique teacher" who had been "gathered in" (xix.35–xx.1; xx.14; *DSS*, pp. 356f). It promises salvation, moreover, to all "who listen to the voice of a teacher" (xx.28; *DSS*, p. 357) or "give ear to the voice of a teacher of righteousness" (xx.32; *DSS*, p. 358). Most interpreters assume that the past teacher of righteousness and the dead unique teacher were the same; many also suppose that he was expected to return in the last days as the Messiah or one of the Messiahs. Two questions, however, must be raised: (1) Will the coming teacher be a Messiah? (2) Are the past and the coming teachers the same person?

Few, if any, have thought that the future teacher would be the royal, Davidic Messiah. Many, however, identify him with the Messiah of Aaron. Milik, for example, says that the priestly Messiah is called the teacher of righteousness, and for evidence cites the Damascus Document vi.10f. There is nothing, however, either here or elsewhere in the Damascus Document, to justify this equation. The commentary on Psalm 37 applies verse 23 to "the priest, the teacher of righteousness," but there is no indication that the future teacher or the priestly Messiah is meant. No passage clearly referring to the Messiah of Aaron calls him a teacher of righteousness. Only from the assumption that the past and coming teachers are the same and the fact that the past teacher was clearly a priest is it possible to infer that the future teacher will be a priest.

Schonfield, to be sure, holds that the Habakkuk Commentary's teacher, who is called a priest, is not the past priest of the Damascus Document but the one expected at the end of days, though he may already have come in the first century A.D., when the Habakkuk Commentary was written. This contention cannot be sustained. The commentator, Schonfield says, speaks so vividly of the teacher of righteousness that he must be referring to a person of his own time. This may be admitted, but it is not necessary to date the Damascus Document's teacher two centuries or more before the time of the Habakkuk Commentary, as Schonfield does. There is really no evidence, in short, that the coming teacher of righteousness was expected to be a priest. This is entirely possible, of course; but even so it would not follow that he was to be the priestly Messiah.

Were the two teachers, then, supposed to be the same person, who had died and was expected to come again? There is nothing to suggest this except the similarity of the designations by which they are known. Even these are not actually quite the same. The first teacher is designated by the noun "teacher," the second somewhat awkwardly by the verb "teaches," as though "He Teaches Righteousness" were his name. This curious verbal form is used also, however, in one of the references to the unique teacher (xx.14); the difference therefore has little if any significance. But even if the titles were exactly the same they would not necessarily indicate the same person. Whether the references to hearing "a teacher" or "a teacher of righteousness" (xx.28, 32) refer to any particular teacher, present or future, is not clear.

Rabinowitz actually finds not only two but three teachers in the Damascus Document. The one who had been raised up in the past he identifies, as we have seen (p. 314), with Nehemiah. The unique teacher who had been "gathered in" he regards as a person of the author's time, "probably one of the not more than two persons" referred to by the commentaries. The one who is to come at the end of days will not be either of the other two. The writers of the commentaries, Rabinowitz says, believed that they were living in the last days; their contemporary teacher was therefore an eschatological figure. The authors of the Damascus Document thought of the last days and therefore of the coming teacher as still in the future, and for the one who had already come, to whom the commentaries refer, they used a new term, "the unique teacher." This rather elaborate hypothesis may not be correct in every detail, but it is preferable to a gratuitous, wholesale identification of every figure referred to as a teacher of righteousness.

Allegro finds ground for identifying the past and future teacher in the use of the same terms for both of them. The founder of the sect and the priestly Messiah, he says, are both called not only "teacher of righteousness" but also "interpreter of the law." One would like to see this statement documented. The priestly Messiah and the interpreter of the law may well be the same, as we have already observed (p. 313). But, unless identity is taken for granted, where is the priestly Messiah called "the teacher of righteousness"? The "last priest" of the Nahum Commentary, Allegro continues, is clearly connected with the "lion of wrath," and since the lion is (according to Allegro) Alexander Janneus, who (according to Allegro) persecuted the teacher of righteousness, the last priest must be the teacher of righteousness. But, says Allegro, the "last priest" "could only refer to the Messiah." All this apparently supports the identification of the historical teacher with the eschatological teacher, who in turn is identified with the priestly Messiah. The reasoning, however, leaps too lightly from conjecture to conjecture to be at all convincing.

Bruce regards it as possible that the resurrected teacher would be the Messiah of Aaron and the interpreter of the law, but he suggests also that the teacher's successors may have been called by the latter title. The last one in the series would then be expected to sponsor the Davidic Messiah and induct him into office. Whether he would then be identified as the Messiah of Aaron, Bruce considers uncertain. Murphy remarks that there were many Messianic claimants, and it would not be surprising if the sect's teacher was one of them, but the evidence does not support this supposition. Nothing indicates, Murphy continues, that the teacher was identified with the Messiah of Aaron or with the priest who would officiate at the Messianic banquet of the last days.

The Thanksgiving Psalm which is commonly believed to refer to the birth of the Messiah (see pp. 317–18) is cited by Oesterreicher as evidence against the identification of the teacher with the Messiah. If the community regarded itself as the Messiah's mother, it could not at the same time believe its founder to be the Messiah. No suggestion that the teacher would come again as the priestly Messiah can be found in this hymn. One may remark that if the Messiah to be born from the community is the royal Messiah, what is said of him will not necessarily apply also to the Messiah of Aaron. Since the two were expected to appear together, however, this distinction does not entirely resolve the difficulty. There is no hint of two Messiahs in this Psalm, in any case.

Licht observes that the Messiah is mentioned only here in the Thanksgiving Psalms, and only rarely in the rest of the sect's literature. This is, moreover, the only passage in the scrolls that deals explicitly with the coming of the Messiah (aside, of course, from bare references to his coming or arising); even here nothing is told about him. Licht concludes that for the men of Qumran the Messiah was only a symbol of the approach of the last days. Their Messianic beliefs were not a strong point of their theology, but were vague and perhaps relatively unimportant.

Vermès regards the "man" referred to in the Thanksgiving Psalm, and also in the Manual of Discipline, not as either of the two Messiahs but as the eschatological prophet associated with them, the prophet promised in Deuteronomy 18. At some time in the course of its history, he suggests, the sect began to identify its teacher of righteousness with this prophet. One point in Vermès' conclusions may, I think, be accepted. If the teacher of righteousness was believed to have any eschatological role at all, it was certainly not that of the Messiah of Israel and probably not that of the priestly Messiah. If he was expected to come again in any capacity, he would come as the promised prophet, who might or might not be the interpreter of the law. Bruce considers it probable that the teacher, resurrected at the end of days, was expected to play the part commonly taken in Jewish thought by the prophet Elijah, though he was not, Bruce thinks, identified either with Elijah or with the prophet of Deuteronomy 18. In any case, he was a forerunner, not a Messiah.

The historic teacher was, it is true, a priest, but this would not prevent him from coming again as a prophet. In Deuteronomy 33, the Blessing of Moses, the blessing pronounced on the tribe of Levi includes this sentence: "They shall teach Jacob thy ordinances, and Israel thy law" (verse 10). Gaster sees here the origin of the title "teacher of righteousness," and he recalls the fact that both this blessing on Levi and the promise of the prophet in Deuteronomy 18:18f are included in the Qumran Testimonia, together with Deuteronomy 5:28f and Numbers 24:15–17. The "star" of the last-named passage, it will be remembered, is explained by the Damascus Document as "the interpreter of the law who came to Damascus" (xix.18f; *DSS,* p. 355). The sect expected, Gaster says in this connection, "a new Prophet and a new Teacher (perhaps, indeed, one and the same person)."

Aside from the references in the Damascus Document to the past and future teacher of righteousness, the text most often cited as evidence that the teacher of righteousness was a Messianic figure is the statement of the Habakkuk Commentary that "into the hand of his elect God will deliver the judgment of all the nations" (v.4; *DSS,* p. 367). Dupont-Sommer holds that "his elect" means the teacher of righteousness, who is therefore to be the judge of the nations. It is more probable, I believe, that the word "elect" in this passage is plural, referring to the whole sect (*DSS,* pp. 146f). The same form appears in the commentary on Psalm 37 (verse 20) in a context which shows clearly that it is plural. Dupont-Sommer, however, continues to defend his interpretation, and it has been accepted by other scholars, including Gärtner, Widengren, and, as we have already seen (p. 329), Michaud. Widengren says that the Micah Commentary calls the teacher of righteousness a teacher of the law. This designation, however, occurs not in the surviving text but in Milik's conjectural restoration of a lost portion. In any case, even if "the elect" is understood to be in the singular, there is nothing in the context to connect this "elect one" with the teacher of righteousness.

In the Old Testament "the elect one" is associated not so much with the Messiah as with the suffering Servant of Isaiah 40ff. In many verses this Servant is explicitly identified with Israel; in others he is believed by many scholars to be the Messiah. Brownlee, as was noted in *DSS* (p. 267), finds both a collective and an individual use of the Servant concept in the Qumran texts. The mention of "his elect" in the Habakkuk Commentary he takes to be a reference to the community as God's servant. Many other allusions to the Servant in this sense are found, especially in the Manual of Discipline. In the teacher of righteousness, Brownlee believes, the conception of the Servant was believed to be realized.

Other scholars have found this interpretation more convincing than I do. There are undoubtedly echoes of the language of Isaiah 40ff in several of the texts. The rejected and persecuted teacher may well have seemed to his followers to be like the suffering Servant of the Lord. Schonfield suggests that memories of the teacher may have colored the Messianic expectations of his followers and helped to produce the idea of a suffering Messiah, as found in Christianity and somewhat later in Judaism. All this may be so, but there is still no evidence that the teacher was the Servant in a Messianic sense.

Possible references to the teacher of righteousness have been seen in other scrolls, but they do not contribute much. A fragmentary collection of prayers from Cave 1 mentions a "faithful shepherd," but there is nothing to show whether he is figure of the past, present, or future, or whether he has anything to do with the teacher of righteousness. The War scroll speaks of those "who hear the voice of him who is honored and see the holy angels" (x.10f). Yadin notes in this connection a similar expression in the Thanksgiving Psalms, "to listen to the voice of him who is honored" (Frag. 12, line 5). Pointing to Deuteronomy 4:12 and 5:21 (English verse 24), he sees here a possible reference to the revelation of the law at Mt. Sinai; the mention of the angels, however, suggests also the possible influence of Ezekiel (e.g., 10:5) and Daniel (8:16; 10:5–7). Dupont-Sommer, however, while recognizing that the expression "he who is honored" is appropriate for God, recalls the references to hearing the voice of the teacher in the Damascus Document (xx.28, 32) and suggests that the honored one here is the teacher of righteousness. To me this seems less probable than Yadin's interpretation, but in any case there is no suggestion of a Messianic function or status.

Comparisons with the Testaments of the Twelve Patriarchs have been adduced in this connection. Not only do we have here both royal and priestly Messianic ideas; in the Testament of Levi there is also a chapter in which Dupont-Sommer sees a description of the teacher of righteousness. The seventeenth chapter traces the history of the priesthood through seven jubilees; this is followed in the eighteenth chapter by the promise of a glorious new priesthood. In chapter 17 Dupont-Sommer finds a condemnation of the Hasmonean dynasty; the new, heavenly priest of chapter 18 he takes to be the teacher of righteousness, restored to life after having been put to death by the wicked priest.

This view is examined and rejected by Otzen; he finds more acceptable an earlier interpretation which regards chapter 17 as a summary of the whole history of the priesthood from Aaron to the corrupt priests of the Hellenistic period. The seventeenth verse of the chapter predicts an unspeakable pollution of the priesthood in the seventh "jubilee." Dupont-Sommer connects this with the high priesthood of Aristobolus II (67–63 B.C.), but the following verses seem clearly to refer to the Babylonian exile and the return to Palestine in the sixth century B.C. The new priest of chapter 18 is then the Hasmonean dynasty itself, or one of the Hasmonean high priests. This interpretation seems to me to fit the text much better than that of Dupont-Sommer.

Three other passages in the Testament of Levi, however, are adduced by Dupont-Sommer in support of his hypothesis. In 10:2 there is a reference to transgression which will be committed "in the end of the ages against the Savior of the world, Christ." In 14:2 it is said that the chief priests will "lay their hands upon the Savior of the world." Dupont-Sommer omits the word "Christ" (10:2) as obviously a Christian interpolation; Otzen protests, however, that "Savior of the world" also is a Christian expression, found in the Testaments only in Christian interpolations and occurring nowhere else in Jewish literature. Murphy remarks also that this expression has not been found in the Dead Sea Scrolls. Dupont-Sommer's third passage, 16:3, says that "a man who renews the law in the power of the Most High" will be called a deceiver and killed. This too is taken to be a reference to the teacher of righteousness, but Otzen maintains that it probably refers to an event in Hebrew history before the Babylonian exile.

Of course, if the whole book is a Christian work, as de Jonge argues, the question of Christian interpolations becomes irrelevant. The picture of the new priest in chapter 18 has unquestionably many contacts with the New Testament. If it originally referred to the Hasmonean priesthood, as Otzen argues, it was retouched by Christians who believed that it spoke of Christ. In verses 6f the allusion to the baptism of Jesus is unmistakable, even if the phrase "in the water" is deleted. Daniélou's thesis that the Testaments were written by an Essene convert to Christianity (see p. 180) comes to mind again in this connection. Whatever theory of authorship may be adopted, Dupont-Sommer's theory that the Qumran teacher of righteousness is the subject of the passages cited must be rejected.

All attempts to identify the teacher with any of the Messiahs mentioned in the Qumran texts leave us at best with tenuous possibilities. It has been claimed, however, that some passages in the scrolls represent the teacher not merely as a Messiah, who by all orthodox Jewish tradition would still be a human figure, but even as a divine being. Dupont-Sommer's earlier inference to this effect from the expression "the body of his flesh" in the Habakkuk Commentary (ix.2; *DSS*, p. 368; cp. p. 152) was not widely accepted and he later abandoned it. Fritsch, however, argues that the teacher "must have been regarded as more than human" because he was "the object of saving faith." This is based on the reference in the Habakkuk Commentary to those who will be delivered from judgment "because of their labor and their faith in the teacher of righteousness" (viii.2f; *DSS*, p. 368). All that this implies, however, is that in order to obey the law correctly the teacher's inspired interpretation must be accepted. Like the prophets, he was the recipient of a revelation, but that did not make him "more than human."

Some scholars believe that the teacher of righteousness was in some sense a Messianic figure not only because of such statements and allusions as we have examined but also on the ground that his followers thought of him in terms of what Allegro calls "a Messianic pattern." This involves particularly the theory that he was put to death and was expected to rise from the dead and return as judge and redeemer. The term "Messianic" may be somewhat misleading in this connection. The "Messianic pattern" of Judaism, so far as there was one, did not involve these elements at all. The word "Messiah," i.e., "anointed," when it did not refer to historic or living kings and priests, meant ordinarily the expected king of David's line, who would be restored to the throne of his ancestors and would lead Israel's armies in the decisive war against their enemies and oppressors. Aside from this, his role was vague; many divergent speculations about him and his coming appear in the rabbinic literature.

There was also "the priest anointed for battle" (see pp. 307–308), and in later times there arose a conception of another Messiah, from the tribe of Joseph, who would be killed in battle before the Davidic Messiah prevailed. The basic tradition of the conquering son of David, however, was the major conception represented by the term "Messiah." To use the term "Messianic pattern" for the three connected ideas of death, resurrection, and return in glory is therefore a Christian rather than a Jewish way of speaking. With this understanding, however, we may now examine the theory that the teacher of righteousness was thought of in such terms.

For the idea that the teacher was crucified, Allegro is primarily responsible. Dupont-Sommer had argued from the beginning that the teacher was a martyr; Allegro developed this idea on the basis of the Nahum Commentary. We have already (pp. 214–17) discussed the question whether the teacher was one of the eight hundred or more men crucified by Alexander Janneus. Here we need only repeat our conclusion that this is not very probable. The teacher may have been crucified, either then or at some earlier or later time. He may have been stoned or put to death in some other way. On the other hand, he may have died a natural death. This is more likely, in fact, if he was the Damascus Document's "unique teacher" who was "gathered in." Neither the Habakkuk Commentary nor any other Qumran text published thus far says or clearly implies that the teacher was put to death. Dupont-Sommer's use of the Testament of Levi 16:3 as reflecting the death of the teacher of righteousness could be used as evidence only if we could be sure that it refers to the teacher at all.

As Bruce points out, to be sure of this we should have to have some other account of the teacher's martyrdom.

However he may have died, was the teacher expected to rise from the dead and appear as redeemer and judge? There is certainly no evidence that he was believed to have risen already. Dupont-Sommer's inference from the word "appeared" in the Habakkuk Commentary (xi.7; *DSS*, p. 370), that the teacher of righteousness appeared in glory after his martyrdom to confound his enemies, cannot be accepted, especially as the subject of the clause is probably not the teacher but the wicked priest (*DSS*, pp. 156f). The question whether the teacher was expected to come again in the future depends on the question of his identity with the coming teacher of the Damascus Document, the priestly Messiah of Aaron, or the expected prophet. This we have already found to be quite uncertain (pp. 329–36).

Bruce suggests that the delay of the expected end after the teacher's death may have led to a belief that he would return to complete his work. "This would be a special resurrection," he says, "in advance of the resurrection of the righteous as a whole." It "would herald the imminent arrival of the Messiahs of Aaron and Israel." Molin, who regards the teacher's martyrdom as possible but uncertain, is quite convinced that he was to be the prophetic forerunner of the two Messiahs.

That the Qumran sect expected a general resurrection of the dead is not admitted by all scholars. Rowley contends that while the sect was acquainted with the belief, as the presence of the book of Daniel among the scrolls attests, "no expectation of any resurrection, either for the Teacher or for any others, appears to have been cherished." Allegro notes, however, that the wicked priest was to be punished in the last days; therefore, he concludes, a general resurrection must have been expected.

We shall consider presently the sect's beliefs concerning the future life and the consummation of the age. In the meantime a warning is in order against inferring too much from such expressions as "the last days" or "the end of days." There are many indications in the scrolls that the community believed itself to be living already in the last days. It was clearly troubled because the promises of the prophets had not been fulfilled. The Habakkuk Commentary says, not that the last days will come soon, but that "the last period extends over and above all that the prophets said," and it encourages those "whose hands do not grow slack from the service of the truth, when the last period is stretched out over them" (vii.9–12; *DSS*, p. 368). There is thus some ground for Roth's statement that the day of the end began when the teacher of righteousness was raised up, and that "raised up" does not mean "raised from the dead."

At the same time, many passages refer clearly to what is still in the future. The use of tenses in Hebrew must be treated with caution, but on the whole the "imperfect" tense, which in classical Hebrew may refer to unfinished action in the past, present, or future, seems to be used in the Qumran texts, as in later Hebrew, for the future. Such expressions as "until the coming" or "until the arising" seem to imply something that has not yet happened. Some texts also, such as the Manual of Discipline, regard the present as still under the dominion of Belial. Every statement must therefore be considered by itself. It is reasonably certain that a teacher of righteousness, an interpreter of the law, a prophet, and two Messiahs were still expected. What connection, if any, the teacher of righteousness who had already come was thought to have with any of these coming persons is quite uncertain.

# XXIX

## *Things to Come*

```
⎿⎾⎿⎾⎿⎾⎿⎾⎿⎾⎿⎾⎿⎾⎿⎾⎿⎾⎿⎾⎿⎾⎿⎾⎿⎾⎿⎾⎿⎾⎿⎾⎿⎾⎿⎾⎿⎾⎿⎾⎿⎾⎿⎾⎿⎾
```

If the Qumran community's ideas concerning the leading characters of the Messianic drama are indefinite and confused, the eschatological program of events is somewhat clearer, though no thoroughly systematic account can be given. As in Judaism at large, there were no doubt many different ideas in circulation, with no effort to reduce them to a system. It cannot be assumed that ideas found in one book were shared by the writers of all the other books. All that we can hope to do for the present is to note some of the ideas that appear in one document or another. No effort will be made to cover the subject exhaustively.

Milik observes that the knowledge revealed to the teacher of righteousness, according to the Habakkuk Commentary, was essentially apocalyptic; that is, it had to do with "the end of days," "the things that are coming upon the last generation" or "upon his people and his congregation," "the consummation of the period," and the like. The whole life of the community was marked by its eschatological expectations. The laws of the sect, however, are explicitly enacted for the present, preliminary age. The Damascus Document refers to the explanation of the law or the ordinance "for the period of wickedness" (vi.10, 14; xv.7, 10; DSS, pp. 353f, 363). The Manual of Discipline, after describing the ceremony of entering the covenant, says, "So shall they do year by year all the days of the dominion of Belial" (ii.19; DSS, p. 373). Later it directs that the sons of Aaron shall govern the community "by the first judgments by which the men of the community began to be disciplined, until there shall come a prophet and the Messiahs of Aaron and Israel" (ix.1of; *DSS*, p. 383). No doubt, says Milik, these laws will be replaced in the coming age by a new law. It is interesting to note that the Rule of the Congregation begins, "And this is the order for the whole congregation of Israel at the end of days."

The people represented by the Dead Sea Scrolls "were conscious," as Schonfield says, "that they were playing a leading part in the last Act of a stupendous Cosmic Drama." The conflict in which they were engaged was "a struggle on two planes"; it was not history, but it included history. The major characters in their literature were both historic individuals and personifications of principles. Details which are given concerning any of them may therefore have been drawn from more than one person; essentially the same series of persons and events might indeed recur in different generations, and material from different times might be inextricably combined in one account. This was made possible by a sense of spiritual kinship uniting earlier and later generations. One is reminded of Gaster's reference to "a stock set of masks" fitted upon "a stock set of characters" (see p. 205). These considerations are not only relevant for the difficult task of identifying historical characters; they also help us to understand the expectations for the future.

The present age, as we have seen, is called "the dominion of Belial." The Damascus Document speaks of a past "period of wrath" before the coming of the teacher of righteousness (i.5; *DSS*, p. 349); the Thanksgiving Psalms use the same expression for the poet's time of trial (iii.28; *DSS*, p. 404). Whether the "period of wrath" of the Damascus Document was ended by the teacher's coming is not entirely clear, but this seems to be implied. Apparently "the period when Israel transgressed and polluted the sanctuary" (xx.23; *DSS*, p. 357) was in the past also. Other passages of the Damascus Document, however, as we have seen, mention a "period of wickedness" which seems to be the present age of the world (p. 342).

A prominent feature of Jewish eschatology, as represented especially by the rabbinic literature, was the time of trouble preceding the Messiah's coming. It was called "the birth-pangs of the Messiah," sometimes more briefly translated as "the Messianic woes." How early this idea arose is a question on which scholars are not agreed. There is no explicit reference to such a period in the Qumran texts, but, as we have seen (p. 317), Gaster interprets the passage in the Thanksgiving Psalms about the woman in travail as expressing the same idea. Some of the other references to trials and torments in the Thanksgiving Psalms may allude to the Messianic woes instead of the poet's own troubles; in that case he must imagine himself in the position of one living in the time of the woes. It is easy to believe that this is the case in the passage beginning, "For I took my stand in the border of wickedness" (iii.24–36; DSS, pp. 404f). Here the idea of a universal conflagration, consuming the whole world, seems to be reflected. It will be recalled that one section of the hymn in the earlier part of the same column has been interpreted as a reference to the loosing of Belial and his hosts before the final consummation (see pp. 317–21).

Where there is a belief in a general resurrection, this naturally precedes the final judgment. Rowley denies that the Qumran sect had such a belief. Like the book of Jubilees, he feels, the Dead Sea Scrolls reflect a belief in the immortality of the soul rather than the resurrection of the whole person, body and soul together. Dupont-Sommer, however, cites as evidence of belief in a bodily resurrection a reference in the War scroll to "those who will rise from the earth" (xii.5). The expression is undoubtedly striking, but its meaning is by no means certain. Literally it means "risers of earth." The Old Testament often has the expression "my risers," that is, "those that rise against me," or "my assailants." In the War scroll, unfortunately, as so often, it is preceded by a gap in the text. Yadin, citing Psalm 18:40, supplies "to subdue," and apparently takes the words in question to mean something like "the assailants of earth." Dupont-Sommer supplies "together with," making the whole clause read, "that they may inherit a monument in battle together with those who will rise from the earth."

The verb presupposed by both Yadin's and Dupont-Sommer's interpretations is not used in Daniel 12:3. It appears in Isaiah 26:19 with reference to the resurrection of the dead, but it is never, there or elsewhere, used with an object in the sense of "rise from," as Dupont-Sommer assumes here. As a matter of fact, it is very doubtful that this is the verb used here at all. Carmignac reads the letters supposed to mean "those who rise from [or against]" as the last part of a quite different verb, the first letters being lost in the gap. The text as he restores it means, "my people from the avengers of earth." As evidence of belief in the resurrection of the dead this passage clearly cannot be considered conclusive.

A line in one of the Thanksgiving Psalms is taken by Mansoor as "a definite reference to the resurrection of the body," which he calls "a belief highly developed by the sect." This is the expression "those who lie in the dust," or possibly "those who dwell in the dust"—the published facsimile is very faint at this point (vi.34). The persons referred to, the line goes on to say, "have raised a flagstaff," and the context suggests that an impious attempt to storm the stronghold of the righteous will be defeated. The words "those who dwell in the dust" appear, as Mansoor notes, in Isaiah 26:19; the expression "lie in the dust" is used three times in Job, clearly referring to death (7:21; 20:11; 21:26). In the highly poetic language of the Thanksgiving Psalms, however, not to mention the fragmentary condition of the text, it is not clear whether this passage speaks of the dead or the living.

Mansoor refers to earlier studies by Vermès and van der Ploeg; but the former finds in the Dead Sea Scrolls not a belief in the resurrection but the idea that the whole person will be taken up to heaven in a purified body, while van der Ploeg's conclusion is that the sect believed in the immortality of the soul (*DSS*, pp. 270f). More recent studies by two other scholars are cited also by Mansoor. One of these, Bardtke, says only that in the descriptions of salvation in the Thanksgiving Psalms the member of the community, delivered from sin, is "like a dead man raised from the dust." In the study by Licht which Mansoor mentions I find no reference at all to the resurrection of the dead. All that Licht says is that the author of the Thanksgiving Psalms expects to be delivered from the impending judgment.

The descriptions of Essene beliefs given by Josephus and Hippolytus differ notably at just this point. The complicated literary relationship between them is not yet clear. They have been carefully compared by M. Black, with incidental reference to the Qumran texts. Josephus attributes to the Essenes a belief that the body was corruptible and mortal, while the soul was immortal and eternal. According to Hippolytus they believed that the souls of the dead went to a bright, airy place to await judgment, and at the judgment their bodies would rise and be united again with their souls.

Black finds that Josephus clearly adapted his account to the ideas of his Greek readers; Hippolytus may have conformed his report to Christian ideas, but what motive he would have for so doing is not apparent, and what he says is more in accord with what would be expected in a Jewish sect. He mentions, moreover, one detail which actually appears in the Dead Sea Scrolls, a "conflagration of everything" at the final judgment (see p. 60). Black's conclusion is that the Essenes may have taught both the immortality of the soul and the resurrection of the body. This possibility must be left open for the present. Even if the Dead Sea Scrolls are assumed to be Essene documents, they do not as yet make clear the belief of the sect on the nature of the future life.

That there will be a universal judgment is clear enough. In the Thanksgiving Psalms the poet acknowledges that a man cannot "recount his sin" to God or "argue concerning his iniquities": "Everything is engraved before thee with a pen of remembrance" (i.24f; DSS, p. 400). In another passage (xvi.10) the poet says, "Thou hast marked the spirit of a righteous man." Gaster translates this, "Thou dost keep a record of every righteous spirit," and interprets it as meaning that God records the deeds of all men for judgment. The Manual of Discipline says that God "has ordained a period for the ruin of error, and in the appointed time of punishment he will destroy it forever" (iv.18f; cp. iii.18; iv.26;

*DSS*, pp. 374–76). The "day of vengeance" is mentioned also (ix.23; *DSS*, p. 384).

The future punishment of the wicked is never specifically described. There are many references to torment and destruction, but it is usually impossible to tell whether they indicate punishment after death or suffering in this life and death itself. The Manual of Discipline mentions "the deep darkness of eternal fire" (ii.8; *DSS*, p. 372). The pit, Sheol, and Abaddon appear in the Thanksgiving Psalms, either as figures of the poet's trials or in connection with the Messianic woes of which we have spoken. After the opening of Sheol and the loosing of Belial, the gates of the pit will be closed on the spirits of nothingness (iii.18). The Book of Mysteries also refers obscurely to a time when the descendants of error will be shut in. An unpublished text from Cave 4 is said to contain a description of the torments of the wicked together with the blessings of the righteous.

A very important item in the program of the last days is the final war with the hosts of Belial described in the War of the Sons of Light with the Sons of Darkness. Eissfeldt observes that in the other texts the victory of good over evil is apparently expected to come mainly if not entirely by divine intervention, but in the War scroll the cooperation of man is considered necessary. Possibly, Eissfeldt suggests, this document may have been written outside of the Qumran community or during a particularly activistic stage of its history, or the eschatological tension may have been especially high with a particular member or group of members. As Milik remarks, however, fragments of four more copies of this work were found in Cave 4, showing that it was very popular in the community. Bits of a similar composition were found also in Cave 2. It was characteristic of the sect, says Milik, that they did not allow cosmic speculations like those of the book of Enoch to absorb their attention but thought of man as involved in the events of the last time. The certainty of victory for the sons of light in the final conflict did not exempt them from exerting all their strength in the fray.

There are passages in the scrolls, as we shall see later, which speak of the elect as sharing the lot of the angels and being united

with them. Combining these with the references to the presence
of angels with the army of the sons of light, Yadin infers that the
conflict was thought of as taking place on two planes, the angels
and the righteous fighting together on earth and the righteous
dead fighting together with the angels in heaven. This is quite in
accord with ideas found elsewhere in apocalyptic literature, but
the passage in the War scroll on which Yadin's interpretation is
mainly based (xii.1–4) does not necessarily imply fighting both
in heaven and on earth. All that is clear is that angels and men
are involved together.

The program of the war is set forth in the scroll in detail, combining biblical material in a curious way with data furnished by
the author's knowledge of the world of his own day. Not only the
issue of the struggle is known in advance but also the amount of
time that each phase of it will require. The conflict will last forty
years. This figure was apparently a fixed item in the community's
tradition. The Damascus Document says that there will be about
forty years between "the ingathering of the unique teacher" and
"the annihilation of all the men of war who returned with the
man of the lie" (xx.14f; *DSS*, p. 357). This, however, cannot mean
the forty years of war unless the teacher's death was thought to
mark the beginning of the conflict. The commentary on Psalm
37 says that the wicked will be destroyed at the end of forty
years; this may or may not refer to the same period that is contemplated by the War scroll.

The war, as shown by Yadin's analysis, is divided into three
major campaigns. The first begins when the exiles of the sons of
light return from the desert of the peoples to encamp in the
desert of Jerusalem. It is directed against three groups of enemies:
(1) the Edomites, Moabites, Ammonites, and Philistines, neighbors and traditional foes of Israel on the east, south, and west;
(2) the Kittim of Assyria, Israel's enemies to the north; and (3)
"the violaters of the covenant," i.e., the Jewish enemies of the
sect. The most formidable of these enemies are evidently the
Kittim of Assyria. The second campaign, immediately following
the first, will be directed against "the Kittim in Egypt." In these
two campaigns, which together will occupy six years, the whole

congregation will be involved. There will be seven phases: in three the sons of light will be victorious, in three the sons of darkness, and in the seventh the enemies will be overthrown. Following these six years, and every subsequent six years of fighting, there will be a sabbatical year, during which the congregation will not fight at all. The extraordinarily supine way in which each enemy is expected to wait to be attacked seems one of the most supernatural (or unnatural) aspects of the whole struggle.

The third campaign will be directed against Israel's more distant enemies, the kings of the north. This will require twenty-nine years of warfare, in which the congregation will fight by divisions, mobilized in turn year by year (ii.9–14; *DSS*, p. 391). With the four interpolated years of rest, this makes thirty-three, completing the total of forty years, thirty-five of fighting and five of rest. The first nine years of this campaign will be used fighting the sons of Shem. These are listed according to Genesis 10 but in the reverse order, and with some adaptation to the writer's point of view, moving from Mesopotamia at the northwest corner, the nearest to Palestine, down to Elam in the southeast, the most distant, and adding at the end the Arabian "sons of Ishmael and Keturah." Included in the list also are Persia and "the people of the east as far as the great desert," i.e., the "easterners" or "Kadmonites" of Genesis 15:19. The next ten years of the third campaign will be devoted to the sons of Ham; the next line in the text (omitted in *DSS*) is incomplete, but it is sufficiently clear that the last ten years will be spent in fighting the sons of Japheth.

An illuminating comparison between this program and rabbinic discussions of the final war has been made by Yadin. In Genesis 15:18–21, known as "the covenant between the pieces" (verse 17), a list is given of ten nations to be dispossessed by the Israelites. Only seven nations were actually conquered; the rabbis therefore concluded that the other three would be overthrown in the days of the Messiah, when the Lord would enlarge Israel's borders (Deuteronomy 12:20; 19:8). The first two campaigns of the War scroll, in which the whole congregation fights, are concerned with the territory of the seven nations; this corresponds to what the rabbis called the obligatory war. The third campaign, directed against the nations outside of that territory, corresponds to the rabbinic category of permitted war to enlarge Israel's boundaries.

The place of the Kittim in this series of campaigns seems to raise a problem. They are named only in connection with the first two campaigns, and in both cases with geographical designations: the Kittim of Assyria and the Kittim in Egypt. Throughout the rest of the scroll, however, the whole war seems to be considered a conflict with the Kittim, who are practically identified with the army of Belial. The resolution of the difficulty has been provided by Carmignac, who has examined all the references to the Kittim in the War scroll and reached the conclusion that in this document the word "Kittim" has become simply a general term for Israel's enemies, corresponding to "Gentiles." In one place, indeed, where the scroll from Cave 1 reads "Kittim," a Cave 4 fragment containing the same passage (xix.10f) reads "peoples."

The Kittim of Assyria and the Kittim in Egypt are no doubt the Roman forces in Syria and Egypt respectively (see pp. 195–203), but not because the word "Kittim" of itself means "Romans." The Kittim of the Habakkuk Commentary also are Romans, but in the War scroll the term has a much wider application. Beginning in Old Testament times as the name of a particular people, it has through the centuries become, as Carmignac says, a common noun like "bohemian" or "vandal."

The descriptions of the trumpets and standards and the mottoes inscribed on them, the various weapons, the organization of the troops and their disposition, the conduct of the battles, and the predominant part taken by the priests were all evidently matters of great interest to the Qumran community. For our purpose they have little significance. It is still difficult to decide whether they represent directions seriously intended to be followed in actual practice or merely the personal daydreams of the author.

The war with the Kittim is mentioned in one of the fragments of a commentary on Isaiah published by Allegro. An earlier portion of the same document refers to the march against Jerusalem from the plains of Acco, which has already been discussed (pp.

321–22). As we have seen, it probably refers to a hostile invasion, perhaps by the Kittim though this is not indicated in the surviving portion of the text. Another fragment of the same commentary says that the branch of David will rule over all the nations and then names Magog, but here the text breaks off. What connection, if any, the events and persons here mentioned may have with the conflict described in the War scroll is quite uncertain. We can say only that the idea of a violent war in the last days evidently played a large part in the thinking of the Qumran sect.

The Thanksgiving Psalms mention "the war of the mighty ones of heaven" which "rushes about in the world and turns not back until the full end decreed forever" (iii.35f; *DSS*, p. 405). A reference to "the tumult of the people" and "the uproar of kingdoms" (vi.7; *DSS*, p. 409) recalls such Old Testament passages as Psalms 2 and 48, which have often been associated with the Messianic war. The last thirteen lines of the same column (vi.24–36) have much to say about some kind of warfare, but, as so often in these poems, it is not clear whether the writer refers to the eschatological war or to his personal experience of deliverance and security in the company of the elect. A part of this passage has already been considered in connection with the resurrection of the dead (pp. 345–46).

The final and eternal bliss of the righteous, with all their conflicts o'er and all their victories won, is pictured in glowing colors, though of course without very precise drawing. The community of the future would be a worshiping community. Bits of what appears to have been a detailed description of the restored temple are preserved in fragments found in Caves 1, 4, and 5. Evidently this composition was very popular at Qumran. Milik suggests that it may have contained also directions for the worship of the new temple. Presumably the sect, like many other Jews, expected the new Jerusalem with its temple to be built on earth, but an earth miraculously renewed. The Manual of Discipline mentions a "making new" in "the period which has been decreed" (iv.25; *DSS*, p. 376). The idea no doubt goes back to "the new heavens and the new earth" promised in Isaiah 65:17 and 66:22. One of the Thanksgiving Psalms speaks of the sons of God's truth, or

God's true sons, as standing before him with the eternal host "to be made new together with all that is to be" (xi.13f). Another passage, echoing Isaiah 43:19 and 48:6, speaks of God's creating new things (xiii.11f).

The individual members of the redeemed people will be refined, purified "with a holy spirit from all wicked deeds," and sprinkled with "a spirit of truth," the Manual of Discipline says; they will "perceive the knowledge of the Most High and the wisdom of the sons of heaven" (iv.20–23; DSS, p. 376). They will have "all eternal blessings and everlasting joy in the life of eternity, and a crown of glory with raiment of majesty in everlasting light" (iv.7f; DSS, p. 375). The crown of glory is mentioned also in one of the Thanksgiving Psalms (ix.25). A passage already cited from the Thanksgiving Psalms says that the elect will stand in their place before God with the eternal host (xi.11f). Thanking God, in another hymn, for his redemption from the pit, the poet voices his assurance of man's hope "for an eternal company," with whom he will "stand in his place with the army of the holy ones" and "come together with the congregation of the sons of heaven," praising God's name and recounting his wonders (iii.19–23; DSS, p. 404). The men of God's counsel, says another Psalm, have a place "in the lot together with the angels of the presence" (vi.13). They belong to the eternal kingdom of God, for, as the War scroll says, he has engraved for them the covenant of his peace "with a living stylus, to reign over them in all the seasons of eternity" (xii.3).

PART SEVEN

# ORGANIZATION AND RITES
# OF THE SECT

# XXX

## *Organization*

The organization of the Qumran community in its general outlines was already fairly clear when DSS was published, but new
texts and further discussion have helped to fill in the picture as
given there (pp. 230ff). The Damascus Document and the Manual of Discipline are still the major sources of information. Fragments of both have been found in the caves; no less than eleven
copies of the Manual are represented by fragments from Cave 4.
In general these agree with the scroll found in Cave 1 in 1947,
except that the text of its fifth column appears in the fragments
in a shorter form which is probably older. The Rule of the Congregation, already known but not yet published when DSS was
written, has somewhat complicated the matter by presenting a
picture that differs at a number of points from what is given in
either the Manual of Discipline or the Damascus Document.
Clearly a detached part of the same scroll that contains the
Manual, it is equally clearly a distinct composition, representing
either a different stage in the sect's history or different ideas of
what it should be in the future.

The Damascus Document is concerned with "the explanation
of the law for the period of wickedness" (vi.14; DSS, p. 354). The
Manual of Discipline also says explicitly that its regulations are to
be observed "all the days of the dominion of Belial" (ii.19; DSS,
p. 373), "until there shall come a prophet and the Messiahs of
Aaron and Israel" (ix.11; DSS, p. 383). The Rule of the Congregation begins with a statement that it is "for the whole congrega-

tion of Israel at the end of days." It legislates, as we have seen (pp. 300–304), for a time when the Messiah of Israel will be present. The final war with Belial's hosts, however, is not yet past. The community is still a military group, organized by "hundreds, fifties, and tens" (i.14) for "the war to subdue nations" (i.21). The references to women and children, the age at which a young man can marry and can be admitted to the army and the community's worship and deliberations, the list of physical and mental qualifications for full membership in the group—all these presuppose a distinctly this-worldly type of life.

Barthélemy, in fact, thinks that this is not the community of the future at all, but a form of organization earlier than that presented by the Manual of Discipline. He suggests that it might fit the Hasidim of the Maccabean period. It is true that the group even then may have thought of itself as already living "at the end of days"; the idea of the Messiah's presence and participation in the common meals, however, would on Barthélemy's hypothesis presuppose an extraordinarily vivid expectation of the imminent coming of the Messiah. Eissfeldt notes that it "almost seems" as though the Rule of the Congregation was intended, like the War scroll, to regulate the community's life in the expected time of the end. Kuhn is convinced that this document contemplates the time of final consummation. Since no one could represent the Messiah at the common meals, there was nothing in the actual meals of the "Essenes" corresponding to the description given in the Rule of the Congregation.

The dominant position of the priest in this document is understood by Milik as a projection of the theocratic organization of Judah during the Persian and Greek periods. Yadin shows that the subordination of the lay Messiah does not reflect any hostility to the house of David, whose victories over Goliath and the Philistines are exalted in the War scroll (xi.2ff; *DSS*, p. 397). The priestly leaders of the community were, no doubt, prepared to welcome the lay Messiah as a military leader, but they were determined that he should be kept in his place.

One cannot help wondering whether the military organization reflected in the Rule of the Congregation and described in detail

in the War scroll corresponds to the actual organization of the
sect at any time. If so, it is a melancholy illustration of the fact
that they who take the sword will perish by the sword. Molin suggests that this form of organization, based on that of the wilderness period as described in the book of Numbers, may have existed
even before the time of the teacher of righteousness. It seems
more likely that the book of Numbers was used as the basis of an
idealistic scheme for the future.

The Manual of Discipline speaks of "thousands and hundreds
and fifties and tens" in connection with the annual renewal of the
covenant (ii.21f; *DSS*, p. 373); the Damascus Document (xii. 23–
xiii.2, *DSS*, p. 361), speaking of "the order of the session of the
camps" for "the period of wickedness," says that those "who walk
in these ways . . . must be as many as ten men at least, by thousands and hundreds and fifties and tens." Otherwise, there is no
indication of a military organization in either of these works, and
not the slightest hint of a martial spirit.

The Manual of Discipline speaks regularly of the "community,"
while the Rule of the Congregation, as its title indicates, speaks
of the "congregation." Barthélemy infers from this fact that the
two groups were not in fact the same. He supposes that an earlier
warlike "congregation" of Hasidim was succeeded by a more
peaceful "community of Essenes." Gaster supposes that the word
"congregation," which actually occurs once in the Manual of
Discipline and often in the Damascus Document, refers to the
sect as a whole, while the word "community" refers to a local
chapter. There is very little in the Manual, however, that suggests
the existence of separate local communities. The mention of "every
place where there are ten men of the council of the community"
(vi.3, 6; *DSS*, p. 378) may imply this, or it may indicate only small
groups within the Qumran settlement. The parallel passage in
the Damascus Document (xiii.1–4; *DSS*, pp. 361f) is equally ambiguous. The Rule of the Congregation also stipulates that its
regulations for the common meal apply only when as many as ten
men are present (ii.22).

The "camps" with which the Damascus Document is largely
concerned were so named, Gaster suggests, to describe both the

situation of the community at Qumran and the sect's military function in the war with Belial. Those who believe that there was a migration to the land of Damascus (see pp. 219–27) understand the term "camp" as a literal designation of the group's temporary settlement there. Gaster's explanation is open to the objection that the military aspect of the sect's life is not otherwise apparent in the Damascus Document. The only certain implication of the term "camp" is that there was more than one settlement of the sect at the time when the Damascus Document was written.

The Manual of Discipline and the Rule of the Congregation differ also in the fact that women and children are mentioned only in the latter. The camps whose life the Damascus Document is intended to regulate were evidently settlements of families (vii.6–10; xix.3–9; *DSS*, p. 354). The Manual of Discipline, however, seems so clearly to reflect a celibate community that the discovery of women's skeletons in the cemetery at Khirbet Qumran was an unexpected development. As was suggested in *DSS* (p. 233), there were probably both celibate communities and settlements of families in the order. The fact that Josephus mentions a group of Essenes who married and had families is often recalled in this connection. Oesterreicher suggests that married groups may have been attached to the celibate community, somewhat as a "Third Order Secular" is affiliated with the "First Order" of Catholic friars.

As there was a priestly and a lay Messiah, so the sect consisted of two main divisions, the priests and Levites and the laity. The priests were called sons of Aaron and sons of Zadok; it was they who ruled, and one of them had to meet with every group of ten members. The assembly of fully initiated members had considerable administrative authority, especially in matters of admission and discipline, but the ultimate power, both legislative and judicial, seems to have been reserved to the priests. The Levites, who are mentioned much more rarely in the texts, apparently served as general assistants to the priests. Milik finds the same division between priestly and lay authority in the Damascus Document. The "superintendent who is over all the camps" is a layman, whose function is administrative; the "priest who is appointed at the head of the many" has the religious function of teaching the law (xiv.7–12; *DSS*, pp. 362f). There is also a "superintendent of the camp" who teaches sacred history and exercises a pastoral oversight which seems to imply that he is a priest (xiii.7–12; *DSS*, p. 362).

At the head of the community, according to the Manual of Discipline, there is a council of twelve laymen and three priests (viii.1; *DSS*, p. 381; cp. p. 232). Milik may be right in suggesting that the twelve laymen represent the twelve tribes of Israel and the three priests represent the priestly families of Gershom, Kohath, and Merari, the three sons of Levi, though the priesthood was actually limited to the descendants of Aaron, the grandson of Kohath. Instead of the council of twelve, the Damascus Document prescribes ten judges, of whom four are priests "of the tribe of Levi and Aaron," and six are laymen "from Israel" (x.5f; *DSS*, p. 359).

Membership in the order was attained only through a period of probation. As described in the Manual of Discipline, this process began with a strict oath of allegiance to the law of Moses and separation from all the wicked; then, after an undefined period of instruction, two years of probation followed, with a review of the candidate's qualifications and conduct at the end of each year and admission to some of the privileges of membership after the first year (v.7–11; vi.13–23; *DSS*, pp. 377, 379).

The fully initiated members are designated by a word which I translated in *DSS* "masters." It was not, perhaps, a very happy rendering; it was, at any rate, open to misunderstanding. What suggested it, as I explained (p. 234), was the distinction between masters and apprentices in the medieval guilds. By "masters" I meant all those who, having successfully completed their novitiate, had been admitted to full membership. Some readers, however, not observing this explanation, took the term to mean a small number of leaders. The late Ralph Marcus, for example, said that the Hebrew word in question designated "the general assembly or membership of the community rather than a small group of rabbis or masters" and twice again on the same page he spoke of "a small group of masters." Marcus recognized, however, that the word might mean "rulers."

The Hebrew word in question is usually translated "many," and that is its ordinary meaning in Hebrew. In this sense, as I pointed out, it is used in Daniel (11:33, 39; 12:2f, 10), and its use there may have suggested the sect's use of the term. This would give it a connotation practically equivalent to "the elect." In the Damascus Document, as a matter of fact, I inadvertently retained the translation "many" instead of "masters" (xiii.7; xiv.7; xv.8; DSS, pp. 362f). In Aramaic the same word means "much" or "great," and so in the plural "great ones."

Milik assumes the meaning "many" for the Hebrew word in the Qumran texts and infers from it that the lay members of the sect were more numerous than the priests. If the use of this word originated with the priestly leaders, they may have meant by it "the crowd" of lay members, but its use in the Manual of Discipline seems to imply a title of dignity. The "many" or "masters," whichever meaning may be preferred, were those admitted to the rights and responsibilities of full membership, including the expression of their opinions and a vote in the deliberative sessions of the community.

Albright has gone so far as to say that the meaning "masters" is "quite impossible in post-Biblical Hebrew." With that opinion not all scholars agree. Dupont-Sommer, while preferring the meaning "many," considers the meaning "great ones" possible. It is true that in the dialect of the rabbis (which is not the dialect of the Qumran texts), when the word is used in the plural in the sense of "teachers" it has a feminine ending, but this form appears only with a personal suffix, "our teachers." In the singular the word means "large," "much," "great"; it is used also for a slave's master and for a teacher. The masculine plural form is sometimes used for "the many" in the sense of the Greek *hoi polloi;* sometimes it designates a whole community or the public; it also sometimes designates the "associates" or members of a religious association. The meaning "great ones" is, no doubt, more Aramaic than Hebrew, but the Hebrew of Qumran was not free from Aramaic influence. The Habakkuk Commentary uses the masculine plural form of the word for the "great ones" who are mocked by the Kittim (iv.2; *DSS*, p. 366).

Interesting suggestions have been made recently concerning an obscure passage in Josephus which says that the Essenes, or their stewards and priests, followed in their manner of living "those of the Dakoi called the most." Instead of "the most" some texts read a similar word meaning "city folk," and many scholars have adopted some such reading. Dupont-Sommer has proposed to retain the word "most" but to emend the word "Dakoi" to "Zadokites." Assuming that the word "most" or "very many" is a translation of the Hebrew term used in the Qumran texts, Dupont-Sommer takes this to mean the members of the sect "or its council." The statement of Josephus then means that all the Essenes conform their way of living to that of "the many," who are thus "the Essene group that serves as a model for all." This interpretation implies a distinction between "the many" and the main body of the sect which seems inconsistent with their designation as "the many." It would be quite in accord with such a term as "masters" or "great ones."

Carmignac proposes a different emendation for "Dakoi," changing it to the possessive pronoun "their" or "of them." The passage thus reads, "those of them called the most." Whatever the original reading was, the suggestions of Carmignac and Dupont-Sommer agree in getting rid of the Dakoi and in implying a distinction between "the most" and the rest of the Essenes. Carmignac agrees also with Dupont-Sommer in supposing that "the most" is a translation of the Qumran term, but he argues that the Hebrew word must mean "the great ones" or "chiefs," those who are respected or venerated. In comparison with all the postulants, novices, and penitents of the sect, he says, the members of the council, who were models of conduct for the rest, were not perhaps very "many," but their dignity deserved the title "great." That the Aramaic rather than the Hebrew meaning of the word should be understood is not surprising in a community whose customary language was Aramaic.

Certainly the word had both meanings; both were developments of the basic meaning "much." For the Qumran sect it may have carried both meanings at the same time. The fully initiated lay members who participated in the formal assemblies of the community were to the priestly leaders "the many"; to the candidates in training and the novitiates under probation, as doubtless also to themselves, they were "the masters."

Those who prefer the meaning "many" are much beguiled by the use of Greek words meaning "more," "most," or "multitude" in the New Testament and the works of Josephus. None of these Greek words actually means "many" (see pp. 114ff). If the Greek writers had our Hebrew word in mind, they had to choose one meaning or the other. The fact that they used words suggesting a large number shows that this interpretation was current, but not necessarily that it was the only interpretation recognized. It is even conceivable that the term may have meant one thing to the members of the sect and something else to those outside. For myself, I am quite willing to give up the translation "masters" if it is misleading, but I am not convinced that the interpretation it was meant to convey is erroneous.

# XXXI

## *Rites*

The religious rites of the sect and their attitude toward the sacrificial worship of the temple have continued to be discussed since the publication of *DSS*, and some new light has been thrown upon them. With regard to the temple worship the result has been to confirm the position suggested earlier in this book (p. 258) and already stated in *DSS* (pp. 237f). Yadin has conclusively shown that the sect was not opposed in principle to the temple and its offerings. For the future, including the forty years of the final war, the full exercise of the priestly office is expected. Early in the War scroll, when the first year of rest following the first six years of fighting is reached, the author pauses to describe the service of the priests and Levites in the sanctuary as it will then be performed (ii.1–6; *DSS*, p. 391). For the present, however, the profanation of the temple by a corrupt priesthood prevents the covenanters from participating in its worship. On the principle that "the sacrifice of the wicked is an abomination to the Lord, but the prayer of the upright is his delight" (Proverbs 15:8; quoted in the Damascus Document, xi.20f; *DSS*, p. 360), they found a temporary and acceptable substitute for the sacrifices of the temple in their prayers and common worship.

A somewhat ambiguous passage in the Manual of Discipline has occasioned some difference of opinion among scholars in this connection. It has been examined by Carmignac in connection with a similar sentence in the War scroll. The ambiguity in this instance lies in a Hebrew preposition, which means "from" but

363

is often used with the meaning "more than." The Manual of Discipline, according to my translation, uses these phrases: ". . . for a ransom for the guilt of transgression and sinful faithlessness, and for acceptance for the land more than the flesh of whole burnt offerings and the fats of sacrifice, and an offering of the lips for justice like the pleasing quality of righteousness, and perfect conduct like a willing gift of an acceptable offering" (ix.3–5; *DSS*, p. 383). Three words used in this passage appear together in a sentence of the War scroll, describing the service of the priests and Levites in the first year of release (ii.6; *DSS*, p. 391). They are "acceptance," "ransom" (or the verb "atone"), and "pleasing quality" (or "fragrance"). The first of these is used only once elsewhere in the War scroll, the other two not at all. This leads Carmignac to the inference that the author of the War scroll was here quoting from the Manual of Discipline, and that therefore he could not have understood it as implying a renunciation of expiation by sacrifice. Hence, Carmignac concludes, the ambiguous phrase in the Manual must mean not "more than" but "from" or "by" the flesh of whole burnt offerings.

A postscript to Carmignac's article by Milik informs us that a Cave 4 fragment containing this part of the Manual reads, after "from the flesh of whole burnt offerings," not "and from the fats of sacrifice" but simply "and the fats of sacrifice." This, says Milik, makes the one preposition "from" or "by" govern all three expressions, "flesh of whole burnt offerings," "fats of sacrifice," and also "offering of the lips." Expiation is then thought to be accomplished by all of these, with the implication that sacrifice was efficacious. If this reading reproduces the original text, Milik concludes, the author of the Manual believed in the efficacy of sacrifice; if it is not the original reading, it at least shows that the Qumran scribe responsible for the change held that belief.

This reasoning does not seem to me cogent. The omission of the preposition before "fats" does not necessarily carry with it the inclusion of "offering" also in the phrase introduced by "from." I seriously doubt that the scribe who omitted or supplied the second "from" had any such subtle considerations in mind. The contrast between sacrifice and praise still seems to me more in accord with the rest of the passage. Gaster's translation brings out this contrast even more strongly than mine: atonement will be made, he reads, "more effectively than by any flesh of burnt-offerings or fat of sacrifices." This has been the understanding of a large majority of interpreters, and I do not believe that Carmignac's and Milik's arguments will convince many of them.

Their major contention, however, that the sect was not opposed to sacrifice in principle, agrees with what many of us already believed. The passage in the Manual refers, I take it, to the period before the purification of the temple and the restoration of pure sacrificial worship. The comparison between sacrifice and praise at the expense of the former no more implies that proper sacrifice under the right auspices will have no value than do the many similar expressions in the Old Testament. As Yadin says, the sect was devoted to the fulfillment of the law, which stressed the obligation of sacrifice. This was impossible for the present at the temple, and sacrifice anywhere else would have been contrary to the law. There was no alternative, therefore, to worship by their own rites until the temple was purified. Their interest meanwhile in the future sacrificial cultus is attested not only by the War scroll but by the Description of the New Jerusalem and the "Mishmaroth" texts.

The sacred meals of the sect are thought by some to have taken the place of the temple sacrifices. Yadin calls attention to the term "honored table" for the altar in the War scroll (ii.6) and compares this with the regulations in the Manual of Discipline for the sacred meal, "when they set the table to eat" (vi.4–6; *DSS*, p. 378). Since sacrifice anywhere but at the temple was unlawful, Kuhn infers that meat could not be offered for sacrifice at these meals, and in fact only bread and wine are mentioned in the text. At the same time, he remarks, the meals were subject to the same rules of ritual purity as the priests' meals at the temple, and he sees here an indication that the meals were regarded as a substitute for the temple sacrifices.

A problem has been raised at this point by the discovery of jars containing animals' bones at Khirbet Qumran (see p. 23). In reporting this find, de Vaux expressed the conviction that these carefully buried bones were certainly the remains of the community's sacred meals. The use of meat must have been in accord with rules which have not thus far been found in any of the texts. Allegro infers from these deposits of bones and from the cooking pots found in the building that the sect had its own sanctuary and offered sacrifices of its own. The teacher of righteousness, he suggests, may have been officiating at the altar when the wicked priest put in his appearance. This is quite incredible: it would be wholly contrary to the law which all the members of the sect had sworn to obey. As has already been observed, until pure sacrifices could again be offered at Jerusalem, no sacrifice at all was possible.

Whatever explanation may be found for the strange jars of bones, it must be one in strict accordance with the ritual law. Their quantity is not sufficient to represent all the meals of the community for any length of time. Some special observance at long intervals, perhaps an annual ceremony, must be assumed. It was certainly not the Passover, as Allegro suggests, for bones of other animals than lambs are included. More probable is Milik's suggestion that the annual renewal of the covenant was the occasion for these feasts.

The Manual of Discipline mentions "reading the book" as an element in the nightly meetings of the sect (vi.7; *DSS*, p. 378). A low, round base or "podium" near one end of the large hall on the south side of the main buildings at Khirbet Qumran has suggested the hypothesis that during the common meals a member of the group stood or sat on this little platform and read to the others, as was done in later Christian monasteries. It has also been suggested that the community's assemblies for worship, study, and judicial deliberations were held in this hall, and the presiding superintendent occupied the "podium." The reference to "reading the book" in the Manual of Discipline does not, in fact, occur in connection with the meals but in connection with the meetings to "keep watch together a third of all the nights of the year." The fact that some eleven hundred bowls were found stacked in a small room adjoining the hall seems to favor the idea that the common meals were held here. The room may have been used, of course, for more than one purpose.

Several writers, in referring to the meals of the Qumran sect, have spoken of their "sacramental character," usually without any effort to define what is meant by that expression. Allegro boldly translates the word for "table" as "communion table." The mere fact that the bread and wine must be blessed by a priest has seemed to some to have "sacramental" significance. Kuhn recalls Josephus's statement that the Essenes went into their refectory "as to some sacred shrine." Essene rites of purification before eating are mentioned also by Josephus, and a Cave 4 fragment refers to such rites.

An Aramaic fragment from Cave 2 published by Baillet describes the placing of the "bread of the Presence" on the altar in the temple, the offering of the two loaves at the Feast of Weeks, and in some obscure connection the assignment of "a ram of the flock to each man." Baillet assigns this fragment to the Description of the New Jerusalem, and this is no doubt correct, for not only are the temple and probably the altar explicitly mentioned, but each stage in the description is introduced in true apocalyptic fashion with the words, "I beheld till . . . ," as often in Daniel. The fragment attests once more the community's ardent interest in the temple offerings, from which it was separated in the present age. Quite possibly the procedure at the common meals and the understanding of their significance were determined by the pattern of the priests' meals after the temple sacrifice.

Kuhn calls attention to the fact that the wine used in the common meals is not designated by the common Hebrew word for wine. The word used for it is often translated in English versions of the Bible "new wine," but it is simply a more poetic term for wine. To the Qumran covenanters it may have seemed more appropriate than the more common word for the wine used at their repasts. No inference can be drawn from it as to the kind of wine used.

Endeavoring to determine the religious meaning of the Qumran meals, Kuhn adduces an Egyptian Jewish legend, the story of

Joseph and Asenath, probably from the first or second century
A.D. This story uses some of the very language used by Christian
writers for the Eucharist: the devout Jew is repeatedly described
as one who "eats the blessed bread of life and drinks the blessed
cup of immortality." These expressions, Kuhn is convinced, are
not Christian interpolations; they repeat the ritual formula of a
cult meal. Some connection with the Essenes is obvious, Kuhn
feels, but in the story a woman partakes of the sacred meal,
whereas the Qumran texts and the classic descriptions of the
Essenes imply that only men participated in their meals.

Kuhn's conclusion is that the story of Joseph and Asenath comes
from the Therapeutae described by Philo, and that these were
an Egyptian offshoot of the Essenes. The sacramental conception
of the meal as conveying immortality is to be attributed to the
Therapeutae, who probably developed it under the influence of
their Hellenistic environment, perhaps even under the influence
of Hellenistic Christianity in Egypt. The "sacramental character"
of the Qumran meals is thus left still undefined, but Kuhn holds
that in some sense they may have been thought to mediate salvation.

Del Medico attributes the section of the Manual of Discipline
which contains the directions for the meals to "a rabbinic association, very different from the associations of the Zadokites and
Zealots." Instead of a meeting of ten or more "masters" or members of the "many" with a priest at their head, Del Medico sees
here a meeting of ten or more rabbis headed by a man named
Cohen, to whom the prerogative of pronouncing the blessing
over the bread and wine is assigned. As for Josephus's description
of the Essene meals, this is an exaggerated satire fabricated by
the first interpolator of Josephus (see p. 266) on the basis of the
quite accurate account given by Hippolytus, which actually describes common Jewish customs. This is all too easy a way of
disposing of the evidence, but it calls attention to the fact that
nothing said about the meals at Qumran is especially distinctive
or significant. All that we are told about them in the Manual of
Discipline, in fact, is that they are taken together and that the
blessing is pronounced by a priest (vi.2, 5; *DSS*, p. 378). And this

applies to all the meals, not simply to a special, occasional observance.

All this is decidedly less than satisfying. One is left with a strong suspicion that the whole idea of anything sacramental in the meals of Qumran is the result of reading Christian conceptions into the texts. Milik, while considering it possible that even the cult meals of the Hellenistic mystery religions had some influence on the Qumran "Essenes," concludes that the sacred meals of the sect were essentially a continuation of the meals accompanying the sacrifices in ancient Israel. This, on the whole, seems as close as we can come to a statement of what their meals meant to the members of the sect, if they can properly be called sacred meals at all. Even this, as a matter of fact, has been shown by van der Ploeg to be very doubtful. All the meals of the community were frugal and orderly, with strict attention to ritual purity. No text clearly attests any special meal of a clearly sacred character.

The whole elaborate ritual system of the Old Testament, it should be remembered, was presented as a divinely provided way of atonement, a series of procedures by which God's people might regain communion with him when it was broken by their sins. Efficacy in making atonement for the sins of Israel is attributed in the Manual of Discipline to the whole life of the community in the desert (viii.4–10; *DSS*, pp. 381f). The common meals were an integral part of that life; if they had any further, more distinct significance, it is not indicated in the texts.

The discovery of the Rule of the Congregation, which explicitly contemplates the presence and participation of the Messiah of Israel at the community's meals, has suggested another kind of "sacramental" significance. Cross apparently believes that the meal described in the Rule of the Congregation is the same as that referred to in the Manual of Discipline. Of the former he says, "It is an order in which the community anticipated liturgically the banquet of the Kingdom"; and he mentions the well-known fact of this "motif in the common meals of the Jerusalem Church." If this means what it seems to mean, the presence of the Messiah must be a matter of liturgical anticipation, either by some kind of symbolic representation or by a spiritual interpretation. Allegro speaks of "the Messianic Banquet" as "the sacramental focus of their worship" and considers it "probable that every communal repast was considered to some extent a rehearsal of the Messianic Banquet." Again it is hard to see just what is meant.

The directions for the order of seating and eating preclude a spiritual interpretation without some kind of realistic procedure. On the other hand, to postulate a dramatization in which the Messiah was impersonated by a member or officer of the sect requires too great a strain on the imagination. The natural inference is that this document deals with conditions and practice in the future, after the Messiah's coming. Even then his coming and presence are hardly more than incidental, so far as the meal is concerned. The present meals have nothing to do with him; when he comes, he will have his part in the proceedings, but the first place will still be that of the priest. True, the order prescribed for the future is to be followed whenever ten men are present. The situation presupposed is evidently not a continual, timeless, spiritual banquet, but a continuing community life not essentially different from that of the present. The one great difference will be that the Messiah of Israel will have come. The situation is apparently that of the period of war, before the final conflagration and renewal of all things.

Schonfield suspects that the whole elaborate ordering of the community, as given in the Manual of Discipline and the Damascus Document as well as in the War scroll, the Rule of the Congregation, and the Benedictions, is an idealistic construction. The authors were "building on a foundation of Essene practice," but what they were describing was not actual practice but "the structure for the Good Society of the Elect." There are expressions in the Manual of Discipline which lend some color to this suspicion. More than once a section is introduced by the puzzling clause, "When these things come to pass in Israel" (viii.4, 12; ix.3; *DSS*, pp. 381–83). What this implies, however, is probably only that the regulations given are not yet fully obeyed. That these regulations are intended for the present age is shown by such expressions as "all the days of the dominion of Belial," the reference to the future coming of a prophet and the two Messiahs, and finally the explicit statement, "These are the regulations of the way for the wise man in these times" (ii.19; ix.11, 21; *DSS*, pp. 373, 383f). In the Damascus Document the reference to present conditions seems obvious.

The same passage in the Manual which prescribes eating together continues, "and together they shall worship, and together they shall counsel"; a few lines lower we read, "And the masters shall keep watch together a third of all the nights of the year, reading the book and searching for justice, and worshiping together" (v.2f,7f; *DSS*, p. 378). As Milik says, this is the only account we have of the sect's liturgical meetings. The expression "a third of all the nights of the year" is not as clear as one might wish. Milik takes it to mean that the meetings are to last for a third of the night, i.e., the whole evening. Del Medico supposes that the "rabbis" were required to moderate their zeal and stay awake for study and worship only every third night. On the basis of the preceding sentence, which speaks of searching the law "day and night, by turns," I interpreted the passage in *DSS* as meaning that the sacred exercise was to be kept going all night by three successive shifts of members (p. 235).

Many bits of liturgical material are contained in the fragments found in the caves, but how they were used is not clear. The Benedictions accompanying the Rule of the Congregation are of this nature, but since they quite plainly envisage a future situation, Milik is no doubt right in pronouncing this document a literary composition rather than a ritual. How far this may be true of other remains of prayers, hymns, and the like it is impossible to tell now. The question whether the Thanksgiving Psalms were used in public worship has already been raised and answered tentatively in the negative (p. 325).

Comparable to the meals in real or supposed "sacramental" significance are the ritual lustrations and ablutions occasionally referred to in the Qumran texts. The Damascus Document forbids attempting purification in unclean or insufficient water (x.10–14; *DSS*, p. 359). The Manual of Discipline sternly warns that no atonement offering and no amount of washing can cleanse one who "walks in the stubbornness of his heart," but at the same time it promises that he who is ruled by "a spirit of true counsel" will find atonement and cleansing, "that he may be sprinkled with water for impurity and sanctify himself with water of cleanness" (iii.4–6, 8f; *DSS*, p. 373). The members of the community must keep apart from "men of error," who "shall not enter the water, . . . for they will not be cleansed unless they have turned from their evil" (v.13f; *DSS*, p. 377). From these passages Kuhn infers that the baths of the Qumran "Essenes" had "the sacramental function of mediating in the divine forgiveness of sin." This is obviously true in some sense, but the "mediation" was no more and no less "sacramental" than it was in the atonement rites of the Old Testament.

According to Josephus, the Essenes had daily baths of purification before their meals. This practice is not attested by the Qumran texts, but Kuhn recalls the fact that the sect originated among priests who withdrew from the temple service, and he mentions the ritual baths of the temple priests before and after every cultic act. Some such association is the more probable if we suppose that the common meals were patterned after the meals which accompanied sacrifice at the temple.

Archeological evidence of the community's lustrations and "baptisms" is seen in the installations at Khirbet Qumran. Allegro refers to the "basins, having the obvious purpose of ritual washing." Instead of "obvious" some would prefer to say "possible." Fritsch thinks that a ritual bath, "probably an initiatory baptismal rite" upon admission to the order, offers the only plausible explanation for the open cisterns with wide steps leading into them. Allegro, however, doubts that they were used in this way, feeling that the running water of the Jordan or Ain Feshkha would have been preferred for such a purpose. Milik reminds us that a great deal of water was needed for the daily use of the community. In the judgment of de Vaux only two "baths," at opposite corners of the ruins, were used for ritual or ordinary bathing, but for them he considers this certain. So far as ritual baths are concerned, the archeological "evidence" is thus reduced to possible archeological illustration.

Not only daily or weekly observances were cherished by the community of Qumran. Great stress is laid on times and seasons in many of the texts. One of the vows taken by the sons of light, as stated in the Manual of Discipline, was "not to advance their times or postpone any of their appointed festivals" (i.14f; *DSS*, p. 371). My late, lamented colleague Julian Obermann, in his last published article, explained the background of this curious vow. While rejecting (wrongly, I believe) the reconstruction of the Qumran calendar by Mlle. Jaubert and others (*DSS*, pp. 239–42), he pointed out that the Pharisees claimed to have, as Moses' successors, the right to regulate the calendar, whereas the covenanters regarded the calendar as divinely established and unchangeable. For the Pharisees it was the official proclamation that determined what day was to be observed as the day of the new moon, and even an erroneous decision duly proclaimed was binding; for the sect of Qumran, God had immutably fixed the course of times and seasons, and no human authority could advance or postpone the appointed festivals.

Advancing an observance is illustrated by the Pharisaic interpretation of "the Sabbath" in Leviticus 23:11, 15f as meaning the Passover. This meant that the waving of the sheaf of firstfruits "on the morrow after the Sabbath" and the observance of Pentecost "seven full weeks" later came on different days of the week in different years. Except when the Passover fell on the seventh day of the week, these observances therefore came earlier than a literal interpretation of the Scripture, which the covenanters championed, would demand.

Postponing sacred times for various reasons was a regular practice of the Pharisees, and they had elaborate procedures for doing this. The Day of Atonement, for example, was not allowed to fall on the day before or after the Sabbath; to prevent this, while still observing it on the 10th of Tishri as required by Scripture, they lengthened the preceding month, the last of the old year, by a day. Both the New Year's Day and the Day of Atonement were thus a day later in the week than they would otherwise have been.

Thus far the argument seems to me both convincing and very

illuminating. From here on it is more open to question, though certainly deserving serious consideration. The article goes on to argue that, apart from not advancing or retarding the sacred times, those who joined the sect "would continue to follow the calendar to which they had adhered hitherto." On the supposition that they were "no doubt converts from the Pharisaic persuasion," this means "that, in its basic structure, the calendar of the sect was identical with that of the Pharisees." Nowhere in the scrolls, Obermann says, is there any hint that entering the sect involved a change to a radically different system of time-reckoning. This is true enough, but for the members of the sect it was their calendar that followed the original divine plan, and it was the calendar of the Pharisees that was new and revolutionary.

More formidable is Obermann's contention that the calendar of the book of Jubilees, which the Qumran sect is supposed to have followed, was based on a year of 364 days and entirely ignored the lunar months. It makes no effort to "bind" the lunar year to the solar year, as the Pharisaic calendar did, so that the Passover could be celebrated year by year at the full moon of the month of Nisan without drifting away from the solar season of the ripening grain. A statement in the closing psalm of the Manual of Discipline is translated by Obermann, "In the occurrence of the festivals on (certain) days of the month, he has joined their circuit with their depending one upon the other" (x.3f; cp. *DSS*, p. 384). In one of the Thanksgiving Psalms the poet, after referring to the eternal divine system of times and seasons, claims to have received knowledge from God and to have listened to his "wondrous secret" (xii.3–12; *DSS*, pp. 414f). In these and similar expressions Obermann sees reason to believe that the "wondrous secret" was the secret of "binding the periods of the moon to the seasons of the sun." This, while not impossible, is certainly not clearly indicated. How the solar and lunar calendars were actually adjusted at Qumran will appear shortly (p. 377).

For the wicked priest's appearance to confound the teacher of righteousness and his followers on "their festival of rest, the day of atonement," as related in the Habakkuk Commentary (xi.4–8; *DSS*, p. 370, but see p. 229 of this book), Obermann accepts the suggestion first made by Talmon (*DSS*, pp. 157, 238f) that the intention of the wicked priest was to make the covenanters desecrate the day which by their reckoning was the Day of Atonement. The story is given, as Obermann acutely notes, in the exposition of a verse which condemns one "who makes his neighbors drink," which suggests that the wicked priest tried to make the sect break their fast on the holy day.

This does not, as Obermann interprets it, involve a different calendar, but merely the refusal of the sect to postpone the Day of Atonement as the official reckoning required. The suggestion that the sect followed the calendar of Jubilees, says Obermann, fails to explain the wicked priest's choice of the Day of Atonement, since every other festival and possibly even every Sabbath would come on a different day from the one designated by the official calendar. Talmon, he continues, might have wondered also how the wicked priest would know when the sect's Day of Atonement would come; Mlle. Jaubert's elaborate calculations only show how difficult this would have been. The answer to that objection is simple: the priest might easily have been informed when the Feast of Trumpets was celebrated by the sect, and he would then know that nine days later they would be observing the Day of Atonement.

One thing which seems to favor the theory that the sect used the calendar of Jubilees is the fact that in the War scroll the priests serve by turn in twenty-six instead of twenty-four courses. By that calendar the year contained exactly fifty-two weeks, divided equally into four quarters of thirteen weeks each. The twenty-six courses of priests would therefore complete exactly two circuits in the course of a year. Obermann dismisses this argument on the ground that the number of courses had not always been twenty-four, and that the heads of the Levites are explicitly said to be "twelve, one to a tribe," showing that the calendar had nothing to do with their number. For the number twenty-six he suggests that in each period of twenty-four weeks two extra divisions may have been appointed to serve at the festivals. These arguments would be more impressive if the twenty-six courses were the only reason we had for connecting the Jubilees calendar with the Qumran sect. The case is more solid than that, however, and new material has now been adduced to support it, as we shall see presently.

That the calendar of Enoch and Jubilees was an old Israelite calendar, as maintained especially by Jaubert and Morgenstern (*DSS*, p. 241), is denied by J. B. Segal for reasons which to me seem convincing; he recognizes, however, that in the second century B.C. this calendar "was no innovation among the Jews, nor was it the fantasy of a heretical sect. It had been recognized by orthodox Jewry." For the authors of Enoch 72–82 and Jubilees it was the normal, time-honored calendar, which pernicious innovators were trying to change. Segal notes that the 364-day year "may have been observed by the Qumran sect," but he refers to the article by Obermann, which, he says, is a warning "against basing conclusions on the scant and obscure passages of the scrolls." That was not exactly the purpose of the article.

What aroused the opposition of the writers of Jubilees and Enoch 72–82, according to Segal, was not the introduction of a luni-solar calendar but the recognition, under Greek influence, that the actual length of the solar year was 365¼ instead of 364 days. This made the solar year 11¼ days longer than the year of twelve lunar months, but the author of Jubilees insists that the moon "comes in from year to year ten days too soon" (6:36). In the light of this suggestion, which seems thoroughly credible, my statement in *DSS* that the calendar of Jubilees and Enoch was "a reaction against the official calendar," and that "the prevalent system . . . was discarded by the author of Jubilees" (p. 239) must be qualified. The system against which he protested had only recently been made "official" and perhaps was not yet "prevalent."

Mlle. Jaubert's reconstruction of the sect's calendar has been further elaborated and defended in an article to which she was able to add, just before it was printed, a postscript noting the signal confirmation of her conclusions by a discovery which Milik announced at the congress of the Old Testament scholars at Strasbourg in 1956. In subsequent publications Milik has given a few more details.

The "Mishmaroth" texts of Cave 4 regulate the weekly turns of service in the temple for the priestly families for a cycle of six years. The script of the manuscript indicates a date early in the first century A.D. It appears that the sect recognized two calendars, which were harmonized by the six-year cycle. The religious calendar followed the year of 364 days, but there was also a lunar calendar by which the twelve months consisted of 29 and 30 days alternately, with an intercalated month of 30 days every third year, making in three years a total of 1092 days, which is three times 364. The two calendars thus come together at the end of three years, but it requires twice that time to make the cycle of twenty-four priestly courses of a week each come out even with the two calendars. The six-year cycle thus brings all three together, and the Mishmaroth texts work out this synchronism in detail.

It may be observed that the twenty-six courses of the War scroll would coincide with both calendars at the end of three years; perhaps they represent a different attempt at synchronization. There is nothing in the texts that shows any effort to make the year correspond with the true solar year of 365¼ days. This would require, as Milik notes, a 24-year cycle with an extra month of 29 days at the end and a supplementary provision for priestly courses.

The Cave 4 texts also list the festivals, giving for each the priestly course in which it occurs in each year of the cycle and the day of the week. In addition to the familiar biblical festivals there is a second Passover, a month after the first, which the Old Testament merely permits for special cases. The autumn festival commonly known as the New Year is called in these texts the day of remembrance. An agricultural feast of oil in the early autumn, otherwise unknown, appears in the remains of one little scroll. There are also references to historical events.

The annual ceremony of "entering into the covenant," described in detail in the Manual of Discipline (i.16–ii.22; *DSS*, pp. 371–73), must have been one of the most important occasions of the year. Milik points out that the reference to a similar rite in Jubilees 6:17 (*DSS*, p. 236) connects it with the Feast of Weeks (Pentecost), and he reports that an unpublished Qumran fragment of the Damascus Document places this ceremony in the third month of the year, when the Feast of Weeks was celebrated. He suggests that on this occasion a reunion of the Essenes scattered throughout the country was held at Qumran, and it is in this connection that he recalls the deposits of animals' bones.

# XXXII

## *The Religious Life*

Some of the material in the Qumran texts may have served the purpose of religious education. Bardtke suggests that the Thanksgiving Psalms may have been used in this way. One of his reasons for doubting that they were used in common worship is that they seem to him to present the doctrines of the sect in something like the form of a catechism. This point is not very impressive: the supposed resemblance between this highly figurative poetry, with no logical sequence of subjects, and a catechism which treats doctrines systematically in the form of questions and answers is not very close. Bardtke remarks also that the constant use of the pronoun "I" makes it less probable that the Psalms were used in worship by the group. The analogy of the Old Testament Psalms and many Christian hymns robs this argument too of much of its force. The possibility that the Thanksgiving Psalms were recited by an individual in the presence of others is recognized by Bardtke.

In any case, he believes, these poems were intended to be repeated by each member of the community at regular intervals and so to direct and control his thinking and spiritual experience. This impression is strengthened by what Bardtke takes to be a deliberate alternation of very lively, moving passages and what seem to be more sober spiritual exercises. The soul, he says, needs such an alternation of tension and relaxation, struggle and peace.

It is entirely probable that these compositions were found useful for edification and inspiration. That they were used in any such systematic way as Bardtke supposes is somewhat less probable, though of course not impossible. That they were composed for the purpose of such use seems to me very improbable. It is quite incredible that the profound spiritual experience which finds expression in the Thanksgiving Psalms could ever have been typical of the group as a whole.

Whether or not they were used in any corporate or systematic fashion, the Thanksgiving Psalms, with other material of a similar nature from the caves, give us our best insight into the personal religious life and experience of at least one member of the community. The question of the authorship of the poems has already been raised in connection with the sect's Messianic beliefs (pp. 324–27). Whether or not the poet was the teacher of righteousness himself, or, as some would have it, one of several leaders who bore that title, he was a man whose whole life was dominated by his spiritual experience. This was an experience, as Licht says, of a "direct, passionate personal relationship with God."

The title "Thanksgiving Psalms" has been given to this collection because of the stereotyped formula with which most of the poems begin, "I thank thee, Lord, because . . . ," which leads to a statement of some favor for which the author is grateful, or a number of such favors. Not everything in the scroll corresponds to this title. As has been noted (p. 294), elements of the type known as the individual Psalm of complaint in the Old Testament are combined with the note of thanksgiving in some of the poems. Their prevailing tone, however, even in the descriptions of past trials or of future disasters, is that of thanksgiving for deliverance, whether already experienced or confidently expected.

The poet is thankful, as we have already seen (pp. 294–95), for his deliverance from the sinfulness and weakness of human nature; he is thankful for the divinely given ability to live a righteous life, which by his own strength he could never have achieved. He is filled with joy and peace and a humble sense of having been brought safely through severe trials; he is thankful for the very possibility of praising God. Licht points out that the references to times and seasons not only reflect the interest of the sect in the calendar but also express the poet's sense of joy in uniting his voice with the chorus of the sun, moon, and stars. In the praise of God he becomes also a member of the angelic host. Thus far everything might apply to the sect as a whole and be appropriated by all its members.

The most distinctive individual element is the consciousness of having received a divine revelation. The poet thanks God for making him "an interpreter of knowledge in wondrous mysteries," and says, "understanding thou didst put in my heart to open the fount of knowledge to all who understand" (ii.13, 17f; *DSS*, p. 401). Michaud points out that this experience of a personal revelation made the poet feel all the more keenly his unworthiness and dependence as a creature, but it also filled him with the sense of God's sovereign power and grace. This feeling was the source of his idea of predestination.

The profound spiritual experience of the poet is ranked by Michaud with that of the greatest mystics. The "terrible obscurities" of style in the Thanksgiving Psalms recall the same phenomenon in the writings of the mystics, who strive in vain to express the ineffable. Gaster interprets the experience and life, not only of this inspired leader but of the whole community, in terms of mystical illumination. The members of the community, he says, considered themselves enlightened; they had achieved the mystic's "unitive state" and were "embraced in the communion of eternal things." The prominence of the concept of light in the Qumran texts and their stress on the knowledge of mysteries are interpreted as expressions of mystical illumination. The passage in the Thanksgiving Psalms which speaks of being brought up "to an eternal height," walking "in an unsearchable plain," and having hope of "an eternal company" (iii.20f; *DSS*, p. 404) does not, according to Gaster, refer to the future life but to that "victory over darkness" which enables a man to "live even on earth in a dimension of eternity." Even the sojourn in the land of Damascus is associated with the mystic's "dark night of the soul."

To many this picture will seem overdrawn. No doubt mysticism has many forms and variations, and it is impossible to draw a sharp line between it and non-mystical types of religious experience. The author of the Thanksgiving Psalms may fairly be described as a man intoxicated with the sense of God's reality, presence, and grace. Certainly the piety of Qumran was not merely formal, mechanical legalism. If mysticism is not identified with the type of experience and thought exemplified by Philo, for example, perhaps the men of Qumran may be called mystics. There is no indication, however, so far as I can see, of that self-absorption, that loss of personal identity in the divine Unity, which is characteristic of mysticism in the strictest sense of the word; nor is there any trace of a spiritual discipline by which the devotee was raised step by step to such an experience. The religious experience of the Qumran community was that of a group taut with expectation of the imminent consummation of the ages, convinced that they were predestined to share in that divine event and must prepare for it, and conscious of a present communion with one another and with God and his angels.

The piety of Qumran was also, of course, a legalistic piety in the sense that strict obedience to the law was both demanded and ardently desired. The spirit of the group was much like that of Psalm 119 in the Old Testament. Otzen finds a difference at this point within the literature of the sect. In the Damascus Document he sees a Pharisaic, rabbinic type of "Halakah" (the definition and elaboration of the law's requirements). It may be noted here that Milik reports other specimens of the sect's Halakah from Cave 4, with statements of the laws for conduct and ritual and proof-texts from the Pentateuch.

In the Manual of Discipline, Otzen finds a different attitude, dominated not so much by legal definitions as by ethical concepts. This is the attitude characteristic of the Testaments of the Twelve Patriarchs. The revealed law is still, however, the ultimate basis of conduct for the Manual and the Testaments. Such characteristic terms as truth, righteousness, and justice are found to be practically synonyms for the law. In these writings, therefore, we have not Pharisaic legalism, Otzen says, but a piety of the law expressed in an ethic of duties to one's neighbor. Sincerity, love of one's neighbor, perfection, chastity, fasting, and charity are found to be the outstanding ethical ideals of these two documents.

Not much that is new concerning the daily life of the sect has come out since *DSS* was published. The fact that marriage and family life are contemplated as normal in the Rule of the Congregation was noted in *DSS* (p. 233). It is not yet possible to go beyond the tentative conclusion suggested there, that the sect probably included both communities of celibates and settlements of families. At any rate, the Rule of the Congregation assumes that there will be families in the community of "the last days."

The general impression that the Manual of Discipline requires a complete sharing of property, thereby differing from the Damascus Document (*DSS*, pp. 233f), is denied by Del Medico and Roth. Bringing everything into the order, as required by the Manual of Discipline (i.11–13; *DSS*, p. 371), means only, Del Medico feels, making no wrong use of one's knowledge, strength, and property. Roth sees here a fundamental difference between the Essenes and the sect of Qumran: property was not held in common, he says, at Qumran. It is impossible to be entirely sure on this point, but whatever may have been true of property in general, the excavations indicate that money was used only at the headquarters of the community. Many coins were found in the ruins of the buildings, but none at all in the caves.

This survey of outstanding points in the religion of the Qumran community is by no means a comprehensive or balanced account. Only important facts and ideas which have emerged since the publication of *DSS* have been considered, leaving entirely untouched many important phases of the subject concerning which there is nothing new to say. The importance of the sect and its literature for the history of Judaism is more and more evident. What was clearly a very important type of Judaism, known hitherto only in late copies of translations of the apocryphal and pseudepigraphic writings and in parts of two medieval manuscripts of the Damascus Document, is emerging now into the light of day in a large portion of its own literature.

It is true that the Qumran group seems to have had little influence on the main stream of Jewish history. For that reason some writers have been inclined to minimize the importance of the Dead Sea Scrolls. Possibly, however, there was at least some

negative influence. At just about the time that the first main phase
of the occupation of Qumran was brought to an end by the earthquake of 31 B.C., Hillel became the leading rabbinic teacher at
Jerusalem. It has been suggested by N. N. Glatzer that some of
the most distinctive aspects of Hillel's work may have been moti-
vated in part by a reaction against the Qumran sect.

Like the covenanters, Hillel stressed humble piety, but he cultivated it in the midst of human society and especially in direct
contact with the common people. In contrast to the sect's sharp
division between the righteous and the wicked, he emphasized
God's mercy to the intermediate group of those who are neither
altogether good nor altogether bad. He revived the ideal of study,
but introduced principles and methods different from those of
the sect. He strove to reform Jewish society and ignored the
Messianic excitement of the times. He was also more hospitable
to proselytes than the Qumran community seems to have been.

Whether or not Glatzer's suggestion is correct, the life and
faith of the covenanters of Qumran represent a type of authentic
religion, well worth studying for its own sake. The variations,
branches, and heresies of any religion are as important for the
history of religion as the form which becomes established as normal and orthodox.

# PART EIGHT

# *TRANSLATIONS*

*Explanatory Note:* Since most of the texts here translated have been recovered only in fragments, there are many gaps in them. Several of them have been published only in part, so that what can be given here does not always represent all that has survived. Dots indicate small gaps in the text; asterisks indicate larger gaps, passages too incomplete to be translated, or portions that have not yet been published. In a few places the sign —?— is used for words which I cannot identify.

In the commentaries, the biblical passages commented on are in italics.

The translation of Text A is based on Avigad's and Yadin's deciphering and transcription, that of B–E and L on the publication of Barthélemy and Milik, that of F on Milik's, and that of H–K and M on Allegro's publications (see Bibliography).

# A. The Genesis Apocryphon
## (Lamech Scroll)

Column i, which is almost entirely lost, must have told of the birth of Noah. At the beginning of column ii, Noah's father, Lamech, is speaking and expressing his misgivings concerning the extraordinary child whom his wife Bath-enosh has brought into the world.

(*Column ii*) Then I thought in my heart that the conception was from watchers, and the . . . was from holy ones and belonged to the giants; and my heart was changed concerning this young man. Then I, Lamech, was alarmed, and I came to Bath-enosh my wife and said, ". . . by the Most High, by the Lord of greatness, by the King of all ages . . . sons of heaven, until you show me everything truly . . . show me, and without lies. . . . By the King of all ages, until you speak to me truly and without lies . . . " Then Bath-enosh my wife spoke to me with great vehemence and with . . . , and said, "O my brother, and O my lord, recall my delight . . . the time, and my breath in its sheath, and I truly everything . . ." Greatly was my heart then changed; and when Bath-enosh my wife saw that my face was changed, then she constrained her spirit and spoke with me and said, "O my lord, and O . . . of my delight, I swear to you by the great Holy One, by the King of heaven, that from you was this seed and from you this conception and from you the implanting of fruit, and not from any stranger nor from watchers nor from any of the sons of heaven. What has so changed and marred your face and so . . . your spirit? I am speaking truly with you." Then I, Lamech, ran to Methuselah, my father, and told him everything . . . his father, that from him he might learn everything with certainty, because he was loved and . . . his lot was assigned, and they showed him everything. And when Methuselah heard it, he ran to Enoch, his father, to learn from him everything truly . . . his will; and he went to Parvaim to Erechmat, and there he found . . . And he said to Enoch, his father, "O my father, and O my lord, what I . . . to you . . . And I tell you in

387

order that you may not be angry with me because I have come here
to . . . fear upon you. . . .

Columns iii–xviii are very poorly preserved, and only scattered sentences
from them have been published. They carry the story down to the time of
Abram.

(*Column xix*) . . . And I said, "You are he." . . . Until now I had
not reached the holy mountain. So I proceeded . . . and I was going
to the south . . . until I reached Hebron. . . . Hebron was built; and
I lived . . . Now there was a famine in that whole land, but I heard
that there were provisions . . . in Egypt; so I proceeded to . . . to the
land of Egypt . . . to the Karmon River, one of the heads of the River
. . . now we . . . our land. And I passed the seven heads of that river,
which . . . Now we passed our land and came into the land of the
sons of Ham, the land of Egypt.

Now I, Abram, dreamed a dream in the night of our coming into the
land of Egypt. I saw in my dream, and behold, a cedar and a palm.
. . . And men came and sought to cut off and uproot the cedar, and to
leave the palm by itself; but the palm called and said, "Do not cut off
the cedar, for accursed is he who . . ." So the cedar was left in the
shade of the palm, and . . . not . . . Then I awoke in the night from
my sleep and said to Sarai, my wife, "I have dreamed a dream . . . and
I am afraid because of this dream." She said to me, "Tell me your
dream, that I may know it." So I began to tell her that dream: ". . . a
dream . . . who will seek to kill me and to let you live on that day.
All the goodness . . . in all . . . say concerning me, 'He is my
brother'; so I shall live in your shade, and my life will be preserved because of you." . . . from me, and to kill me. And Sarai wept because
of my words that night . . . and Sarai toward Zoan . . . in his soul,
lest any might see her . . . And after those five years . . . three men
of the nobles of Egypt . . . of Pharaoh Zoan concerning . . . and concerning my wife; and they gave . . . goodness and wisdom and truth.
And I proclaimed before them . . . my words . . . how . . . in the
famine which . . . and did not . . . and they came to the place, until . . . with much eating and drinking . . . wine . . .

\* \* \*

(*Column xx*) . . . how . . . and beautiful was the expression of her
face and how . . . was the hair of her head; how lovely were her eyes,
how delectable her nose, and the whole bloom of her face . . . ; how
lovely her breast, and how beautiful all the whiteness of her; her arms

how beautiful, and her hands how perfect; and . . . the whole appearance of her hands; how lovely her palms, and how long and slender each finger of her hands; her feet how beautiful, and how perfect her legs. Of all the virgins and brides that go into the bridal chamber none is more beautiful than she; yea, above all women is she beautiful, and her beauty is high above all of them; yet with all this beauty she has great wisdom—but the—?—of her hands is lovely.

When the king heard the words of Hyrcanus and the words of his two companions, all three of whom spoke as with one mouth, he loved her very much; and he sent in haste to have her brought. When he saw her he was amazed by all her beauty and took her to himself to be his wife; and he sought to kill me. But Sarai said to the king, "He is my brother," that I might be benefited because of her; and I, Abram, was left alone for her sake and was not killed. But I, Abram, wept with strong weeping, both I and my nephew Lot with me, in the night when Sarai was forcibly taken from me. That night I prayed and supplicated and entreated, saying with grief, while my tears flowed down, "Blessed art thou, O God Most High, Lord of all ages; for thou art Lord and Ruler over all; yea, over all the kings of the earth thou art Ruler, working judgment with all of them. And now I complain to thee, O Lord, against Pharaoh Zoan, king of Egypt, for he has taken my wife from me with might. Exact justice for me from him, that I may see thy great hand against him and against his whole house; and let him not have power this night to defile my wife. So may it be known, my Lord, that thou art Lord of all the kings of the earth." So I wept, and was silent.

That night God Most High sent to him a crushing wind to crush him and every man of his house, an evil wind; and it crushed him and every man of his house. So he was not able to approach her, and did not know her, though he was with her two years. At the end of two years the crushing afflictions and blows became mighty and prevailed over him and over every man of his house. He therefore sent word and summoned all the wise men of Egypt and all the enchanters, together with all the physicians of Egypt, to find whether they might be able to heal him of this crushing affliction, and heal the men of his house. But all the physicians and enchanters and all the wise men were unable to rise and heal him, for that wind was crushing all of them, and they fled.

Then Hyrcanus came to me and requested of me that I come and pray for the king and lay my hands upon him, that he might recover, for in a dream . . . But Lot said to him, "My uncle Abram cannot pray for the king while Sarai, his wife, is with him; go, therefore, tell the king to send his wife from him to her husband, that he may pray for him and he may recover."

When Hyrcanus heard Lot's words, he went and said to the king, "All these crushing afflictions and blows which are crushing and smiting my lord the king are on account of Sarai, Abram's wife. Pray, give Sarai back to Abram, her husband, that this crushing affliction may—?—from you and the wind—?—. So he summoned me to him and said to me, "What have you done to me because of Sarai? You said to me, 'She is my sister,' but she was your wife, and I took her to be my wife. Here is your wife who was with me; go, get you out of the whole country of Egypt. But now pray for me and my house, that this evil wind may leave us." So I prayed for this . . . , and laid my hands on his head; and the crushing affliction was taken away from him, and the evil wind departed from him, and he recovered. The king rose and informed me . . . and the king swore to me with an oath that . . . And the king gave him much . . . and much raiment of fine linen and purple . . . before her, and also to Hagar. . . . And he appointed men with me to lead me out.

So I, Abram, went with very much goods, and also with silver and gold; and I went up from Egypt, and Lot my nephew with me. Lot too got much wealth, and he took to himself a wife of . . .

(*Column xxi*) . . . every place where I camped until I reached Bethel, the place where I had built the altar; and I built it again. I offered on it a burnt offering and a meal offering to God Most High, and there I called on the name of the Lord of the ages, and praised the name of God, and blessed God; and there I gave thanks before God for all the wealth and goods he had given me, and for doing good to me and bringing me back to this land in peace.

After that day Lot separated from me because of what our herdsmen did. He went and settled in the valley of the Jordan, taking all his herds with him. I also added much to him over and above what he had. He pastured his herds and came to Sodom, and built him a house in Sodom and lived there, while I lived on the mountain of Bethel. But it grieved me that Lot, my nephew, had separated from me.

Then God appeared to me in a vision of the night and said to me, "Go up to Ramath Hazor, which is to the north of Bethel, the place where you are dwelling; and lift up your eyes and look to the east and to the west and to the south and to the north; and see this whole land, which I give to you and to your descendants for all ages." So I went up the next day to Ramath Hazor, and I saw the land from that height from the river of Egypt to Lebanon and Senir, and from the great sea to Hauran and all the land of Gebal to Kadesh, and all the great desert east of Hauran and Senir to the Euphrates. And he said to me, "To your descendants I will give all this land, and they shall possess it for all ages. I will increase your descendants like the dust of the earth, so that no son of man will be able to number them, and your descendants will be unnumbered. Rise, walk, go and see how great is its length and how great is its breadth, for to you and to your descendants I will give it after you to all the ages."

So I, Abram, went to travel about and see the land. I began to travel from the river Gihon, and I came by the seaside until I reached Ox Mountain; then I traveled from beside this great sea of salt, and went by the side of Ox Mountain to the east across the breadth of the land until I reached the river Euphrates. I traveled along the Euphrates until I reached the Red Sea to the east. I came on beside the Red Sea until I reached the tongue of the Sea of Reeds which goes out from the Red Sea. I traveled to the south until I reached the river Gihon; then I turned back and came to my house in peace, and found all my men well. I went and dwelt at the oaks of Mamre at Hebron, to the northeast of Hebron; and there I built an altar and offered on it a burnt offering and a meal offering to God Most High. I ate and drank there with all the men of my house, and I sent word and invited Mamre and Arnam and Eshcol, the three Amorite brothers, my friends; and they ate together with me and drank with me.

Before those days Chedorlaomer king of Elam, Amraphel king of Babylon, Arioch king of Caphtok, and Tidal king of nations (that is, Mesopotamia) had come and made war with Bera king of Sodom, and with Birsha king of Gomorram, and with Shinab king of Admah, and with Shemiebed king of Zeboiim, and with the king of Bela. All these were mustered together for war in the Valley of Siddim. And the king of Elam and the kings who were with him overcame the king of Sodom and all his allies, and imposed upon them tribute. For twelve years they paid what was exacted of them to the king of Elam, but in the thirteenth year they rebelled against him. In the fourteenth year the king of Elam brought all his allies, and they went up by the way of the desert, and smote and plundered from the river Euphrates. They smote the Rephaim who were in Ashtaroth-karnaim, the Zumzamim who were in Ammon, the Emim who were in Shaveh-kirioth, and the Horites who were in the mountains of Gebal, until they reached El-paran, which is in the desert. And they returned . . . in Hazazon-tamar.

Then the king of Sodom, the king of Gomorram, the king of Admah, the king of Zeboiim, and the king of Bela went out to meet them, and they joined battle in the Valley of Siddim against Chedorlaomer king of Elam and the kings who were with him. But the king of Sodom was beaten and fled, and the king of Gomorram fell into the pits . . . . all the herds of Sodom and of . . . and they took Lot, Abram's nephew, (*Column xxii*) who was living in Sodom together with them, and all his wealth. But one who tended the flocks that Abram had given to Lot escaped from captivity and came to Abram. (Abram was then living at Hebron.) And he told him that his nephew Lot had been taken captive with all his wealth, but had not been killed, and that the kings had gone ahead by the way of the great plain to their country, capturing and plundering and smiting and killing and going to the country of Damascus. Abram wept for his nephew Lot. Then Abram strengthened himself and arose, and chose from his servants three hundred and eighteen mighty men, picked for war; and Arnam and Eshcol and Mamre went along with him. He pursued them until he reached Dan; and he found them encamped in the Valley of Dan. Then he fell upon them at night from all four sides of them, and killed some among them by night and routed them; and he pursued them, and they all fled from before him until they reached Helbon, which is situated to the north of Damascus. So he delivered from them everyone who had been taken captive, and all the plunder they had taken and all their goods; he also saved his nephew Lot and all his wealth, and brought back all the captives they had taken. When the king of Sodom heard that Abram had brought back all the captives and all the plunder, he went up to meet him. And he came to Salem, that is Jerusalem. Now Abram was encamped in the Valley of Shaveh, that is the King's Valley, the plain of Beth-karma. Then Melchizedek, the king of Salem, brought out food and drink for Abram and for all the men who were with him. He was priest of God Most High; and he blessed Abram, and said, "Blessed be Abram of God Most High, Lord of heaven and earth, and blessed be God Most High, who has delivered those who hate you into your hand." And he gave him a tenth of all the wealth of the king of Elam and his allies.

Then drew near the king of Sodom and said to Abram, "My lord Abram, give me the persons that belong to me who are captives with you, whom you have delivered from the king of Elam, and let all the wealth be left to you." Then Abram said to the king of Sodom, "I lift my hand this day to God Most High, Lord of heaven and earth, that I will take nothing, from a thread to a sandal-thong, of all that belongs to you, lest you might say, 'Abram's prosperity is all from my wealth'— except what the young men who are with me have already consumed and the share of the three men who went with me: they can give you of their share." So Abram returned all the wealth and all the captives and gave them to the king of Sodom; and he released all the captives from that land who were with him, and sent them all away.

After these things God appeared to Abram in a vision and said to him, "Behold, it is ten whole years since the day that you went out from Haran. Two you spent here, seven in Egypt, and one since you returned from Egypt. So now examine and number all that you have, and see how everything that went out with you on the day when you went out from Haran has increased twofold. So now be not afraid; I am with you, and I will be your stay and strength. I am a shield over you, and will—?—for you him who is stronger than you. Your prosperity and your wealth will increase greatly." And Abram said, "O my Lord God, my prosperity and wealth are great, but of what use are all these things to me, for I shall die naked and go without sons, and one of the sons of my house will be my heir. Eleazar son of . . . will be my heir." And he said to him, "This man shall not be your heir, but one who will issue . . ."

Here the scroll ends, but needle-holes in the edge of this column show that there was originally at least one more column.

# B. The Rule of the Congregation

(*Column i*) And this is the order for the whole congregation of Israel at the end of days, when they are gathered together to conduct themselves as directed by the judgment of the sons of Zadok the priests and the men of their covenant, who turned back from walking in the way of the people. They are the men of his counsel who have kept his covenant in the midst of wickedness to atone for the land. When they come, they shall cause all who come to assemble, including infants and women, and shall proclaim in their hearing all the statutes of the covenant. They must be made to understand all their judgments, lest they go astray in their errors.

And this is the order for all the hosts of the congregation, for every native in Israel. From his youth he must be taught in the Book of Hagi, and according to his days they shall instruct him in the statutes of the covenant. He shall receive his training in their judgments ten years . . . when he is twenty years old, he shall be numbered in the census, to enter the lot in the midst of his family for community in the holy congregation. But he shall not approach a woman to know her by lying with her except when he has fully reached the age of twenty years, when he knows good and evil; and then she shall be allowed to invoke against him the ordinances of the law and to take a place in the hearing of the judgments. And when he has completed—when he is twenty-five years old, he shall come to take his place among the foundations of the holy congregation, to serve the service of the congregation. When he is thirty years old he shall draw near to take part in pleading and judgment, and to take his place among the chiefs of the thousands of Israel, with the commanders of hundreds, commanders of fifties, commanders of tens, judges, and officers for their tribes in all their families, at the direction of the sons of Aaron the priests. Every head of the fathers of the congregation for whom the lot comes out to take his place in the service, to go out and come in before the congregation, according to his understanding together with the perfection of his conduct let him gird his loins for his position to perform the service of his work among his brethren. Great and small, this man with that man, they shall be honored, one more than another. When a man's years become many, according to his strength shall they give him his task in the service of the congregation. No simpleton shall enter the lot to take a place over the congregation of Israel for contending and judgment, to take up the task of the congregation or to have a place in the war to subdue nations; only in the order of the host he shall register his family, and in the service of task-work he shall perform his service according to his work. The sons of Levi shall stand, each in his position, as directed by the sons of Aaron, to bring in and bring out the whole congregation, each in his order, under the guidance of the heads of the fathers of the congregation, for commanders and judges and officers, according to the number of all their hosts, as directed by the sons of Zadok the priests and all the heads of the fathers of the congregation. If there is a convocation of the whole assembly for judgment, for common counsel, or for a convocation for war, they shall consecrate them three days, so that everyone who comes shall be ready for these things. These are the men summoned for the council of the community, from the age of . . . , all the wise men of the congregation and the perceptive and knowing, perfect in conduct, and the men of valor, together with the commanders of the tribes, and all their judges and officers, and the commanders of thousands and commanders of hundreds (*Column ii*) and of fifties and of tens, and the Levites, each in the midst of his division of service. These are the men of renown, summoned for the assembly, those appointed to the council of the community in Israel in the presence of the sons of Zadok, the priests. Any man afflicted with any one of all the uncleannesses of man shall not enter the assembly of God; and any man afflicted with these so that he is not able to hold a position in the congregation, anyone afflicted in his flesh, injured in his feet or hands, lame or blind or deaf or dumb or afflicted with any blemish in his flesh visible to the eyes, or an old man who stumbles so that he cannot hold himself up in the midst of the congregation—these shall not enter to take a place in the midst of the congregation of the men of renown. For holy angels are in their congregation. If one of these men has anything to say to the holy council, they shall inquire of him about it, but the man shall not come into the midst of the congregation, because he is afflicted. This is the session of the men of renown, summoned to the meeting for the council of the community, when God begets the Messiah: with them shall come the priest at the head of the whole congregation of Israel, and all the fathers of the sons of Aaron, the priests, summoned to the meeting, men of renown; and they shall sit before him, each according to his rank. Next shall come the Messiah of Israel, and before him shall sit the heads of the thousands of Israel, each according to his rank, according to his position in their camps and according to their journeyings. And all the heads of the fathers of the congregation, with the wise men of the holy congregation, shall sit before them, each according to his rank. And if they are met for the common table or to drink the wine, and the common table is set, and the wine is mixed for drinking, let not any put forth his hand on the first of the bread or the wine before the priest, for it is he who shall bless the first of the bread and the wine, and he shall put forth his hand on the bread first; and next the Messiah of Israel shall put forth his hand on the bread. And then all the congregation of the community shall pronounce the blessing, each according to his rank. And according to this statute they shall do for every meal when there are met as many as ten men.

# C. The Benedictions

### Blessing of the Congregation

Words of blessing for the wise man, that he may bless those who
fear God, who do his will, who keep his commandments and hold fast
to his holy covenant, and who walk perfectly in all the ways of his
truth; and he chose them for a covenant eternal which shall stand forever. May the Lord bless you from his holy dwelling, and an eternal
source which will not lie may he open to you from heaven . . . in your
hand . . . and may he be gracious to you with all blessings . . . you
in the congregation of the holy ones . . . a source eternal; and may he
not . . . the thirsty. And you . . . May he deliver you from all . . .
hate without . . . adversary

❁     ❁     ❁

### Blessing of the Chief Priest

❁     ❁     ❁

. . . may he make you glad and be gracious to you. . . . May he be
gracious to you with a spirit of holiness and steadfast love . . . and
may he graciously grant you an eternal covenant and . . . and may he
be gracious to you with righteous judgment . . . and may he be gracious to you in all your works . . . with eternal truth . . . on all your
descendants.

❁     ❁     ❁

May the Lord lift up his countenance to you, and a sweet fragrance
. . . may he choose; and may he visit all your holiness and in . . . all
your seed; may he lift up his countenance to your whole congregation.
May he place on your head . . . with glory . . . sanctify your seed
with eternal glory . . . eternal may he give to you, and kingdom . . .
from flesh, and with the holy angels . . . may he fight before your
thousands . . . generation of error . . .

❁     ❁     ❁

## Blessing of the Priests

* * *

Words of blessing for the wise man that he may bless the sons of Zadok, the priests, whom God chose to confirm his covenant forever and to assay all his judgments in the midst of his people, and to instruct them as he commanded. And they established his covenant in truth, and in righteousness observed all his statutes; and they walked according to what he chose. May the Lord bless you from his holy dwelling, and make you a perfection of glory among the holy ones. A covenant of eternal priesthood may he renew for you, and give you your place in a holy dwelling. By your acts may he judge all nobles, and by what drops from your lips all princes of peoples; may he cause you to inherit the dominion . . . , and may he bless by your hand the counsel of all flesh.

* * *

. . . And you shall be like an angel of the Presence in the holy dwelling, to the glory of the God of hosts . . . round about, serving in the royal temple and casting the lot with the angels of the Presence, and the common counsel . . . for an everlasting time and to all the periods of eternity, for true are all his judgments. And may he make you holy among his people, and for a luminary . . . to the world in knowledge, and to enlighten the faces of many . . . a diadem for the holy of holies; for . . . and you will glorify his name, and his holy ones. . . .

* * *

. . . who has consecrated you for an everlasting time and for all the periods of eternity, and your glory he will not give to another. And God will put the dread of you on all who hear the fame of you, and your glory. . . .

## Blessing of the Prince of the Congregation

For the wise man, that he may bless the prince of the congregation, who . . . his . . . , and may he renew for him the covenant of community, to establish the kingdom of his people forever . . . to reprove in uprightness the meek of the land, and to walk before him perfectly in all the ways of . . . , and to establish his holy covenant when those who seek him are in distress. May the Lord exalt you to an everlasting height, and like a strong tower with a high wall. And . . . with the strength of your hand; with your rod you shall lay waste the land, and with the breath of your lips you shall slay the wicked, with a spirit of counsel and everlasting power, a spirit of knowledge and the fear of God. And may righteousness be the girdle of your loins, and faith the girdle of your waist. May he make your horns of iron and your hoofs of bronze. You shall gore like a bull . . . and tread down peoples like the mire of the streets, for God has established you for a rod of rulers; before you . . . and all nations shall serve you. By his holy name he will strengthen you, and you shall be like a lion . . . the prey, and none shall take it back. Your steeds shall spread out over . . .

\* \* \*

# D. The Book of Mysteries

\* \* \*

They do not know the mystery that is to be, and the things of old they do not consider; they do not know what is coming upon them, nor how to save themselves from the mystery that is to be. And this shall be to you the sign that this will come to pass. When the descendants of error are shut in, wickedness will depart from before righteousness as darkness departs from before light; and as smoke is destroyed and is no longer, so will wickedness be destroyed forever. And righteousness will be revealed like the sun, the fixed order of the world; and all who hold back the wondrous mysteries will be no longer. Knowledge will fill the world, and folly will be there no more forever. The word is sure to come, and the oracle is true. From this will it be known to you that it will not turn back: Do not all the peoples hate iniquity? Yet by all of them it is practiced. Does not the fame of truth sound from the mouths of all nations? But is there any lip or tongue that holds fast to it? What nation is glad to be oppressed by one stronger than itself? What one is glad that its wealth is wickedly plundered? Yet what nation does not oppress its neighbor? Where is a people that does not plunder the wealth of another?

# E. The Scroll of Prayers

. . . the season of our peace . . . for a season . . . our souls for the
circuit of . . . the earth in the season . . . like showers on the grass
. . . to all generations. Blessed be the Lord who has made us glad.
. . . A prayer for the Day of Atonement. Remember, O Lord, . . .

❖   ❖   ❖

. . . and command . . . in the lot of the righteous, but for the wicked
the lot . . . in their bones, disgrace for all flesh; but the righteous . . .
fat with the delights of heaven, and the produce of earth for the beasts
. . . between the righteous and the wicked. Thou hast given the
wicked for our ransom, and the treacherous . . . destruction of all that
afflict us. And we will praise thy name forever. . . . Because for this
thou didst create us, and it is this that . . . Blessed . . .

❖   ❖   ❖

. . . a great luminary for the season . . . and their statutes are not to
be transgressed; and all of them . . . and their dominion in all the
world. But the seed of man did not perceive all that thou didst cause
him to inherit; they did not know thee whenever thou didst speak; but
they did more wickedly than any; they did not perceive thy great might.
Therefore thou didst reject them, for thou hast no pleasure in error,
and wickedness shall not be established before thee. But thou didst
choose for thyself a people in the time of thy good pleasure; for thou
rememberedst thy covenant. Thou didst . . . them, separating them
for thyself as holy from all the peoples; and thou didst renew thy
covenant for them in a vision of glory and the words of thy holy Spirit
with the works of thy hands and the writing of thy right hand, to make
them know the discipline of glory and the ascents of eternity . . . to
them a faithful shepherd . . . meek . . .

❖   ❖   ❖

# F. The Prayer of Nabonidus

The words of the prayer which Nabonidus, king of Assyria and of Babylon, the great king, prayed when he was smitten with a severe inflammation by the command of the Most High God, in the city of Teima: I was smitten for seven years and I was put far from men. But when I confessed my trespasses and my sins, he left me a seer. He was a Jew of the exiles in Babylonia. He gave his explanation and wrote that honor should be given and great glory to the name of the Most High God. And he wrote thus: When you were smitten with a severe inflammation in the city of Teima by the command of the Most High seven years, you prayed to the gods made of silver and gold, of bronze, of iron, of wood, of stone, of clay . . . of the gods . . .

# G. The Testimonia

After quoting Deuteronomy 5:28f; 18:18f; Numbers 24:15–17; and Deuteronomy 33:8–11, the fragment that has been published concludes with the following selection from the apocryphal Psalms of Joshua, other fragments of which were found in the same cave.

At the time when Joshua finished giving praise and thanks in his songs, he said, "Cursed be the man that rebuilds this city. At the cost of his first born may he lay its foundation, and at the cost of his youngest may he set up its gates. For, lo, an accursed man, one of Belial, will arise to be a fowler's snare to his people and the ruin of all his neighbors. He will arise . . . that they may both be instruments of violence. They will return and rebuild . . . for it a wall and towers, to make it a stronghold of wickedness . . . in Israel, and a horror in Ephraim and in Judah. They will commit ungodliness in the land and great blasphemy among the sons of . . . blood like water on the bulwark of the daughter of Zion and in the bounds of Jerusalem.

# H. The Florilegium

Only the following excerpt has been published.

. . . . *Moreover the Lord declares to you that he will build you a house. And I will raise up your seed after you, and I will establish the throne of his kingdom forever. I will be his father, and he shall be my son* [II Samuel 7:11–14]. He is the branch of David, who will arise with the interpreter of the law who . . . in . . . in the latter days; as it is written, *And I will raise up the booth of David that is fallen* [Amos 9:11]. That is the booth of David that is fallen; but afterward he will arise to save Israel.

# I. The Commentary on Genesis 49

[10] *A ruler shall not depart from the tribe of Judah* while Israel has dominion, nor shall one who sits on the throne for David be cut off. For the staff is the covenant of kingship; the thousands of Israel are the feet, until the coming of the Messiah of righteousness, the branch of David, for to him and to his seed is given the covenant of the kingship of his people until the generations of eternity, because he kept the . . . the law with the men of the community. For . . . that is the synagogue of the men of . . .

# J. The Commentary on Psalm 37

❉ ❉ ❉

. . . shall perish by the sword and by famine and by pestilence. [8] *Refrain from anger, and forsake wrath! Fret not yourself; it tends only to evil.* [9] *For the wicked shall be cut off.* This refers to all those who turn to the law, who do not refuse to turn from their wickedness. For all who are rebellious against turning from their iniquity *shall be cut off, but those who wait for the LORD shall possess the land.* This means that they are the congregation of his elect, those who do his will. [10] *Yet a little while, and the wicked will be no more; though I look well at his place, he will not be there.* This refers to all the wickedness at the end of forty years: when they are finished there will not be found in the land any wicked man. [11] *But the meek shall possess the land, and delight themselves in abundant prosperity.* This refers to the poor who will receive the season of affliction, but will be rescued from all the snares of . . . the earth . . . all affliction . . .

\* \* \*

[14] *The wicked draw the sword and bend their bows, to bring down the poor and needy, to slay those who walk uprightly;* [15] *their sword shall enter their own heart, and their bows shall be broken.* This refers to the wicked of Ephraim and Manasseh, who seek to put forth a hand against the priest and against the men of his counsel in the time of testing which is coming upon them; but God will redeem them from their hand, and afterward they will be delivered into the hand of the tyrants of the nations for judgment. . . .

\* \* \*

. . . those who return from the desert, who will live for a thousand generations in . . . man and to his seed forever. [19] . . . *in the days of famine* . . . [20] . . . *perish.* This means that he will keep them alive in famine in the season . . . will perish by famine and by pestilence, every one who does not go out . . .

*But those who love the LORD are like the glory of the pastures.* This means . . . the congregation of his elect, who will be chiefs and princes . . . sheep in the midst of their pastures.

*They vanish like smoke, all of it.* This refers to the princes of . . . who have oppressed his holy people; they will perish like the smoke of a lamp in the wind. [21] *The wicked borrows, and cannot pay back, but the righteous is generous and gives;* [22] *for those blessed by the LORD shall possess the land, but those cursed by him shall be cut off.* This refers to the congregation of the poor, who . . . the inheritance of all. . . . They will possess the lofty mountain of Israel, and his holy people will delight themselves . . . *shall be cut off.* They are the tyrants of . . . the wicked of Israel, who will be cut off and destroyed forever.

[23] *The steps of a man are from the LORD; he establishes him, and*

*he delights in all his way; though* . . . This refers to the priest, the teacher of . . . He has established him to build for him a congregation of . . . [25] . . . , *and now am old, yet have I not* . . . [26] *giving liberally and lending, and* . . .

❖ ❖ ❖

[32] *The wicked watches the righteous and seeks* . . . *let him be condemned when he is brought to trial.* This refers to the wicked . . . who . . . to kill him . . . and the law, who sent to him [or which or whom he sent to him]. But God will not . . . and will not . . . when he is brought to trial. He will render to the wicked his requital, delivering him into the hand of the tyrants of the nations to do to him . . .

❖ ❖ ❖

# K. The Commentary on Isaiah 10-11

. . . [28] *he has come to Aiath; he has passed through* . . . [29] . . . *the pass, at Geba they lodge for the night;* . . . [30] . . . *aloud, O daughter of Gallim! Hearken* . . . [31] *Madmenah* . . . ; *the inhabitants of Gebim flee for safety.* [32] *This very* . . . *his fist at the mount of the daughter of Zion, the hill of Jerusalem* . . . word for the latter days to come . . . when he goes up from the plain of Acco to fight against . . . and there is none like him. And in all . . . to the border of Jerusalem . . . in all . . . the Kittim, who . . . all the nations and . . . [33] . . . *height will be hewn down* . . . [34] *He will cut down the thickets* . . . for the war of the Kittim . . . the Kittim, who will be delivered . . . *with an ax, and Lebanon with its majestic* . . . Israel and the meek of . . . And they will be terror-stricken; and their hearts will melt . . . are the mighty men of the Kittim . . . *forest with an ax* . . . *and Lebanon with* . . . by the hand of his great one . . . Jerusalem, when he fled before . . . [11:1] . . . *Jesse, and a branch* . . . *out of his roots.* [2] . . . *upon him,* . . . *and understanding, the spirit of counsel* . . . *the spirit of knowledge* . . . [3] . . . *the LORD* . . . *what* . . . *see* . . . [4] . . . *he shall judge* . . . of David who will arise in the latter . . . And God will sustain him with . . . law

. . . a glorious throne, a . . . wreath, and many-colored robes . . . in his hand, and over all the nations shall he rule; and Magog . . . his sword will execute judgment on all the peoples. And as for what it says, . . . *or decide by what his ears hear;* this means that . . . as they teach him he will judge, and at their direction . . . one of the renowned priests shall go forth, and in his hand the garments . . .

✷  ✷  ✷

# L. The Commentary on Micah 1:5-7

[1] . . . This means the prophet of the lie . . . simple. And what are the high places of Judah? . . . the teacher of righteousness who . . . those who volunteered to be added to the elect of . . . in the council of the community, who are delivered from the day . . .

✷  ✷  ✷

# M. The Commentary on Nahum 2:11-13

[11] . . . dwelling for the wicked of the nations. *Where the lion went, the lioness, the lion's cub* . . . Demetrius; king of Greece, who tried to come to Jerusalem by the advice of the seekers of smooth things . . . frightened the kings of Greece from Antiochus until the rulers of the Kittim arose; but afterward . . . shall trample . . . [12] *The lion tore enough for his cubs and strangled prey for his lionesses* . . . refers to the lion of wrath who smites with his great ones and the men of his counsel . . . *and his dens with torn flesh.* This refers to the lion of wrath . . . by the seekers of smooth things, who hangs men alive . . . in Israel before; because one hanged alive . . . [13] *Behold, I am against . . . and the sword shall devour your lions; I will cut . . . prey* . . . Your multitude are the troops of his army . . . and his lions are . . . and his prey is the wealth which . . . of Jerusalem, who . . . Ephraim; Israel will be delivered to . . .

✷  ✷  ✷

# APPENDIX
# BIBLIOGRAPHY
# INDEX

# Appendix:
# The Non-biblical Manuscripts of Qumran

*Note:* These are arranged alphabetically by the titles under which the works are referred to in this book. Unless otherwise noted, the language is Hebrew. Many compositions of which little is yet known are omitted.

*Apocalypse of Jubilees.* Cave 4. Perhaps one of the sources of the Testament of Levi in the Testaments of the Twelve Patriarchs.

*Beatitudes.* Cave 4. A series of pronouncements beginning with the word "Blessed"; also a description of the torments of the wicked.

*Benedictions.* Cave 1. Five (originally six) columns, which had been part of the same scroll that contained the Manual of Discipline, but became separated from it and were bought by the Palestine Museum from a dealer in Bethlehem in 1950.

*Damascus Document.* Large portions of two medieval manuscripts were found in Cairo near the end of the nineteenth century; for translation see DSS, pp. 349–64. Fragments of ancient copies were found in Cave 4 (seven different manuscripts, one written on papyrus), and others in Caves 5 and 6. The text agrees with the Cairo manuscript A, except that there are several sections at the beginning and end and in the course of the text which are not contained in either of the Cairo manuscripts.

*Enoch.* One of the works known as "pseudepigrapha," preserved in an Ethiopic version and also partly in Greek. Fragments in Cave 4 in Aramaic (ten different manuscripts). Other Aramaic works belonging to the Enoch literature are represented also in Caves 4 and 6, and a Hebrew manuscript of Cave 6 contains a similar apocalyptic work.

*Florilegium.* Cave 4. Verses of Messianic or supposedly Messianic import from Exodus, II Samuel, the Psalms, Isaiah, Daniel, and Amos, with brief comments.

*Genealogy of priests.* Cave 6.

*Genesis Apocryphon,* formerly called the Lamech scroll. Cave 1. One of the scrolls found in 1947 (see pp. 387ff).

*Jeremiah, Apocryphal Book of.* Cave 4 (five or six different manuscripts). A work resembling the book of Baruch and the Epistle of Jeremiah in the Apocrypha.

*Jubilees.* One of the "pseudepigrapha." Fragments in Caves 1, 2, and 4 (six manuscripts). Two other manuscripts from Cave 4 contained a work of the same nature, possibly a source or a recension of Jubilees. See also *Apocalypse of Jubilees.*

*Lamech scroll.* See *Genesis Apocryphon.*

*Manual of Discipline,* also known as *Rule of the Community.* Cave 1. One of the scrolls found in 1947; for translation see *DSS,* pp. 371–89. Fragments in Cave 4 (eleven manuscripts, two on papyrus). Two of the manuscripts present a shorter and probably earlier form of the text contained in column v of the scroll from Cave 1. There are also other variations in the text.

*Midrash of the Book of Moses.* Fragments in Cave 4 of a papyrus manuscript in a cryptic alphabet.

*Mishmaroth.* Fragments of several manuscripts in Cave 4. Directions for the courses or turns of the priestly families in the temple worship, with specific assignments for each festival, each year, and each week of the year. A similar document lists the priestly families assigned to each Sabbath and the beginning of each month. Sometimes the Babylonian names of the months are used, and there are a few references to historical events.

*Mysteries, Book of.* Caves 1 and 4 (two or more manuscripts); see translation of an excerpt, p. 398.

*New Jerusalem, Description of the.* Caves 1, 2, 4, and 5. An Aramaic work which describes the Jerusalem and temple of the future. It is not certain that all these fragments belonged to the same work.

*Noah, Book of.* Cave 1. Possibly one of the sources of Enoch. A similar work in Aramaic was represented in Cave 6.

*Prayer of Nabonidus.* Cave 4.

*Psalms of Joshua.* Fragments in Cave 4 and a quotation in the Testimonia.

*Rule of the Community.* See *Manual of Discipline.*

*Rule of the Congregation.* Cave 1. Two columns which were originally, with the Benedictions, part of the same scroll that contained the Manual of Discipline.

*Sayings of Moses.* Cave 1. Directions for the observance of the festivals.

*Tanhumim.* Cave 4. Passages from Isaiah, one of which is described as *tanhumim* (comfort).

*Testament of Levi.* Caves 1 and 4 (three manuscripts). An Aramaic document, more extensive than the Testament of Levi in the Greek Testaments of the Twelve Patriarchs in the pseudepigrapha; perhaps one of the sources used by the author of that work. Portions of a later copy of this Aramaic work had been found in the Cairo genizah that contained the manuscripts of the Damascus Document (*DSS,* pp. 187–201, 349–64). The text of the Qumran fragments, where it covers the same passages, agrees closely with that of the genizah manuscript. One fragment, published by Milik in 1955, includes a prayer of Levi which appears in only one Greek manuscript of the Testaments of the Twelve Patriarchs and has been commonly regarded as a late addition to the text; another supposed interpolation appears in one of the other fragments.

*Testament of Naphtali.* Cave 4. Perhaps another source of the Testaments of the Twelve Patriarchs, but in Hebrew. (No fragments of the Testaments of the Twelve Patriarchs were found in the caves; see pp. 179f.)

*Testimonia.* Cave 4. A collection of Messianic proof-texts, including Deuteronomy 5:28f and 18:18f; Numbers 24:15–17; then Deuteronomy 33:8–11; and finally a passage from the Psalms of Joshua (q.v.).

*Thanksgiving Psalms.* Cave 1. Part of the first discovery of scrolls in 1947; for translation of major selections see *DSS*, pp. 400–415. Also fragments of six manuscripts in Cave 4, including one on papyrus. At some points these fragments fill gaps in the text of the Cave 1 scroll. The order in which the Psalms appear in the fragments is not always the same as in the scroll. There are also fragments of several other manuscripts containing similar psalms not found in the scroll; whether they belonged to the same collection is an open question. A collection of less individualistic psalms, exhibiting more interest in Israel's history, was represented by other fragments; still another collection contains psalms or hymns which end, "Amen, Amen."

*Three Tongues of Fire.* Caves 1 and 4. Liturgical directions with mysterious references to "tongues of fire," apparently three in number.

*War of the Sons of Light with the Sons of Darkness* (also referred to sometimes simply as the War scroll). Cave 1. One of the scrolls found in 1947; for translation of major excerpts see *DSS*, pp. 390–99. Also fragments of four manuscripts in Cave 4, making it possible to fill some of the numerous gaps in the scroll. There are many variations in the text. Fragments of a similar composition were found in Cave 2.

*Words of Michael.* Cave 4. An Aramaic work beginning, "The words of the book that Michael spoke to the angels."

# Bibliography

~~~~~~~~~~~~~~~~~~~~~~~~~~~~~~~~~~~~~~~~~~~~~~~~~~

*Note:* For the most part, only publications which have appeared since *DSS* was written are included here. A few works already mentioned in *DSS* are named again because they are referred to in this book also. Several items which appeared too late to be used in this book are here included for the benefit of readers wishing the most recent references. See also the Supplement at the end. For an exhaustive bibliography through 1956, the work of Burchard, listed here, may be consulted.

## ABBREVIATIONS

Books included here are more fully noted in the Bibliography.

| | |
|---|---|
| AO | *Archiv Orientální* |
| BA | *Biblical Archaeologist* |
| BASOR | *Bulletin of the American Schools of Oriental Research* |
| BJRL | *Bulletin of the John Rylands Library* |
| BNTE | Davies and Daube (editors), *The Background of the New Testament and Its Eschatology* |
| IEJ | *Biblische Zeitschrift* |
| JAOS | *Catholic Biblical Quarterly* |
| JBL | *Cahiers Sioniens* |
| CBQ | Burrows, M., *The Dead Sea Scrolls* |
| HTR | *Ephemerides theologicae Lovanienses* |
| CS | *Harvard Theological Review* |
| ETL | *Israel Exploration Journal* |
| BZ | *Journal of the American Oriental Society* |
| DSS | *Journal of Biblical Literature and Exegesis* |
| JBR | *Journal of Bible and Religion* |
| JJS | *Journal of Jewish Studies* |
| JQR | *Jewish Quarterly Review* |
| JSS | *Journal of Semitic Studies* |
| JTS | *Journal of Theological Studies* |
| NRT | *Nouvelle revue théologique* |

NT      *Novum Testamentum*
NTS     *New Testament Studies*
PEQ     *Palestine Exploration Quarterly*
RB      *Revue Biblique*
RHPR    *Revue d'histoire et de philosophie religieuses*
RHR     *Revue de l'histoire des religions*
RSR     *Revue des sciences religieuses*
SNT     Stendahl, K. (editor), *The Scrolls and the New Testament*
ST      *Studia Theologica*
ThLZ    *Theologische Literaturzeitung*
TS      *Theological Studies*
TZ      *Theologische Zeitschrift*
VD      *Verbum Domini*
VT      *Vetus Testamentum*
VTS     *Vetus Testamentum, Supplements to* (Volumes I–IV)
ZAW     *Zeitschrift für die alttestamentliche Wissenschaft*
ZDPV    *Zeitschrift des Deutschen Palästina-Vereins*
ZNW     *Zeitschrift für die neutestamentliche Wissenschaft*
ZRG     *Zeitschrift für Religions- und Geistesgeschichte*
ZTK     *Zeitschrift für Theologie und Kirche*

Albright, W. F. "New Light on Early Recensions of the Hebrew Bible." BASOR, December 1955, pp. 27–33.

———. "Recent Discoveries in Palestine and the Gospel of St. John." BNTE, pp. 153–71.

———. "The High Place in Ancient Palestine." VTS IV, 1957, pp. 242–58.

Allegro, J. M. "A Newly Discovered Fragment of a Commentary on Psalm XXXVII from Qumrân." PEQ LXXXVI, 1954, pp. 69–75.

———. "Le Travail d'édition des fragments manuscrits de Qumran." See Benoit, P., et al.

———. "Further Light on the History of the Qumran Sect." JBL LXXV, 1956, pp. 89–95.

———. "Further Messianic References in Qumran Literature." JBL LXXV, 1956, pp. 174–87.

———. "Addendum to Professor Millar Burrows' note on the Ascent from Accho in 4Qp Isa*." VT VII, 1957, p. 183.

———. *The Dead Sea Scrolls and the Origins of Christianity*. Hammondsworth: Penguin Books Ltd., 1956. New York: Criterion Books, 1957.

Avigad, N., and Yadin, Y. *A Genesis Apocryphon*. Jerusalem: The Magnes Press of the Hebrew University and Heikhal ha-Sefer, 1956.

———. "Last of the Dead Sea Scrolls Unrolled." BA XIX, 1956, pp. 22–24.

Baillet, M. "Fragments araméens de Qumran 2. Description de la Jérusalem Nouvelle." RB LXII, 1955, pp. 222–45.

———. "Fragments du Document de Damas. Qumran grotte 6." RB LXIII, 1956, pp. 513–23.

———. "Le Travail d'édition des fragments manuscrits de Qumran." See Benoit, P., et al.

Baker, H. W. "Notes on the Opening of the 'Bronze' Scrolls from Qumran." BJRL, 1956, pp. 45–56.

Bammel, E. "Zu 1QS 9, 10 f." VT VII, 1957, pp. 381–85.

Bardtke, H. "Considérations sur les cantiques de Qumran." RB LXIII, 1956, pp. 220–33.

Barthélemy, D., and Milik, J. T. *Qumran Cave I (Discoveries in the Judaean Desert I)*. Oxford: Clarendon Press, 1955.

Baumgärtel, F. "Zur Liturgie in der 'Sektenrolle' vom Toten Meer." ZAW LXV, 1953, pp. 263–65.

Baumgarten, J., and Mansoor, M. "Studies in the New *Hodayot* (Thanksgiving Hymns)." JBL LXXIV, 1955, pp. 115–24, 188–95; LXXV, 1956, pp. 107–113; LXXVI, 1957, pp. 139–48.

Benoit, P., et al. "Le Travail d'édition des fragments manuscrits de Qumran." RB LXIII, 1956, pp. 49–67 (English translation in BA XIX, 1956, pp. 75–96).

Black, M. "The Theological Conceptions of the DSS." *Svensk Exegetisk Årsbok* (Uppsala) XVIII–XIX, 1953–54, pp. 72–97.

———. "The Account of the Essenes in Hippolytus and Josephus." BNTE, pp. 172–75.

Bowman, J. "Contact between Samaritan sects and Qumran?" VT VII, 1957, pp. 184–89.

Brown, R. E. "The Qumrân Scrolls and the Johannine Gospel and Epistles." CBQ XVII, 1955, pp. 403–19, 559–74 (reprinted in SNT, pp. 183–207).

Brownlee, W. H. "John the Baptist in the New Light of Ancient Scrolls." *Interpretation* IX, 1955, pp. 71–90 (revised and enlarged in SNT, pp. 33–53).

———. "The Habakkuk Midrash and Targum of Jonathan." JJS VII, 1956, pp. 169–86.

———. "Messianic Motifs of Qumran and the New Testament." NTS III, 1956–57, pp. 12–30, 195–210.

———. "Muhammad ed-Deeb's Story of His Discovery." JNES XVI, 1957, pp. 236–39.

Bruce, F. F. "Qumrân and Early Christianity." NTS II, 1955–56, pp. 176–190.

———. *Second Thoughts on the Dead Sea Scrolls*. Grand Rapids: Wm. B. Eerdmans Publishing Co., 1956.

———. *The Teacher of Righteousness in the Qumran Texts*. (Tyndale Lecture in Biblical Archeology, 1956). London: Tyndale Press, 1957.

Buchanan, G. W. "The Old Testament Meaning of the Knowledge of Good and Evil." JBL LXXV, 1956, pp. 114–20.

Burchard, C. *Bibliographie zu den Handschriften vom Toten Meer*. (ZAW Beiheft 76). Berlin: Töpelmann, 1957.

Burrows, M. *The Dead Sea Scrolls*. New York: Viking Press, 1955 (abbreviated *DSS*).

———. "The Ascent from Acco in 4QpIsa^a." VT VII, 1957, pp. 104f.

Carmignac, J. "Précisions apportées au vocabulaire de l'hébreu biblique par la Guerre des fils de lumière contre les fils de ténèbres." VT V, 1955, pp. 345–64.

Carmignac, J. "Les Kittim dans la 'Guerre des fils de lumière contre les fils de ténèbres.' " NRT LXXXVII, 1955, pp. 737–48.

———. "Les Citations de l'AT dans 'La Guerre des fils de la lumière contre les fils de ténèbres.' " RB LXIII, 1956, pp. 234–60, 375–90.

———. "L'Utilité ou l'inutilité des sacrifices sanglants dans la 'Règle de la Communauté' de Qumrân." RB LXIII, 1956, pp. 524–32.

———. "Conjectures sur les écrits de Qumrân." RSR, 1957, pp. 140–68.

———. "Conjecture sur un passage de Flavius Josèphe relatif aux Esséniens." VT VII, 1957, pp. 318f.

Casey, R. P. "Gnosis, Gnosticism and the New Testament." BNTE, pp. 52–80.

Chamberlain, J. V. "Further Elucidation of a Messianic Thanksgiving Psalm from Qumran." JNES XIV, 1955, pp. 181–82.

———. "The Functions of God as Messianic Titles in the Complete Qumran Isaiah Scroll." VT V, 1955, pp. 365–72.

Cross, F. M., Jr. "The Scrolls from the Judean Wilderness." *Christian Century* LXXII, 1955, pp. 899–901, 920–22, 944f, 968–71.

———. "The Oldest Manuscripts from Qumran." JBL LXXIV, 1955, pp. 147–72.

———. "Le Lettre de Simon Ben Kosba." RB LXIII, 1956, pp. 45–48.

———. "Le Travail d'édition des fragments manuscrits de Qumran." See Benoit, P., et al.

———. "The Scrolls from the Judaean Desert." *Archaeology* IX, 1956, pp. 41–53.

———. "A Report on the Biblical Fragments of Cave Four in Wâdī Qumrân." BASOR, February 1956, pp. 9–13.

———. "A Footnote to Biblical History." BA XIX, 1956, pp. 12–17.

———. *The Ancient Library of Qumran and Modern Biblical Studies* (The Haskell Lectures, 1956–57). New York: Doubleday, 1958.

Cullmann, O. "The Significance of the Qumran Texts for Research into the Beginnings of Christianity." JBL LXXIV, 1955, pp. 213–26 (reprinted in SNT, pp. 18–32).

Dahl, N. A. "The Origin of Baptism." *Interpretationes* (Mowinckel Festschrift), Oslo, 1955, pp. 36–52.

Daniélou, J. "La Communauté de Qumran et l'organisation de l'église ancienne." RHPR XXXV, Cahier 34, 1955, pp. 104–16.

———. *Les Manuscrits de la Mer Morte et les origines du Christianisme.* Paris: Éditions de l'Orante, 1957.

Daube, D. *The New Testament and Rabbinic Judaism.* London: Athlone Press, 1956.

Davies, A. P. *The Meaning of the Dead Sea Scrolls.* New York: New American Library of World Literature, 1956.

Davies, W. D. *Paul and Rabbinic Judaism: Some Rabbinic Elements in Pauline Theology*, 2nd ed. London: Society for the Propagation of Christian Knowledge, 1955.

————, and Daube, D. (editors). *The Background of the New Testament and Its Eschatology* (In Honour of Charles Harold Dodd). Cambridge, England: University Press, 1956 (abbreviated BNTE).

————. "Paul and the Dead Sea Scrolls: Flesh and Spirit." SNT, pp. 157–82.

de Boer, P. A. H. *Second-Isaiah's Message.* (*Oudtestamentische Studiën,* Deel XI.) Leiden: E. J. Brill, 1956.

de Contenson, H. "In the Footsteps of St. John the Baptist, Notes on the Rolls of the Dead Sea." *Antiquity and Survival* (The Hague, Netherlands), No. 1, 1955, pp. 37–56.

Delcor, M. "La Guerre des fils de lumière contre les fils de ténèbres ou le 'Manuel du parfait combattant' de Qumrân." NRT LXXVII, 1955, pp. 372–99.

————. "L'Immortalité de l'âme dans le livre de la Sagesse et dans les documents de Qumrân." NRT LXXVII, 1955, pp. 614–30.

Del Medico, H. E. "La Traduction d'un texte démarqué dans le Manuel de Discipline (DSD X 1–9)." VT VI, 1956, pp. 34–39.

————. "L'État des manuscrits de Qumran I." VT VII, 1957, pp. 127–38.

————. *L'Énigme des manuscrits de la Mer Morte.* Paris: Librairie Plon, 1957.

de Moor, J. C. "Lexical Remarks Concerning *Yaḥad* and *Yaḥdaw*." VT VII, 1957, pp. 350–55.

de Vaux, R. "Les Fouilles de Khirbet Qumrân." *Comptes Rendus des Séances de l'Académie des Inscriptions et Belles-Lettres,* 1955, pp. 378–85.

————. "Fouilles de Khirbet Qumrân. Rapport préliminaire sur les 3°, 4°, et 5° campagnes." RB LXIII, 1956, pp. 533–77.

Driver, G. R. "Three Difficult Words in *Discipline* (iii.3–4, vii.5–6, 11)." JSS II, 1957, pp. 247–50.

Dupont-Sommer, A. "Les Manuscrits de la Mer Morte; leur importance pour l'histoire des religions." *Numen* II, 1955, pp. 168–89.

————. "Le Problème des influences étrangères sur la secte juive de Qoumrân." RHPR XXXV, Cahier 34, 1955, pp. 75–94.

————. "La Mère du Messie et la mère de l'Aspic dans un hymne de Qoumrân (DST iii.6–18)." RHR CXLVII, 1955, pp. 174–88.

————. "Règlement de la guerre des fils de lumière: traduction et notes, No. I, II." RHR CXLVIII, 1955, pp. 25–43, 141–80.

————. "'Le Chef des Rois de Yawan' dans l'Édit de Damas." *Semitica* V, 1955, pp. 41–57.

————. "On a Passage of Josephus Relating to the Essenes." (*Antiquités* XVIII, §22.) JSS I, 1956, pp. 361–66.

————. "Les Esséniens." *Évidences* 54, 1956, pp. 19–25; 55, pp. 27–34; 56, pp. 11–25; 57, pp. 9–23; 58, pp. 27–39; 59, pp. 13–27; 60, pp. 25–36; 62, 1957, pp. 32–47; 63, pp. 19–32; 65, pp. 19–28; 67, pp. 27–33.

————. "Le Livre des Hymnes découvert près de la Mer Morte (1QH)." *Semitica* VII, 1957, p. 120.

————. "Les Rouleaux de cuivre trouvé à Qoumrân." RHR CLI, 1957, pp. 22–36.

Eissfeldt, O. *Einleitung in das Alte Testament.* Tübingen: Mohr, 1956.

Farmer, W. R. "The Economic Basis of the Qumran Community." TZ XI, 1955, pp. 295–308.

―――. "A Postscript to 'The Economic Basis of the Qumran Community.'" TZ XII, 1956, pp. 56–58.

―――. "The Geography of Ezekiel's River of Life." BA XIX, 1956, pp. 17–22.

―――. *Maccabees, Zealots, and Josephus.* New York: Columbia University Press, 1956.

Fitzmyer, J. A. "The Qumran Scrolls, the Ebionites, and Their Literature." TS XVI, 1955, pp. 335–72 (reprinted, in slightly abridged form, in SNT, pp. 208–31).

Flusser, D. "Healing through the Laying-on of Hands in a Dead Sea Scroll." IEJ VII, 1957, pp. 107–108.

Fohrer, G. "Zum Text von Jes. XLI 8–13." VT V, 1955, pp. 239–49.

Freedman, D. N. "The Prayer of Nabonidus." BASOR, February 1957, pp. 31–32.

Fritsch, C. T. "Herod the Great and the Qumran Community." JBL LXXIV, 1955, pp. 173–81.

―――. *The Qumrān Community, Its History and Scrolls.* New York: Macmillan, 1956.

Gärtner, B. "The Habakkuk Commentary (DSH) and the Gospel of Matthew." ST VIII, 1955, pp. 1–24.

Gaster, T. H. *The Dead Sea Scriptures in English Translation.* New York: Doubleday, 1956.

Ginsberg, H. L. "The Dead Sea Manuscript Finds: New Light on *ERETZ YISRAEL* in the Greco-Roman Period." In *Israel: Its Role in Civilization* (New York: Harper, 1956), pp. 39–57.

Glatzer, N. "Hillel the Elder in the Light of the Dead Sea Scrolls." SNT, pp. 232–44.

Gordis, R. "The 'Begotten' Messiah in the Qumran Scrolls." VT VII, 1957, pp. 191–94.

―――. "The Knowledge of Good and Evil in the Old Testament and the Qumran Scrolls." JBL LXXVI, 1957, pp. 123–38.

Graystone, G. *The Dead Sea Scrolls and the Originality of Christ.* New York: Sheed and Ward, 1956.

Greenberg, M. "The Stabilization of the Text of the Hebrew Bible, Reviewed in the Light of the Biblical Materials from the Judean Desert." JAOS LXXVI, 1956, pp. 157–66.

Guillaume, A. "Some Readings in the Dead Sea Scroll of Isaiah." JBL LXXVI, 1956, pp. 40–43.

Hardy, E. R. "The Dead Sea Discipline and the Rule of St. Benedict." JBR XXV, 1957, pp. 183–86.

Howlett, D. *The Essenes and Christianity.* New York: Harper, 1957.

Huntzinger, C.-H. "Neues Licht auf Lc 2:14 ἄνθρωποι εὐδοκίας." ZNW XLIV, 1952–53, pp. 85–90.

―――. "Le Travail d'édition des fragments manuscrits de Qumran." See Benoit, P., et al.

————. "Fragmente einer älteren Fassung des Buches Milḥamā aus Höhle 4 von Qumrān." ZAW LXIX, 1957, pp. 131–51.

Hvidberg, F. "The Masseba and the Holy Seed." *Interpretationes* (Mowinckel Festschrift), Oslo, 1955, pp. 97–99.

Hyatt, J. P. "The View of Man in the Qumran 'Hodayot.'" NTS II, 1955, pp. 256–84.

————. "The Dead Sea Discoveries: Retrospect and Challenge." JBL LXXVI, 1957, pp. 1–12.

Iwry, S. "Maṣṣēbāh and Bāmāh in 1Q Isaiahᵃ 6:13." JBL LXXVI, 1957, pp. 225–32.

————. "The Qumrân Isaiah and the End of the Dial of Ahaz." BASOR, October 1957, pp. 27–33.

Jaubert, A. "La Date de la dernière Cène." RHR CXLVI, 1954, pp. 140–73.

————. "Le Calendrier des Jubilés et les jours liturgiques de la semaine." VT VII, 1957, pp. 35–61.

————. *La Date de la Cène, calendrier et liturgie chrétienne.* Paris: Librairie Lecoffre, 1957.

Johnson, S. E. "Paul and the Manual of Discipline." HTR LXVIII, 1955, pp. 157–65.

Kandler, H.-J. "Zum Problem des Verhältnisses der Sekte von Chirbet Qumran zu den Essenern." In *Festschrift für Prof. Dr. Viktor Christian, Vorderasiatische Studien* (Vienna, 1956), pp. 55–64.

Kapelrud, A. S. *Dødehavs rullene.* Oslo: Universitetsforlaget, 1956.

Kelso, J. L. "The Archeology of Qumran." JBL LXXIV, 1955, pp. 141–46.

Klausner, J. *The Messianic Idea in Israel.* New York: Macmillan, 1955.

Kuhn, K. G. "The Lord's Supper and the Communal Meal at Qumran." *Evangelische Theologie* X, 1950–51, pp. 508–27. (English translation with revision and enlargement, SNT, pp. 65–93.)

————. "New Light on Temptation, Sin, and Flesh in the New Testament." ZTK XLIX, 1952, pp. 200–222. (English translation with revision, SNT, pp. 94–113.)

————. "The Two Messiahs of Aaron and Israel." ThLZ LXXIX, 1954, cols. 76of; and NTS I, 1954–55, pp. 168–79. (English translation with some revision, SNT, pp. 55–64.)

————. "Beiträge zum Verständnis der Kriegsrolle von Qumrân." ThLZ, 1956, cols. 25–30.

————. *Phylakterien aus Höhle 4 von Qumran.* (*Abhandlungen der Heidelberger Akademie der Wissenschaften, Philosophisch-Historische Klasse* 1957, 1. Abhandlung.) Heidelberg: Universitätsverlag, 1957.

Laperrousaz, E. M. "Remarques sur les circonstances qui ont entouré la destruction des bâtiments de Qumrân." VT VII, 1957, pp. 337–49.

La Sor, W. S. "The Messiahs of Aaron and Israel." VT VI, 1956, pp. 425–29.

————. *Amazing Dead Sea Scrolls and the Christian Faith.* Chicago: Moody Press, 1957.

Leach, E. R. "A Possible Method of Intercalation for the Calendar of the Book of Jubilees." VT VII, 1957, pp. 392–97.

Licht, J. "The Doctrine of the Thanksgiving Scroll." IEJ VI, 1956, pp. 1–13, 89–101.

———. *Megillat ha-Hodayot.* Jerusalem: Bialik Institute, 1957.

Mansoor, M. "Studies in the New *Hodayot* (Thanksgiving Hymns) I–IV." See Baumgarten, J.

Marcus, R. "*Mebaqqer* and *Rabbim* in the Manual of Discipline vi.11–13." JBL LXXV, 1956, pp. 290–302.

———. "On the Text of the Qumran Manual of Discipline, I–IX." JNES, 1957, pp. 24–38.

Metzinger, A. "Die Handschriftenfunde vom Toten Meer und das Neue Testament." *Biblica* XXXVI, 1955, pp. 457–81.

Meyer, R. "Das Problem der Dialektmischung in den hebräischen Texten von Chirbet Qumran." VT VII, 1957, pp. 139–48.

Michaud, H. "Une Apocalypse nouvelle. La guerre des fils de lumière contre les fils de ténèbres." *Positions Luthériennes,* 1955, pp. 65–76.

———. "A propos du nom de Qumrân." RHPR XXXV, Cahier 34, 1955, pp. 68–74.

———. "Le Maître de la Justice d'après les hymnes de Qumran." *Bulletin (trimestriel) de la faculté libre de théologie protestante de Paris,* 19° année, 1956, pp. 67–77.

———. "Un Livre apocryphe de la Genèse en Araméen." *Positions Luthériennes* V, 1957, pp. 91–104.

Milik, J. T. "Note additionnelle sur le contrat juif d l'an 134 après Jésus-Christ." RB LXII, 1955, pp. 253–54.

———. "Le Testament de Lévi en Araméen; fragment de la grotte 4 de Qumran." RB LXII, 1955, pp. 398–406.

———. " 'Prière de Nabonide' et autres écrits d'un cycle de Daniel." RB LXIII, 1956, pp. 407–15.

———. "The Copper Document from Cave III, Qumran." BA XIX, 1956, pp. 60–64.

———. "Le Travail d'édition des fragments manuscrits de Qumran." See Benoit, P., et al.

———. "Esseni et historia populi Judaici." VD XXXV, 1957, pp. 65–74.

———. "Le Travail d'édition des manuscrits du Désert de Juda." VTS IV, 1957, pp. 17–26.

———. *Dix ans de découvertes dans le Désert de Juda.* Paris: Les Editions du Cerf, 1957.

Molin, G. "Die Hymnen von Chirbet Qumran (1 Q T)." In *Festschrift für Prof. Dr. Viktor Christian, Vorderasiatische Studien* (Vienna, 1956), pp. 74–82.

———. *Lob Gottes aus der Wüste.* Freiburg/München: Karl Alber Verlag, 1957.

Moscati, S. *I manoscritti ebraici del Deserto di Giuda.* Roma: Istituto per L'Oriente, 1955.

Mowinckel, S. "The Hebrew Equivalent of Taxo in Ass. Mos. ix." VTS I, 1953, pp. 88–96.

———. "Some Remarks on *Hodayot* 39.5–20." JBL LXXV, 1956, pp. 285–86.

Murphy, R. E. *The Dead Sea Scrolls and the Bible*. Westminster, Md.: Newman Press, 1956.

———. "The Dead Sea Scrolls and New Testament Comparisons." CBQ XVIII, 1956, pp. 263–72.

Mussner, F. "Einige Parallelen aus den Qumrān-Texten zur Areopagrede." BZ—NF I, 1957, pp. 125–30.

North, R. "The Damascus of Qumran Geography." PEQ LXXXVII, 1955, pp. 34–48.

———. "The Qumrân 'Sadducees.' " CBQ XVII, 1955, pp. 164–88.

———. "Qumran 'Serek a' and related fragments." *Orientalia* XXV, 1956, pp. 90–99.

Noth, M. "Der alttestamentliche Name der Siedlung auf *chirbet ḳumrān.*" ZDPV LXXI, 1955, pp. 111–23.

Nötscher, F. "Zur theologischen Terminologie der Qumran-Texte." *Bonner Biblische Beiträge* X, 1956, pp. 201ff.

———. " 'Wahrheit' als theologischer Terminus in den Qumran-Texten." In *Festschrift für Prof. Dr. Viktor Christian, Vorderasiatische Studien* (Vienna, 1956), pp. 83–92.

———. "Die Handschriften aus der Gegend am Toten Meer." *Theologische Revue* LIII, 1957, cols. 50–58.

Obermann, J. "Calendaric Elements in the Dead Sea Scrolls." JBL LXXV, 1956, pp. 277–84.

Oesterreicher, J. M. "The Community of Qumran." In *The Bridge* (New York: Pantheon Books, 1956), pp. 91–134.

Orlinsky, H. M. "Notes on the Present State of the Textual Criticism of the Judean Biblical Cave Scrolls. In *A Stubborn Faith* (Dallas: M. A. Irwin Festschrift, 1956), pp. 117–31.

———. "Madhebah in Isaiah xiv.4." VT VII, 1957, pp. 202–203.

Otzen, B. "Die neugefundenen hebräischen Sektenschriften und die Testamente der zwölf Patriarchen." ST VII, 1954, pp. 125–57.

Parrot, A. "Les Manuscrits de la Mer Morte. Le point de vue archéologique." RHPR XXXV, Cahier 34, 1955, pp. 61–67.

Pfeiffer, C. F. *The Dead Sea Scrolls*. Grand Rapids, Mich.: Baker Book House, 1957.

Rabin, C. "The Dead Sea Scrolls and the History of the Old Testament Text." JTS, N. S. VI, 1955–56, pp. 174–82.

Richardson, H. "Some Notes on 1QSa." JBL LXXVI, 1957, pp. 108–22.

Rigaux, P. B. "Les Documents de la Mer Morte." *La Revue Générale Belge,* 1956, pp. 65–82.

Roberts, B. J. "The Qumran Scrolls and the Essenes." NTS III, 1956, pp. 58–65.

Roth, C. "A Solution to the Mystery of the Scrolls, Adding a Chapter to 1st-Century Jewish History." *Commentary* XXIV, 1957, pp. 317–24.

Roth, C. "The Teacher of Righteousness, New Light on the Dead Sea Scrolls." *The Listener,* June 27, 1957, pp. 1037–41.

——. "Le Point de vue de l'historien sur les manuscrits de la Mer Morte." *Évidences* 65, 1957, pp. 37–43.

Rowley, H. H. "The Origin of the Dead Sea Scrolls." In Robertson, E., and Wallenstein, M., *Melilah, A Volume of Studies* V (Manchester, England: University Press, 1955), pp. 51–61.

——. *The Dead Sea Scrolls and Their Significance.* London: Independent Press, Ltd., 1955.

——. "The Kittim and the Dead Sea Scrolls." PEQ LXXXVIII, 1956, pp. 92–109.

——. "4 QpNahum and the Teacher of Righteousness." JBL LXXV, 1956, pp. 188–93.

——. *Jewish Apocalyptic and the Dead Sea Scrolls* (Ethel M. Wood Lecture). London: Athlone Press, 1957.

——. "The 390 Years of the Zadokite Work." In *Mélanges Bibliques rédigés en l'honneur de André Robert,* 1957, pp. 341–47.

——. *The Dead Sea Scrolls and the New Testament.* London: Society for Promoting Christian Knowledge, 1957.

Rubinstein, A. "Conditional Constructions in the Isaiah Scroll (DSIa)." VT VI, 1956, pp. 69–79.

——. "Notes on Some Syntactical Irregularities in Text B of the Zadokite Documents." VT VII, 1957, pp. 356–61.

Schmitt, J. "Les Écrits du N. T. et les textes de Qumran." RSR XXIX, 1955, pp. 381–401; XXX, 1956, pp. 54–74, 261–82.

Schoeps, H. J. "Die ebionitische Wahreit des Christentums." ST VIII, 1955, pp. 43–50; BNTE, pp. 115–23.

——. *Urgemeinde, Judenchristentum, Gnosis.* Tübingen: J. C. B. Mohr, 1956.

——. "Die Opposition gegen die Hasmonäer." ThLZ, 1956, cols. 667–70.

Schonfield, H. *Secrets of the Dead Sea Scrolls.* London: Jewish Chronicle Publications, 1956.

Schubert, K. "Zwei Messiasse aus dem Regelbuch von Chirbet Qumran." *Judaica* XI, 1955, pp. 216–35.

——. "The Sermon on the Mount and the Qumran Texts." *Theologische Quartalschrift* CXXXV, 1955, pp. 321–37. (English translation, SNT, pp. 118–28).

——. "War Jesus ein Essener?" *Wort und Wahrheit* XI, 1956, pp. 687–97.

——. "Der alttestamentliche Hintergrund der Vorstellung von den beiden Messiassen im Schrifttum von Chirbet Qumran." *Judaica* XII, 1956, pp. 24–28.

——. "Die ersten beiden Kolumnen der Kriegsrolle von Chirbet Qumran." In *Festschrift für Prof. Dr. Viktor Christian, Vorderasiatische Studien* (Vienna, 1956), pp. 93–99.

Schweizer, E. "Gegenwart des Geistes und eschatologische Hoffnung bei Zarathustra, spätjüdischen Gruppen, Gnostikern und den Zeugen des Neuen Testamentes." BNTE, pp. 488–94.

Segal, J. B. "Intercalation and the Hebrew Calendar." VT VII, 1957, pp. 250–307.

Segert, S. "Zur Habakuk-Rolle aus dem Funde beim Toten Meer IV–VI." AO XXIII, 1955, pp. 178–83, 364–73, 575–619.

———. "Die Gütergemeinschaft der Essaer." In *Studia Antigua Antonio Salão, 70 oblata* (Prague, 1955), pp. 66–73.

Silbermann, L. H. "The Two 'Messiahs' of the Manual of Discipline." VT V, 1955, pp. 77–82.

———. "Language and Structure in the Hodayot (1QH3)." JBL LXXV, 1956, pp. 96–106.

Sjöberg, E. "Neuschöpfung in den Toten-Meer-Rollen," ST IX, 1955, pp. 131–36.

Skehan, P. W. "The Text of Isaias at Qumrân." CBQ XVII, 1955, pp. 38–43, 158–63.

———. "Exodus in the Samaritan Recension from Qumran." JBL LXXIV, 1955, pp. 182–87.

———. "Le Travail d'édition des fragments manuscrits de Qumran." See Benoit, P., et al.

———. "The Qumran Manuscripts and Textual Crticism." VTS IV, 1957, pp. 148–60.

Smith, M. "The Jewish Elements in the Gospels." JBR, 1956, pp. 90–96.

Sonne, I. "Remarks on 'Manual of Discipline,' col. vi.6–7." VT VII, 1957, pp. 405–408.

Spares, D. "The Books of the Qumran Community." JTS, N. S. VI, 1955–56, pp. 226–29.

Starcky, J. "Le Travail d'édition des fragments manuscrits de Qumran." See Benoit, P., et al.

Stauffer, E. "Der gekreuzigte Thoralehrer." ZRG VIII, 1956, pp. 250–53.

Stegemann, H. "Die Risse in der Kriegsrolle von Qumran." ThLZ XVIII, 1956, pp. 205–10.

Stendahl, K. (editor). *The Scrolls and the New Testament.* New York: Harper, 1957 (abbreviated SNT).

———. "The Scrolls and the New Testament: An Introduction and a Perspective." SNT, pp. 1–18.

Strugnell, J. "Le Travail d'édition des fragments manuscrits de Qumran." See Benoit, P., et al.

Teicher, J. L. "The Essenes." (*Texte und untersuchungen zur Geschichte der altchristlichen Literatur* Band 63) *Studia Patristica* (Berlin) I, 1957, pp. 540–45.

Toombs, L. E. "The Early History of the Qumran Sect." JSS I, 1956, pp. 367–81.

van der Ploeg, J. "La Règle de la Guerre. Traduction et Notes." VT V, 1955, pp. 373–420.

———. "Les Manuscrits trouvés depuis 1947 dans le Désert de Juda. III." *Ex Oriente Lux* XIV (Leiden), 1955–56, pp. 85–116.

———. "The Meals of the Essenes." JSS II, 1957, pp. 163–75.

Vermès, G. "Quelques Traditions de la Communauté de Qumran." CS IX, 1955, pp. 25–58.

———. "L'Araméen palestinien et le langage des Évangiles." CS IX, 1955, pp. 98–102.

———. "A propos des Commentaires bibliques découverts à Qumran." RHPR XXXV, Cahier 34, 1955, pp. 95–103.

———. *Discovery in the Judean Desert: The Dead Sea Scrolls and Their Meaning.* New York: Desclée Co., Inc., 1957 (translated from the French; see *DSS* p. 434).

Vogt, E. " 'Peace Among Men of God's Good Pleasure' Lk. 2:14." *Biblica* XXXIV, 1953, pp. 427–29 (translated with revision in SNT, pp. 114–17).

———. "Effossiones in Ḥirbet Qumran." *Biblica* XXXVI, 1955, pp. 562–64.

———. " 'Mysteria' in textibus Qumran." *Biblica* XXXVII, 1956, pp. 247–57.

Walker, N. "Concerning the 390 Years and the 20 Years of the Damascus Document." JBL LXXVI, 1957, pp. 57–58.

Wallenstein, M. "A Hymn from the Scrolls." VT V, 1955, pp. 277–83.

———. "A Striking Hymn from the Dead Sea Scrolls." BJRL XXXVIII, 1955–56, pp. 241–65.

———. *The Nezer and the Submission in Suffering Hymn from the Dead Sea Scrolls.* (Reconstructed, Vocalized and Translated with Critical Notes.) *Publications de l'Institut historique et archéologique néerlandais de Stamboul,* No. 4, 1957.

———. "Some Aspects of the Vocabulary and Morphology of the Hymns of the Judean Scrolls." VT VII, 1957, pp. 209–13.

Wernberg-Møller, P. "Some Reflections on the Biblical Material in the Manual of Discipline." ST IX, 1955, pp. 40–66.

———. "Some Passages in the 'Zadokite' Fragments and their Parallels in the Manual of Discipline." JSS I, 1956, pp. 110–28.

———. "Pronouns and Suffixes in the Scrolls and the Masoretic Text." JBL LXXVI, 1957, pp. 44–49.

Widengren, G. "King and Covenant." JSS II, 1957, pp. 1–32.

Wieder, N. "The Doctrine of the Two Messiahs among the Karaites." JJS VI, 1955, pp. 14–25.

———. "The Idea of a Second Coming of Moses." JQR XLVI, 1955–56, pp. 356–66.

———. "The Qumran Sectaries and the Karaites." JQR XLVII, 1956, pp. 97–117, 269–92.

Wieluch, D. "Zwei 'neue' antike Zeugen über Essener." VT VII, 1957, pp. 418f.

Wiesenberg, E. "Chronological data in the Zadokite Fragments." VT V, 1955, pp. 284–308.

Wildeberger, H. "Der Dualismus in den Qumranschriften." *Asiatische Studien* (Bern), 1954, pp. 163–77.

Wilson, E. *The Scrolls from the Dead Sea.* New York: Oxford University Press, 1955 (revised and enlarged from *The New Yorker,* May 1955, pp. 45–131).

————. "More on the Dead Sea Scrolls." *Encounter* VI (London), 1956, pp. 3–9.

Wilson, R. M. "Simon, Dositheus and the Dead Sea Scrolls." ZRG IX, 1957, pp. 21–30.

Winter, P. "Twenty-six Priestly Courses." VT VI, 1956, pp. 215–17.

————. "Ṣadoqite Fragments IV 20, 21 and the Exegesis of Genesis 1:27 in Late Judaism." ZAW LXVIII, 1956, pp. 71–84.

Yadin, Y. *Megillat Milḥemet Bne 'Or bi-Bne Ḥošek.* Jerusalem: Bialik Institute, 1956.

————. "Three Notes on the Dead Sea Scrolls." IEJ VI, 1956, pp. 158–62.

————. *The Message of the Scrolls.* New York: Simon & Schuster, 1957.

Zeitlin, S. "Additional Remarks." JQR XLV, 1954–55, pp. 218–29.

————. "The Propaganda of the Hebrew Scrolls and the Falsification of History." JQR XLVI, 1955–56, pp. 1–39, 116–80, 209–58.

————. "The Dead Sea Scrolls." JQR XLVI, 1955–56, pp. 389–400.

————. *The Dead Sea Scrolls and Modern Scholarship.* (JQR Monograph Series, No. III) Philadelphia: Dropsie College, 1956.

————. "How Ancient are the Hebrew Scrolls from the Dead Sea?" *Judaism* VI, 1956, pp. 55–58.

————. "The Dead Sea Scrolls: A Travesty of Scholarship." JQR XLVII, 1956–57, pp. 1–36.

————. "Revealing Data on the So-Called Discovery of the Dead Sea Scrolls." JQR XLVII, 1956–57, pp. 183–87.

————. "Recent Literature on the Dead Sea Scrolls." JQR XLVII, 1956–57, pp. 196–211.

————. "The Dead Sea Scrolls: 1. The Lamech Scrolls—A Mediaeval Midrash; 2. The Copper Scroll; 3. Was Kando the Owner of the Scrolls?" JQR XLVII, 1956–57, pp. 245–68.

## Supplementary Bibliography

Baumgarten, J. M. "On the Testimony of Women in 1QSa." JBL LXXVI, 1957, pp. 266–69.

Brant, W. *Wer war Jesus Christus?* Verändern die Schriftrollenfunde vom Toten Meer unser Christusbild? Stuttgart: Union Verlag, 1957.

Carmignac, J. *Le Docteur de Justice et Jesus-Christ.* Paris: Editions de l'Orante, 1957.

Kutscher, E. Y. "Dating the Language of the Genesis Apocryphon." JBL LXXVI, 1957, pp. 288–92.

Livur, Y. *ha-mašiaḥ mi-bet dawid bimegillot midbar yehudah* ('iyyunim bimegillot midbar yehudah, pp. 53–76). Jerusalem: Qiryat Sepher Press, 1957.

Mowinckel, S. "The Copper Scroll—an Apocryphon?" JBL LXXVI, 1957, pp. 261–265.

Rowley, H. H. "Some Traces of the History of the Qumran Sect." TZ XIII, 1957, pp. 530–540.

―――. "The Teacher of Righteousness and the Dead Sea Scrolls." BJRL XL, September 1957, pp. 114–46.

Rubinstein, A. "Observations on the Old Russian Version of Josephus' *Wars*." JSS II, October 1957, pp. 329–48.

Wernberg-Møller, P. *The Manual of Discipline*. (*Studies on the Texts of the Desert of Judah*, edited by J. van der Ploeg, Vol. 1) Leiden: E. J. Brill, 1957.

# Index

Figures in italics enclosed in parentheses
indicate pages in *The Dead Sea Scrolls.*

425